A PART OF MYSELF

Carl Zuckmayer

A PART OF MYSELF

Translated from the German by
Richard and Clara Winston

A HELEN AND KURT WOLFF BOOK
HARCOURT BRACE JOVANOVICH, INC., NEW YORK

First American edition

ISBN 0-15-170970-X

Library of Congress Catalog Card Number: 70-126526

Originally published in Germany under the title *Als Wärs Ein
Stück von Mir* by S. Fischer Verlag, Frankfurt am Main

Printed in the United States of America

B   C   D   E

CONTENTS

How often are we to die before we go quite off this stage? In every friend we lose a part of ourselves.

Alexander Pope

1926-1934
A MOMENT IN PARADISE

WHERE IS OUR HOME? Where we are born, or where we wish to die? In those days I thought I knew. I thought I could pinpoint the tiny spot on the globe that was my chosen home, the one I had made my own and where I hoped contentedly to live out my life. It was the village of Henndorf, near Salzburg; or to be precise Wiesmühl House with its two acres of land and water rights. If I had been asked at the time where the Garden of Eden was situated, I would have answered without hesitation: In Austria, ten miles east of Salzburg along the national highway, close to the lovely lake called Wallersee. Perhaps it stretched as far as Thalgau and Mondsee on the one side, and to the banks of the river Inn on the other—a piece of country which could be walked from end to end in a day. Not that it was a place of dreamy contentment without desires, but it harbored the essence of happiness. For the only lasting kind of felicity consists in consciousness of productivity. Today, in a different landscape, I work again at the same desk with the heavy oak top that stood in my study in Henndorf. At night I lie in the same gaily painted peasant bed where I was so often lulled to sleep by the Wiesmühl brook. But if I am asked where I want to die, I must say: I don't know. I know only this: once we lived in Paradise, and it does not matter whether it lasted twelve and a half years or no longer than it takes to open and close one's eyes.

After the success of my play *The Merry Vineyard* I paid off all my debts and had been touched by all my friends, but to my amazement I still had money left—more than I could carry in my pocket. On the other hand the Austrian poet Richard Billinger had none. Author of a thin volume of enchantingly beautiful poems, he was at the time in Berlin, struggling with plays he was trying to write. He had used up all his advances, run through all his prospects for further loans. And so I invited him to spend the spring of 1926 with us on the Baltic island of Hiddensee, where we had rented a small house in the dunes, fairly near to where Gerhart Hauptmann lived. One stormy night, when a cold sea wind was roaring and we had fortified ourselves with huge quantities of grog, Billinger spoke

3

of that rather remote mill near Henndorf in the countryside around Salzburg. It was empty and for sale, he said—the transaction was in charge of the owner of the famous Kaspar Moser Bräu in Henndorf, one of the oldest inns in Austria.

He described the mill and its environs in the most idyllic terms. As a matter of fact, we would never have recognized it from his description, let alone been able to find it. All the facts about its whereabouts, size, and condition were absolutely wrong. But what he said about it excited us enormously, and the more he talked, the more tempting the property sounded. My wife was Austrian by birth, and I had always had an affinity not so much for the sea as for farming country, regions of woods and mountains. Moreover, I fully realized that Billinger's description probably corresponded with a higher reality, even if none of his facts were correct. What is more, after a few more drinks he knew the exact price. Of course that was wrong too. But it seemed to me that our problem of where to live was completely solved. In the middle of the night we sent a telegram to the innkeeper Carl Mayr, whom we had never met: 'Will buy Wiesmühl. Send contract at once.' The reply came next day: 'Better look at it first. Mayr.'

In the light of day and without the benefit of alcohol, that did seem rather sensible. We promptly left the Baltic and headed south.

I shall never forget how Herr Carl Mayr received us under the shady chestnuts of his terraced garden at the old Kaspar Moser inn. It was like being a guest of the last grand duke of some ancient, highly civilized vest-pocket principality. Mayr's head, already somewhat graying, was a curious blend of sturdiness and delicacy. But his outstanding quality was a kind of natural aristocracy. His neck and nose testified to a strong element of the robust peasant type, but his mouth, chin, forehead, eyes, and hands suggested artistic refinement of the kind that Coleridge called androgynous. He wore an elegant version of the local costume and silver-buckled gray suède shoes. Still as slender as a young man, he moved with the grace of a dancer between the kitchen, the tables, and his own quaint little house at the end of the tavern garden. He had the air of an amiable sovereign and a mouth always ready to break into a smile, but occasionally the roughest rustic curses would fall from it—when, say, a patron behaved badly or was drunk at the wrong times. It was a kind of test to be one of his guests, and not everybody passed. If he didn't like someone, he might order him to leave the table: 'You needn't pay, but you needn't come back either.' Yet he did not belong to the notorious species of rough innkeepers. On the whole he had a friendly word for everyone, radiating good cheer in the lovely wood-paneled public room, and made a particular impression on the children who spent summer holidays with their parents in Henndorf. To them he seemed like a king out of some fairy tale.

We quickly realized that it was by no means certain that we could buy Wiesmühl and become Carl's neighbors. That depended not so much on whether we liked the house as on whether he liked us. His family, a dynasty of innkeepers and brewers, had become prosperous. Both he and his brother Richard had completed Gymnasium, subsequently studied art, and traveled a good deal. As a result, he possessed a distinctive worldliness, both in his personality and in his way of life, along with the traditional rustic qualities of the district. When I returned from America and found him no longer alive, I visited his grave in the family vault of St Peter's Cemetery in Salzburg. I have been to it often since. On the stone slab, in lettering he himself designed, is the inscription: 'Herr Carl Mayr, Artist.'

He was in fact extremely proficient in painting, drawing, embroidery, and weaving, and considered himself an artist by vocation, whereas the inn was more of an inherited estate or family castle which he ran with a kind of playful generosity, though never foolishly. Cuisine and cellar were of the highest quality, and it was a pleasure to watch him write out the daily menus in the same fine but energetic hand in which he was later to trace the inscription for his gravestone.

Carl Mayr was a bachelor, and underneath the aristocratic equability and quiet grace of his life you sensed a strain of tragic loneliness, the detached melancholia of the late-comer, the last descendant of a line. That sadness, that sensitive but never cold aloofness, made his friendship all the more precious. Although he was strongly subject to moods, there was nothing capricious or the least unreliable about him. His moods were those of an extraordinary instrument which will not yield its proper music when touched by a coarse or unskilled hand. Knowing him brought an enduring enrichment of our lives.

*

5

Here, across a torrent of years, I must insert an experience that for me belongs to the realm of the miraculous, although there is nothing the least 'supernatural' about it. On the ground floor of Carl Mayr's small house, situated at one end of the tavern garden, there was a 'garden room' with glass door and wide windows. These looked out on his own private garden, which had a carefully calculated air of luxuriant wild growth. He had decorated the entire rear curved wall of the garden room with a hand-painted panoramic wallpaper which was undoubtedly rare and of some value. It was of French provenance, but it pictured life in America in a series of fanciful vignettes: ladies and gentlemen, white and black, in elegant or popular dress; riders, chaises, and stagecoaches; the outlines of old New York and sailing ships in a blue inlet; a primitive, toylike early railroad train drawn across a bridge by a locomotive with a funnel-shaped smokestack and high spoked wheels; white houses with pillared porticoes amidst great trees; distant mountain ranges with lightning flashing about their crests; and in the center a frost-bound Niagara Falls, its great masses of water glittering with ice—while in a dim grotto beside the Falls a beautiful Indian maiden wearing a marvelous feathered headdress and many golden bracelets lay sleeping. Finely drawn and delicately tinted, the whole composition, called *Le Voyage en Amérique*, was so entertaining that one never tired of looking at it and discovering still another quaint detail.

Carl Mayr had bought the panels in Munich, Vienna, or Paris and installed them so artfully in his garden room that they seemed a mural executed especially for the room. I recall the way he would take up brush and paints between the coffee and liqueur and restore its damaged spots: adding a highlight on the boot tip of a gallant Negro cavalier, or a touch of red to the Indian princess's crown of feathers. Evenings, with the candles lit or the moonlight streaming through the glass panes, the *Travel in America* shimmered with all kinds of oddities, and many a night we saw our own shadows dancing upon it. A few years later, after Carl had given up the inn and retired to private life, he decided to sell the wallpaper—perhaps he felt that he had looked at it long enough. At any rate, one day it was carefully removed and rolled up. Soon afterwards it was replaced by an Empire paper, a good deal less fantastic, and which Carl again repaired with the same minute care. In our memories, however, the garden room was still animated by the figures and quaint visions of *Le Voyage en Amérique*.

Many years passed. I had long ago taken flight from occupied Austria. The war was nearing its end; all communication by mail, all direct contact with the countries beyond the 'Atlantic Wall' had been severed. I was living in America, on my Vermont farm. One day some friends fetched me from my sylvan solitude to meet an American writer who lived in a colonial village a few hours' drive away. Charles Jackson was his name; he had just had a sensational success with his book, *The Lost Weekend.*

From the proceeds of the sale of its movie rights he had bought a magnificent Early American house. He was what we Europeans call a typical Yankee, a most intelligent and sensitive man, but totally without links to the European character or to what we consider European culture. I was shown the house with its pillared porch and its huge fireplaces. They were the only source of heat, and since it was winter, brisk fires were crackling in them. The house was furnished as a modern American of some taste would furnish it; in the master bedroom college banners and football emblems adorned the wall. I was therefore not expecting any aesthetic thrill when I was told that there was an unusually beautiful room on the ground floor, a kind of garden room, which however could not be heated and so was not being used right now. Without any particular curiosity, but as if I were somehow drawn by a scent, I went to see the room. When we entered I shivered—but not because the room was unheated. I was standing in Carl Mayr's garden room. The furniture was missing, of course—but the whole of the curved rear wall was covered with a frescolike wallpaper. For a moment I scarcely dared look at it closely. Then, faintly wondering whether all this was not some dream, I stepped closer and recognized all the details, all the familiar figures of the *Travel in America*—as if Carl Mayr had just dabbed on the final spots of color. My host, observing my special interest in the paper, although he could not guess just how stirred I was, began explaining: 'This is something rather rare—it was done by a French painter in the early part of the nineteenth century.'

'It's called *Le Voyage en Amérique*,' I said. 'Has it always been here?'

'No,' Jackson said. 'It was installed here by the previous owner of the house.'

'Do you know if there were many prints of it?'

'Only three—an original and two copies made by the painter

7

himself. This one was sold to someone in Europe and only came back to America a few years ago, thanks to an art dealer who found it in Austria.'

I went up closer to the panel, and I do not think it was an illusion that I recognized flecks of color I had seen Carl Mayr putting on with his fine brush.

This happened about the time Carl Mayr died in Henndorf. I still feel as if I had visited him in his garden room just before his death.

We spent our first evening in Henndorf in the wood-paneled public room of the inn, which has flanked the main highway for about a thousand years. It has burned down and been rebuilt several times, and with its massive walls and large rooms rather resembled an old castle. It also had a 'ghost room' that was haunted —everybody in Henndorf firmly believed in the ghost, and we ourselves had various brushes with it.

In the course of the evening peasants dropped in and took their places at the solid wood tables over a mug of beer or a pitcher of wine, puffing at their pipes. Suddenly the sounds of a zither began in the vaulted entrance hall, and a fat man who was sitting among the peasants and looked just like the rest of them started singing local songs in a wonderful bass. The others soon chimed in. The fat man was our host's brother, the famous concert artist Richard Mayr, first basso of the Vienna Opera—probably unsurpassed to this day in the parts of Leporello and Rocco.

The hours passed, and at about midnight our host said that now was the right time to look at the mill. Carrying lanterns, down we all went. The meadows were hushed, the brook rippled, the fountain in the courtyard splashed. The house, hidden behind a row of dark pines, had been uninhabited for twenty years. Magnificent painted peasant chests and beds, things that had been the miller's, still stood in the upstairs rooms. But the big living room on the ground floor was bare; grass was growing at the doorway and even into the hall. There was no light in the house; we placed our lanterns on the ledge of the stove and sat down on the built-in bench. We had brought wine with us. The pitcher was passed round, and we began to feel more and more at home in the empty, shadowy room. After a while our imaginations, guided and inspired by Herr Mayr's knowledgeable suggestions, filled the room with furniture, utensils. 'The sideboard should go here. The dining table there. An old grandfather clock would look good between those windows—perhaps about this big, with a painted face, the kind you find in old taverns. And a shelf with pitchers and pewter plates over on that wall. And for a ceiling light an iron wheel or a painted wooden yoke wired for electricity. And the chairs should be . . . and the curtains . . . and the tablecloths . . . and the dishes . . .'

A few weeks later it actually looked exactly as we had conceived it that night, amid the dust and spiderwebs.

The old mill needed all sorts of repairs before we could move in. In the interval, during which our task was to become acquainted with our Henndorf surroundings and learn to feel at home, Herr Mayr had quartered us in the haunted room—for it was the finest room in the house, with darkened old paintings, high-backed armchairs upholstered in velvet or needlepoint, and an immense Renaissance bed reached by a wooden step and roofed by a brocade canopy. It was also the quietest room, where you were not disturbed by the occasional choruses in the public room or the cars passing on the highway—few and far between in those days. Since there were two of us, and we generally went to bed slightly tipsy after the lively evenings in the garden or the public room, we weren't afraid. But my wife was expecting a baby, and I suppose her condition made her unusually susceptible to parapsychological influences. Every night, in the deep darkness that precedes the first glimmerings of dawn, she would awake gripped by such dread that she dared not extend her hand for the light switch or to me. She felt sure that she would touch something cold or corpselike. Later on I occupied the room alone, and I must admit that I often had similar sensations towards morning. The first cockcrow from the nearby farmyard would free me of them. Perhaps the old paintings contributed their mite to the charming eeriness of the room. The aged face of a long-forgotten Hapsburg monarch acquired cruel, piercing eyes in the crepuscular light cast by the old-fashioned lampshades; and there was a Madonna whose swollen abdomen contained a Christ child: through what seemed to be transparent gauze you saw Him holding a tiny cross, His head already surrounded by a nimbus. Certainly that was not a wholesome sight for a pregnant woman. We did not meet the traditional ghost—for the tale was told that an old woman, murdered by her two sons in this

9

bed in the sixteenth century, would appear through a walled-up
door, search under the bed for her money-box, and then depart
through the door, locked though it was. Nor did we see a bloody
figure said to appear at times behind the screen near the stove, its
head trembling. But footsteps and knocking could often be heard
in the walled-up corridor, produced by who knows what natural
causes. And on warm August nights an inexplicably cool draft
would sometimes blow through the room. Early one morning,
moreover, we were awakened by a wind whistling into the room
and blowing the heavy plush curtains almost to the ceiling. I
remembered that I had closed the long windows opening on the
balcony before going to bed. When I got up and checked on them,
I realized that there was not a breath of wind outside. Not the
slightest sign of a rising or fading storm could be felt. There were
still stars in the sky, a first streak of dawn in the east, and the first
cock was crowing. . . . Reassured, I went back to sleep and did not
worry about whether the phenomenon was 'ghostly' or physically
explicable.

We grew used to it, just as Herr Mayr himself had done. For he
lived in peaceful coexistence with his hauntings. To him there was
nothing supernatural about them. They were traditional fellow
inhabitants of the house, as much a part of it as the heirloom
furniture and the beautiful old tiled stoves. After all, he would say,
in a house like this so many ancestors had lived and died, so many
grandchildren had been born. Who could say whether some essence
of them, of their thoughts and their anima, might not be still alive.
Yet he was not in the least superstitious; he tended rather towards
a cheerfully rational irony, and often it was hard to say whether in
telling his ghost stories he was making fun of his audience or of
himself. Thus he once asserted—with a perfectly straight face but a
whimsical little glint in his eyes—that one of the ghosts must have
caught cold, because while he was doing his accounts in his little
office he had heard something sneezing behind him three times. He
had said: 'Bless you,' whereupon he heard a little snuffling, and
after that, silence.

Late one January evening, however, with the snow falling noise-
lessly outside, I was sitting with him in the public room, which was
already closed. There was no one in the kitchen. He was doing
some needlepoint, a favorite nocturnal occupation of his, working
on a tapestry based on an old print depicting Judith striking off the

head of Holofernes. I was reading a book over a mug of wine. Suddenly there was a loud knocking in one dim corner of the big room. Three times it sounded, as if someone were striking a walking stick against the floor. 'Good evening, Grandmother,' Carl said without looking up from his work, in a perfectly even voice. I said nothing, but watched the corner of the room and simultaneously kept one eye on his face. He looked exactly as if a belated guest had knocked on the door. After a short while the same three knocks came from the same corner, only now, it seemed to me, somewhat more insistent and impatient. 'Yes, yes,' he said in the same even voice, 'everything is all right and business is fine. Now be quiet.'

'Would you mind telling me whom you were talking to?' I asked after a silence.

'With my Grandmother Moser,' he said as if it were perfectly natural. 'Today is January eleventh, the anniversary of her death— she's almost always heard from on this day. During the last few months of her life she sat over there in the corner. She was paralyzed and always pounded with her crutch when she wanted to hear what was going on. So she still does it. She was a real fanatic about business.' With that, the episode was dismissed and we went to bed.

This lighthearted uncanniness was just as much a part of Henndorf and its charm, as caroling on Epiphany and the wild mummery during the Twelve Nights after Christmas. Our own house, Wiesmühl, we were told half jokingly and half in warning, also was haunted. In 1806, when the French occupied the country and the miller was off to war, his wife had killed an importunate grenadier and buried him in the cellar. He could be seen sometimes, we were told, and during the autumn Ember days his old regiment would come marching up to fetch him. However, the ghostly grenadier never showed up, although many a night the sound of bells came from the millstream, as if church bells were tolling the alarm for a fire in the village, or sometimes the stream drummed against the old wooden vanes of the water wheel with a noise like a marching regiment. Nevertheless the old house behind its sheltering pines, and tucked into the hill, was a cosy place for us; and if there were ghosts in it, we must have made life miserable for them with our bustling and in no way phantasmal life. Certainly we were not peering around looking for ghosts. And perhaps we spoiled things for them by the clear, daylight current of work that poured through the house throughout those years.

11

It remained true, of course, that Berlin was the center of my professional life. There all my premières and rehearsals took place. There my publisher and many of my friends lived. Such fantastic experiments as 'sound movies' were going on in Berlin, and a good many other activities and social occasions lured me there. But for my writing I had to be in the country. In the past, too, I had gone off into some rustic retreat whenever I could. Now an incredible stroke of luck—a surprise hit like nothing else in this period, apart from Brecht's *Threepenny Opera*—had made it possible for me to move into my own eyrie. And some bourgeois or peasant instinct told me that a house was better than money and perhaps the one thing you could hold on to in difficult times—as long as you could hold on to anything. And so, year in, year out, I thereafter sat like a broody hen on the eggs I had laid.

We lived at the mill for the larger part of the year. In the beginning we had to go out to the well with its neat shingled roof and carry water back into the house. It was quite a while before I could afford piped water and a bathroom. The children grew up there, played with the children of the peasants, and when they were bigger went to the village school. The natives called us 'the Wiesmüllers'—everyone was called after his house or farm—and throughout all those years many of the villagers never knew my real name. Nor did they ask what anyone did 'outside,' that is, outside the village—whether he had a name in the world, wrote plays, painted, or sang in opera. We talked with them about wind and weather, grass and cattle, and all sorts of everyday concerns. We bought our fish from Roider the fisherman, who had his solitary hut in a clearing in the forest, and went to Göpfringer's farm for fragrant dark bread fresh from the oven. We attended weddings, baptisms, and funerals, drank and danced with the people at their festivals, learned their customs and their songs. At Christmas we set up a tree freshly cut in the woods, in a corner of our living room, and a crèche with traditional wooden figures. The peasant children would come in to perform an old play about the birth of Christ; among the dramatic bits were scattered many Salzburg folk songs that Mozart probably heard in his youth. Sometimes as many as thirty children between the ages of four and fifteen participated. My wife had to break them in like half-wild foals, or train them like puppies, and sometimes the process involved a good deal of clouting and thumping. Then came the presents, followed by the carp dinner, and at midnight we tramped with lanterns over the hard-frozen snow to Mass in the brightly illuminated church. The village band played loudly, solemnly, and out of tune; the schoolmistress battled with her choir and her own tendency to rise into falsetto; all the music-makers preferred different keys; steam rose from heavy boots and damp coats; there was a rather strong smell; and it was all as beautiful, as serious, and as joyous as could be. Long after the Mass we would sit in Herr Mayr's lovely and well-heated garden room over würst and wine or beer, sometimes until dawn broke.

There were three clubs in the village, each of which displayed its own flag on holidays: the Volunteer Fire Department, the Rifle Club—which made a tremendous racket with their brass-bound old rifles at church and other rustic festivals—and the Veterans. The Veterans were those of the First World War. Every year on the anniversary of the outbreak of the war they drank themselves stupid—because, they reasoned, if the war had not broken out, they would not have been able to survive it. Henndorf people seldom let an opportunity for celebrating slip by. They were jovial and relaxed in temperament, good-natured, hard-working, curious, and above all talented. The fisherman would be singing loudly as he rowed his dory out on the pike-gray lake towards evening. And at certain jobs, such as installing the corner posts for a new building, age-old craftsmen's verses were recited in a ritual singsong by leader and chorus, verses that regulated the pace and rhythm of the movement far back in the Middle Ages. When our young gardener was laying out our rock garden by the brook, when the carpenter was constructing a new fence, they did their work with style and a kind of artistic *élan*. In this region, in which every stable door and the ridge of every roof reminds you of the late baroque's delight in forms, a feeling for sound craftsmanship and a love of the real thing still persisted. The peasant women took pleasure in the flowers in their windows. Glass paintings adorned the whitewashed walls, and in the kitchens copper flashed and pewter gleamed. Even dirty old Lena, half crazy and still wild about men at eighty, decked herself out with silver chains and bright beads. She would borrow such jewelry from Carl Mayr, and when she shuffled through the village with her wrinkled brown face, muttering to herself and pounding heavily with her cane, she looked like the shaman of some Indian tribe in full regalia. The people in this village still had faces, individual, distinctive, idiosyncratic faces such as you see in the paintings of medieval masters and in the wooden sculpture of Michael Pacher and Tilman Riemenschneider.

I have seldom met so blithe, balanced, and reliable a person as our caretaker, Josef Eder, who with his bright-eyed wife Justina helped us with heavy jobs. Josef was also the village gravedigger. But having to do with corpses and graves had not stamped him with the slightest trace of morbidity. Rather, it seemed to have given him a kind of unconscious dignity and gentleness. Yet he was a strong, healthy man who could show his brawn at work, in dancing, and in brawls as well. These Catholic peasants had a very simple and natural attitude toward death. It was part of the process of life; it belonged to the seasons and the change of generations. The idea of transcendence and eternity had stripped death of its grimness. Death was respected, mourned, paid homage to by solemn ritual, but people did not fear it or hide from it. Even the children were accustomed to the sight of corpses lying peacefully on their biers; the children went up to them, perhaps with a thrilling shudder, to pay their last visit and make the sign of the cross. Similarly, our domestic gravedigger was wholly unsentimental about his trade, though he was by no means rough or heartless. 'Lord Jesus,' he once exclaimed when he had been digging a new manure pit for us and we expressed our surprise at the long narrow shape, 'I turned it into a grave by mistake. Just force of habit.' Or when crazy old Lena limped by he would murmur indulgently: 'I'll be burying you soon.' And to a sick friend when he was feeling better: 'You've slipped away from my shovel again.' Often he used to say to me: 'That will be my finest day, when the time comes to bury you. . . .' It sounded enormously reassuring. Yet he was ten years older than I and unfortunately died before he had that honor.

Joking or serious, idling or working, his powerful body and his strong, plain face with its red mustache were always as composed as they were alert and cheerful. With their somewhat astringent features and their rustic manner, both Josef and Justina were good-looking after their fashion. It was a pleasure to see them because they were natural, proud, and in harmony with themselves.

The longer we lived there, the more closely integrated we became with the people and the country. There were no quarrels and no sour notes. And then, one night in the summer of 1934, the village

14

was awakened by a low crashing and booming that made the windowpanes rattle. It was no thunderstorm or avalanche. It was the first act of terror, a bridge being dynamited by the Nazis.

Most of the villagers were honestly outraged. Under the leadership of the brave young constable, Hans Lackner, a sizable group set out to hunt for the 'snotnoses.' For the hate propaganda had as yet made little impact on the local peasants. It had gained ground chiefly among the members of the rural middle class who wanted to be more than they were, the storekeepers, salesmen, and petty officials. The people in this region were neither very rich nor very poor. There were no large landowners; the populace consisted of fairly well-established farmers. They had their own farms and kept a few hired men or maids, whom they treated in the traditionally patriarchal way like members of the family. The devastating unemployment which had prepared the way for extremism in Germany was virtually unknown in these parts. The situation was quite different in certain areas of Alpine Austria, where real misery prevailed, or in the larger cities and industrial centers. But the farmers of the lower valleys knew nothing of this. They eyed one another or grinned with embarrassment when over beer someone began giving them 'political enlightenment.' In February of that same year the desperate rising of the socialists in Vienna had been bloodily repressed. The cruel end of the leftist peasant leader, Koloman Wallisch, whom the victors had hunted down and hanged, aroused a certain amount of anger here and there. But on the whole the farmers had little sympathy for the 'Reds'; the word was that they wanted to burn down the churches and take the land from the peasants. If driven to make a choice the peasants preferred the 'coxcombs,' as they called Prince Rüdiger von Starhemberg's militia, the *Heimwehr*; at least they made music or held torchlight parades and left everything unchanged. The statesmanlike shrewdness with which tiny Chancellor Dollfuss conducted foreign relations, and after 'restoring order' tried to effect some compromises in domestic affairs, gave an attractive cast to the new regime—even though it was a variety of Fascism, tempered by Austrian sloth and not at all terroristic. To intellectuals, and especially to refugees from Hitler Germany, 'independent Austria' seemed distinctly the lesser evil. And later, under sensible and liberal Kurt von Schuschnigg, who began on a policy of a 'window to the left,' there was even the prospect of a return to democratic forms of administration, which had by no means been completely eliminated.

After Hitler's seizure of power there was a great deal of whispering in Austria to the effect that things were now much better in the Reich and that the only people he had expelled or imprisoned were harmful vermin and corrupters of the *Volk*. The concept of Greater Germany was nothing new in Austria. The postcard painter and paperhanger Adolf Hitler had left his native haunts for Germany, where he had effectively sold this notion of predestined union; in time, thanks to this principle, both countries would know the blessing of total devastation. Nevertheless Austrians were a far more balanced people. Centuries of political education in holding together a community of nationalities had given them a certain distaste for the way 'they over there' were carrying on, making a big noise and rattling their sabers. Austrians were emotionally averse to militarism and strict organization. They preferred to wait and see. They would rather have their butter and cream than honor and glory—or at least so it seemed then. The agitators and climbers who counted on making careers and exercising power under Nazism had to go about their business with conspiratorial secrecy—in contrast to Germany, where under the shield of the freest kind of democracy they had been able to rage and incite against that democracy for years. Or else they had gone across the border and been organized into an Austrian Legion, poised for invasion. But that was something we heard little about.

In Henndorf itself and in the neighboring rural communities there were few malcontents, few people infected by envy and hatred—and it was precisely among these few that the supporters of the movement for 'national liberation' were to be found. Naturally, almost every one of them was well known. The intimacy of a village and of farm life provided, in microcosm, a model of the development and structure of the 'national rising.' There was the owner of the cheese plant, an ambitious, narrow-minded fellow from Allgäu in Bavaria who was aggrieved because he was not regarded as a real manufacturer or captain of industry, roles that might have come his way in the course of the German 'boom.' In the village he treated everyone with the same loud joviality, while hating those who were superior to him in culture, education, or anything else. Then there was a peasant with a medium-sized farm who was jealous of his brother-in-law, the mayor. He dreamed of replacing him, becoming a freehold farmer, as it was called 'over there in the Reich,' and assuming the leading role in the village. There was the former supervisor of the bathing establishment on the lake, the second son of a farmer with a sizable place. He was embittered because he was not the principal heir. He was also lazy, quarrelsome, and a drinker and in addition suffered from inferiority feelings because of a minor leg injury. He had lost his job at the baths because of unreliability, then had tangled with the law for collecting his invalid's pension twice over, and from then on lived heart and soul for 'the movement.' For the movement promised him revenge and unlimited legitimate power over others. He was exactly the type from whom the notorious concentration-camp sadists were recruited. If you look, you can find his sort in every country.

Anti-Semitism was, of course, the Nazis' cleverest—because most effective—psychological stroke. Moreover, the leaders and forerunners of Nazism really believed in it—for we must not imagine that any propaganda line will ever make headway unless its early spokesmen are themselves convinced of its truth. All political extremists mean what they say and shout. All of them, on both right and left, will carry out what they have promised in their wildest proclamations. For if they ranted only to win votes, or out of pure calculation, they would never be able to incite the masses to fanaticism. That is a truism we have learned through many painful lessons.

Race theory, of course, was completely idiotic in a country whose *élan vital* and whose nobility as well sprang from the continuous mixing of German with Slavic, Magyar, Romanian, and Asiatic blood. Nevertheless, both race theory and anti-Semitism were given a powerful impetus in old Austria (although, of course, both these follies may flourish in other nations). For it was in Austria that the unforgivable Georg Schönerer, a charlatan in every field, provided it with a base in popular—or rather vulgar—politics. This happened at about the same time that (again in Austria) Theodor Herzl was creating the intellectual foundations of Zionism.

But in the farming country of western Austria, unlike Vienna and the eastern frontier areas, the people knew few if any Jews. There the Jews had not become, as they had in Germany, a stimulating element in economic, social, and intellectual life. Or, if and where they had, no one paid any attention. The whole matter did not emerge in public affairs. *The* Jew was something fabulous, like a wizard or a witch. 'Is Schuschnigg a Jew?' That question was once put to me by a 'woods farmer,' one of those who lived on isolated farms a few miles above Henndorf, in the foothills or the valleys of the heavily forested mountain range. I liked to drop in on them when I went hiking. 'What makes you think so?' I said. 'Because the Nazis blast away at him the way they do.' I explained that Schuschnigg was not a Jew, but a Catholic like himself. He seemed reassured. But then, after brooding a while longer he asked: 'Are the Jews really so bad?' I reassured him about that also. 'Someday,' he said pensively, 'someday I'd rather like to see one.'

The country folk were quite indifferent to the fact that there were some Jews among the people who were musicians and who produced such great theatrical performances at the Salzburg Festival, thereby attracting monied tourists to the area. But anti-Semitic propaganda made its mark by providing every fool with the pleasure of despising someone below him. There was, for example, Crookbacked Anderl, a somewhat deformed, mildly feeble-minded butcher's boy, with a slobbering mouth and staring eyes, obsessed with impotent lewdness. He would creep around at night to spy on lovers, or peer through windows to catch a glimpse of maids undressing. Now he could regard himself as a better class of human being, one of a nobler race, than Max Reinhardt, Bruno Walter, or Stefan Zweig. The thing spread slowly like a hidden plague, while we ourselves hardly noticed what was going on. On the contrary, we thought the disease was being overcome after Chancellor Dollfuss had been assassinated by a Nazi gang. In honor of his funeral the electric lights were turned off in all the cities of Austria, and in the countryside as well. Burning candles were placed in every window, the churches were jammed, and people gathered in the streets to march in processions of mourning. It was a moving occasion, and we imagined we saw all of Austria united in self-defense against the violence threatening her from without and within. The worst danger seemed over. Even the police took action. A few Nazi ringleaders were arrested, including our loud-mouthed cheesemaker. But they were released after brief questioning for lack of 'evidence.' Afterwards they felt like martyrs and looked forward with redoubled fervor to their future vindication.

But the people we loved and respected, like the Mayr family, like

18

our caretakers, like the majority of the ordinary country folk, were, and remained, incorruptible. They formed closer ranks around the pastor, a small, unassuming, courageous man who Sunday after Sunday thundered from the pulpit in his eternally hoarse voice against those whom he called the 'new pagans,' and who disregarded the incident with a shrug when a few louts smashed his windows. He dreamed of the day when the Tower of Babel in the Reich would collapse and be replaced by a form of Christian socialism. Besides, the story went, Mussolini stood armed at the Brenner Pass because he did not want Hitler for a neighbor. Mussolini would surely guarantee—that was the word people used so lightly—the independence of Austria.

That first bridge blown up was on the main highway to Vienna. After that incident Willy, a miller's son who worked as gardener for us and the Mayrs, grew increasingly pale, nervous, and restless. He was a fine lad, tall, slender, with a special grace of movement. He did his work so skillfully and imaginatively that it was a joy to watch him or to plan something new with him. During the days after the unsuccessful attempt at a Nazi uprising, and the successful assassination of Dollfuss, he was so confused and depressed that he could no longer look anyone in the face. And one morning the police came and arrested him, charging him with being chiefly responsible for the dynamiting of the bridge.

Now his life was at stake, for under the prevailing martial law there was a death penalty for crimes involving explosives. We all feared for him, although he was a Nazi. For—why was he a Nazi? It was fairly simple. His girl friend worked for the cheesemaker, who employed a few dozen people. The cheesemaker was the local Führer, and the people who were dependent upon him, along with the members of their families, had to follow along whether they liked it or not. That was how it had begun. And our Willy, who had a rather imaginative nature, had probably been intrigued by the mood of adventure, the cops-and-robbers spirit of conspiracy. That was a large part of the appeal of the Nazi movement for young people. The Nazi leaders filled them with flattering notions of what fighters, heroes, saviors of the people they were—while at the same time dropping a threatening hint: anyone who didn't go along would have a few surprises awaiting him later on. At first it was pretty much a game—what fun to light a swastika fire on a mountain, then hide in tree tops and watch the police searching for clues. Young people, of course, always have a leaning toward illegality (and sometimes they are quite right about it). Most of these boys had nothing so serious in mind as killing and brutality. But then there was no turning back; one day the orders came.

During the weeks that Willy was waiting for his sentence, with the prospects that it might be immediate execution by hanging, a letter came to us from him. He enclosed a small, neatly drawn sketch of our garden. Shortly before his arrest he had installed a new underground water line to the vegetable garden, and he was the only person who knew where it could be turned on and off. That bothered him—for if he were to die we would not be able to regulate the water and the garden might suffer considerable damage. I myself was one of the favorite targets of Nazi propaganda: my plays and books had been banned or burned in the Reich, and our house was on the list of those that were to be blown up or seized in case of an uprising in Austria. But none of these facts made any difference to Willy, with his rather childishly decent mentality.

He was not condemned to death; the sentence was reduced to a long term of imprisonment with hard labor. We were truly glad, and I sometimes sent books to him in prison. To express his thanks, for Christmas he painted a charmingly primitive picture of our house which to this day hangs in my room, for I found it again after the war.

He was released from prison when Hitler annexed Austria. Later, long after I had fled, I learned that during those days of the Anschluss he had drawn a gun to drive off a mob that had begun to plunder my house, since it could no longer lay hands on me. But that came too late. Such loyalty had lost all meaning. The Gestapo wrecked what he had saved from the looters.

In retrospect I can say that we were never disappointed by our neighbors in Henndorf. They all behaved as we might have expected. Our good Frau Justina, the caretaker's wife, expressed this best in a letter she sent me while I was in Switzerland:

'It's April, raining one minute, sun shining the next, snowing the next, and the people are like the weather. The ones that were a nuisance before are worse nuisances than ever, and the ones that were decent are better than ever now.'

*

20

But at the time we celebrated the great festival, that rural community which is fundamentally indestructible was still flourishing. It was only half a year before disaster descended upon Germany, and the seventh summer I had lived in Henndorf. To be exact, it was the feast of the Assumption, that is, August 15th in the year 1932.

The Rifle Club—the oldest club in the village, whose president was our caretaker-gravedigger—had been after me for a very long time to donate a new flag to the village. For their hundred-year-old banner, as venerable as the club itself, was slowly shredding to tatters. The most flattering proposals were made to me: if, for example, I bought that new flag I would be entitled to have three salvos fired over my grave. But I knew the peasants and that it is not wise to yield to them too quickly, especially in material things. If you do, you lose their respect and are regarded as a fool or a spendthrift. Now, however, as a kind of offering for seven happy years in this village, I agreed to make that gift. The enthusiasm was enormous. The banner was ordered from the best flagmaker in Vienna. It was to be hand-embroidered, red and white in the national colors, of heavy silk, edged with gold, with a vignette of the landscape in the center. But the main thing was the festival, to which the whole village had been looking forward for months. As the date drew near, everyone was gripped by a veritable fever of anticipation. There were endless conferences to plan the proceedings. Everything was considered: invitations to neighboring communities, decoration of the village, illumination, the church ceremonies, the parade, the food and drinks. The festival was to go on for three days and three nights. They wanted people to be talking about this festival for the next thirty years, the Henndorfers said. And so they would have been—had not so many other topics of conversation arisen in the meantime. . . .

On the eve of the festival there was not a house in the vicinity without its flowers, wreaths and lights. For days the horses had been curried and combed to look their best when they pulled the floats. Their manes and tails were braided and tied with red and white silk ribbons. Our house, too, shared in the festive spirit. All the doors and windows were open; the warm summery air wafted through the rooms; the door to the outside staircase leading up to the kitchen was also open, and our living room had been converted into a rustic utopia. Eatables stood everywhere, on the heavy

21

wooden tables, the window sills, the sideboard—a whole ham in one place, a whole cheese in another. Sausages hung from the ceiling beams. The slabs of butter were the size of loaves of bread, and the huge round black loaves lay on wooden plates. Our caretaker incessantly drew beer from a barrel that stood outside the front door. His red mustache dripped with foam, for he felt obliged to taste the beer before presenting it to guests. A keg of Lagrein Kretzer, which should be of a light-brown shade if it is genuine, was set up in the room. And for those who needed a quick pick-me-up, aged golden Slovenian slivovitz stood by in large pitchers.

There were sixteen guests in the house, and more and more kept arriving, for it was festival time in Salzburg and the area was swarming with friends. Some of them stayed with us, and it remains a mystery to me where we found room for all of them. Most of the ladies, especially the younger and prettier ones, had donned the local costume. The farther away they came from, the more traditional and local were the dresses they had bought from Lanz, in Salzburg. Our guests were a colorful mixture, and yet there was a kind of hidden harmony among them. Companions of a dream life, where have you all gone? There was Chaliapin, the great Russian singer, with his wife, several friends, and his lovely daughters, brunette Dasya and wheat-blonde Marina—a whole band of Russians. There was a Dutch scholar who had recently set up a precious music archive in Vienna. There was a theater director, a Catholic prelate from Germany, a few writers, some actors and artists with their wives or girl friends.

But the principal personages were the peasants, and the whole content and meaning of the festival was the village itself. Day and night there was singing in the taverns, the beat of dancing feet, the blare of music. The children took part too. The little girls had had their hair stiffened with sugar water and lard, then put in paper curlers overnight. On the eve of the festival they marched into our yard in their starched white batiste dresses to honor my wife, who as co-donor of the flag was officially called the Flag Mother. The first notes of the recorders piped out. But just as the girls were beginning a traditional dance, in which the schoolmaster had carefully drilled them, the inevitable thunderstorm broke. At the first clap of thunder the dancers flew in all directions like a flock of frightened partridges. This wholly spontaneous sight was certainly more amusing for our guests, who had gathered to watch it at all the windows of our house, than the traditional ballet would have been. Thunderstorms belong to rustic festivities like salt in soup. The grand nocturnal torchlight procession also took place amid thunder and lightning, and the rain beat down on our heads when we stopped at the veterans' memorial and removed our hats for three minutes in honor of the dead. But brilliant moonlight suddenly thrust through the clouds, which scattered rapidly. Everything smelled of leaves and wet earth, and thereafter not a drop of rain fell as long as the festival lasted.

The stamina of farmers during such celebrations is almost incredible, and we did our best to keep pace with them. But after we had gone to bed near three o'clock in the morning, only a few of my guests awoke with me when the brass band came marching up again at four, to begin its morning concert after another pint of beer. At six the parade of affiliated clubs began. They had come from thirty-two other Austrian villages to pay tribute to the new Henndorf flag, and such was the blare of trumpets and thunder of drums that the horses reared up. The special carriage which took us to the open-air Mass for the solemn consecration of the flag was drawn by two young stallions, the finest in the village, and we could call ourselves lucky to have come through that ride alive. The Mass took place under the open sky, in a large meadow encircled by trees. My paternal friend Friedrich von Erxleben, called Petrus, had come all the way from Germany to preside. He looked splendid, with his white hair, his glowing eyes, and his handsome face shining with earthly and heavenly love. He intoned the Latin text with an Italian accent he had learned during his stay among the Jesuits in Rome. Flanked by two massive peasant women who had provided the streamers for the flag—a brightly colored embroidered one for weddings and a black one for funerals —my wife had to recite some lines of verse. She suffered more stagefright than an actress who is playing Joan of Arc for the first time. All the thirty-two flags from the visiting clubs bowed and 'kissed' the fresh, newly consecrated banner by way of salute. Henceforth it would be borne in the midst of the townsfolk on all solemn and joyous occasions. It was meant to make people glad; its bright cloth would confer upon them the strong and simple sense of belonging, a consciousness of mutual trust and mutual aid. It would remind them that they were not only ordinary selfish human beings, but that the sky above them and the hard earth they

23

tilled beneath them were common to all, so that each man should help the other because in this world everyone needed everyone else. This was the burden of my friend Petrus's address; its tempo quickened somewhat towards the end because Petrus had been fasting since midnight and it was by this time close to noon.

The festival lasted from Saturday night until the small hours of Monday morning. Tens of thousands of litres of beer and wine were drawn and drunk, and even the poorest ate their fill. The bands ran through their entire repertoire, group photographs were taken, and nobody absented himself from the jollities except to go out under the trees to the call of nature or to kiss a girl. The dancing went on without a break. As guest of honor I had to waltz with the wife of the leading farmer of the district; she weighed two hundred and fifty pounds and sweated like a horse. But there were many lovely girls and women whirling lightly, tilting their heads as they danced, their eyes half closed.

On the second night, during a coffee break in our house, a breathless small boy came running from the inn to report that the music had stopped. The forester who was our village conductor had fallen from the podium. But the mishap proved to be no tragic accident, merely a pause, the inevitable result of sheer exhaustion. For the forester drank a glass with every waltz and a pint to accompany every polka. Everyone wanted to go on dancing, and I sent word that there was cold water in the well, in case they had forgotten, and black coffee in the kitchen at the restaurant. An hour later another messenger appeared, even more out of breath, to report happily that the conductor was back and the band playing again. We all went out to see. But at midnight the forester again tumbled off the podium, out cold, this time for good. To the accompaniment of solemn singing from the members of the Rifle Club, he was carried home. By then everyone was too tired or too drunk to dance anyhow. Lights went out and all was suddenly still in the village. The full moon shone over the meadows and showered silver into the rollicking brooks. Only we and our guests were still awake and merry; habitual night owls, we were further stimulated by the excitement of the festival. We stood in the wide village street in front of the closed inn and tried to lift the staggering theater director into his room through his window, because he had lost his key. But he kept tumbling down.

Suddenly we heard a strange noise in the night, a chirping and trilling that sounded more like an animal than a human being. Two shadows appeared, approaching along the bright, deserted highway, for now, after midnight, there were no longer any cars on it. They were two itinerant musicians—one of them blowing a kind of old-fashioned clarinet, the other with a fiddle tucked under his chin. In the days of Schubert or Eichendorff they might have come tramping along a road just as they were doing on this night. Back in the town of Frankenmarkt, sixteen miles away, they had heard that our town was having a festival, and so they had set out on foot to earn a little cash. Now they were bitterly disappointed at having come too late. But they were just in time for us. I directed them; they led the way, playing, and a procession formed of its own accord, a kind of polonaise made up of our guests. To music, we tramped back home to the mill. When we had crossed the dark bridge over the brook to our own property, the musicians sat down on a bench in front of the house and without being asked immediately began playing a waltz. The meadow looked like a scoured white floor in the moonlight, and we all started dancing. The dew wet our shoes, the grass tickled the ladies' ankles, but we danced and sang on the meadow until the morning mist steamed up and full daylight appeared. Then, dreamy and blissful, we sat over coffee in the first rays of sunlight.

We provided a bed of hay for the musicians, in our attic. There they slept long and well until noon. Then the village policemen awoke them and put them under arrest for disturbing the peace at night and practicing a trade without a license. He did that only because they came from another village, of course. The poor fellows came to me and said they were going to have to pay a fine of twelve schillings, which would ruin them, or spend three days in jail. Naturally, I gave them the twelve schillings. The older of them weighed the money in his palm thoughtfully for a long time, thanked me, then pocketed it and said: 'If you haven't any objection, sir, we'd just as soon go to jail anyway. . . .' I heard them still playing as the constable marched them off. And I can still hear them. That music rings with homesickness and joy, with youth and age, with all the seasons of memory, with time and eternity. It is the sound of Austria.

1934-1939
EXPULSION

SOONER OR LATER in every human life there comes the catastrophe of banishment or expulsion with which, according to the Book of Genesis, all earthly travail begins. For many people, it happens almost unnoticed. Or else some seemingly trivial event, perhaps a change of school, or town, or apartment, a family quarrel or a new career, makes them belatedly aware that they have passed through this universal experience, this re-enactment of a prototypal episode. Yet it is as much part of the development of human beings as metamorphosis is for many animals.

In many lives and on many occasions the catastrophe takes all too brutal a form, a rejection, persecution or ruination. Those who are fortunate go through the shock at an age when it is not yet too shattering, but has the effect of making them aware of the forces of resistance and metamorphosis within. Those who understand the meaning of friendship discover its special grace at such times, for friendship proves stronger than all hatred and even stronger than death.

When we had to leave Henndorf we thought we were losing everything that was dear to us, everything that made life worth living. For our departure meant the loss of all natural and acquired ties, a disappearance of all the sense of 'belonging' that background, education, tradition, community of work, even the habits and style of daily life, had formed within us. Even more, it meant the loss of language, which for the writer is the very element in which he works, and so the source of his livelihood, and for every man the basic substance, wellspring, and root of all knowledge, experience, communication—of his humanity and thus of humanism in general.

Or so it seemed. For we had not yet learned that in reality there is no losing anything we have grasped and possessed in its essence, neither happiness nor sorrow. I remember one time when I sat with my mother and my friend the poet Schiebelhuth on the edge of a lonely clearing on the Henndorf mountain called the Zifanken. As we sat quietly looking across the top of the high grass, suddenly a handsome red fox came trotting towards us. He was running with the wind and saw us only at the last moment, so that he leaped

29

high in the air in fright and bounded towards the bushes. Such spontaneous encounters with shy animals who are rarely to be seen running freely, whether the otter, the martin, or the badger in Europe, or the wildcat or even bear in Vermont, always have moved me in a special way, as if I had caught a glimpse of one of the mysteries of the Creation. So, too, at that time I was seized with a curious, inexplicable emotion, although I neither knew nor imagined that this was one of our last walks in the countryside that had become so much my home. Then Schiebelhuth said, as if he had somehow sensed what was going on within me: 'You will always have this fox and this place on the margin of the woods, wherever you go. They belong to you; no one can ever take these things from us. The image within is everlasting.'

We had been more or less at home in Henndorf ever since I bought Wiesmühl in 1926. But from 1933 on, after Hitler's seizure of power in Germany, it became our permanent residence. Only during the last two years did we also maintain an apartment in Vienna. The nearness of Salzburg, which Reinhardt and Hofmannsthal as well as the high level of its music had transformed into a world center during the summer months, preserved us from too much rustication. In fact, our circle of friends and acquaintances during those years was enormously rich and varied. It extended from great artists, men of the world, celebrities who arrived like rare migratory birds, sometimes in flocks, sometimes in solitary flight, and alighted near us for a time, to the nesters and residents of the native populace. It extended from the Herr Professor (in those days the term could refer only to Max Reinhardt, whereas nowadays it has become virtually an epithet for anybody engaged in 'cultural activity') and his famous or distinguished visitors, to the young ladies from England and America who horrified the natives by displaying red-lacquered toenails in open sandals; from the Abbot of St Peter's Monastery to the waiter Franz in the Café Bazar or the old doorkeeper in the Österreichischer Hof and the 'hostess' of the tavern on Kaigasse, in whose comfortable public room with its Tyrolean stove I spent many afternoon hours. It was empty at those times, and I would sit with my notebook and then, over an evening pint, read aloud what I had done to my always receptive friend Kapsreiter.

In the early days, when we had no car of our own, we could

reach Salzburg only by being rowed across the lake, which was fifteen minutes from our house, to Wallersee Station, where we caught a local train that crawled slowly over the countryside. Later there was a bus that left Henndorf at long intervals and was always overcrowded. It was certainly jolly to take it and listen to the rough jokes of the farmers and peddlers who were jolted around inside it. But often it lurched into the ditch, or stopped on account of motor trouble—always in front of a tavern, of which there were half a dozen in a stretch of ten miles. The upshot was that I preferred walking. I did not mind the three-and-a-half-hour hike. In the Salzburg suburb of Gnigl there was an old inn surrounded by chestnuts and linden trees. It was called Dachslueg—'Badger Lookout'—and lay on a country road impassable to automobiles. From this vantage point you could see the whole of Salzburg couched between the fortress, the Kapuzinerberg, the Mönchsberg, and the Nonnberg, and all the way out to the open hills and the tower of the pilgrimage church, Maria Plain. The city would usually be bathed in a shimmering mist which in these parts comes after the notorious rainy season and precedes the fair weather of late summer. Suddenly the air would shake with a tremendous boom, for at noon all the clock towers came to life. Before their thunderous assault and the energetic tolling of the smaller bells at higher pitches, the mist would be torn asunder—even that sallow cloud compounded of hearth smoke and other exhalations which always hangs over old, closely built-up cities. Then I would proceed swiftly down to the city, saunter along the lively Linzergasse, step into a shop here and there, and meet my friends.

Among these there were two groups: the aforementioned migrants and birds of paradise who put on their private artistic performances chiefly during the period of the Festival, and the permanent group of resident friends. We counted among the latter our Henndorf gravedigger and Rifle Club president as well as the writer Stefan Zweig, who lived on the Kapuzinerberg (his house filled with priceless collections of manuscripts and relics, including letters and scores of Mozart and Beethoven, and even Beethoven's rickety writing desk and his last piano!); Alexander Lernet-Holenia, Austria's foremost writer since Hofmannsthal; and the great German actors Werner Krauss and Emil Jannings. Emil had come home from Hollywood laden with dollars, not caring to expose himself to the hazards of the new talking movie in a language not his own. I thereupon wrote the scenario for his first sound movie, based on Heinrich Mann's novel *Professor Unrat—The Blue Angel*, which has held its interest to this day. Marlene Dietrich, who had just been discovered, helped make it a worldwide success. What is more, she created a character which has since been imitated over and over again, in a thousand variations, but never with her originality and style.

We exchanged regular visits with the Jannings's, and whenever we went to their house we returned home stuffed, having overeaten woefully. For his wife Gussy knew how to turn sauerbraten, goose, a plate of cold meats, or corned beef with herb sauce into a Rabelaisian banquet. Emil, for his part, was larger than life; normal human standards simply did not fit him, in the physical sense as well. There on his country property he was like a Renaissance prince in his *castello*. Money meant power to him, the power to savor life to the full, and to play a leading role in his circle. As host and tablemate—surrounded by friends who could at least attempt to match him mentally and physically—he revealed his finest talents. He outdid everyone not only in appetite, but also in down-to-earth wit and burlesques. Except for Maxim Kopf, the painter from Prague who was later to marry Dorothy Thompson, I never knew anyone who had Jannings's way of pronouncing the most obscene and unprintable words and phrases with such poise and naturalness that even well-bred young ladies did not have to blush. In fact, they could laugh freely; no one was in the least embarrassed. Jannings carried it off by a sparkling devilry. I myself am rather repelled by obscenity, and especially by sexual jokes, when they are manifestly surrogate satisfactions, forms of exhibitionism, or cerebral lewdness. Lusty language that does not come from natural vigor I find embarrassing. But Emil's Rabelaisian crudities were completely authentic. Sensitive though he was, sometimes even hypochondriacal, and spontaneous, his talent came from his guts.

Werner Krauss, his boyhood friend, whom I still regard as the greatest actor of our times, had a completely different temperament. He was a man who delighted in fooling around and acting, in life as well as on the stage. For him, make-believe was the expression both of an ever active creative imagination and of a genuine naïveté, a truly childlike character. Whereas Jannings had a keen understanding of the rising and falling pressures, the norms and fluctuations of this world, in everything from the stock market to modern art, Krauss was really unworldly—so much so that for a while he loyally believed in the Führer and in the purity of his aims. Emil was never taken in; what impressed him was success. And after all Hitler had that to his credit (until he abused it).

To suggest something of the demonic quality of Krauss's art, I must mention an incident that took place in my house in Henndorf, where he often visited me, coming over from his home at Mondsee. I owned a mask, a very rare and remarkable piece, more than two hundred years old, of the kind that is still worn in Austrian mountain villages for caroling, at carnival and Advent processions, and on all sorts of other occasions that go back to ancient pagan customs. The mask is supposed to frighten off ghosts or devils. I had discovered it in the attic of an old country inn and had bought it. It was a gruesome thing—a huge face carved from smoothly polished wood, rather like an African devil mask; an immensely long nose, evil, squinting slits for eyes, a horribly toothed mouth, and pale flaxen hair. A savage troll that lived on the flesh of children would have such a face. It gave one such shivers that nobody in my family wanted to see it. I felt the same way and kept it hidden in a chest in the attic, as its former owner had done. If a maid or cleaning woman happened to come across it up there, we were sure to hear a piercing scream and the thumps of headlong flight.

In the course of a long afternoon together, during which we kept our wine glasses filled, Krauss began talking about the problem of miming, especially the facial expression of the actor on stage and in motion pictures. Close-ups in movies, he said, had given an undue importance to this aspect of acting, and this was something about movie-making that he hated. For he did not like accomplishing his effects by facial expressions seen through a telescope, so to speak. He hadn't become an actor for that kind of thing. What he wanted was ... he reflected for a long time and then said in a curiously obstinate intonation: to conjure. Yes, to conjure like a magician. He despised actors who had to do everything by miming, he said. That was no more than making faces. Great works of art hadn't been written for that purpose. It should be possible to play great dramatic roles with masks. That was true acting. In classical antiquity, remember, the actors had worn masks—not only the gods, but the great tragic human characters also. That was something he had always secretly wanted to do. 'As a matter of fact, I'm convinced that if I were really inside my part nobody in the audience would notice whether I was wearing a mask or masking my real face in some other way. After all, that's the real meaning of make-up; we actors call it putting on our masks. And behind a mask I'd really be able to conjure.'

It suddenly occurred to me to test him, and I produced the horrible mask from the attic. Krauss was fascinated. He turned the mask back and forth, held it up in front of his face several times, and mumbled under his breath, while the rest of the group at table went on talking. But suddenly he put the mask on, tying it behind his ears with the leather thongs attached to the sides—and instantly everyone fell silent. For a while his head swayed; we saw only the mask and his expressive hands poking out of his shirt sleeves, looking strangely naked. Suddenly he said: 'Oh, I'm terribly sad. There's nothing I can do about it. I have to weep. I am filled with sorrow. I could weep for the rest of my life.' He spoke almost in a monotone. But we all saw the mask weeping. He went on like that for a while. He told a story about the death of his sweetheart. He defended himself in a dialogue with an invisible person who held him guilty of that death. He admitted it. 'Yes, I know, it is my fault, I caused it,' and the mask took on an expression of utter despair, of terrible incurable unhappiness. Then he suddenly gave an embarrassed chuckle and removed the mask. But he himself seemed to have no face. His eyes, ordinarily a radiant blue with a sly twinkle in them, were as if switched off and not looking at anyone. 'You're wonderful,' I said, handing him a glass of wine. 'Go on.' He drained it, leaned back, replaced the mask, and suddenly —without laughing, without uttering a sound—slapped his thigh. He merely drew in his breath like someone so amused that he is choked with laughter. Then, 'Fellows,' he gasped, 'what a joke!' And I could swear, like everyone else at the table, that the mask grinned, that laughter spread across its whole face.

We had a totally different but equally memorable and pleasant relationship with Stefan Zweig. He was by nature not an emotional person, or rather he preferred not to express his feelings directly and make a show of them. But once he felt close to anyone, he offered unlimited, brotherly affection. I think he counted friendship among the highest forms of happiness that he was capable of experiencing. Above all, he was a person of extraordinary, perhaps unique, generosity and helpfulness. He came from a well-to-do family and from his childhood had never known material anxieties, so that he could pursue his career as a writer unhampered by such concerns. But his understanding of the needs and worries of others was all the greater, and he was always ready to lend a helping hand, especially to young writers and artists. He supported a tremendous number of them when they were starting out—never out of a vain mania to play the Maecenas, never with condescending charity, but out of a perfectly natural feeling of comradeship. He also helped many artists in their old age. All this he did unobtrusively, with the greatest discretion; the slightest publicity horrified him, and expressions of thanks embarrassed him. Wherever he could he went beyond financial aid, giving recommendations and advice, making connections. No amount of letter writing, telephoning, or traveling was too much for him if he could smooth the way for a young writer whose career he thought deserved backing. At the time we met I no longer needed such help, but the beginning of our friendship sprang from similar motives. As soon as he learned that I intended to settle in the vicinity of Salzburg, he, older than I and known throughout the world, arranged to meet me. He invited me to his house, drove to Henndorf to look at ours while it was still in its roughest shape, and drew me into his circle of notables who would scarcely have been accessible to me at the time.

Giving was so much part of his nature that he did not confine it to those in need; he regarded it as a form of human association. He was always ready to assist a writer who was running into difficulties with the plan and structure of a work. Stefan would freely contribute his experience, his knowledge and his inspirations without—as others do when they have added no more than a fart to a creative work—boasting of being a 'collaborator.' On the other hand he came to me with a play whose prologue was giving him trouble because it dealt with the 'common people'—not his usual subject. Moreover, it was set in my native region. With the same naturalness with which he gave help, he accepted it when I spent an hour completely rewriting the scene for him. There is nothing special about that; such co-operation ought to prevail among creative people, and in good, unconstrained periods it probably always has been that way.

The first time he came to Henndorf, we were just confronting the problem of installing a new stove in our living room, since the old one was unusable. We wanted to furnish the whole room in a single style that would be in keeping with the character of the house and the landscape. Therefore, a real rustic tiled stove was the only possible choice, and such stoves were hard to come by, except for a brand-new one of the arty-crafty type. Stefan beamed when we described our problem. He asked for the measurements and mysteriously disappeared. Next day a team of truckers appeared with an old Salzburg tiled stove, dark green, charmingly ornamented. It fitted the corner where it was to go to perfection. Stefan's story was that it came from the storeroom of his home on the Kapuzinerberg, where it was lying about among other 'junk.' To this day I wonder if he had not run around Salzburg for hours in order to hunt up such a stove and make us a present of it.

We were also indebted to him for the dogs, and these were the finest of gifts. He owned a superlative specimen of a long-legged, long-eared, and marvellously proportioned springer or water spaniel (unlike the cockers, which I do not much care for). This animal was the father of many generations of dogs. He was called Kasper. With characteristic consideration, Stefan provided him with a bitch, to keep him company. The latter was a purebred (there is such a thing as racial purity among dogs), and a beautiful animal. At regular intervals a litter resulted from this perfect marriage. I know by experience how hard it is for a real dog lover, who is not just interested in the commercial end of breeding dogs, to find proper owners for puppies. Nevertheless, I shall never forget how Stefan, in our second year at Henndorf, presented us with the most beautiful pair of spaniels imaginable. They were called Flick and Flock, were spotted white and dark brown, and had tails like ostrich feathers. In defiance of convention I refused to have their tails cropped. The pair displayed incredible canine intelligence. Among all the many dogs I have had, I have never known such personalities, except for a St Bernard and a female dachshund— but then she was a cross between a child and an angel.

The spaniels increased and multiplied in charming and enviable incest, which at the outset does not necessarily lead to symptoms of degeneracy. I allowed them offspring only once a year, and the litters were flawless. Incidentally, the pair provided me with a chance for some observations on marital psychology. Flock, the male, used to go half mad with desire when Flick was in heat. But during the third or fourth year of their life together he lost interest and became too lazy to cover her. Evidently familiarity had cooled his libido. I had to fetch a neighbor's male and chain him nearby. Then, stimulated by jealousy, Flock mounted his mate at once, and seemed more ardent than ever.

Stefan Zweig was a catalyst; he took keen pleasure in bringing together the people he liked. Thus it was through him that I first met Joseph Roth, whom he was especially fond of, as well as Bruno Walter and Toscanini. Later, in London, he introduced me to Joachim Maass; still later, in our American exile, Maass and I became close friends and have remained so to this day. Instigating friendships between people was another aspect of Stefan's generosity of spirit. For the rest, he was an 'odd bird.' The image suits him because he actually had small, dark, sharply flashing birdlike eyes; you recognized the warmth as well as the melancholia in them only after you had known him well for some time. He loved women, revered women, liked talking about women, but he rather avoided them in the flesh. When he was having tea with me in Henndorf and my wife or a woman friend of ours wanted to keep us company, he was apt to show signs of nervousness, shied away from their attempts to start a real conversation, politely declined when the ladies offered him something to eat or drink. The result was that after a while they tactfully left us alone, whereupon he thawed immediately; among men he was always intensely and stimulatingly talkative.

Once, when Stefan had left after one of these intimate dialogues, my wife asked me: 'What was Stefan telling you about so animatedly today?' 'The latest gossip of the French Revolution,' I replied. For he was working on his *Marie Antoinette* at the time, and he knew as much about every case of phimosis, syphilis, or gonorrhea among the personalities as if he had been official dermatologist in Saint-Germain. He even mentioned such matters with the same sort of discreet smile, hand slightly shielding his mouth, as the Saint-Germain skin specialist might have done among friends.

One of his most peculiar characteristics—perhaps it foreshadowed the tragedy of his later suicide—was his inexplicable fear of aging. I have never seen it so intense in any other person, not even in women. At the time of his fiftieth birthday he fell into a profound depression. That was before the beginning of the reign of terror in Germany, and he himself was perfectly healthy, never having weakened his sound constitution by any sort of excess, not even in his work. Nevertheless, he felt downcast and restless for weeks. He considered travel, but decided against it because he was starting another book. Finally he asked me to perform what he called an act of friendship. He wanted to avoid all the congratulations, celebrations, and honors that are usually connected with the fiftieth birthday of a famous and well-beloved person. Instead, he wanted the two of us to go to Munich in total secrecy and celebrate the day in a small Jewish restaurant known only to connoisseurs. He loved good food and had discovered that this place surpassed all others in the preparation of blue carp, braised goose, and all the traditional side dishes.

Sitting with me in the restaurant, he did justice to the staggering feast and chattered away gaily about this and that without the slightest suspicion that the restaurant owners, who adored him, knew perfectly well that it was his birthday and pretended not to notice merely out of discretion and respect. Finally, over a glass of brandy, he suddenly said: 'You know, we've about had what life has to offer. From now on it's a downhill course.'

Since I was fifteen years his junior, I did not contradict him; I thought he was merely speaking for effect. About half a year before his sixtieth birthday I heard him say something similar when, on the occasion of a short visit to New York, he asked me to a French restaurant. As we parted he remarked: 'However the war turns out, there's a world coming into which we won't fit any longer.' Then, too, he was still perfectly healthy, not suffering from physical troubles or the financial anxieties that harassed most of us exiles. But before long we received the news from Brazil of his suicide.

In the spring of 1934, during the struggles between the Dollfuss regime and the Viennese socialists, among whom he had several close friends, the Austrian police came and searched his house. Next day Stefan packed his bags and went to London, never to return. I met him there shortly afterwards—at the time I was earning my bread doing movie work for Alexander Korda, but spending that money in Henndorf, for it bought me freedom to do my own work. Stefan pleaded with me not to go back home. I ought to send for my family and stay in England, he said. For my part I could not see why, now that Austria had quietened down politically and there seemed to be no immediate danger.

He did not return to his beloved house, still under the care of his wife Friederike, and to his collections. But the latter were already carefully packed and on the way to him, and he had started transferring his fortune. 'I could no longer sleep there,' he said to me. 'At night, I kept hearing the roar of tanks rolling up from the German border.' Insistently, with a desperate note in his voice, he warned me against staying on. 'You're returning to a trap,' he said. 'And sooner or later it's going to be sprung. There can't be any other outcome. Why not leave now, when you can still take your possessions with you, instead of waiting until you'll have to run for it? You'll be lucky if you can get away then.'

Of course he was right, and my view was shortsighted. Or rather, it was sheer stupidity. But sometimes the gods give their consent to stupidity. I bless them and it today, for they—the gods and my stupidity—presented us with four good, fulfilled years. And perhaps those years stored up within us the spiritual reserves of strength that made us able to endure the frightful things that came afterwards.

Those last few years in Austria widened and deepened our many friendships. Those who came to Salzburg and to our home in Henndorf were not only the prominent figures in the world of letters, such as Franz Werfel with his vital and redoubtable wife Alma Mahler, and Gerhart Hauptmann, Thomas Mann, Bruno Frank, to mention only the most eminent. There were also many less favored by fortune, or already deprived of their homeland, stopping off at the first station of exile. We ourselves were fortunate in having already made our home here, so that we were not yet thrown into a foreign environment but were on a secure footing in a German-speaking territory. Except for the small territory of German Switzerland, Austria could be regarded as the last enclave of an intellectual freedom that had been lost in Germany. Of course we knew what was slowly brewing among the narrow-minded philistines of Austria too, but we were not directly affected by it; we knew too little about these people, did not take them seriously, and in spite of what had happened in Germany, which should have taught us a lesson, we thought we could laugh it away.

Eastward, our network of neighborly relations extended as far as Kammer Castle on the Attersee, one wing of which was occupied by lovely Eleonora von Mendelssohn and her husband Jessenski.

A former hussar captain in the Austrian Imperial Army, he still sat his horse magnificently, white-haired but trim and youthful in his red silk riding tunic. In the other wing lived Raimund von Hofmannsthal, a son of the great Austrian writer Hugo von Hofmannsthal. It seemed as if all of Austria and half the world gathered there in the castle at night, after a boat ride to the accompaniment of zither music over the crystal-clear lake. After such parties we never reached home before dawn. Today, as a matter of fact, it seems to me that the Salzburg nights went on forever, like parties in Berlin. Even though there are no 'white nights' like those of Stockholm or Oslo, the nights seemed illuminated by a festivity that ignored fatigue, and before we realized it, they merged with daybreak.

A reception at Max Reinhardt's splendid Leopoldskron Castle was almost always preceded by some great artistic event—a performance in the Salzburg Festival House under Bruno Walter or Toscanini, a song recital by Lotte Lehmann, a Mozart serenade at the Salzburg Palace, or a Reinhardt première with the best actors of his Berlin and Vienna ensembles. Artists, writers, and theatrical people mingled with celebrities and aristocrats; it was usually midnight before we went to dinner in rooms lit only by candles. The jokes that have come down about these occasions are world-famous, but are nevertheless authentic. I think it was the Hollywood movie magnate Louis B. Mayer who, taking alarm at the sight of the thousands of glittering candles, asked: 'A short circuit, Mr. Reinhardt?' Mayer, so Max Reinhardt related, sat utterly dashed, his brow beaded wih sweat, during the performance of *Everyman* which bore the subtitle: 'A Play about the Rich Man's Death.' He was still reeling from the shock when the play was over. 'You can't put that on in America,' he told Reinhardt. 'There are too many rich people there.'

Another Hollywood mogul seemed excessively impressed by the names of all the archdukes, dukes, counts, and barons present at a supper. The playwright Ferenc Molnár, whose spiteful witticisms would fill volumes, whispered to him that actually they were only extras from Reinhardt's theaters who had been drilled for their parts as aristocrats, and that their evening dress and decorations were hired, whereupon the magnate lost interest in this 'fake' party and left. The truth was that this mixture of real artists and genuine aristocrats—who have always made an essential contribution to the

40

cultural life of their times and for whom the snobs are a very poor substitute—made an altogether delightful amalgam. Over champagne and caviar, Burgundy and saddle of venison, revolutionaries and monarchists got along beautifully. For in this world of doomed enchantment politics were underplayed—perhaps because everyone knew that in the long run he would not be able to escape their iron grip. It was somewhat like Versailles in the days of the Bastille, only more alert, more aware, intellectually more lucid, as is only proper for an elite devoted to the Muses. For it was just such an elite that had set the tone in Salzburg and that gave those days and nights their unique glory.

It was always two or three in the morning before the first vehicles drove up to the flight of stairs at Leopoldskron Castle to take the guests home or to their hotels. During the twenties those vehicles were frequently, still, carriages with teams of elegant horses, or simple hansom cabs. But then came the finest part of it, the true witching hour of such a night. During the general and rather chaotic breakup of the party, amid the endless goodbyes, Reinhardt found an opportunity to murmur to one or another member of his intimate circle: 'Do stay on for another hour,' or, 'Wait for me in the library.'

That hour often stretched on to five or six in the morning. We sat in the small, dusky room above the baroque gallery and the stairway to the already darkened library, drinking vintage cognac and smoking imported cigars. The time was spent in conversation, anecdotes, stories, improvisations, inspired whimsicalities and parodies. The mood was one of contemplative serenity, of wholly personal gaiety arising out of a common medium: art, literature, and the theater. Reinhardt could laugh to the point of tears when the actors told their green-room jokes. At other times he might listen with the keenest intensity, tongue pressing against the inside of his cheek, when our wise little clown, Vladimir Sokoloff, talked about his youth in the Russian theater and his years with Stanislavski, or when an actor recited something unusual on request, or a writer read from a new work. Reinhardt was a master of the art of creative listening. Sometimes, too, he would talk about his own plans for future work, and I am convinced that during those early-morning hours he often conceived crucial ideas for his productions.

In this small circle, beautiful women were treated like goddesses. The maestro—in those days the name belonged only to

Toscanini—usually stayed up late after one of his great concerts, or a performance of an opera. He too preferred working at night. In America, for example, when he decided to conduct Gershwin's *Rhapsody in Blue*, he learned the score by heart in the course of a single night, and never had to look at it again. A small circle had gathered around him; it usually met in one of the quieter taverns that stayed open to all hours. He would talk exuberantly and indefatigably in Italian, English, French, and broken German all night long. Towards morning this man of seventy, who might well have a rehearsal at ten o'clock, would lead his exhausted youthful satellites on a brisk walk along the banks of the Salzach River.

The first bus to Henndorf departed at half past seven. We would usually spend the few intervening hours in the station restaurant over goulash and beer. Sometimes such breakfasts would continue until noon—I remember one especially exciting one with Erich Maria Remarque and Thornton Wilder in the summer of 1937. Sometimes a hardy soul, man or woman, would accompany me back to Henndorf, where we promptly went down through the dewy woods to my solitary bathing cabin to swim in the cool lake before our coffee.

A few of my personal and literary friends lived and worked for weeks and even months in our small guest cottage or in the nearby Mayr inn. A good many friendships soared as suddenly as rockets on New Year's Eve, but they did not burst; they lasted for years. The first time Chaliapin came to see us, brought by his daughter Marina, he arrived at five in the afternoon for tea and stayed until ten the following morning. Late that night he began to sing, although he had been strictly forbidden to use his voice when he had been smoking and drinking. '*Mais, Feodor,*' his wife remonstrated, '*tu ne dois pas chanter maintenant!*'

'*Chérrie,*' he replied with his rolling Russian accent, '*je chante pourre mes amis quand il me faut chanter!*'

We thought our rafters might crack from the power of his voice. Our daughters, who in those days were still condemned to going to bed early, crept out on the stairs in their nightgowns and listened.

I must mention one special encounter which, though we did not know it, presaged the darkest shadow of the later tragedy, but also the elements of later heroism. This was during our early period in Henndorf, the summer of 1927, and we had as house guests my

German socialist friends Carlo Mierendorff and Theodor Haubach, and the courageous Swiss socialist Joseph Halperin. At our house the three met Count Hellmuth James von Moltke. Though by tradition and rearing Moltke should have been a Christian conservative, he was even then leaning towards socialism. The three socialists as it happened were keenly interested in the ideas of English neoconservatism. During the conversations of that night, the groundwork was laid for what was later to be the Kreisau Circle, a group that played a large part in the German resistance to Hitler. Early in 1945 Haubach and Moltke were sentenced to death by Hitler's People's Court, and hanged. Mierendorff, after enduring five terrible years in German concentration camps, fell victim to an English bomb just as he was preparing an uprising against the tyranny.

Late one afternoon about a year before the downfall of Austria, an agreeable gentleman dressed in the local Salzburg costume called upon Reinhardt. He introduced himself as Baron Trapp, and presented his wife, an ascending scale of children, and a private chaplain who conducted the family in the kind of singing that is now world-famous. In those days, before the expulsion, that was still a purely domestic Salzburgian affair, like so many of the unusual and inspired aspects of that period.

When the season was over, when the fine automobiles with their foreign license plates and their babble of languages had vanished over the Salzburg bridge, the natives emerged from their holes. The Salzburgers themselves, who had been swamped by the overwhelming numbers of 'celebrities,' once more peopled the markets, streets, and taverns, and chatted with each other in their own way. This was really the loveliest time of year in the town and in the countryside. In the spring the fighting cocks hissed in the moss at Seekirchen. In the fall there was partridge and pheasant shooting. In the winter you could ski on fresh untracked snow, without the benefit of cable cars or lifts, or the hindrance of crowded runs. And almost every day work moved along gradually. For the prolonged nights and sociable days I have spoken of were only the exceptions, of course. We were living; we thanked God we were and that there were such things as life and art.

Was this our Golden Age? I don't really think any such age exists. There are moments when one lives in paradise, but on the whole one can never live outside one's own times. This merciful respite was already filled with the portents of the coming disaster. All the problems and conflicts of approaching dissolution, reshufflings, and transformations of the world were already working within us. Perhaps for that very reason these years seem so fantastically vital. When Max Reinhardt celebrated his sixtieth birthday on September 9, 1933 (he spent the day very quietly in the mountains with his wife, Helene Thimig), he had already lost his Deutsches Theater in Berlin. The controlled press there sneered at him as 'the Jew Goldmann.' Great conductors like Bruno Walter and Otto Klemperer could not or would not return to Germany. That firebrand Toscanini kept clear of Fascist Italy, after a scandalous incident there.

And yet the Salzburg magic continued for a while—for half a decade longer. Once, at a late hour, I heard Reinhardt say almost with satisfaction: 'The nicest part of these festival summers is that each one may be the last.' After a pause, he added: 'You can feel the taste of transitoriness on your tongue.'

Late in the autumn of the year 1937 a quiet party for a small group was given at Eleonora von Mendelssohn's and Jessenski's Kammer Castle. That wonderful violinist Arnold Rosé and his Vienna String Quartet played. To end the evening they played part of Haydn's Emperor Quartet, the movement which gave rise to the Austrian Imperial anthem, which in turn subsequently became the *Deutschlandlied*, the German anthem.

The Viennese artists played it as Haydn had meant it, as a simple, devout melody—almost a prayer. Tears filled the eyes of most of the listeners. And half a year later most of the people I have spoken of in these pages were scattered to the four winds.

How and why Austria was destroyed can be read in the schoolbooks of today. When Chancellor Schuschnigg went to Obersalzberg to attempt negotiations with Hitler, he was presented with conditions that amounted to capitulation. Schuschnigg thereupon called for a plebiscite in which the Austrians themselves were to decide whether they wished annexation to Nazi Germany or independence. The voting was set for Sunday, March 13, 1938. In spite of tremendous Nazi propaganda and the dissatisfaction of many Austrians with existing conditions, it was fairly certain—and Hitler knew this too—that the result would be a clear majority for an independent Austria, which in turn would presumably force the Western Powers to abide by the guarantees they had given Austria. For that reason Hitler did not permit the plebiscite to take place. On March 11th German troops crossed the Austrian frontier. Simultaneously, in a well-prepared treasonous coup, the Viennese government was overthrown and arrested, along with all the reliable government officials in the country. Those are the bare facts.

But what it was like in reality (or rather, in the lived dreams which we are wont to call reality), how it actually happened—this is something that only those who went through it can possibly know.

A number of omens preceded the catastrophe. Several weeks before, a display of northern lights appeared over all of Austria. The aurora borealis is extremely rare in this part of the world; most people have only heard about it, never seen it. It was said that none had been seen since 1866, the year in which the Austrians were defeated by the Prussians. The display in January 1938 flamed so mightily and flickered so glaringly that it looked like a tremendous conflagration. It appeared at midnight, and in Henndorf the fire department came clanging out of the station because the firemen thought something was on fire in the next village.

Around the same time the 'plague bird' was seen in Vienna. Its appearance was actually confirmed by ornithologists. This is an albino variety of the sparrow, its plumage strangely flecked with white. It is said to show itself only before great epidemics or an outbreak of war.

The weather during this period was also unusual. For weeks neither snow nor rain fell. The sky was radiantly clear day in and day out; in midwinter it was possible to lie on the stubble in the sun, and the sun blazed with such summery heat during that grim March that all vegetation, fruit, grapes, lilacs, everything, began to bud and blossom weeks too soon. Later, during a raw May, the heavy artillery of hard frost mercilessly blasted all this premature beauty.

The atmosphere in Vienna was very peculiar during those spring-like days. Outwardly, there was something of the gaiety of Carnival. For the Nazi Party had received a fiendishly clever order from Germany: Send the children into the streets! Adults stay home! Thus, in those last days, while the German invasion troops were already massing at the border, the streets of Vienna filled with swarms of young people of all ages, carrying swastika flags, shouting 'Heil Hitler!' and blocking the traffic arteries of the city. The police were helpless—which for the police in such situations may be a welcome condition. They stood around with loaded weapons and did not dare use them. After all, the new policy of 'social reconciliation' that the government had proclaimed could not very well begin by shooting at children. And everyone knew quite well that a dead twelve-year-old on a Viennese street would have served as a welcome pretext for Berlin to 'restore order'—the phrase used to this day whenever a Great Power would like to swallow up a weaker country.

The children were not altogether peaceful among themselves. 'Your father was a Schuschnigg up to yesterday, mine's always been a Hitler!' 'Aw go on, at New Year's yours was still a snotty Starhemberg!' 'And his was with the Reds then!' In a moment a knot of youngsters would be rolling in the gutter with their flags—an apt allegory of their parents and teachers. But except for such squabbles, nothing happened. The children marched around and shouted; the grownups stood silently by, partly amused, partly embittered, partly waiting malevolently for the next move.

What seemed to be a simliar symptom of breakdown, though in reality it was a trick carefully planned by the Nazis, was the enormous increase in the hordes of beggars. Beggars had already been a problem in the capital, but on a smaller scale. Now, as was later learned, the illegal Nazi Party paid them wages to appear en masse, in as wretched and ragged a state as possible, in the finest parts of the city, particularly those favored by foreigners: the First District between the Ring, Kärntner Strasse, Stephansplatz, Graben, Kohlmarkt. Here they pestered every passer-by. Evidently the Nazis had learned something from *The Threepenny Opera.*

In spite of all this there was still a majority in the city who believed Schuschnigg would win the plebiscite and thus fend off Hitler. The Viennese were counting on Mussolini, who had saved Austria once before, in 1934. But the Duce was now a prisoner of the growing German military might. Thanks to a Popular Front crisis, France was without a government at the time. England had one, but it was treating Hitler with what was considered to be statesmanlike prudence.

At the time we did not realize that. We too were among the credulous. We thought it our duty at this critical moment neither to doubt nor to run away. This attitude had become so much a matter of principle with me that when I received a considerable sum for a movie scenario I had done in England, I had the money transferred to the Austrian National Bank. For, I told myself, if I wanted and hoped for an economically viable Austrian state, I must not undermine its economy by keeping my money abroad. Every skilled dialectician would laugh at me, and yet he would be wrong. . . . I am not telling these stories as a warning or a lesson—men have never learned anything from the experiences of others, certainly not from those of earlier generations. I am telling them only in order to capture something that otherwise flows and flees away: life.

About three weeks before the end, the Schuschnigg government granted me Austrian citizenship. I was supposed to pick up my new passport at police headquarters in Salzburg, but I was unable to go because I was busy in Vienna with the production of one of my plays. That was my good luck, as later events proved. Incidentally, after the war and after the collapse the passport was still there at the Salzburg police headquarters, with a note from the Gestapo attached: Owner to be arrested immediately when he comes to collect this passport.

Towards noon one day I ran into our friend Egon Friedell, the cultural historian and philosopher, on Kärntner Strasse. He was also an actor, and although he made fun of himself and the theater, acting was his special ambition and probably also a good part of his sustenance, for his *Cultural History of the Modern Age*, a book highly regarded today, probably brought him more admiration than royalties during his lifetime. He lived in his Vienna apartment with a housekeeper and a small dog of indefinite breed whom he called Herr Schnack and who was trained to tear to shreds newspapers containing foolish articles or irritating reviews. Friedell was esteemed for his original, sardonic, but never cheap wit as much as for his intellect. In those days there were few people—there are even fewer today—who could lay claim to vast, comprehensive culture. Egon was one of those few; but he hated the professional tone and concealed his erudition behind his magnificent sense of humor.

He was a plump, broad-shouldered man with a massive head whose nose merged with his brow like the profiles of Caesars on antique coins. His lips seemed soft above his strong chin, soft but also sarcastic, and there was always a trace of whimsicality around his eyes and mouth. He fancied that he looked like Louis XV and was fond of imitating that monarch, but to my way of thinking he rather resembled one of the Encyclopedists. He was marvelous company for the people he liked. Those he disliked had a hard time with him, for he could become angry and aggressive over some casual stupidity or platitude. Sometimes he was intolerable, especially when he guzzled. For he did guzzle. The word 'drink' would be a euphemism. To attempt to explain his heavy drinking humorously or psychologically would be impertinent. He drank heavily, and it was his own affair. Every so often he poured incredible quantities of the strongest possible liquor into himself, without the slightest regard for his often delicate health. He did not care what he guzzled, so long as it was strong. Sometimes the alcohol produced in him a wonderful lucidity and alertness of mind, sometimes total stupor.

On this day in early March of 1938 he stopped me in the street. He had heard that a new play of mine, *Bellman*, was to open in the theater in Josefstadt, and he wanted to be in the cast. I was expected home for lunch and pressed him to come with me, but in vain; he was one of those drinkers who stop eating. Instead he lured me into the nearby Reiss Bar on Neuer Markt, a tavern patronized by many artists. Just for a glass, he said. After two hours and many glasses I telephoned home to say that I would be along for lunch somewhat later. My wife had already ceased expecting me, and so I sat on with Egon. That afternoon, along with much merriment and wit, we had a serious talk which shook me to the core, and which I have never forgotten.

'What will you do when the Nazis come?' he asked abruptly in the midst of a disquisition on Reinhardt's theater.

'They won't come.'

'But suppose they do, anyhow?'

'Then,' I said, 'I suppose there'll be nothing else but to make for the frontier.'

He shook his head. 'I won't go,' he said in a tone at once obstinate and frightened. 'What would I do in another country? I'd only be a beggar and cut a ridiculous figure.' And then he leaned forward as if he felt a need for confession and confided to me, under seal of secrecy which has lost its point by now, something he had been keeping to himself. In Germany his works were considered antimaterialistic and therefore anti-Marxist as well, and thus had not been banned in spite of his being a Jew. Consequently he had some highly placed patrons and admirers who had the ears of the powerful men in Germany. And they had let him know that if Austria were annexed he would be accorded special treatment. 'I could live quietly and work undisturbed, they've told me,' he said several times. 'Though not in Vienna. But what I don't know, what I don't know is whether I can accept.' As he spoke he wore an indescribable expression of stoic tragedy. Then he asked me to forget the whole thing, ordered more drinks, and changed the subject. Later that afternoon my wife joined us, and toward evening Alma Werfel came by with Anna, her daughter by Gustav Mahler, who has since become a gifted sculptress.

We sat together until late at night. When we left, the bill for him and myself (I kept it) listed thirty-eight glasses of barack, a Hungarian brandy, and twenty-six small glasses of Pilsner. But the evening had not been quite so jolly as Alma Mahler represents it in her book. Ten days after the occupation of Austria—we heard about it after we were in Switzerland—Friedell jumped from the window of his apartment when two SA men who were not looking for him at all entered the building. He died on the pavement.

The night before March 11th a violent south wind arose, a foehn storm, hot and dry. It blew all the next day, under a cloudless sky, and whipped the innumerable plebiscite leaflets through the streets like withered leaves. Papers whirled everywhere, bundled, crumpled, smooth or shredded—the whole city was swamped with paper. It fell like dirty snow from the trucks on which bands of workmen rolled slowly through the city from Wiener Neustadt, shouting in wavering choruses against Hitler and demonstrating for the government. Word had gone around that even the socialist working class was prepared to vote for Schuschnigg and Austria, although the workers had not forgotten the bloody repression of February 1934. For Schuschnigg was seeking reconciliation; he had promised political liberty; and anything seemed better than Hitler. '*Rot-Weiss-Rot—Bis in den Tod!*' ('Red, white, red—until death'), the choruses shouted. The corners of houses and the sidewalks were painted with the Austrian colors. Arguments and battles broke out in the taverns. A fever of excitement spread through the paper-strewn city.

On the morning of March 11 I experienced something that had nothing to do with politics, rather with the imagination, and that in memory seems tragicomic. It was the first blocking rehearsal of my new play, with a cast of Vienna's best actors, Paula Wessely, Attila Hörbiger, and Anton Edthofer, under the direction of Ernst Lothar. And so, on the morning of the catastrophe, on the stage of a dusky theater, a handful of persons completely forgot the world outside, the peril, the crisis on which all our fates depended, and for several hours succumbed completely to the magic spell of the theater. We discussed and quarreled over cuts, positions, and changes as if there were nothing more important in the world. When we left the theater that afternoon, stepping out of its dimness into the brilliance of the still radiant spring sky, into air still whirling with paper, everything was over. Two hours later, as the sun was setting, Schuschnigg delivered his last message on the radio: 'I am yielding to force. God protect Austria!' He was standing, as we learned later, between two guards with swastika armbands, members of his own bodyguard, who then placed him under arrest.

That night hell broke loose. The underworld opened its gates and vomited forth the lowest, filthiest, most horrible demons it contained. The city was transformed into a nightmare painting by Hieronymus Bosch; phantoms and devils seemed to have crawled out of sewers and swamps. The air was filled with an incessant screeching, horrible, piercing, hysterical cries from the throats of men and women who continued screaming day and night. People's faces vanished, were replaced by contorted masks: some of fear, some of cunning, some of wild, hate-filled triumph. In the course of my life I had seen something of untrammeled human instincts, of horror or panic. I had taken part in a dozen battles in the First World War, had experienced barrages, gassing, going over the top. I had witnessed the turmoil of the postwar era, the crushing of up-risings, street battles, meeting-hall brawls. I was present among the bystanders during the Hitler *Putsch* of 1923 in Munich. I saw the early period of Nazi rule in Berlin. But none of this was comparable to those days in Vienna. What was unleashed upon Vienna had nothing to do with the seizure of power in Germany, which proceeded under the guise of legality and was met by parts of the population with alienation, scepticism, or an unsuspecting nationalistic idealism. What was unleashed upon Vienna was a torrent of envy, jealousy, bitterness, blind, malignant craving for revenge. All better instincts were silenced. Probably revolution will always be horrible; but the horror may be borne, understood, assimilated, when it has sprung from genuine need, is conceived out of conviction and true intelligence, if what has brought matters to the boiling point is a true spiritual flame. But here only the torpid masses had been unchained. Their blind destructiveness and hatred were directed against everything that nature or intelligence had refined. It was a witches' sabbath of the mob. All that makes for human dignity was buried.

Oddly enough—I can scarcely explain it today, but I can testify that it is so, that memory is not playing me false—I felt no fear during these hours and days. I felt nothing but rage, disgust, despair, and a complete indifference towards my own survival. Yet on earlier occasions I had tasted the fear of an individual confronted by a horde of enemies, by a fanatical mob. In 1932 I was recognized at a Nazi meeting in the Berlin Sportpalast. The crowd started shouting abuse; with the help of a few friends I got away, but barely escaped a beating. I felt it even more when I left Henndorf, after Hitler was already in power, and crossed the border to Freilassing in order to vote against Hitler—taking a pointless risk, since the election was a farce. I was not threatened that time; I remained anonymous and unmolested in a group of Germans from abroad. But while I stood in the voting booth crossing out the Yes and underlining the No on my ballot, cold sweat poured down my face. I felt as if I were being observed by an invisible eye, as if everyone outside knew just what I had done—this, long before before George Orwell had written his *Nineteen Eighty-Four*.

But in Vienna in these March days I was filled with an iciness that utterly extinguished the natural sensation of fear. Something inside me, some normal component of human nature, had been completely frozen, or killed. I had never experienced such a state of indifferent alienation and contempt before, and I never felt it again. My friend Dr Franz Horch, who was then a reader for Reinhardt and for the Zsolnay publishing house, was affected quite differently. That evening we took a cab through the city, for we were planning to meet in an apartment with others in the same predicament and discuss the situation. Horch was a man of nervous temperament anyhow, and today his whole body was shaking and he was constantly repressing tears. It was no pleasure to ride through Vienna in a cab at this time. The streets were so jammed with shouting and gesticulating crowds that we could scarcely move. In the square near the Opera we became stuck in the mob. Tough louts, typical rowdies, pressed against the cab windows and stared banefully

inside. Already they suspected every cab of containing a fugitive or
a 'bloodsucker.' 'Ridin' a cab—must be Polish Jews. Get 'em out—
beat 'em up.' While my friend almost threw up from sheer terror,
I rolled down the window, abruptly thrust my arm stiffly through it
almost into the men's faces, and shouted something that sounded
like 'Hei'tler!', putting on the sharp Prussian accent of an army
sergeant. I had already realized that this was the only effective feint.
And so we finally reached the apartment. There a small, woeful
group had gathered, almost all of them people who within the hour
had seen the foundation of their lives knocked out from under
them. How often, in exile, have I witnessed such scenes: brooding,
despairing people blown together by an evil wind and sitting like
victims of a shipwreck on a sinking vessel or a reef. Ödön von
Horváth was there, as well as Franz Theodor Czokor and our
friend Albrecht Joseph. Alexander Lernet-Holenia had come also;
although he himself was not directly threatened, he felt he belonged
with us. Very soon a kind of gallows humor came to the fore. We
were concerned with the question of saving our lives, but being together for the last time this way we felt obliged to rise above the
situation with a modicum of wit. When we parted, we all felt that it
was for ever. Yet almost all the friends who met that evening
would see each other again later on.

Several of my friends departed that same night. They were the
wiser ones, for the frontiers were not effectively closed for several
days. I did not want to go. Perhaps I was suffering from a kind of
paralysis, of defiance or shame—such reactions may well be a form
of nervous shock. In any case, I told my wife that I did not intend
to go abroad. 'I'm not getting into any refugee train,' I said. I
talked the wildest nonsense. I had a right to my native land, I said.
I hadn't 'done anything.' (Apparently I repressed the things I had
done, my Berlin speech against Goebbels and my membership in the
Iron Front, the opposition to the Nazis.) I hadn't 'committed any
crime' that would justify persecution. Yet by then justice had
vanished from Germany and persecution was raging blindly, bar-
barously, though under the cloak of 'order and discipline.' There
was no safety in having done nothing against the tyrants; one's
crime was in not having joined up with them. Quite aside from
political or racial principles, anyone was liable to persecution. It
might be that you only smelled different. For the moment they de-

cided you were different, you were an outlaw—which meant being exposed to a kind of annihilation far worse than death. The fear by which dictatorships keep their subjects in check is by no means the fear of death. A person who opposes the revolutionaries in a time of upheaval must count on being killed, and to my mind that is not the worst that can happen if you feel that all human decency and dignity is going to the dogs all around you. But to be shattered physically and spiritually, to be trampled under, crushed, crippled by humiliation and torture, and still have to go on living as a slave, without identity, condemned to continuing life in its most painful and hopeless form, with no end in view and no prospect of rescue, only to die at last more miserably than an animal in the slaughterhouse—that was the real horror that awaited us under the new regime. I mention all this for those who have not experienced those times or else—and this, too, seems to happen—no longer remember what it was like. What it was like surpassed the limits of imagination for the inhabitants of other countries at the time, especially the Western democracies. At this moment of confusion it also surpassed the limits of my own imagination, although I knew enough about it.

But I had another mad notion. I wanted to return to Henndorf, to my house. In a bureau drawer there I had an old army revolver from the First World War, and some ammunition. 'If they come for me,' I said, 'I'll take a few of them with me first.' My wife was in despair. She knew that in this state of temporary madness I would have been capable of something of the sort—in other words, of a form of suicide. And she was determined to do everything to persuade me to flee. I would not be alive today if she had not succeeded.

The next several days, from March 12 to 15, were filled with such tension that in retrospect they seem to me as compressed as the last scene of a drama.

Around noon on Saturday, March 12, Emil Jannings telephoned. He was taking a rest cure at the Vienna Cottage Sanatorium. Owing to his compromises with the German rulers, he and I had had some differences of late. Now he was sincerely concerned about me, and anxious to be of help. Since he enjoyed great prestige in 'the highest quarters,' he thought he would be able to, and his feeling for friendship was stronger than all political disagreements. He saw my conflict, saw that my whole being rebelled against the idea of flight, although all logic and the rush of events argued in favor of it. In my presence he telephoned the German Embassy in Vienna, then headed by that equivocal personality Herr von Papen, to ask its estimate of the situation. Was a man like myself in any immediate danger, he wanted to know.

There followed one of the strangest, most absurd conversations in those absurd times. I was of course known to the German Embassy. I had occasionally met the German Ambassador at official receptions in Vienna. We used to greet each other and pretend that nothing was in the least out of the way. But I was somewhat better acquainted with Clemens von Ketteler, the attaché with whom Jannings spoke that day. As a Catholic and a cultivated man, at the moment he probably sympathized more with the defenders of Austria than with his Führer. He was in charge of the official information service of the German Embassy, and in that capacity was in constant touch with both the new Viennese government and Berlin. Now he assured us that to the best of his knowledge there was no danger for me. Everything was going to be different in Austria, he said. For diplomatic reasons, in order to placate foreign opinion, a 'liberal' version of Fascism was to be practised here. Even the racial laws would not be applied with full severity. Anyhow, Zuckmayer was Catholic and certain arrangements were being made with the Church to protect its members. My most prudent course would be to stay where I was and await events.

Two hours later this man was dead. When he left the Embassy for lunch, a mobile squad arrested him. He was taken in a car to Modena Park, a small park in the middle of the city, and killed. His body was later fished out of the Danube. The background of this murder has remained obscure, like so much else of that period. Probably the chief reason was his 'political unreliability.'

On Sunday, March 13, hundreds of heavy German bombers landed at Vienna's Aspern Airport. All day long their motors thundered. Squadrons incessantly circled low over the city, like angry hornets. Along with the clamor in the streets and the roar of loudspeakers continuously battering the ears with Hitler's latest proclamations, and the endless chanting of 'Sieg Heil, Sieg Heil, Sieg Heil!' from throats already hoarse from shouting, the aeroplane motors added a last straw to the nerve-racking, truly diabolic noise. You ceased to think of it as human or machine sounds. The din of a world going down to its doom saturated the air.

Meanwhile the arrests had begun. Already Jews, as well as aristocrats, either because they had defended the indepedence of Austria or simply for the fun of it, were being herded through the streets and forced to wash the election slogans from the pavements. As I was riding to the railroad station on Tuesday morning I saw a frail old gentleman with a scrub pail and a far too small brush kneeling in the filth of the streets, kept at his task by an SA guard, with a group of hoodlums standing around him. But even in this group the sight did not arouse unadulterated pleasure. They merely stood there looking on with the air of idlers at a traffic accident. Perhaps a few were ashamed. Some of them may also have felt a touch of fear.

The mobile squads were also dashing around the city calling on the homes of blacklisted people, or those who had been denounced by malicious neighbors. What followed was well known. People were taken away; afterwards they might be found in hospitals, horribly beaten or mutilated. Others disappeared forever. When the squads went too far, caught the wrong man or stole too flagrantly, the police reports stated that the culprits had been 'Communists disguised as Storm Troopers.' No one believed such preposterous excuses. People believed only in what they could see: naked violence.

The day before our telephone had been ringing constantly: calls from well-meaning acquaintances who wanted to warn me. Now it suddenly became silent. It stood in its corner, a small, black, ominous instrument that had already been seized by the evil spirits. When you lifted the receiver you heard a strange crackling. The wire-tappers were already at work.

That night I had a talk with my wife of a kind that occurs only once in a lifetime. I remember every word, and yet it seems to me like something I have read about. By now I had developed a new delusion: that I must make my way into Germany in order to go underground and help prepare an uprising against Hitler—an uprising whose prospects of success had never been smaller than at this moment. All those who might have joined in such an enterprise were in concentration camps or awaiting the executioner.

Instead of trying to bring me to my senses by the use of logic, my wife merely said: 'I want you to do something for me. Give me a year of your life. Try to make your way out of the country and wait out this one year abroad. Then, if you still think the way you do today, return and do whatever you think you you must do. I vow that I won't oppose your decision; I'll even take part in it, once the children are safe. But I beg you, give me this year.'

At that moment common sense and sanity returned to my mind. In a flash I realized that my new-found obstinacy and audacity were not heroism, were nothing but an inverse form of the same kind of terror my friend Horch had shown—a failure of nerve. I saw that it would be the greater cowardice to throw away my life now instead of painfully, patiently preserving it for the better hour and the greater task that might still be in the offing; that in the name of resistance to the present victors, and in the name of ethics and human values also, the only reasonable resolve was to try to survive.

It was literally the last moment. Although we did not yet know it, our house in Henndorf had already been seized and Hans Lackner, the loyal young constable who was an unswerving anti-Nazi and who had often played his zither for us in the evenings, had been beaten half to death. *They* turned up in our Vienna apartment the day after my flight, and when they found me already gone they stripped the place, carrying off, among other things, a library of several thousand volumes which included dedication copies from most of the writers of our time, from Gerhart Hauptmann to Brecht. I never saw any of those possessions again.

We were in no mood for leavetakings. We would have preferred to focus on nothing but practical details, and to behave as if we were merely setting out on some ordinary journey. But there were people who belonged to us. At such times you realize fully who really belongs to you. In our case there was, among others, our cook, who had run our household for many years in city and country and was forever scolding us, which in her case was an evidence of close affection. Her name belongs in this catalogue of true friendships: Anna Buchendorfer. She and her seventeen-year-old niece, who had come into our house when she was almost a child, wept copiously as they helped us to pack. Towards evening our dearest friend in Vienna, Grete Wiesenthal, came. We thought we were bidding her goodbye for ever, and yet we celebrated a glorious reunion after the war and to this day still remain happily and affectionately attached to one another. Alfred Ibach, who holds a permanent place in our hearts, also came; he was then a playreader for Hilpert and later became director of the theater in Josefstadt. He stayed overnight and accompanied me to the railroad station next morning, prepared to stay by my side until departure time, in case he was needed. I asked Anna and her niece to bring in whatever cold food we had in the refrigerator—no one had been able to think of cooking all that day—and to stay with us. I also had some champagne in the cellar, and brought that up. Observing myself, I found that I was reasonably calm and steady. In fact I had been shaken up too thoroughly for sentimental feelings to arise. First of all I requested the maids to do me a great favor and stop crying. They bravely tried, and only snuffled occasionally. Then I poured the champagne, and we all drank a glass. Over the second glass we cheered up, and began talking about all kinds of things we had experienced together.

Two years before, we had rented the former servants' quarters in the handsome Palais Salms, and had furnished them with great care. Mine, where I used to live alone during working spells, was on the ground floor, off the front door; the family apartment was on the topmost floor, in the attic. As a precaution I spent this night upstairs. We fell into bed dead tired; we had hardly slept the night before. 'This is the worst,' my wife murmured, already half asleep, 'the worst thing that can happen to people. But we must go through...' And then she suddenly gave a gasping snore, her mouth open, like an overstrained hunting dog. I held her hand, and that night passed too.

I traveled alone, by the direct Vienna–Zurich train, which had a connection to London. This was the only sensible idea that had come to me in the course of those days. If we had all left together, it would have been clear that we were trying to make an escape. My single chance to cross the border unhindered lay in my making the flight seem like a brief journey—and shortly before I had received a telegram from Alexander Korda asking me to come to London as soon as possible to discuss plans for a new movie script. I kept that in my pocket as a kind of alibi. My family was to travel to Berlin by plane. There, in contrast to Vienna, relatively orderly conditions prevailed, and we had friends there who would help them. Arresting of families was not yet usual in such cases, and we could count on the fact that in Germany the border check would be carried out by decent old-style officials and not by Nazi Party men. The family was to wait in Berlin to see whether I made it through, and then to follow me. My passport, fortunately, was still my German one—a brand-new Austrian passport would certainly have

57

aroused suspicion. And it was 'in order.' By some inexplicable interpretation of the Nuremberg Laws, in spite of my descent on my mother's side I did not belong to that category of persons whose passports were stamped with a large J to signify 'Jew' or 'of Jewish origin.' I therefore had some prospect of making it, although you never knew what names might be on the border guards' lists. The chances were about fifty-fifty.

The railroad line from Vienna to the Swiss or Liechtenstein border at Feldkirch-Buchs passes through all of central and western Austria. It was a radiant early-spring morning. I had seldom seen the countryside looking lovelier. Snow still lay on the mountains, but the margins of the woods were already turning green. Towards noon the train passed by Wallersee; Henndorf is across that lake. I stood in the corridor of the express and looked out. The blue sky was reflected in the lake. I saw my bathing hut, with its bit of clearing behind it. I imagined I could hear my dogs barking.

Then, with a loud clatter, a troop transport train blocked the view; it was lumbering eastward on the adjacent track. German batteries were being transported to Vienna. The artillerymen sat on the flatcar beside their light field howitzers. In their field-gray uniforms they looked as young and fresh as we had done when we marched towards France in 1914. The people in my train rolled down the windows and waved at them. Many shouted 'Heil Hitler!' and pointed to the swastika they wore in their buttonholes, out of genuine or hypocritical enthusiasm. The German soldiers, who in their own country were more accustomed to depressed silence and set faces—such outbursts of jubilation had long since ceased inside Germany—laughed a little. It seemed to me that they responded to the greetings with a touch of embarrassment. Many of them went on spooning up their soup and did not raise their heads.

The Salzburg station resembled an army camp. Invasion troops were camping everywhere. They looked calm, disciplined, soldierly. Neither in their appearance nor in their manner did they seem to have anything in common with those Party gangs who had just taken over governmental and police power in Austria, against whom even the highest-ranking military officers were now powerless. The same kind of mob I had seen in Vienna was surging around the station, yelling 'Sieg Heil!' or singing the Horst Wessel song, the Party anthem, in which the words 'The time for freedom and for bread is dawning' sounded like sheer mockery. I wanted

58

to buy cigars, but the woman who ran the tobacco stand and who had served me for years, a widow of fifty, was rushing after a few German soldiers to thrust cigarettes into their pockets. 'German brothers!' she screeched, her eyes rolling ecstatically. She seemed to be foaming at the mouth. I heard later that when the first German unit marched in, she had knelt in the street. A few weeks earlier I had heard her screaming, 'Loyalty to Austria,' at a parade of the Fatherland Front. At the sight of her, I felt a good deal easier about leaving this country.

When the train at last began moving again, I became aware of how my heart was thumping. A few hours later we halted in Innsbruck. From there it is about three hours to the border. But at this point the first Nazi control entered the car. A fat man in civilian clothes, wearing a swastika armband and a police badge, suddenly appeared in my sparsely occupied compartment. Behind him stood two brownshirts, revolvers at their belts.

'Passports!'

At first he nodded with satisfaction when he saw the German eagle on the face of the passport. Then he looked closer at the identification. He read my occupation, 'Writer' (and I thought, why didn't I call myself farmer or dog breeder?), and stared suspiciously into my face.

'Take your baggage and leave the train.'

'Why?' I asked.

'Our Führer doesn't like the press,' he snapped.

'I don't work for the press,' I said.

'We'll see about that,' he said sharply, cutting me off. 'Get off.'

I still tried to protest. 'I'm expected in London. I can't miss my connection.'

'Get off the train!' he roared at me. The two brownshirts came a step closer.

On the platform a small group of other delinquents or suspects had been herded together. I was led to them. All of them, including the women, were carrying their baggage, as I was.

'Forward, march!' someone ordered.

As we left the station I saw my beautiful express train start.

We were led across the Innsbruck Bahnhofsplatz. People turned their heads to look at us. I saw the handsome Hotel Tirolerhof where I had often stayed and spent pleasant hours. And I felt an enormous thirst for a bottle of red wine. I was choking with fury.

As we were led up the broad stairway of the police station, an elderly gentleman who had also been taken out of the train came up to my side and suddenly whispered a number. It was *A-16023.* I wrote it down later, but would never have forgotten it anyhow. 'Please telephone there,' he whispered without moving his lips, 'if you get out of this. Say I was arrested. They're looking for me; my name is . . .' He did not have the time to speak his name, but I suddenly recalled having seen his picture in a history of Austrian Social Democracy. I nodded and repeated the number under my breath. Later, when he was led away, he saluted me with his eyes.

For hours we sat in the bare corridor on our luggage. A guard stood by, watching to make sure that we did not talk to one another. Inside the police station there was constant restless movement. Again and again pallid-looking persons were brought in between two brownshirts and vanished behind one door or another. This was the day on which Schuschnigg's organization, the Fatherland Front, was being rounded up.

My hunger, thirst, and fury mounted steadily. When I was at last taken into an office for interrogation I was beside myself. I knew what was at stake, and I had nothing to lose. Besides, I knew the type of subordinate official I would be dealing with and had made up my mind to behave like a member of the ruling class.

So as soon as I entered the office, I at once began to bellow. 'This is an outrage!' I shouted in my flintiest army German at the policeman on duty, who sat at a desk flanked by several Storm Troop officers. 'I am being held here without any reason and have missed my connecting train. You'll have to pay damages. . . .' And so on.

As I spoke I tossed my German passport, that frail.lifesaver, onto the desk and tried to shout even louder: 'See for yourself whether there are any charges against me!' I could feel that my strategy was working. These uniformed men were all Austrians; the whole thing was still new to them, and their hearts sank into their boots in these days when confronted with any German who shouted at them. I showed them my telegram from London, which they could not read because it was in English, and went on berating them for loss of time and urgent business, and then calmed down.

The man who had fetched me from the train was standing by, looking at me with some uncertainty, but still hostile.

'He's a writer,' he said. 'That's suspicious. Our Führer doesn't like the press.'

'But I write for the movies,' I said, 'and the Führer does like them.'

'Yes,' the officer at the desk said, 'he does.' He addressed me in a friendly tone: 'I know your house in Henndorf. I often go to the lake for swimming. A beautiful place.'

'That it is,' I said. 'What do you want of me now?'

The man stood up. Evidently I had persuaded him. 'In times like these mistakes are made,' he said. 'We're only doing our duty. Go quickly now—but out the back door. That bunch out there'—he waved his hand toward the corridor, where some of my companions from the train were still waiting—'won't be getting off so easy. Them's Jews,' he added in the local dialect. 'Heil Hitler!' And I was released.

As I descended the rear stairs I heard footsteps—tap, tap, tap— following at my heels. But I did not turn around. Suddenly I felt a hand on my shoulder—an SA man in his brown uniform. A shiver ran down my spine. He took a thin volume from his pocket. I recognized the binding of a short novel I had published the previous year: *A Summer in Austria.*

'I've just finished reading this,' he said, smiling confidentially. 'Would you mind autographing it for me?' I did so with the pen he handed me.

Suddenly he leaned forward close to my ear.

'It won't be summer in Austria any more,' he murmured. 'Goodbye, and don't come back. Be careful at the border,' he added, clicked his heels, and vanished. The swastika on his armband gleamed.

By the time I reached the railroad station again, I was soaked with sweat, and not only because I was carrying my suitcases. I went to the post office and sent a telegram to Berlin, where my wife would be waiting in the apartment of Mirl and Peter Suhrkamp for my telephone call from Zurich—for I should have been in Zurich by now. 'Manuscript on the way, somewhat delayed,' I wired. No signature.

Night had already fallen by the time I stood on the platform awaiting the next train to the border. It arrived late and was over- crowded; probably most of the passengers were refugees. Guards in brown and black uniforms were posted on the footplates.

I tried to push my way into one of the jammed compartments, and since I was hot, I opened my trench coat for the first time that day. Immediately, something startling and acutely embarrassing happened. A lively conversation had been going on in the compartment, but it stopped abruptly as soon as I entered. In the sudden silence an elderly gentleman of unmistakably Jewish appearance stood up, pointed to his seat, and said with a note of humility in his voice:

'Wouldn't you like to sit down, sir?'

'But it's your seat,' I said. 'Thank you, but keep it.' He refused, and the others moved apart, trying to make room for me.

Suddenly I realized what it was all about.

During this period in Austria everyone who did not want to expose himself to unpleasantness on the street had been wearing a swastika in his buttonhole—you could buy them for ten groschen at every newsstand. Anyone who was not wearing one was taken as being 'against' and could expect to be challenged—which, if he were lucky, meant being subjected only to verbal abuse. The result was that people stared at buttonholes. I could not and would not wear a swastika, of course, not even for sham. But in order not to endanger my escape needlessly I had fastened something else to my lapel: a clasp with my war decorations and the pin with the Iron Cross, First Class. People might call it outmoded romanticism, but I had saved these things. All politics aside, to me they represented memories of difficult, grave years lived through at the side of comrades I could never forget, and of many dangers to what was then my young life. I had no foreknowledge that they were destined to save my life.

During the war we ourselves disrespectfully referred to these decorations as pieces of tin, and at the moment I had quite forgotten I was wearing them like protective amulets on my jacket under my coat. But as soon as I unbuttoned the coat I read their effect in the nervous looks of my fellow travellers. As Austrians they did not know exactly what the decorations were. But they saw something black and white and black, white, and red, and obviously decided that I was a particularly dangerous and savage madman. Soon someone offered me a drink, and when I politely accepted and began a conversation, they became more at ease and apparently decided that I was human too. They were fearful of the border, and by their talk I realized that they envied me for my presumable sense of security. They had no idea how shaky I felt, or what good reason I had for feeling uneasy.

It was a three-hour journey in the middle of the night, and the closer we came to the border the weirder, more hectic and frenzied the mood in the train became. Patrols kept pushing through the crowded aisles, entering the compartments, checking individuals, asking for names, destinations, and the sums of money the passengers carried. No one was allowed to have more than ten German marks or twenty Austrian schillings with him—that was the total fortune I had taken on my departure. Severe penalties could be imposed for the slightest excess, and the new laws actually threatened death for attempts to smuggle large sums out of the country. The Nazis had reason to suspect that some refugees would try to take out considerable amounts. Special rewards were being offered to officials for discovering money or valuables. But in addition, these continuous and really needless controls—needless because the crucial check would take place at the border—were being carried out in a spirit of cruel harassment. In a small way this practice reflected the whole system of dictatorship, which is built on planned intimidation. The idea was to convince everyone that he was under surveillance all the time and might be caught at any moment.

My fellow passengers were all persons who were probably not yet being persecuted individually, but who had good reason to fear that they would be on the grounds of race or ideology. A number of them may well have belonged to that class of ruthless profiteers who like jackals haunt the battlefields of politics and economics. It flashed through my mind that it must be very easy for decent people to swallow the Nazi slogan: 'The good of the commonweal takes precedence over the good of the individual.' It sounds so just. How many credulous souls have been taken in by it, and how bitterly they have been deceived and disappointed by it, or would be in the future. As a fugitive I felt a kind of pity for the others on the train who would be staying behind to live under the dictatorship.

Most of those in my compartment seemed innocuous and distraught. There was a short, well-knit man with a round blond head —his first name was Baldur, and he was as 'Aryan' as the Nordic god from whom the name had been taken. By profession, he said, he was a center on a Viennese soccer team. But he was fleeing along with his Jewish girl friend Rebecca, who was two heads taller than him and wore glasses. They rightly feared, aside from separation, the penalties connected with the ban on 'miscegenation.' They sat

63

there like chickens tied to a pole, and whenever one of the officials approached they shrank as if the cook were approaching with her knife. Again and again they conferred nervously about what they had best say at the border. I gave them the advice to say nothing and to act as if they did not know one another. But immediately afterwards, when a martial SS man came along to make a preliminary check of passports, they instantly aroused suspicion by exchanging looks and nods. 'Do you know this man?' the SS man asked abruptly. 'Yes,' she stammered, 'he's my fiancé.'

The SS man took both their passports, pocketed them, and went out into the corridor, where he dreamily lit a cigarette. Terrified, the two sat there, their faces pale and guilty. Baldur kept shaking his head and saying meditatively: 'My fiancé! It's a psychological riddle to me. We aren't—I mean, we've never used the word before. We're just together. And now she suddenly says: my fiancé. To that fellow!'

'But I can't say we're lovers,' she stammered. She turned frightfully red: 'You know our relationship is more of a spiritual thing.' The two were so touching in their anxiety and their unconsciously comic quality that I could scarcely endure it—and in defiance of all the laws of suspense I want to anticipate and say that they made it through, and I hope they are 'lovers' to this day, and perhaps the parents of many 'half-breeds,' to use the Nazi term for the offspring of mixed marriages.

The man who had offered me the whisky kept drinking heavily from a canteen and squirming more and more nervously in his seat. 'My father was a commanding general,' he kept saying loudly, 'so what can happen to *me*?' He was perspiring; his forehead was a mottled red. In the course of the various questionings in the train he had alleged, like everyone else, that he had no more than ten marks with him. But five minutes before the border, when the train was already slowing, he suddenly turned green, as if he was nauseated. He jumped up, wrenched the window down, pulled a bundle of bank notes from some inside pocket of his coat, and threw it out into the night. It was a very thick bundle; certainly it would have gone ill with him if that amount of money had been found on him. Then he settled back in his seat, breathing heavily.

Now and then, at smaller stations, names were called, and people taken from the train. Suddenly my own name was called, and I started in alarm, although the voice was a woman's. Then a Polish lady who had seen me in the corridor appeared; she had recognized my face from theater posters in Vienna and the illustrated magazines, and wanted to inquire about Max Reinhardt's plans; she had such admiration for his work, she said, and was wondering whether *Everyman* would continue to be performed in Salzburg. She herself was escaping, but she seemed to find that less momentous than our discussion of theater and literature, and talked about art, culture, and society as if these matters still existed. I could not help thinking of the marquises in the dungeons of the French Revolution. But the current crisis seemed to me a tasteless parody of that situation. Perhaps it seemed the same way to the aristocrats of those days. Such experiences take on a romantic cast only after they are over. Fresh blood smells vulgar.

As the train slowly pulled into Feldkirch and we caught sight of the glaring beams of searchlights, I had little hope. Actually I felt nothing at all, and my head seemed empty of all thought. Cold suspense had taken possession of me. But all my instincts were mustering for self-defense. Today I wonder whether the fox must be in such a state when it hears the pack baying.

'Everybody out, with baggage. The train is being cleared.'

'Porter!' I called.

'Carry your own stuff!' someone barked. 'There aren't any porters for you people.'

The passenger on this train existed only in the plural. And so I took up my two suitcases, packed with everything I would need for the interim. With failing heart, I saw the border officials consisted almost entirely of Hitler troopers in brown and black uniforms. The station was swarming with people. Everywhere, large tables had been set up, and the suitcases and pocketbooks of the passengers were being unceremoniously dumped onto these tables. The suitcases were tipped up or overturned; then they were tapped to make sure they had no double bottoms. After that every single item of the contents was examined, every pair of stockings unrolled, shoe trees taken out of the shoes, every folded shirt taken out, every compact or powder box opened. And this was done for hundreds of passengers; in addition some of them were personally searched—that is, sent to a cell where they were stripped to the skin and virtually turned upside down like the suitcases. I told myself that this display of German thoroughness would have to take hours, and prepared myself for a long period of painful waiting.

By and by it occurred to me that in one of my suitcases I had a quantity of handwritten manuscripts and poems and drafts. It had been an act of incredible stupidity to take such things along, yet they were what mattered most to me. Anything written was especially suspect; that was well known. If they want to read every single page, I thought in horror, I'll never get away from here.

While one man with clumsy hands was dumping out my first suitcase, another, in a black shirt, demanded my passport. I handed it to him innocently, and covertly watched his reaction.

He stared at my name for a long time. Then he abruptly raised his head as if he had caught a scent.

'Zuckmayer?' he asked.

I nodded.

'*The* Zuckmayer?'

'What do you mean by that?'

'I mean, the notorious one.'

'I don't know whether I'm notorious. But I don't suppose there's any other writer with my name

His eyes narrowed like those of a man taking aim and sure of hitting his target.

'Come along,' he said.

'I must stay with my baggage,' I replied.

'You don't have to,' he said with a mocking smile, as if to say: You won't need baggage any more.

I was led down the whole long platform while my baggage remained behind, at the mercy of German thoroughness. At the far end of the station, where it was pitch dark, there were several barracks. The area smelled of garlic and the moist carbide of a bicycle lamp which swayed above the door to one of the barracks.

Inside, a lean, blond fellow in the uniform of the SS sat behind a desk. He wore steel-rimmed glasses and looked overstrained and undernourished. In front of the desk stood a man with turned-up coat collar and bowed head, who had obviously just been interrogated.

'Take him to the precinct for shipment,' I heard the official's voice saying. 'If it's overcrowded, to the local jail. Next.' Two SA men led the man out; he looked utterly crushed and seemed to be weeping.

I was next. I stepped before my judge. The man who had brought me had been whispering to him. Now he looked up.

'Carl Zuckmayer,' he said. 'Aha.'

He stared at the passport, leafed through it; his face grew thoughtful. Again and again he stared at the first page. I realized that the five-year period of validity irritated him. Jews in those days were receiving passports valid only for six months, if they could get them at all. Mine had been made out by the German Consulate in Salzburg a good while ago; the officials there were well disposed towards me.

Then he asked for some paper or other; it probably contained the names of people on a political blacklist. He turned to the letter Z, but did not find my name, and again began examining my passport. 'Odd,' he said, shaking his head, 'I'm sure I've heard something about you, but I can't remember exactly what it was. So you're not a Hebrew at all.'

He laughed jovially, and I grinned faintly. There was no need for me to confide to him that my mother's maiden name was Goldschmidt.

'Catholic,' he read. 'Oh well, we'll take care of the papists too one of these days.'

'I don't live in celibacy,' I said, with a semblance of a laugh. He chuckled at the joke, and came up to me, passport in hand, as if ready to return it to me.

'Where are you bound for?'

'To London, to write a movie script.'

'Movie? That's interesting. Have you written many of those? Any I might know?'

'My latest was called *Rembrandt*,' I said.

'Oh—I saw that. Politically clean enough. It was running in Vienna last winter when I was detailed there for an SS training course. Illegally, of course,' he said confidentially. Then he leaned closer to me.

'Are you a Party comrade? Do you have a Party card?'

'No,' I said, 'I'm not a member of the Party.'

Instantly, all his joviality vanished. He pulled away the passport, for which I had already stretched out my hand.

'I see,' he said sharply. 'A German writer and not a Party member, eh? But you are a member of the Reich Writers' League?'

'No,' I said. 'Not that either.' There was no point to lying, since I had no papers to identify me as as a member of anything, and in those days anyone who had such papers would carry them.

67

'And why not?'

His face had turned stiff and menacing.

The answer I gave was not something I had considered for so much as the fraction of a second. I did not know why I spoke so or what the consequences would be. But I have understood since why people tend to believe in the inspiration of guardian angels or beneficent spirits.

'I cannot be a Party member,' I answered quickly, 'because my works are banned in Germany. They are said not to accord with National Socialist ideology. That is why I am working in London, where incidentally I also made the Rembrandt film. I am allowed to travel freely abroad; you can see that from my passport. Otherwise I wouldn't have it. That will have to satisfy you.'

Again I held out my hand for my passport.

The Sturmführer was staring at me in a very strange way. His mouth gaped, his eyes were large and round. Suddenly he seized my outstretched hand and shook it.

'Marvelous!' he exclaimed. 'This frankness! This honesty!'

I seized my advantage: 'Do you think that everybody who comes in here is a liar?'

'Most are,' he replied. 'But you—you're a true German, that's all. I never would have believed that today of all days anyone would admit frankly that he isn't a Party member, that his works are banned. You—you'll make a Party member one of these days, I guarantee!'

'Thanks,' I said, taking my passport. 'Can I go for my baggage now?'

'I'll come with you,' he said. 'I need a breather. Marvelous. I respect you. Nothing amiss with your baggage, I hope?'

He raised his eyebrows and his forehead furrowed again. I thought of my manuscripts, and turned hot and cold at the thought of a second round of this dangerous game. Moreover, outside the door I could see the man who had brought me here and who was staring balefully at me.

This is the moment, I thought, quite consciously and calculatingly this time. I opened my coat wide, throwing it back as if I were trying to find my handkerchief in my pocket, and incidentally exposing my left lapel with its military decorations. His eyes instantly fixed on them.

'You were at the front?' he asked.

'Of course,' I said casually. 'For almost four years.'

'Were you an officer?'

I nodded.

'Isn't that ... the Iron Cross, First Class?'

'Yes.'

'And what's that?'

'The Hessian medal for bravery. I come from Mainz. They awarded that to you for having been in action for a while.'

'What about this—with the swords?'

It was the Zähringen Lion with Oak Leaf and Swords—a decoration specially for officers who had done something outstanding or made themselves popular, I explained.

'Why, you're a hero!' he said, round-eyed again.

'Not that,' I said harshly, 'but at any rate these things can't be bought in the street for ten groschen.' The allusion was pretty audacious, but it had its effect.

'Right you are,' he exclaimed, laughing excessively. 'You mean the fellow travellers. The opportunists. That's German humor all right. Magnificent.' He removed his cap and wiped his forehead. I saw that his hair was clipped close at the back of his head; in front was a fashionable forelock.

'We of the younger generation,' he began as if about to launch on a speech, 'we who didn't have the good fortune to take part in the war, know what we owe to our heroes. Attention!' he suddenly barked through the door. 'SA and SS, line up!'

We left the barracks, and his men came dashing toward us. He made them line up in front of me. 'We honor a hero of the World War 1914—18!' he bellowed. 'Heil Hitler!'

A row of brownshirts and blackshirts had lined up in front of me as if they were being inspected by a general. They clicked their heels so that the dirt spurted out in all directions, and rapped out 'Heil Hitler!' into my face as if I were the Führer in person. I had suddenly become the great man at this border station, and felt like the Captain of Köpenick in my own play.

'Where is this gentleman's baggage?' the Sturmführer demanded. 'Close it and take it into the Swiss train.' I did not have to lift a finger. The suitcase containing my manuscript was not even opened.

'This gentleman hasn't been searched yet,' an SA man said.

'It won't be necessary,' my protector retorted. 'This gentleman has been checked out.'

He turned to me. 'You had better wait in the station restaurant. We still have hours of work with the others.'

The result was that I alone of all the passengers did not have to undergo that procedure which, as I heard, was highly embarrassing for the ladies in particular; it was conducted by the wives of the guards or by female officials who behaved with utmost coarseness.

I might never have told this story just as it happened (and was even chary of telling it all to my wife when we met again, for it sounded even to me like so much braggadocio) had I not had a witness. For while my 'friend' was escorting me to the station restaurant, and zealous Storm Troopers were carrying my baggage into the train and bespeaking my seat, a man came up to me and whispered: 'I met your wife at the Schwarzwaldschule Rest House; she knows me well. My wife is still lying in the train, with a broken leg. I don't know how we're going to make it through—she's Jewish. Perhaps you can help me.'

I turned to my Sturmführer, who had been giving orders to his men. 'This gentleman is an acquaintance of mine,' I told him. 'He's absolutely all right on politics. His wife has a broken leg and is in no condition to go through all the checks. Could you oblige me by waiving some of the formalities?'

'If you vouch for these people, that's good enough for me,' my protector said. He gave instructions, and shortly afterwards I saw a woman with her leg in a cast being helped by her husband and a railroad official into the Swiss train.

A few days later this man ran into my wife and me on Bahnhofstrasse in Zurich and lavished thanks upon me. That is how my wife heard, for the first time, the blow-by-blow story of my adventure at the border.

It was not over yet. I sat in the station restaurant. The hours crept by. But at least I was able to have the red wine for which I had been craving, and I became aware that I had not eaten since I left Vienna. Nevertheless I had no appetite. I was also not tired, although I had scarcely slept for days. The first light of day was already beginning to show. My pulse beat with the ticking of the clock. If only I were out of this. Any moment might change the situation. If a new border guard came on duty, new suspicion might crop up and the whole farce would have been in vain. Now that I was almost safe, I was frightened to death.

My Nazi friend sat beside me, drinking up my last twenty

schillings, and acquiring a glassy stare. Again and again he be-
moaned the fact that he had not had the opportunity to fight in the
war, where he would have been able to 'prove himself.'

'There'll be another,' I consoled him.

'Yes,' he exclaimed enthusiastically. 'Let's drink to that!'

Suddenly I saw him, without hatred but also without pity, lying
in a pool of blood, with the pinched look of death on his face, that
I had seen on so many men. From time to time an SA man rushed
into the restaurant to report that they had caught another who had
hidden ten thousand schillings in his shoe or a diamond in his
anus.

'Well—we'll give him the business. What a swine!'

'When is the train leaving?' I asked the SA man.

'It will be a while longer. We're doing a thorough job today.'

'That gives us more time to enjoy each other's company,' my
companion said.

As the train crossed the border, the sky was a glassy green, and
cloudless. The perpetual snow glittered in the early-morning sun.
The Swiss customs officials entered the car and uttered friendly
gutturals. It was all over. I was in a train, and it was not headed
toward Dachau.

I sat at the window thinking: You ought to be happy now. Or at
least feel something like relief. But I felt nothing at all. Not even
pain. I only thought: I'll never be happy again. I am absolutely
indifferent to everything—whether I am here or anywhere else in
the world. It will never change from now on.

But it always does change. It changes as long as we live. Time
certainly does not heal all wounds. But it teaches us a dialectic of
change, of inescapable metamorphosis. The thesis of that dialectic
is: the will to live. Its antithesis: despair. Its synthesis is
friendship.

In those days we kept hearing the anecdote of the widely
traveled Englishman who was asked which people he liked best.
The French? 'No,' he said. Then the Germans? Or the Italians?
Perhaps the Indians? The Russians? Even the Americans? He
answered every question with the same laconic No. 'Does that
mean you like only Englishmen?' 'No,' the man said. 'I like my
friends.'

71

That is an axiom to cling to—although for my part I must confess that I have an insurmountable partiality for Germans, even for their faults (I am not speaking here of the crimes with which the henchmen and lackeys of the tyranny tainted our nation), and that I have always felt that I belong to them without reservation. But what good are such feelings when you are no longer at home among them? Exile should not be regarded as an evasion. It is not something that can be taken lightly. Has its real psychological misery ever been described—the degree of self-deception, vain hopes, false confidence, lives shattered in mid-course? Yet we had before us a good example of how not to behave in exile. There were the Russians who had left after the October Revolution of 1917 and were now sitting around in all the big cities of the world, forever feeding each other rumors about the imminent collapse of Bolshevism, and celebrating every Easter with the toast: Home by Christmas. They went on in this way until they were old and gray. But these Russian exiles were everywhere a well-received group. The Berlin of the twenties is inconceivable without them (I shall have something to say about those years later on). Even in poverty there was something aristocratic about them, and a quality of tragic dignity. They had the air of banished noblemen of the eighteenth century, even if at home they had only been grooms, café musicians, or valets.

Nothing of the sort could possibly be said for our group of exiles. There was nothing noble or appealing about us. We were not welcomed, and at best aroused pity mingled with a slight contempt, at least collectively—for until the war, the world cherished a dreadful respect for Hitler's dazzling successes. And collectively, whether Christians or Jews, we all brought with us the old German vice: dissension.

In Hollywood the saying was: If at the beginning of a movie production there is one Hungarian on the team, at the end there will be only Hungarians; but if at the beginning there are ten Germans, at the end there will be only one left. Certain political groups, such as the Communists, might maintain cohesiveness, but national groupings scarcely ever did. Yet it is my belief that no German ever forgets his native region, whether it lies on the Oder or the Vistula, on the Rhine or on the Danube. Even those who are successful in a foreign country, and choose to remain there, always carry that crack in their hearts and that invisible burden upon their backs. And we others will always bear in our blood the toxins of those years in exile. In fact we cultivate those toxins, whether we know it or not, as of a disease we have grown accustomed to and can no longer do without. The only remedy for those deep-seated feelings of insecurity, for that sense of homelessness, is the existence of friendship: both those old, settled friendships which continue without a break over decades, and those that flare up when we meet certain people who from the start seem to have been our comrades always, as if we had been closely linked in some earlier life.

Through the darkness of the ages, through the history and prehistory of the human race, the saga of friendship is scattered like the strings of lights of peopled towns and streets over a nocturnal landscape. Castor and Pollux have been translated to the stars. The song of Achilles and Patroclus is a lyric note in the ten-year struggle for Troy. The somber story of the Nibelungs is illuminated by the ballad of the friendship between young Giselher and Volker. From his dungeon tower Richard Coeur de Lion hears the voice of the singer Blondel. It is a voice that goes to the heart more purely than the sweet accents of courtship, the mellifluous lines of the minnesong, for it is without lust. The feelings of friendship are more intense than those of sensual passion. Its goal is not possession or fulfilment, but constancy, the continual act of fidelity. In love between the sexes, fidelity is sustained by the marital bond, which is to say by a vow, an obligation, a moral law, but it does not spring from the original nature of the feeling. Friendship, on the other hand, is synonymous with fidelity. It is the soil in which fidelity grows. And the cruelest failure in human relations is when the fidelity of friendship breaks down—not in the struggle between the sexes.

When I think of the brightest and the darkest hours in my life, and in the lives of those who are close to me, friendship is intertwined among them like a strong, visible, unbreakable chain. In the good times it was strengthened by mutual giving and receiving. In times of distress it became an anchor, pilot, sometimes a life preserver, and always, even in storms, even in defeat, it remains a beacon light, a signal in the fog. Whenever death has snatched a friend away —and that, alas, began happening too early in my life and goes on happening—I have felt every time as if I have lost a part of myself.

There is the elevated form of friendship that begins with esteem

73

and is based upon mutual understanding and appreciation. There are the timid or tempestuous advances made by personalities of differing talent and character, that attraction of opposites which must survive severe testing and becomes firm in the process. There are the variable stages of comradeship resulting from shared experiences or dangers, sometimes fading when those experiences pass, sometimes growing into genuine attachments. Such encounters seem to lie largely in the realm of chance, arriving as they do out of natural changes in the circumstances of life, and may take the most varied forms, whereas a firm rule like that of a monastic order seems to govern the fraternity of like-minded people. There are the cometlike epiphanies of new friends at the right moment, and there are partings, the painful and almost ritual partings such as we went through when we became exiles and had to bid goodbye, often forever, to friends remaining behind. Friendship with simple people, with workmen, woodcutters, and farmers, such as I enjoyed in the Green Mountains of Vermont, is like a hearth fire over which we warm our hands on an autumn night. There are no intellectual bonds with such people, but there is mutual trust, manly respect, and also a kind of reserve which is a safeguard for the durability and reliability of the relationship.

'Friends in need'—we hear this phrase spoken in the ironic tone of the embittered, in the whine of the disappointed who did not realize that they themselves had caused disappointment and were casting the blame on others. We lived through days in which evil and treachery were commonplace. Many people have preserved from those days only black memories of baseness and meanness. But I have kept a *white list* of those who withstood the test, who testified by their lives and deaths that fidelity and faith are realities, in spite of all differences of nation, class, and race.

The canon in the great choir belongs to dead friends. We have lost them and do not cease to mourn them, but they still live among us. Often we hear their voices, in sleep or waking; often we feel the firm, calm pressure of their hands, like no one else's handshake. Even if we do not know where their graves are, we keep their memory green. They are with us; they drink from our glasses and walk through our rooms. For friends do not die.

'Switzerland,' Friedrich Engels wrote in a memoir of the stormy years 1848–49, 'showed the exiles its rough side at that time.'

74

Ninety years later, in 1938–39, that side of Switzerland had become no smoother. I shall not forget how I was greeted by the *Fremden-polizei,* the department of the Swiss police force in charge of aliens, when I first went to report my presence as a political refugee. Switzerland has a long tradition of offering political asylum. Nevertheless, I was snarled at in dialect and treated as if I were a potential embezzler, swindler, forger of checks, possibly even a Communist. How much money did I have? Could I prove that I had a bank account? At the moment I couldn't, of course. Indigents were not welcome here; why hadn't I stayed where I belonged? What crime had I committed (this is literal) that I had been forced to take flight?

I said, knowing it was wise to be cautious about making any political declarations, that my mother was of Jewish descent. That would not be sufficient reason, I was told, since I was not a Jew myself. And Jews were only running away out of cowardice or because they wanted to do business outside Germany, since nothing was happening to them there if they behaved properly; it was just that the authorities were now keeping an eye on their activities, and high time too. I mentioned the occupation of Austria and the conditions prevailing there. But I wasn't an Austrian at all, I was told —which was true enough according to my passport. So if things were a bit hectic in Austria, I should have gone back to the Reich, which was thriving now, instead of coming here to be a burden on the Swiss. I would not be a burden on anyone, I said, and would earn my own livelihood. But not here, the police officer snapped at me, I was not entitled to earn anything here! A fine state of affairs, if anyone could come along and take the bread out of the mouths of the natives. And I was told that for the present they could not expel me, but my residence permit would be good only for a limited stay and was cancelable at any time. They would see about the future, but I was not to imagine that I would be granted permission to settle in Switzerland. And with that I was ungraciously dismissed.

Well, that was one group of officials. In Bern, too, we later came across an undisguised display of anti-Semitism and sympathy for the Nazis. In Vaud, in French Switzerland, our experiences were more pleasant—although by then we were able to produce evidence of a sum of money earned in England. But the pilgrimages to the authorities, and even to the various consulates I had to see in connection with some trips to London and Paris, were occasions of penance and entreaty every time.

The behavior of a number of eminent individuals was entirely different. For example, the Swiss writer Caesar von Arx, whom I did not know personally, at once offered me all the aid and support that his prestige and influence in the country afforded. Robert Faesi, the Swiss professor of literature, likewise threw his full energies into helping the German and Austrian writers who were seeking refuge in Switzerland. Then there was the group around Zurich Schauspielhaus. These were the days in which this small theater with its close-packed rows of seats and skimpy backstage space outgrew whatever provincialism it may have had and became the last stronghold of the free German theater. There no one asked whether a man was rightist or leftist, Catholic or Communist, Christian or Jew, but only whether he was a good artist. And the Swiss public, both intelligentsia and ordinary theatergoers, in their affection for the troupe proved that they had their hearts in the right place.

Our friends stood by us magnificently. The moment I sent word to Alexander Korda, the *grand seigneur* among movieland's adventurers, that I had got through to Zurich and my family was to follow, he telegraphed me a handsome sum in sterling—although he owed me no money and I had asked for none, our next project being only in the planning stage. We would work it out sometime later, he told me over the telephone—on the contract after next; I needn't fear that he would deduct it from the next contract. Without that advance I would actually have been stranded high and dry and unable even to pay my hotel bill, for my publisher, Bermann Fischer, had himself fled from Austria and was on his way to Sweden to re-establish his publishing house. On the same day I received a telegram from Elisabeth Bergner, then as celebrated on the stage and the cinema in London as she had earlier been in Berlin. She had probably heard from Korda where we were, and wanted to know whether I needed money, and how much. This prompt kindness on the part of more fortunate friends was enormously heartening at this time.

Of course I did not deceive myself. I realized that these friends were extending a kind of first aid, like a bandage after an accident. But the urgent thing was for me to launch upon an entirely new struggle for existence. Quite aside from all the emotional factors, that first year of exile was one of the most strenuous years in my life. For what was involved was not just the work which had long since become the content of my life, but a kind of rushed and obstinate forced labor for the purpose of self-preservation and building a future. I soon realized that we would have to be moving on, that we could not stay in lovely Switzerland, and that I would need funds for transporting a family of five—four people and our elderly dog, whom we had brought with us—to the land of all hope, America. During that one year I turned out, in addition to my own writing, six movie scenarios: three for London, one for Paris, and two for Amsterdam. The fact that I found the strength, and the inner and outer repose, to work at such an insane pace was due solely to a piece of good luck—what I have called the 'epiphany of new friends at the right moment.' In this case it was my meeting Pierre and Françoise Pelot, the owners of the ancient, gloriously old-fashioned and traditional Hotel Belle-Vue in Chardonne, near Vevey, about a thousand feet above Lake Geneva.

A dozen or so quiet places in western Switzerland had been recommended to us, places where, in those days, it was still possible to live relatively cheaply. While I was 'job hunting' in Paris, London, and Amsterdam, my wife looked around for a suitable home for us. For—quite aside from the rude and hostile attitude of the authorities—we could not stay in Zurich, although we had quickly moved from the comfortable hotel to a modest pension. Zurich was not only too expensive, it was also hard on the nerves. On Bahnhofstrasse you ran daily into fellow victims, newly arrived refugees. Each one would be greeted with exclamations— for there was no keeping track of each other in these confused times. And each new arrival brought some item of terrible news: Auernheimer was in Dachau. Friedell had committed suicide, Louis Rothschild had been imprisoned, Rudolf Beer, director of the Vienna Volkstheater, had been horribly beaten and tortured, and had finally taken poison in the hospital. So-and-So had been arrested at the frontier. Stories of this sort made us rejoice the more over everyone who had escaped. There were constant hailings and reunions on elegant Bahnhofstrasse. The native Zurichers, their mouths always pursed somewhat crossly since they had no real worries, looked on in astonishment as they waited for the streetcar while we refugees embraced one another and conducted loud, excited conversations. You hardly heard the local dialect, Züridütsch;

Bahnhofstrasse echoed with German and Austrian speech, much like many cafés in Paris, the London suburb of Hampstead, and later certain districts in New York. This emanation of a shared destiny was moving and comforting at first, but there was also something depressing about it. We did not want to become like the Russian exiles whose conversations always circled around the same subject. Therefore, and not simply for financial reasons, we felt impelled to seek other spheres.

For the present we did not think about America. At that time the immigrant visa could have been obtained without any special difficulty; the quota was not yet overfilled. Our friend Franz Horch, in well-founded fear of what awaited Europe, had already secured his visa. He also made out an application at the American consulate for me and for Franz Werfel—for Werfel and Alma Mahler were already in Zurich, and often asked us to dine with them at one of the city's splendid restaurants. But when Horch came to a bar at eleven o'clock in the morning, according to plan, in order to take us to the consulate for a personal interview, he found us so much under the influence of dry sherry and mutual sedition that we were entirely deaf to his arguments. No, we said like obstinate children. One flight is enough. We're Europeans and we'll stay in Europe. What would we do in a country where people pour ketchup on beef and where our greatest linguistic achievement would be to say in English: 'I am not able to express myself'?

We still clung to the fable of the invulnerable Maginot Line, which Hitler would not even dare to attack, with the threat of a growing Soviet power at his back. That was half a year before the Munich Pact, in which England and France abandoned Czecho-slovakia and thus gave Hitler free rein in the east; it was not quite a year and a half before the equivocal Nonaggression Pact between Moscow and Berlin. But we chose to loll in the old Zurich Bodega on Fraumünsterstrasse and think of ourselves as the last bulwarks of European culture, rather than set out for unknown and uncongenial parts.

Both of us later had to pay the price for this nonchalance—I by going through a complicated immigration procedure via Cuba, Werfel by a harried six-day scramble across all of France and over the Pyrenees.

In May of 1938, then, we moved to the pretty village of Char-

78

donne, which looks down on Lake Geneva, with terraced vineyards below and the wooded height of Mont Pèlerin above. When I returned from my trip with two separate film contracts, a couple of pounds of Dunhill tobacco, and a fantastic schedule, I found that my wife had already rented two comfortable rooms in the Hotel Belle-Vue. One of the rooms had an old stone fireplace in the corner. Outside each room was a spacious balcony, wreathed in wisteria, and a writing table was already waiting on mine. The hotel was a large rustic stone building, not at all like ordinary Swiss hotels. It rather resembled an old French provincial inn. To this day an eighteenth-century engraving of the building hangs in my room; it shows the place exactly as we found it, except for the smaller trees. From the balconies you looked out over the lake, ever changing in its tones and light, to the summits of the Dent du Midi and the mountains of Savoy.

I really cannot explain how it happened that so lively and lasting a friendship sprang up within a few days, perhaps only a few hours, between ourselves and the Pelots, our hosts, who were about ten years younger than we. Such things are natural phenomena. Within a short time we had become more than friends; we were like blood relatives, and our relationship remained ever afterwards like that of brothers and sisters. Lovely Françoise—her father was a gentleman's tailor in Vevey and her family stemmed from Sicily— was at that time in the last stages of pregnancy. On May 31 she brought her second child into the world, Anne-Françoise. The infant was so pretty that I fell in love with her during her first toothless months, and although it often happens that extremely pretty babies grow up plain, Anne-Françoise is even more beautiful today. Whenever I had time I pushed her perambulator along the garden paths and sang her lullabies from my Hessian homeland.

But in those weeks before her birth, her mother Françoise, with her rounded belly and full breasts, was, in my view, which not everybody may share, a picture of perfect womanliness. I would have liked to paint her. Despite her condition, she was, like her husband Pierre, always cheerful, displaying a wonderful cordiality toward every guest, and never tired. Or at least she never showed it. The two largely ran their hotel themselves, although they had several employees and even a cook at the height of the season. In the autumn, winter, and early spring they attended to the cooking and together carried the meals into the pleasant, light dining room with its large windows looking out over the landscape. Guests were served in patriarchal fashion by the *patron* himself, and Pierre poured the local white wine from such a height, without ever spilling a drop, that it bubbled like champagne in the glasses. While he worked, he whistled or sang. Often, with complete lack of self-consciousness, he walked whistling loudly through the restaurant and down the halls, but no one felt in the least disturbed by this or by the shouts of glee with which his three-year-old son, Jacquie Trésor, rushed towards his father in the early morning, dashing down halls and staircases.

Soon, on special occasions, we were sharing meals with the family, which included also Mère Pelot, a woman of great good sense and charm, and two of Pierre's sisters, Madeleine and Annie; the former was a gardener and *vigneronne*, the latter a deaconess. We ate in the *lingerie*, where the hotel's ironing was done, sitting together at the great oblong table. The insouciant, loud, but always good-natured bustle in the place never got on our nerves. For me, even when I was at work, there was something soothing about it, like the twitter of birds or the tinkle of cowbells. In those days we were not inclined to talk very much about Henndorf and our expulsion from our lost paradise, but our hosts sensed and guessed everything. One day I came back from London with a guitar that a kind lady had given me—my old one, a valuable instrument, had been smashed out of sheer spite when our house in Henndorf was searched. Thereafter we sat through many long evenings playing music together. With his wife or his sister Madeleine, Pierre sang the lovely French folk songs of the region, and into our distraught lives there returned a measure of good cheer, confidence, even of feeling at home, such as we had scarcely any right to expect. Thus the first year of exile gave us something to cling to, and this strengthened our inner forces. As yet we were not uprooted, not yet *vis-à-vis de rien*. That was still to come.

We had many predecessors in our present location. The shores of Lake Geneva were rich in the traditions of exile. Through the centuries Frenchmen, Englishmen, Irishmen, Italians, Germans, Russians—refugees from virtually every country in Europe—had found asylum here for longer or shorter periods. In Vevey a plaque commemorates the house in which Rousseau lived. Victor Hugo spent the years of his exile in the very same Hotel Belle-Vue in Chardonne where we were now staying; he had even left an old suitcase there. During the First World War the French pacifists Marcel Martinet and Henry Guilbaux (who had been condemned to death in France) and, after two years of war service, Henri Barbusse stayed in Geneva. Lenin and Trotsky were also there for a while; later the leaders of the Mensheviks and Social Revolutionaries took their place. Fellow exiles and ancestors went back almost a thousand years. On one of my first walks from Chardonne through the vineyards to the quaint village of St Saphorin I found at the entrance to the village the arms of the canton of Vaud chiseled in stone, painted in the green and white colors of the canton and bearing the cantonal motto: *Liberté et Patrie.* I stood before it for a long time. Where freedom and fatherland are one, I thought, there it is possible to live. And perhaps someday this fusion would be attained in unhappy Germany. I am not ashamed to say that my eyes overflowed with tears—for the first time, I think, since my flight.

The high point of this hard-working summer was my parents' golden wedding anniversary. We had all looked forward to their celebrating this day with us in our Henndorf home, where the guest cottage had been built specially for them. That could no longer be. Now we tried to obtain a visa for them to visit Switzerland—and encountered great difficulties. In those days new emigrants were more dreaded than rabies or typhus bacilli—and this, too, we must try to understand. It is not so easy for a small country, which in the event of war has all it can do to provision its own citizens, also to have to provide for a stream of refugees. My parents, I should add, did not want to emigrate under any circumstances. Naturally, I had offered to help them. At the age of forty-two I felt the strength and resolution to provide for their livelihood, all the more so because I had no idea how difficult that would be in America. But my father did not want to go abroad without funds, dependent on his son; he would not have wanted to even if I had been in better circumstances. He was attached to his country with his whole soul. At that time he was in his seventies, and the thought of dying on foreign soil was unendurable to him. Nevertheless he might have done it for my mother's sake—but she was even more determined to stay than he. She had unshakable confidence that nothing would happen to her, despite the fate of one of her brothers. A convert like herself, a bachelor, and a distinguished district judge, he had recently committed suicide in Mainz when he was ordered to leave his apartment for transportation to a 'resettlement' area. But she felt protected by her fifty years of marriage to an 'Aryan,' and in the end her confidence was justified. But what might have become of her if my father had not survived those times of terror alongside her is still a nightmare to me. Another of her brothers had died for Germany in 1914 and the third met a natural death, fortunately, before encountering humiliation or worse. Above all, she wanted to spare my father, who by that time had almost entirely lost his sight, the vicissitudes of exile. Separation from her two sons—my brother had been living in Turkey for several years, where he was head of the state music schools—was a deep pain to her, but for countless people in this period suffering was an everyday part of existence.

With the aid of our old and some of our newly acquired Swiss friends we were able to convince the authorities that they wanted to enter Switzerland only as tourists and not as refugees. And I shall never forget the celebration we were able to arrange for them in Chardonne, solely because of the kindness, the tact, the endless helpfulness of our friends the Pelots. And yet we had known them less than two months at that time. Pierre was fairly well aware of the state of my finances. I am convinced that he figured the feast he produced from his kitchen and cellar at fifty percent of the cost, although he insisted otherwise. After all, I knew the going price of fresh lobster and filet de boeuf, Burgundy and champagne. What it amounted to was that the Pelots gave a party for us. My brother had come from Turkey. In the morning we and the children assembled outside our parents' bedroom door to sing a canon he had composed for the occasion. The Pelots had decorated my parents' chairs at the banquet with gilded ears of corn and roses. All that was lacking was our native land. And on that day we all had it in our hearts. Late that evening my father, who was not ordinarily fond of speechmaking, stood up with a glass in hand and turned to his sons, my brother and myself. 'You boys are expelled from your country today for no fault of your own. Don't lose heart and keep your pride and your confidence, because you are good boys. You have not deserved such treatment from your country. But keep your love for it in spite of everything. And I tell you now —at this moment I am sure of it—everything is going to change. You will see your country again and will be honored and respected there, as you ought to be. Let us drink to that.'

We embraced, and did not know that this was goodbye—for many long years.

It is hard to realize how many events and experiences can be compressed into a single year. If I were to describe the time span from the spring of 1938 to the next spring, from our expulsion from Austria to our more decisive expulsion from Europe, with all the low and high points, with all the turbulence, shocks, and upheavals, with all the encounters and all my jaunts, some of them highly adventurous, to Paris and London—that alone would fill two fat volumes. But I am not concerned here either with remembrance of things past or the snows of yesteryear. I am telling the story of hours of friendship, recalling the memories of what remains imperishable and what became for me a source of faith and trust in spite of everything, even when the devil put his hoof into things. And the devil did his utmost to put his hoof in, as vigorously and protractedly as possible.

To his interference I must attribute the terrible and utterly senseless—if we may ever rightly say that, since we do not know better—death of our friend Ödön von Horváth, the playwright and novelist.

For me the story begins on the afternoon of Friday before Whitsun. We had been awaiting Ödön's visit for a whole week. He was planning to stay for a while and then look for a congenial place where he might work either in our neighborhood or in the vicinity of Zurich. We were hoping that Chardonne would appeal to him, that he would become a neighbor as he had been in Henndorf, where during the previous several years he had written most of his major works, and we were looking forward eagerly to his arrival. Then we received a telegram from Amsterdam that he had first to go to Paris and would arrive at Chardonne on Whitsunday. His room was waiting.

It was the time of the wild narcissi, which were blooming in great masses on the tranquil pastures of Mont Pèlerin, perfuming the whole area. On this Friday I had gone up to the mountain early in the afternoon, along with my daughter Winnetou, to pick flowers for the Sunday table, and for Ödön's room. The weather was good, though somewhat sultry as it often is before thunderstorms. But there were no particular signs of a storm. My daughter and I were alone in the middle of a rather large meadow rimmed by forest. Suddenly, from the west, the direction of France, black clouds came rushing towards us with uncanny speed. Within barely a minute a rainstorm was lashing down upon us. The woods were loud with the creaking of trees, and we could not hear our own voices. I am not ordinarily frightened by elemental forces, and a violent thunderstorm, even if I have to walk right through it, usually fills me with a certain gaiety. But in this case, perhaps because the child was with me, I became almost frightened, and we ran as fast as we could to a hay loft for shelter. I am not speaking out of hindsight when I say that during this storm, with its sudden flashes of lightning and booming thunderclaps, I had a curious feeling of menace, of some mysterious danger in the air, although we were in a relatively safe place.

This was the same storm that had come up from the Atlantic and swept across all of France, and that had hit Paris an hour or a half hour before. Shortly after we returned to our hotel, I was called to the telephone. The call was from a mutual friend in Paris who informed me that Ödön was dead. Apparently he had had some kind of accident in the street during the storm and had been taken to the morgue; there were no details yet, but his parents had been informed.

The background of this accident was very strange. Ödön had not actually planned to go to Paris. He had been in Amsterdam negotiating with Landshoff and Landauer, the publishers of the exiles, about a new novel. From there he meant to come directly to Switzerland. Now, there was a clairvoyant in Amsterdam who was the talk of the town. It had become the fashion, especially among intellectuals, to consult him, even though most intellectuals went merely out of curiosity or for amusement. But Ödön had a special weakness for everything out of the ordinary. Clairvoyants appealed to him, and the day before his intended departure he went to see the man, accompanied by a friend. I heard from the eyewitness that the clairvoyant fell into a curious state of agitation as soon as Ödön entered; his excitement mounted to a kind of trance, and in this state he repeatedly said: 'You must go to Paris. You absolutely must go to Paris at once. Something is awaiting you there'—he could not say exactly what, but repeated again and again—'the decisive event of your life.'

At this time Ödön happened to be corresponding with the producer Siodmak, who had stopped in Paris on his way to Hollywood and who had shown an interest in making a movie of Ödön's novel *The Age of the Fish*. He had urged Ödön to come to Paris for a discussion, if that were possible. Ödön had not taken the matter too seriously. People in the movie world always want to talk with somebody about projects that ultimately come to nothing, and there was no firm offer behind Siodmak's request. But the clairvoyant's trance made a great impression on Ödön. Perhaps he really can see into the future, he said to his Amsterdam friend; a Hollywood movie would certainly be a decisive event in the life of an exiled writer. And so he went to Paris.

A few days after his death I arrived in Paris for his funeral. Various friends told me that on the fatal day Ödön had been going about as if haunted by a strange nervousness. He had visited one person after another, staying nowhere, leaving quickly without any special reason. In the course of the morning he had walked across almost the whole city. He had made an appointment to meet Siodmak and his wife for an early afternoon performance at a movie house on the Champs Élysées where the Disney film *Snow White* was then opening in Europe. The Siodmaks already had the tickets and were waiting for him in the lobby. Outside, the storm had begun. Ödön appeared soaked through, at the last moment before the beginning of the performance, but only to say that he couldn't join them, he had something urgent to do. Immediately afterwards he rushed out again into the downpour. He must have quickly crossed the broad boulevard and walked along the Rond Point, which is encircled by tall trees. There, a heavy branch from a tree shaken loose by the storm crashed down upon him. It struck the back of his head and the nape of his neck, killing him instantly. At that time a few elms still stood at the Rond Point; I myself saw the half-uprooted elm that caused his death, for it had not yet been removed. Elms are trees touched by disaster. In Europe they had for some time been prone to a mysterious sickness, the Dutch elm disease, which seemed to condemn them to extinction, and the disease has since spread to the noble elms of the eastern United States.

All of Ödön's close friends remember that he had always had a phobia about objects that might fall on him. In cities he would make wide detours around all building sites. He often remarked that someday he would be killed by a falling roof tile. How much of all that is coincidence lies beyond human conjecture.

But all those omens, especially in the gloomy atmosphere of exile, had a sinister, disturbing effect. Every one of us felt affected by the fate of one of our most promising fellows: each of us felt as if some bit of hope had been snatched away. And few persons had been so loved by women, friends, and children, scarcely anyone had had so few personal enemies, as this gifted writer who met his end at the age of barely thirty-seven. If this memoir were directed only towards the few dozen literary and theater people who know of Ödön, I would not have to be retelling a story whose outlines are generally known to them. But I am afraid that the name of this writer who was not destined to reach maturity remains largely unknown today. He possessed, after Brecht, the strongest dramatic talent of his age. And yet he left behind no work that will in the long run be counted part of the classical stock of German literature. 'Everything about him,' I said in my address at his grave, 'was beginning, incipience, promise. The work that he has left for us was a sketch, a draft, the secret plan for greater work of lasting beauty and importance that he was not permitted to create.'

His parents, whom we had met in Berlin years before, had asked me to speak at Ödön's grave, and since I thought that would be some small comfort to them, I agreed, in spite of our own difficult circumstances.

We saw our dead friend once more on the bier. Since the blow that felled him had struck him from behind, his face was unchanged, only of a yellowish pallor. But he looked beautiful, terribly still, and seemed to be smiling ironically. Before the coffin was closed, his mother leaned toward him with outstretched hands, as if she wanted to lift him out—a gesture that I often see before me and that will remain in my mind forever.

Tragedy mingled with the grotesque at this funeral. After the obsequies in a Catholic church in the heart of the city we rode in a long procession of cabs to the distant cemetery near the Gare du Nord. All the exiles in Paris were present, and most of them had become involved in hopeless feuds and hatreds among themselves. As soon as we arrived, in fact, the most distracted discussions had begun as to the order of the speakers at the grave. The family had expressly requested Franz Werfel, Walter Mehring, and myself to speak, but in addition to us there were many others who felt that they had to be heard on such an occasion. There was a rather sizable crowd, and argument raged as to who ought to give precedence to whom, or who would feel insulted if someone else spoke first. I suggested alphabetical order—which was perhaps in my favor, since I would have the last word.

The only available grave was at the extreme end of the grounds. And so, after leaving the cabs, the entire funeral procession tramped across the whole of the wide cemetery to where it became barren and treeless. Ödön's parents walked somberly behind the coffin— Ödön's brother, whom he dearly loved, supporting their mother. Alongside the French priest came a Hungarian chaplain, a family friend, who had flown from Budapest. Behind him were two young women who disputed the honor of having been Ödön's last sweetheart. And then we came—miserable band of plucked birds, even those of us who still had some decent clothing and sound shoes left. Rudolf Leonhardt, one of the early Expressionist writers, limped along on a cane. Many wore those vague, shabby scarves that are the mark of an incipient wretchedness. Joseph Roth, the greatly gifted novelist, staggered along completely drunk, as he almost always was at this period, with stained suit, leaning on two youthful admirers. And the Paris rain dripped incessantly down upon the whole absurd procession—that rain conventionally known as silvery. But it was only wet and a dirty gray.

The cemetery was bounded by the tracks of a railroad yard, and as background to the long and short funeral orations there was the constant rattling and screeching of brakes as freight trains were shunted, and the clamor of railroad workers giving instructions, exchanging jokes, laughing, making appointments: '*Ou vas-tu, Gaston?*' '*Au bistro. Viens pour un verre!*' '*Entendu*'—and so on, their calls resounding and sometimes drowning the speakers whose voices did not carry. If Ödön were alive he would die laughing, I thought. At the end the inconspicuous little chaplain stepped up to the grave, took a paper bag from his pocket, and poured the contents down upon the coffin, saying in a low voice: 'Soil from Hungary.' But everyone heard him. It seemed as if the noises from the railroad yard had suddenly ceased.

We celebrated Christmas, our first since we no longer had a home of our own, in the Belle-Vue at Chardonne. But the jollity and domestic happiness of the Pelot family counteracted all impulses of melancholy or sadness in us. We shared their happiness as if it were ours, and I began to apprehend that in life as in the Church a kind of 'deputyship' exists among people, a vicarious participation in sorrow and in gladness extending beyond mere sympathy. Also that this deputyship, not mere community of interests, is the real source of all humanitarian evolution, both in the sense of the social contract and in that of international peace.

We celebrated New Year's Eve together, as well. The snow was heavy; I went skiing with Pierre whenever there was a bit of free time, and in the early darkness we tobogganed with the children down the serpentine highway—which in those days had little traffic and almost none after a snowfall—to the station of the funicular railway in Vevey, on which we rode up again.

At the beginning of the fall I had been in Zurich, where my *Bellman* was being rehearsed. There I had watched, along with the rest of the world, the unfolding of the Czechoslovak crisis, which ended feebly in the ominous Munich Conference and British Prime Minister Chamberlain's returning home crying, 'Peace in our time,' as he waved the sheet of paper bearing Hitler's and Mussolini's signatures. That was the first great act of appeasement, and it was fraught with terrible consequences. Hitler had been given a free hand, and he did not stand with it resting idly in a pocket, at least not his own.

Those were dispiriting days. In Zurich a practice blackout of the city was ordered. Sirens howled, the lights went out, and the local young people took it all as a colossal joke. Crowds of them jostled through the streets laughing and screeching, or used the darkness for amorous amusements. But even I realized, though hitherto I had been inclined to optimistic illusions, that the avalanche was on its way—and that it would just be a case of delayed action. 'Delayed action' was the phrase we applied to howitzer shells that buried themselves in the ground before exploding with all the greater force. Friends from Germany, it was true, reported that in Berlin, during the partial mobilization that had been ordered in the crisis, the reservists had cursed and the people had been gloomy and refractory. There was no sign of eagerness for war on the part of the German people, they said. But we could no longer be taken in by such stories. We knew that dictatorship cares little about popular mood when grave decisions are made, and that propaganda would bring the people into line when the time came. I had the clearest feeling, when my play was staged, that this would be my last performance in a German-language theater, perhaps the last altogether. And even as we celebrated its first night, sitting up until dawn with our friends, we were aware all the time that our merriment was a form of dancing on a volcano.

In the course of my visits in Paris and London during that year, moreover, I had been forced to see what a lax, indifferent, cynical attitude people in the leading circles in those capitals had towards the 'phenomenon' of Hitler and his escapades, cannonades of threats, and acts of illegality. That was true for statesmen, politicians, intellectuals, and journalists. The thing was to let him bark, then he wouldn't bite, they said. Or else: he must not be provoked or he might bite after all. A good many people were hypnotized by his successes and his blatant displays of power; they were rather envious. As for the common people, they are so easily blinded the world over. In Paris pissoirs you found swastikas chalked on the walls, and in heavy letters the wordes *LA MORT AUX JUIFS!* It felt like home. And in England, when I first went there after the occupation of Austria and had not yet learned to hold my tongue about it, a distinguished gentleman, a member of the House of Commons, patted me forbearingly on the back and said: 'This man Hitler—why, isn't he quite a good chap? I think we need him, all of us, as a bulwark against Communism.'

There were others, of course, in France as well as England, who knew what was brewing and warned against it. I never had the good fortune to meet Winston Churchill. But I was introduced into one oasis of the best in British tradition and culture: the home of Duff Cooper, then First Lord of the Admiralty. His wife, the beautiful Lady Diana Manners, had formerly acted in *The Miracle* for Reinhardt in Salzburg. Duff Cooper was a great cavalier, not of the old school but of a timeless school, a man of high intellectual accomplishments and political wisdom who also proved himself, in his *Talleyrand*, a writer and historian of distinction. He and some others, like the writer and diplomat Harold Nicolson, have remained for me impressive examples of what lasting, what far from devalued sterling qualities the Empire has contributed to Europe and the world since the days of the first Elizabeth and her poets.

Nicolson could be met in the Café Royal on Regent Street, others in the Hungarian, Greek, and Scandinavian restaurants of Soho. In Paris the French literary and theater people forgathered at Fouchet's or in the small restaurants on the Left Bank. It was an improbable era, seen from a contemporary viewpoint. There was the feeling that we were experiencing world history every day, and helping to bring it forth, simply by our existence. I recall one evening in March 1939 when I was strolling with friends along the Boul' Mich' in Paris. Suddenly the city throbbed and resounded with the bells of all the churches. We walked to the Île, and as we approached the cathedral of Notre Dame we heard from its towers, amid the flourish of trumpets, a chorus of youthful voices singing: '*Habemus Papam.*'

It was the day on which Cardinal Pacelli, the former papal nuncio in Berlin, had been elected Holy Father of the Roman Catholic Church—an election that imposed upon him the burden of infinite problems and endless misunderstandings. We were all moved by the fatefulness of the moment, and along with countless others doffed our hats and knelt in the street as the Bishop of Paris appeared on a balcony and gave his blessing.

Shortly afterwards I had a decisive experience in Paris. My wife was meeting me there, for I was coming back from London and needed some time to complete a movie script for the producer Max Ophüls. The project took a week more than I had counted on, and my visa had run out. Since a special recommendation was needed for prolongation of a visa, I called on the writer Jean Giraudoux, whom I knew from Berlin. He received me warmly, and asked whether I did not want to stay in France, where after all I had greater opportunities for work and better cultural connections than in Switzerland and where in addition I was only an hour's flight away from London. But what would become of the exiles here should the war break out? I asked him. Would we be locked up? Or were the authorities already considering other alternatives? 'But my dear sir,' Giraudoux said, smilingly alluding to the title of his famous play about the war for Troy, '*this* war will not take place.'

He was someone who had access to the most secret archives of world politics. I left his office firmly resolved—for the first time—to leave Europe as soon as possible.

Next day, equipped with Giraudoux's recommendation, we went to the Préfecture. Closely packed in one waiting room sat a large number of foreigners, most of them refugees from Spain. There were not enough benches; many had to stand. An official sat behind a desk staring into space with a bored expression and toying with his pencil. I went up to him, handed him our passports and the letter of recommendation, and asked how long it would probably take. He shrugged and with a gesture indicated that I should join the other people waiting.

Although so many were standing, there was one relatively comfortable upholstered chair that was unoccupied. I was told that there, only the day before, an old man from some country or other, who had been waiting for weeks, had slit open the arteries in his wrists. He had sat with his hands hidden behind his back and was not noticed until he had bled to death. We too preferred not to use the chair, and resigned ourselves to an endless wait. Suddenly my name was called out; it was Lajos, Ödön von Horváth's brother. He too was here to see about extending his *carte d'identité*. 'Did you slip a bank note to the man at the desk?' he whispered to me. I looked at him in astonishment. Such an idea had not occurred to me. 'Unless you do, you never get your turn,' Lajos said softly. 'Your recommendation won't help at all.'

I moved unobtrusively back to the official and asked him to let me have my passport again; I'd forgotten something, I said. He pushed it towards me without looking, and I tucked a rather sizable bank note in it. Now, too, he continued staring into space and playing with his pencil, but after a while he had wormed the passport under his desk. I did not have to wait much longer; I was soon called in and was able to settle my business in the adjoining office without any trouble. My decision to leave this continent grew firmer.

In the evening we attended the première of an operetta in which the émigré Austrian actor Oskar Karlweis was playing the lead. The performance was torture for him. In his dressing room cold sweat poured down his face as he repeated his lines again and again, with trembling lips. On the stage he beamed, danced, and pranced as his part required, sang chansons with impromptu additions, carried on rapid-fire dialogues, even improvised—all this in a language which he must have known quite well before, but which up to a year ago had not been the language of his profession—and how sensitive the French of all people are to hearing their language spoken incorrectly or clumsily. I saw Karlweis a few years later in much the same situation, and radiating the same self-confidence. This time he had the lead in a play in New York. His part was tremendously long and difficult, and had to be played in English. How could any human being endure so much stress without damaging his heart? And in fact Oskar died of heart disease, though not until he had survived the tests of exile and was once more able to act in his mother tongue. At that time, in Paris, his performance reminded me of an acrobat's walking a high tightrope without balancing pole and net.

But he made it. The Paris audience was enthusiastic, his performance a smash hit. We celebrated late that night in a newly opened Taverne Viennoise where the Parisians were finding their substitute for the Mirabell Bar in Salzburg. But throughout the festivities I was in thought already at the American consulate.

Back in Geneva, I had no great difficulty obtaining—with generous aid from America, which I shall have to tell about later—a visitor's visa, though only for a limited time. But that satisfied us. My sole aim now was to get away before it was too late. My period of naïve credulity was over. I knew that the 'unknown corporal' of the First World War would not rest until he had become Supreme Commander of a second world war. I could already smell the pungent odor of ecrasite, that Austrian explosive specialty. Our breathing spell in Switzerland and Western Europe, the peace and sense of shelter in the home of our dear friends in Chardonne, were over.

Since we could not take with us all we had accumulated in the course of this year—books, for example, and our small stock of dishware and silverware—my friend Pierre brought down an old-fashioned wooden trunk with curved lid and metal bands in which to store our things. On the lid were large initials: V. H. After the war these possessions were still safe in Victor Hugo's old trunk.

It was May. Lake Geneva shone in the full splendor of a perfect spring. Never had the landscape seemed so peaceful, so harmonious —a fabric woven of north and south, the heart of the old Continent. The world we belonged to. Across the lake, in the French spa of Evian, an International Refugee Conference was taking place at the time. The conferees were not refugees, but envoys and officials of various nations, and of the League of Nations also, who discussed the fate of the refugees now pouring across all the borders. They dealt above all with the question of formalities, such as the issuance of Nansen passports. As so often with conferences, all the discussion came to nothing that we, the affected persons, ever noticed. But at the end of the conference a banquet and a great display of fireworks were arranged.

We stood under the ancient lindens of the terrace of the Hotel Belle-Vue, with its view over the entire lake, and watched the rockets shoot into the sky and print their fantastic configurations on the darkness. Nice of them after all, I said, to give us such a brilliant send-off.

We had arranged to sail from Rotterdam. Friends came to see us off. We spent the day walking in The Hague, looked at the Vermeers in Maurits Huis, and we ate and drank together cheerfully. On board ship we found letters from friends, from the lands vanishing behind us, among them an unforgettable one from Alexander Lernet-Holenia. 'Don't lament your fate,' he wrote to me. 'I envy you for it. You will see the world, whose law is change; you will be a new man in a new world. Change! Change! Change alone is life.'

Before our departure we spent a short while in Paris, where I had a job to finish and my remaining fee to collect. With a small private movie company, that can be a problem. Whenever I turned up, the cashier or the boss was always out to lunch. . . .

Our actual departure from Paris took a dramatic turn. With our prodigious amount of baggage we needed two cabs to get to the railroad station, and we were careless enough to load ourselves, along with the dog, into the first cab, and have the second follow with our belongings. In the traffic we lost sight of the second one, and we found ourselves standing on the platform, with the train about to leave and no sign of our possessions. The cab-driver said that he did not know the other driver, and we had not even bothered to note the license plate. Cabs loaded with baggage often did not turn up, our driver told us—it happened all the time. Instead, the cabs would head for Marseilles, where such goods could be disposed of at the best prices. Already we could see our entire wardrobes on the way to the Mediterranean. But at the last moment the other driver appeared; he had merely had a minor breakdown. While the compartment doors were already being closed, he helped the porters hurl our suitcases into the train.

Friederike Zweig had appeared on the platform to bid us goodbye. She was very distraught and brought the sad news that Joseph Roth had died in a delirium during the night.

The night before, our last in Paris, the producer G. W. Pabst had invited us to the exquisite restaurant Le Vert Galant, on the Île de la Cité. Wonderful wine was served. We drank a great deal, first a dry white Sancerre from the Loire, then Burgundy, then several glasses of cognac. When the party broke up, we decided not to ride in the cab with our friends. We needed fresh air, we said, and preferred to walk. We wanted to be alone. My wife and I first walked along the left bank, then crossed one of the bridges to the right bank. In the middle of the bridge we paused, sat on the railing, and held one another close. We were tipsy and did not know whether we were laughing or weeping. The lights of the city were mirrored in the rapidly flowing black water. From Notre Dame and other towers the hour struck twelve. Couples in close embrace huddled by the pillars of the bridge; under it we thought we could see a clochard rolling himself up in his tattered coat. From anchored barges we could hear laughter and song, the music of an accordion, a shrill woman's voice. We heard the city, saw it glittering and sparkling. At such moments you do not know exactly what is taking place in others, or even inside yourself. I heard my wife stammering: 'All this—perhaps never again—perhaps destroyed, in ruins—all that we—' She waved in a wide gesture over the river, the city, our continent. 'It's so beautiful,' she exclaimed, pointing to the shimmering, glittering waters of the Seine.

But it was not the Seine I saw, or the City of Light. I saw the Rhine.

1896-1914
A LOOK AT THE RHINE

LONG CRACKS gaped between the wooden planks of the walk-way on the old railroad bridge at Mainz. The planks smelled depressingly of soot, tar, and lubricating oil, so that the child forgot the lilacs and chestnuts in the park. Also, a cold gust came up through the cracks. They were too narrow to fall through. You couldn't even get your shoe stuck in them; in fact, the tip of an umbrella would barely fit between the planks. But underneath them was an abyss. It was an incomprehensibly frightful abyss, even more terrible than those in dreams; and within that abyss was a constant violent rocking and rushing that you could feel in your spine and stomach as though everything fixed were gliding away, everything solid slipping, the ground itself racing furiously away under your feet, or as though you were being sucked like bread crumbs from a plate into a tremendous drain. The bridge itself seemed to the child's eye infinite. Its iron arches, tall as a house, soared menacingly on and on, never stopping. One bank had vanished behind you, the other was still out of sight—and the sky and horizon seemed suddenly filled with that horrible rocking and rushing, as if everything were topsy-turvy and you were walking with your head downward.

Then, above him, the boy heard his father's voice. 'When I was a little boy,' it said, with a wry laugh, 'and had to cross the Rhine bridge for the first time, I was awfully frightened because I didn't know how strong such bridges are. I began fretting and crying, and everybody laughed at me.'

Suspiciously, the boy peered up at him, not understanding the man's tact and delicacy, his going so far as to lie out of kindness in order to make the fear more tolerable—for when the father was small the bridge had not yet been built. The boy looked up with a child's healthy distrust of a grownup's facetious tone, behind which there was apt to be some hidden design, some concealed trap. But the voice went on earnestly: 'Yes, just imagine, they had to carry me over the bridge, and I kicked and struggled, even though I was already four years old. But of course you would walk across alone; you don't have to be carried.' At the same time the large, warm, masculine hand closed firmly and gently around the small, surely rather cold and tremulous little hand. And the fear lessened, and gave way to a slightly shivering dread which already contained the germs of excitement and a prickling curiosity. That tugging sense of dizziness was now mingled with a secret pleasure and the beginnings of a dreamy courage. Suppose a train came now! Would the planks still hold? And a train did come; the whole bridge shook and rocked and thumped and thundered. For minutes you were swathed in smoke and steam, as if walking through hell. But the fear was gone and did not return. The small feet pattered gaily, daringly, to either side of the crack. Without fear, the boy looked through it, looked down. It was his first conscious look at the Rhine.

My native soil is Rhenish Hesse, which means that as far as landscape goes it has little of the romantic grandeur associated with the Rhine. In its rich, sunlit fertility this region has a very simple, very sober cast. The poles in the vineyards stand in neat, orderly rows; the fruit trees are set out in perfect alignment. All the land is tilled. Red is the basic color of the soil, especially in the vicinity of my birthplace, Nackenheim. The tint of red crops up everywhere in the vineyards, fields, and paths: the dullish damask of crumbled brick, the spotted tawniness of rusty bicycle wheels, the glow of the bullfinch's breast feathers, the faded carmine of the evening sky when the south wind is blowing—all that is fused in that fertile soil, and is outdazzled by the autumnal change of the grape leaves and the foliage of the trees. Modest clustered villages, many with a handsome old church and a few half-timbered houses, most built of plain grayish-yellow brick, snuggle into the slopes of the vineyards along the stretch of the Rhine extending from Mainz to Worms. The broad curves of the wavy or humpy plowland around Thunder Mountain, which is not much more than a hill, the stretch of orchard country on the left bank of the Rhine from the bend in the river near Mainz almost to the mouth of the Nahe; Ingelheim with its Carolingian imperial palace; and the delightful Church of St Roch towering over the slate roofs of Bingen; the sandy asparagus fields; the smooth channel of the river, which here has only a few small islets breaking its flow; the busy towns, which in spite of their long ages of history and their ancient buildings have nothing of the museum, nothing of the tourist trap about them—what other landscape so quietly and restrainedly presents a picture of intensive settlement and lush fruitfulness? The imagination can people it with Roman armies, with Celtic and Frankish tribes, with pagans and saints, with the splendid train of medieval emperors, with the baroque pomp of the electoral princes, with marauding Swedes and Cossacks, with French bandit, revolutionary, and occupation troops, with all the figures and all the confusions of two thousand years of history. But the face of the countryside remains tranquil and undemanding.

Birthplace is no fiction of the emotions, no intellectual construct. It governs growth and speech, sight and hearing; it animates the senses and opens them to the breath of the spirit. To be born by a stream and to grow up under the spell of a great river is a special blessing. Rivers sustain the land and keep the earth in balance, for they connect the seas and make the network of communication within the continents. It is in riverland, in floodland, in the mist-dampened meadows along fruitful shores, that peoples have always settled, built their cities and markets, temples and churches. It is along rivers that trade routes and languages meet. To be in the stream of things means to stand amid the fullness of life.

The Rhine, we learn in childhood, rises in the Alps and flows into the North Sea. But what does that mean to the eyes of a growing boy? What affects him is the living quality of its water, the force of its current, in which he learns early to swim and sail, and the rich vegetation along its streams and water-meadows. Its geography and history do not much interest him.

Children are aware of a landscape in microcosm; they cannot take in the full scope. Forests of reeds, ponds teeming with frogs and tadpoles, fallen fruit by shaggy hedges, brown and green lizards by fences, the plump pods of milkweed, a pine grove temptingly marked 'Private. No Trespassing!,' piles of stones, sand pits, a garden, part grass and part gravel, the ridged bark of a poplar tree, the iron banisters of stairs going down to a laundry room which gives out a cool and soapy smell—that is the infinitely vast landscape of childhood.

The Rhine itself, in those days unpolluted and free from diesel oil, so that it did not matter if you swallowed a mouthful of water when you went swimming or diving, was part of the fabric of every-day life. Reluctantly, dressed in your best suit, you joined the family Sunday walks along the broad avenue that bordered the river, in October kicking the leaves from the old piebald plane trees into huge heaps in front of you. The Rhine became an adventure only when you could swim secretly from the bathhouse out to one of the

barges being tugged slowly upriver and could try to pull yourself up
on its railing, which lay low in the water, in order to catch a ride.
If the sailors caught you, you were likely to be speeded back into
the river with a kick. The fact that both clambering up and tumbling into the water involved risking life and limb, because of the
strong suction of the barge and the current of the river, only added
to the fun. That children manage to stay alive at all can only be
explained by the wildest good luck or a host of guardian angels.
Only merciful forgetfulness prevents adults from trembling in eternal
fear for the welfare of their young.

There was, for example, somewhat off the beaten track in the
Gonsenheimer Forest, where the people of Mainz liked to take
walks, a deep sand pit rimmed by a tangle of willows. We children
had a secret name for the place: the Schinderhannes Cave.* It had
curious pipes and shafts leading from it. Probably it was nothing
but an abandoned building site. We loved to carry out illicit ex-
cavations in one of the shafts of this pit. More alluring than the
hope of finding anything—an old pistol, say, or a rusty, bloodstained
knife, a pot of gold, or even a skull—was the danger. As soon as
you made your way to any depth into one of these shafts, the sand
began trickling in with a soft rustle, and once it came rushing down
on me with an alarming roar. Luckily, a schoolmate pulled me out
by my legs, for the sand had already clogged my mouth, nose, and
ears. But before this happened my sense of smell had already told
me that this was probably not a robber's hiding place, but an
abandoned fox's den, or a forgotten military latrine, abandoned
after one of the maneuvers frequently carried out in this area. Of
course we also considered the possibility of a buried corpse, but
even so we called a halt to our speleological investigations—one of
those happy chances by which a boy survives to tell his tale.

Our favorite locale for daredevil exploits was the Old Rhine.
Above the mouth of the Main a wide, straight channel, suitable for
shipping, has been dredged almost all the way to the city of Worms.
But the winding old bed of the river is still there, creeping through
a jungle of willows and alders, rotting poplar trunks and vigorously
sprouting second growth. Here was an unexplored, almost impenetrable web of brooks, branches, stagnant inlets, swampy patches,
standing pools, and stony tributaries which at high water are filled
with roaring torrents. These places along the Old Rhine are known

* See footnote, p. 257.

only to fishermen and prowling boys. Here was our Ontario with its tricky rapids, here the cloudy yellow waves of the Amazon, here the morasses, depths, crocodiles, and mosquito swarms of the upper Congo. Here we were explorers and natives, prey and hunters, conquerors and cannibals all at once. The fishermen, who rightly regarded us as nuisances and pilferers of nets, became rogue elephants and one-eyed Polyphemuses. We would have loved to plant some bullets in their backsides, but fortunately we had no rifles. As for the swarms of mosquitoes, we carried their marks visibly on our faces, arms, and calves, not to speak of the bruises on our shins from dragging our outriggers and paddleboats onto land. We even went down with sleeping sickness; it assailed us irresistibly during maths classes or when we were doing our homework.

The Old Rhine—that is the Rhine River of high-spirited and unpolitical boys. It has no history; there are no lines of verse or songs about it. No wars have been fought over it; it played no part in the peace conferences of Versailles and of Potsdam; its residents raise no claims, and it is skipped by Europe's maternal eye. Fish spawn there, and many wild ducks as well as herons nest among its thickets of reeds. The children know it well and love it.

When I was born in the winter of 1896 the Rhine, so I have been told, was frozen over so hard that on New Year's Eve there was dancing by torchlight in the middle of the stream, and later the Mainz Carnival procession crossed on the ice. There were other such times in my boyhood; nowadays the Rhine seems to lend itself to such excesses more rarely.

It was a Sunday night, three days after Christmas, when I came into the world in the Hessian village of Nackenheim, where my father operated a small factory that made crown corks for wine bottles. The country doctor was out of reach—he lived in the next district town, and there were neither telephones nor Volkswagens. The midwife, understandably enough on so bitter a Sunday, had been warming up at the tavern and could scarcely be persuaded to move. But the birth went rapidly and well. My mother had slipped on a steep staircase that morning and fallen a good two stories, which jolt had apparently speeded the process, so that I made my appearance on the day of St John instead of on the day of the Holy Innocents. My only brother, to whom my mother had given birth far more painfully six and a half years earlier, relates that he heard the midwife tramping and thumping about angrily, presumably because she had to make up for lost time. All those odd noises in the darkness were frightening, but suddenly he heard the loud wailing of a baby and a sudden sense of gladness pierced his heart, as if a miracle had happened.

It is said that a child born on one of the seven nights between Christmas and the New Year, and what is more on a Sunday, can hear the animals talking. And I wish to claim in all seriousness that I can. Not quite so precisely as Konrad Lorenz, the investigator of animal behavior. But I can do it my own way, and would even venture to assert that this ability decided my profession. For one who understands, who is prepared to listen to, the voice of animal creation, can sense what men really mean and are aiming at via their language—which is a logical structure only in appearance. In reality it is a polyphonic composition of sound and tone, concealing its truths behind noun and pronoun, beneath grammar and syntax. You become most aware of that in a foreign country when you hear people talking in a completely unknown tongue. Suddenly you understand the basic meanings of the way someone is speaking, not by the words themselves. A child's understanding is even closer to the roots of language. I have been told that the first words I was able to say, aside from the sounds for mother, father, and brother, were *horse*, *cat*, and *dog*; to these I soon added *cow*, *goat*, and an imitation of the cock's crow. One day, after I had barely learned to walk, I was found in the neighbor's stable. I had slipped through a gap in the garden fence and lay unconcerned between the hooves of a big roan whose moist, warm nostrils were snuffing at me.

In the summer of 1952, when I entered my native village and birthplace for the first time after an interval of decades—the house had meanwhile been partly rebuilt and totally refurnished—I stood still in astonishment, in a room filled with people, and looked at a particular window. I suddenly realized that I knew this window, knew it perfectly. I can see it through the bars of a crib, through the white mesh of a mosquito netting; at night it forms a dark blue rectangle, and behind it, along the slopes of a vineyard, is the magic sparkle of innumerable fireflies. My mother, who came along with me on this visit, confirmed my sense that I had slept in this room as a baby. When I went over to the window and looked out, there was no vineyard at all, but a field planted with fruit trees. But old Lorenz Horn, one of my father's earliest associates, told me: 'You're quite right, Carl. The apple trees have been there only thirty years. In those days that was where your vineyard was.'

That must have been in or before my fourth year, for in 1900 we moved to the big city, to Mainz. My father, who had bought the cork factory in the eighties at a low price and at a correspondingly high risk, had within a short time modernized and expanded it. When he took over, the machinery was still driven by a mill wheel. Soon the whole plant changed to steam, and later to electric power. The number of workers steadily increased, and today, still set in the midst of the vineyards and without significantly detracting from the rural character of the landscape, the factory stands as probably the most important enterprise of the kind in the German wine country. Unfortunately, for a long time our family has had no connection with it. My father, suffering from age and deteriorating eyesight, had to give up the ownership and eventually all participation in it. And his two sons had turned to profitless arts.

But in those days, when the family moved to Mainz at the beginning of the new century, everything was still in the stage of growth. In spite of their city quarters, both my parents remained intimately connected with the Nackenheim factory in ways that went beyond purely business matters. There they had begun their life together; there lay their common concern, their lifework. Quite contrary to stereotyped notions of the class struggle, the spirit of the entrepreneur was combined in my parents with a kind of socialistic idealism. My mother, at barely twenty, had set up the first health service in the area, especially for the women workers of the factory. She also instituted voluntary health insurance. Throughout the many years that my father ran the factory, she knew virtually every employee as an individual, even when the labor force had grown by leaps and bounds.

I treasure a photograph of my parents at this period, one of those carefully posed studies on stiff cardboard which are somehow so expressive. My mother looks small and fragile, with lively, intelligent eyes and so mobile a mouth that in photographs her lips always seem forcibly shut as if she were fighting the impulses to say something during the time exposure. Even people who knew her in old age still had the impression of a vivacious temperament, quick sympathies, humor, and affection for the world. My father, who can well be called a handsome man—his manly good looks tempered by a hidden tenderness and sensibility—takes the proud stance of a

103

young husband and factory owner, chest somewhat thrust out, head boldly raised, with thick hair, flashing eyes, and well-groomed mustache, the tip drawn far across the cheek. How splendidly self-assured, vital, and conscious of success mustaches were in those days. My father's style of mustache must not be confounded with the bombastic handlebar which Kaiser Wilhelm II made unpopular throughout the world. The younger man's mustache at the turn of the century was not any forced imitation of some so-called feudal style. Rather, it reflected that naïve faith in progress, that still unalloyed delight in the results of enterprise, which marked the period between the war of 1870 and the war of 1914. For in those days it was really true that anyone possessing a modicum of skill and industry could take up almost anything and turn it to gold or profits, or at least to bread and wine.

The grandparents had had a harder time of it. My father's father had to finance his law studies by tutoring. My mother's father had suffered hunger as a boy, and only attained a degree of prosperity in manhood, after great efforts. But the good heritage, the solid basis, the assured education, fell to their sons and daughters, who had reached their thirties and forties around the turn of the century. Subsequent upheavals have thoroughly undermined all that, have knocked it to smithereens. But those who have some roots in that period feel the continuity of their inheritance and their values, even across the then inconceivable abysses of dread, horror, and destruction.

I know I am violating all literary convention in saying what I am about to say, that I am incurring the charge of sentimentality, of banality, but still I am going to say it: I had a happy childhood. I know that people don't like to hear it; I know it is a rash assertion—but anything else would be a lie. Yet I have forgotten none of the anxieties and miseries, the griefs and depressions, the experiences of injustice and indignation; I have not repressed any of the bleak, frightened, despairing hours, any of the pangs which go along with youth, which are part and parcel of the difficult process of growing up. But is not this alternation of highs and lows essential if there is to be any weather at all? And when I speak of happiness, I also mean the sorrow without which it can no more appear than white without its complement of black. What loss will ever be as poignant as the death of a bird, a bullfinch that took its feed from a boy's hand and nibbled his fingers, that fluffed its feathers and began twittering when the boy came near the cage, that whistled a song after him and flew to his shoulder? And who can feel so bitterly misunderstood, so mocked in his grief, when the parents present him with a new bird, thinking that will put everything to rights again? The boy knows that another bird can never be the same. At the period when I was growing up adults knew little about children, never bothered their heads with child psychology, and that was just as well. Thanks to their obtuseness, the child remained in a world of his own. Nobody but another child could possibly share it with him. What children expect from grownups is not to be 'understood,' but only to be loved, even though this love may be expressed clumsily or in sternness. Intimacy does not exist between generations—only trust.

For example, for years I was afflicted with a fear of ghosts. In the days when I had to go to bed early and my older brother, who shared the room with me, was allowed to stay up longer, that dreadful dusk which was not yet night was the very culture medium in which ghosts spawned. I heard them in the quietude that is filled with noises unknown to daytime. I knew that the chalky skeleton behind curtain was only the light from neighboring houses filtered through the louvers of the green blinds, but still I had to keep my eyes open, for otherwise that ghost would creep out of its hiding place and fall upon me. And there were others, with specific names, which came out of the wardrobe or through the crack at the bottom of the door. One was called the 'thread ghost'; I even drew its picture—a completely abstract drawing, showing arms, legs, body, a triangle of a head, the whole composed of hair-thin lines. But the drawing itself had the power to frighten me, even though I had made it myself; like a grinning totem, it had become all the more terrifying. I knew that the monotonous, incomprehensible murmuring from the next room was my parents talking, and yet it became the whispering of ghosts, and so unnerving that in the end, after heroic efforts at self-control, I began to scream. But I never blamed my father when he came in, upset and irritable, and called me a stupid or bad boy, or sometimes even gave me a few slaps on the backside because he thought that I 'wouldn't go to sleep' out of sheer naughtiness. He knew no better, and there was no way to make him understand; in fact, I rather pitied him for being so dense and unaware of the lurking dangers. The denseness of others can be reassuring; the scolding and spanking were real and banished the

105

ghosts. Tearfully, I fell asleep. When I awoke later and heard my brother's deep, even breathing from the other bed, the ghosts were gone. Even grownups often find that a dog sleeping in the room will by its mere presence quell the abstract fear of the invisible and banish the demons.

I think I was lucky not to have been an only child, or a first child. The second child receives his full measure of love but is spared the excessive anxiety and solicitude most parents spend on their first-born. My mother was anxious by nature, not for herself, but for her loved ones. Whenever she could not gather them around her, like a mother hen, she was vividly conscious of disasters and accidents. If a train was late, she had visions of some terrible derailment which she imagined down to the last realistic detail, with the result that when the anxiously expected person innocently came walking in, she vented all her nervousness upon him. Such incidents were the cause of the otherwise rare altercations between my parents. When my brother or I came home late from playing or swimming, or something of the sort, she would be standing tensely at the window looking down the street as if she expected us on a stretcher or in an ambulance at any moment. More ruthlessly inclined than my brother in this respect, I did my best to cure her of this habit by loafing around so long and so late that she came to realize her vigils were foolish. A fortunate adaptation, for with two sons in the war for four years, she would scarcely have lasted out the First World War. As it was, she developed a thyroid disturbance from sheer anxiety.

Our parents suspected nothing of the real dangers, aside from the risks of our play, that we were actually exposed to during our early schooldays. I attended the 'fashionable' new Gymnasium which had three elementary classes to prepare pupils for the course in the humanities. My fellow pupils all came from prosperous middle-class homes and were therefore well dressed and cared for. But on the way to school we had to pass the *Volksschule*, the ordinary elementary school of Mainz New Town. That was the school for the sons of less favored classes, workmen, artisans, people who could not afford the sizable fees of the superior private schools. The boys of the *Volksschule* ran around in worn suits, many with patches on their sleeves and trousers, for which I secretly envied them. I would have felt much easier in such clothing than I did in my well-pressed sailor suit, let alone my velvet jacket with its turn-down collar and tie.

We did not wear school caps, but our status was clearly proclaimed by our clothing as well as our school bags covered with sealskin or our leather briefcases. And so there took place among the boys from six to twelve a primitive but by no means innocuous rehearsal of the class struggle. In the mornings we were relatively safe, for both proletarian and middle-class boys were usually equally late and had to run to make their prisons, in which the bells were already pealing. But at noon the *Volksschule* boys obviously had more time than we, who had to be home punctually for a regular family meal. They lay in wait for us on our way home, first to provoke us by shouting insults (any boy who was especially well dressed, without distinction of religion or race, was called 'Jew boy!'). Then they threw stones at us, or blocked our way, usually in a close-knit group. Running away was impossible; one would be forever despised by friend and foe, and by oneself as well. And so we had to march past them or straight through their threatening phalanx with heads defiantly raised and with expressions of contempt. Sometimes they contented themselves with spitting at us or throwing horse manure at our backs, but often they fell upon us to tear off the knot of a sailor collar, or the fine satchel we carried on our backs, or the cord from our hoods. We defended ourselves, and the result was a brawl in which we could be badly punched, or else, on days of rain and slush, rolled in the filthy streets. We might have chosen another, safer way home by way of the fashionable Kaiserstrasse, but that would have besmirched our honor. We behaved like certain warfaring countries which would rather incur defeat than 'lose face.'

If after such an encounter I came home late, dirty and with torn clothes, I might be scolded for being an incorrigible rowdy and a street urchin myself. Sometimes my parents would even punish me by, for example, not allowing me any dessert—a cruelty I bore with feelings of haughty martyrdom. I would nurse my sprained thumb, which some torturer had twisted, in secret, holding it under cold water. I would sooner have swallowed my tongue than explained the true state of affairs, for then my father might have written to the principal of the *Volksschule* or done something else intolerably embarrassing, such as having me fetched from the Gymnasium. And my big brother was going to the 'old Gymnasium' in another part of the city. His way to school was in a totally different direction from mine, so that I could not even threaten my assailants with him.

But oddly enough, I felt neither hatred nor contempt for them. I envied them a little for their freedom and wildness, and was proud when ultimately—either because they were tired of badgering me, or because I stood up for myself bravely and could match them swearword for swearword—they invited me to join in their rough cops-and-robbers games in Mainz's 'Garden Field.'

This Garden Field had a special attraction for me. When we were given a day off from school because of the heat, we crossed the Field at a run—later on bicycles—because it was the quickest way to the bathing huts. The Field was a patchwork of new suburban, fenced-in allotment gardens and ramshackle cottages. There was a slight odor of depravity about it; the better people did not live there. But at the beginning of the century it served as winter quarters for the Wolf Circus, one of the early enterprises of the Wallenda family of acrobats who later became world-famous. Sometimes, on cold nights, you could hear the hoarse, distant howling of the troupe of wolves who were presented at the spring and autumn fairs. You could imagine that you were in Russia or the Wild West. In other respects, too, the Garden Field was an exciting place for those too young to take an interest in the sailors' district with its notorious taverns, and the Kappelhof, the brothel alley behind the cathedral, whose name was spoken only in whispers. It was not safe to walk in the Garden Field after dark, so it was said; there were gangsters and men with knives about, as well as sluttish girls. Moreover, the Mandafitts lived there. They were a notorious gang of juveniles, all sprung from the same mighty womb. Old Mandafitt, their father, no doubt one of those with a knife, often lurched through the streets bawling drunkenly. Unless he happened to be doing time, his chief activity seemed to be begetting children. He had produced innumerable urchins of all ages. But these were not just run-of-the-mill proletarian youths. They were systematically preparing themselves for a career of crime, and we middle-class boys regarded them with a mixture of nervousness and admiration. The girls of the family were equally glamorous, and behind a fence teenager Babette Mandafitt gave me one of my earliest kisses. I did not understand why she bit my lower lip. But it was an experience.

I have a special recollection of one of those houses, small, one-story, with a roof already sagging. Above the door was a tin sign with a painting of a poodle that looked like a sheep, and of some beast part calf, part lion, which was probably meant to be a St

Bernard. Between these effigies, in clumsy lettering stood the inscription: *MATTHIAS LEISES, DOG BARBER.* Underneath, scrawled in pencil, were the words: 'Fixed prices.' This sign inspired me to write one of my first poems. I dashed it down on scrap paper during a boring class, and it passed from hand to hand.

> The dog barber Matthias Leises
> Operates only at fixed prices
> Last night he clipped a dog that bit
> And rudely on his table shit.
> The dog barber Matthias Leises
> Is a man the city prizes
> Because he clipped a dog that bit.
> He shears them with and without lice
> And always at a fixed price,
> Even those that on his apron shit—
> O dog barber Matthias Leises.

My schoolmates regarded this as an avant-garde masterpiece, because of the repetitive rhymes and the frank use of the word relating to the digestive processes. We were, it is plain, in advance of our time, and few of my poems have achieved anything like such popularity.

Apart from the street urchins, who had the alluring exoticism of wild aboriginals, Indians, or Bushmen but were also somewhat menacing, I felt drawn to boys who came from the simpler classes—this in spite of my precocious leanings toward music, poetry, and the theater. The living-room-kitchen and the stuffy, gloomy stairwell in the home of a boy whose father was 'only' a locomotive engineer and whose mother did her own laundry seemed to me a far more enjoyable playground, and more attractive surroundings, than our more elegant dwelling with its gardens in front and rear on the 'good side' of Bonifatiusplatz. I loved the boy of the house, who went about all winter long in the same woolen sweater. But my greatest pleasure were the visits to a peasant boy in Gonsenheim, Lobesam Becker, whose father had conceived the notion that his son should study Latin and become a pastor. When I visited the Beckers I was allowed to put on a mud-smeared long apron and help cut asparagus. For that purpose we used a specially broad knife and first had cautiously to dig the soil away from around the asparagus

109

tips, which would just be poking through the ground. Afterwards, in the low-ceilinged farmhouse, I would sit at an oilcloth-covered table and eat potatoes in their jackets, with pot cheese, washed down with a little home-made, sourish cider which for me was the peak of delight. I infinitely preferred such occasions to the always rather painful invitations to elegant children's parties at which there would be chocolate and whipped cream, and which would end in vexation and tears every time.

The servant girls exerted a totally different kind of attraction on me. As yet sex played no part in it, or at most a quite unconscious one. I was fascinated by the girls' long-drawn-out, sometimes sad, sometimes bold and wanton singing. These were genuine folk songs which I imitated ironically but nevertheless learned, as I did their highly figurative, tart dialect, for most of them came from small villages. I loved their strange, mysterious personalities, which veered between inexplicable spells of weeping and wild hilarity, between earnest piety and the queerest superstitions. I observed with awe the embarrassed soldiers who sometimes visited them towards evening, who would be fed in the kitchen and who would stand with them in the hall holding their rough hands. I wondered about the big wicker trunks in which they kept their linen and their secrets. They lived in our house, were loyally devoted to the family, and yet seemed to have come from an entirely different world. Outside the kitchen they wore dazzling white aprons, and when they served at table they carefully pinned up their long braids. There was a sweetish-sourish smell in their room with its iron bedsteads and checked feather beds. At Christmas they received large plates of 'goodies' and fabrics for dresses, or earrings. They were deeply moved and kissed my mother's hand. Sometimes one of them left to be married, and then there would be a good deal of weeping.

The quiet, orderly house with its maids. The bells of St Boniface's Church and, on Corpus Christi Day, the solemn procession. The military band that frequently went blaring through the streets or which I heard—with a faint shudder, for someday I would have to join them—drumming and tootling on the drillgrounds. The terrors of school. The family festivals. And the storm already blowing up around our heads.

In Mainz before the First World War sex education did not exist. I scarcely think there is anything of the sort there to this day. So far as I know, such education is given only in other parts of the country, or in a few progressive schools, with dubious success. Public clarifications of 'the facts of life' to a group, presumably of both sexes, might well have a paralyzing effect upon the emotions and imaginations of young people. It would separate love from sex, neutralizing those instinctual and psychic forces and reducing the whole thing to a hygienic procedure or a matter of free-style gymnastics. But the consistent obscuring of the question such as was customary in our youth often led to another kind of degradation or depravity, although it did not give free reign to the charm of mystery. In school and household everything connected with sex was strictly taboo. We read the Latin classics, including Ovid, Horace, and Catullus, in bowdlerized editions, and when in Homer the master of the house lay down with his maids, the passage was abashedly skipped over in reading. Religion demanded chastity—a word that in itself led to antithetical thoughts and fantasies. For to be chaste it was necessary to know what unchastity was. The Protestant boys, a minority among us, had the unabbreviated Bible at their disposal. They marked all the risky passages that referred to begetting, pregnancy, or lechery and gave them to us to read. But even in Luther's vigorous old-fashioned German there remained something mysterious about concubines and the goings-on in Noah's family. Most of us, therefore, had to depend on conjectures, on secret observations and eavesdropping, on the encyclopedia, and on the misinformation we passed on to each other.

In former times the matter had been relatively simple for young men of prosperous Mainz society. There was Madame Beauri, famous throughout the city, a lady of mature years who walked the streets bejeweled and bedizened with the swish of a Parisian *grande cocotte* and was reputed to have introduced several generations of well-heeled young gentlemen to the art of love. She was passed on from fathers to sons, from uncles to nephews. But I know about her only from hearsay. By my time she had gone into retirement and left a gap which was not filled. There remained three major possibilities for adolescent boys. Some lost their innocence in barns to dance-sweaty peasant girls in the course of the many country fairs, which often took a saturnalian turn. Others had their first experience in the beds of servant girls. And then there was Kappelhof Lane. There stood a row of old, narrow-gabled, half-timbered houses, marked by large numbers and red lanterns. Otherwise the street was fairly dark; only dim gas lights illuminated either end, since most of the visitors did not want to be seen and recognized. With coat collars turned up and hats drawn down low, they moved rapidly towards their destination. The steep stairways of these houses were covered with red plush carpets. On the lower floor was a 'salon' with a potted palm, worn easy chairs, and a phonograph with a big funnel. Here the half-dressed attractions presented themselves for choice. But you had only to order a dubious sweet wine, or, in a more spendthrift mood, a bottle of German sparkling wine, if you did not care to engage in activities at close quarters. Sometimes whole groups of the outlawed student associations, inspired by beer and braggadocio, went there in a body. Other adolescents came alone, stealing timidly and surreptitiously around the corner of the street. Out of sheer curiosity these temples of Venus had to be seen at least once, even if only as a salon patron. It was the thing among Gymnasium seniors, students, and young soldiers to talk about them with the swagger of the habitué. All this was done under the seal of strictest secrecy as far as adults were concerned. That was the unspoken rule of the game, mutually accepted by the youth and their elders. Some young men reached their university city still uninstructed. There, if they were lucky, they might fall in love with a willing daughter of their landlady, or else undergo the dreary and brutul initiation of the streets along with, frequently, the corresponding disease, which in those days called for savage methods of treatment.

I was spared all that, and the disillusionment associated with it. Such disillusionment awaited me, in the direst of forms, during wartime.

'The facts of life' were no dark mystery to me, thanks to a precocious keen-eyed relationship to nature. I understood in general, and without too much mental toil, how both animals and men went about reproducing themselves, before the details of the matter became too engrossing. With a wholesome simplicity I grasped the duality of the sexes, the natural miracle of union in love. I did not trouble my parents by asking questions and saved them the embarrassment of explanations. Nor did I feel that there was any serious schism between sexuality and religion; religion existed to illuminate life, not to veil its processes. A kindly Providence sent me an instructress in the guise of a sophisticated woman some years older than myself. She appeared while I was still in the

Gymnasium and vanished leaving behind neither sorrow nor disenchantment. Soon afterwards came first love.

The happiness of my youth was founded on the unconstrained but by no means uncultivated naïveté of my parents, on the total security of our home life. The best times were our holiday trips in summer, to Switzerland, to southern Tyrol, to the Bathic, to Holland. There my parents were changed people, released from everyday cares, my father as happy to be free of the factory and business for a few weeks as I from school, my mother grateful at every meal in the hotel for which she had not had to plan the menu and do the marketing. And both of them suddenly ceased to be ordinary citizens of Mainz, but became in my eyes people of the world, travelers with cosmopolitan airs. Above all, both of them became almost like children again, venturesome and full of curiosity, and tenderly playful towards each other—a mood for which habit otherwise left no room. Before we crossed a frontier my father concealed small packets of cigars carefully in his inner jacket pockets—even though the cigars across the border were just as good or better. But on holiday Father became a smuggler. And I acquired respect for him. In those days few people traveled so far; there were no cars and camping areas. Hence you ran into a kind of international elite when traveling, and acquired a precious fund of experience and knowledge of the world. I was bored to death when I was dragged through the art museums in Munich, but something stuck: Dutch, German, and Italian painting, classical sculpture, French rococo. The didactic aspects were forgotten, but a foundation had been laid for an ability to make distinctions. And then all the naked breasts and backsides! Suddenly they were no longer a forbidden sight, but art; and being allowed to feast the eyes on them made up for all the still lifes or historical portraits one also had to look at.

I found school oppressive, except for the flaring up of friendships, the adventures of alliances, feuds, and struggles for power. I learned easily but my mind was too imaginative and preoccupied with my own interests to have allowed me to be anything but a careless and rebellious pupil. We had little respect for our teachers, with a few notable exceptions. We made fun of them and tried to annoy and trick them as far as possible. We spied out their weaknesses and considered how we could exploit these with the merciless and wary eye of prisoners keeping watch on their guards and warders. Presumably the generation gap was greater in those days than it is now; to us the teachers were a comical but somewhat dangerous group of eccentric individuals, driving drillmasters, and monsters. One such teacher was named Grünschlag. He was in charge of the third elementary class, and everyone dreaded him two years in advance—rightly so, for in those days the rod was still customary, and he never spared it. On school walks he made us march in military formation and plagued us with the routines of a tough company sergeant.

Later, when we ourselves became soldiers at the outbreak of the war, we agreed that if we returned as officers we would take fearful revenge on Grünschlag. He himself had not been a 'one-year volunteer' and would therefore have to stay in the rank of a non-com. We'd make him feel our power, we vowed. In the army you can always find some reason to come down hard on an enlisted man.

Sure enough, I did return home on leave as a young lieutenant, and sure enough, I did meet Herr Grünschlag on the street, just as in our daydream—an elderly, depressed-looking garrison non-com. He prepared to obey regulations—at attention six paces before and three paces after passing an officer—and to walk past me with hand on cap, eyes fixed. The moment had come: I could have sent him running back on the double, before the eyes of everyone, on the pretext that he had come to attention a step too late, or had not saluted snappily enough. Instead, I went up to him, shook hands, and had a few friendly words with him. It seems to me that humiliating a man, even if he thoroughly deserves it, gives pleasure only to born underlings.

I was Catholic—that was a matter of course among us; there were few persons of other faiths in the vicinity, and my father's family had been Catholic as long as anyone could remember. But I consider that another blessing of my youth. It is fortunate to feel yourself a member of a religious community whose rites are rooted in age-old forms, of a church in which the mystery of the Incarnation, the miracle of the Transfiguration, takes place anew in every Mass. But the child goes to church as he goes to the bakery. There is nothing pietistically solemn about it. In the one place is the smell of warm bread, in the other of stone-chilled incense. Genuflection, kneeling, clasping hands, making the sign of the cross, the tinkle of the Mass bells, the raising of the monstrance, and the

114

thumping of the heart during the profound silence of the transubstantiation—all that fits as easily into daily life as going to sleep, getting up, learning, playing. Sunday belongs to all, and on that day the fat man in black from the parsonage is transformed into a sanctified figure in glorious robes. Not that I thought other religions were less good. But this one was mine, and it awakened in my child's being an inner life that permeated me through and through —bringing me for a while the happiness of unconditional belief, later, when I was growing up, all the struggles, doubts, spiritual crises, which are a part of a productive existence, leading to apostasy but never to indifference, and finally, beyond all intermediate stages, to serene knowledge of the truth of childhood belief.

There is a special power inherent in the mystery of the Sacraments, from the whisper of first confession to swallowing the Host at First Communion. Even rituals that are often ridiculed as superstitious, akin to the turning of prayer wheels or the invocations of shamans, such as dipping the fingertips into holy water, such as the rosary, the eternal light at the altar—these rituals too exert a symbolic force and enrich the heart with a simple confidence. To this day I am moved by recollection of the peal of boys' voices at the end of a High Mass, when a *Te Deum* or the chorale, *Fest soll mein Taufbund allzeit stehen*, was jubilantly sung. Those choruses filled me with an elation that was comparable to no other joy. It sprang not from any casual sense of pleasure, but from the physically tangible presence of a creative power that a Kantian or neo-Kantian may possibly be able to demonstrate, but that most of us, and especially most young persons, can only believe in. Even in mysticism and Mariolatry there was nothing stupefying and certainly nothing narcotic. Living faith does not check but stirs and stimulates the urge towards knowledge, towards understanding. This synthesis is as old as the primal questions of humanity, as old as philosophy and theism; but it is also newer and more inexhaustible than any other experience or doctrine offered to men nowadays. No more idiotic slogan has ever been adopted than the one proclaimed by the early Bolsheviks: 'Religion is the opium of the people.' Yet the Bolsheviks were clever people who surely knew that it was untenable historically as well as dialectically. They needed it as a propaganda maxim in a country where religious mysticism had been misused and where there had been no 'enlightenment' outside its literature.

We too, in our humanistic early years, were rebels against dogmas and creeds, which suddenly seemed to us outmoded and no longer comprehensible. At thirteen I was attending devotions to St Aloysius every Sunday; at fourteen I was a positivist, a fervent believer in Darwin's theory of evolution, which I opposed to the Biblical story of Creation, and took Ernst Haeckel's monism as a new religion, although Professor Mayer, our brilliant teacher of religion, tried to build a bridge for us between the Pentateuch and scientific cosmogony—this, long before the days of Teilhard de Chardin. Then, at fifteen, I came upon Nietzsche's *Joyful Wisdom* in my parents' locked bookcase, for I had long since learned where the key was hidden. I succumbed to *Zarathustra*, succumbed to the most seductive and brilliant 'anti-Christian' of our era. I gave myself up to him body and soul, like Faust yielding to the devil. Nietzsche seemed to me the great Lucifer. Nor did I want to keep him to myself—I passed him on to enlightened schoolmates like an anarchist handing on dynamite. Before a religious-instruction class I wrote his *GOD IS DEAD* on the blackboard. Instead of punishing me, Professor Mayer gave me St Augustine's *Confessions*, which were ordinarily not read in school, and demonstrated to me that I was more intoxicated by the poetic qualities in Nietzsche than by his philosophical logic.

I see the city in which I grew up as clearly as if it existed unchanged to this day. For in my youth it looked as it must have looked fifty or a hundred years earlier. The streets of the basketmakers and ropemakers—Korbgasse and Seilergasse—were still inhabited by real basketmakers and ropemakers. I could look into their vaulted basement shops and see them weaving their cane. I could touch the thick skeins of twisted cords that hung out on the street, just as I could watch at the *Fischtor* (Fish Gate) for the freshly caught large Rhine salmon (the polluted Rhine has no salmon nowadays; we must rely on Scotland and Sweden) or a load of silvery sea fish and live lobsters being carried into the slippery yard at our Uncle Wallau's fish store. But the heart of the city was the market, itself stretching on like a river. Here everything came together; it was the culminating point of the narrow streets and lanes in the midst of which, some framed by tiny parsonage gardens, the old churches stood. From Fischtorgässchen where it intersected with Rheinallee the market ran past the sandstone-red cathedral and Liebfrauenplatz, around the magnificent old market fountain to 'Höfchen,' where in spring the booths and baskets overflowed with vegetables and where the fragrance of greenery and fruit always mingled with the heartier smells of onions and *Handkäse*. Here, at the monument to long-bearded Johann Gensfleisch, who called himself Gutenberg, the grand boulevard of Mainz began: Ludwigstrasse. It was the place for strolling on Sundays at noon. Here was a little pavilion where the town band played graceful medleys or pompous marches. Here, too, were the finest shops as well as the best *confiserie*; here, on the three days of Carnival, the masked revelers eddied back and forth; and from here it was a short walk past the episcopal palace and the Weihergarten (where since Beethoven's day the music publishers Schott and Sons had been located) to Eppichmauergasse, where my paternal grandparents lived.

Both sets of my grandparents, the aged Zuckmayers and the aged Goldschmidts, were still alive in the summer of 1914 when I dashed directly from the school bench to the barracks. They used to walk, unobtrusively but unmistakably, through the Old Town. They signified to me visible origin and descent, and formed a living bridge to the previous century, for they were all born in the 1850's. It produces a kind of vertigo to make these backward glances and then to consider the rapid forward rush of the stream of time to the present day. As children, we knew people who were themselves children during Goethe's latter years, who were born during Napoleon's latter years, and they seem to me no more remote, at most a little less strange, than the astronauts who have now visited the moon.

If I concede my grandparents a modest flashback in this story, I do not do so with the intent of opening up a family album. Family sagas may be interesting to some people, but I am ordinarily bored by them, even at the movies. I speak of my grandparents because I think they were typical, and therefore illuminating; typical of an era long gone, but also of the fateful times only just past, whose cacophonies still ring in our ears.

For my Grandparents Zuckmayer were 'Aryans,' which is to say a species which has no real existence, a classification which does not apply to the peoples of Central Europe and cannot stand up to serious investigation. These grandparents came of Rhenish Franconian and South German families, originally from Austria, so it was said. An Italian ancestress also contributed a drop of Latin blood to the stock, which presumably did it good.

My Goldschmidt grandparents, however, were so-called non-Aryans. Their family had lived in Rhenish Hesse for centuries—recordedly since the sixteenth century—and also had its Latin admixture, in this case French. They had long since converted to Christianity, so that my mother was a 'passive Christian'—this, in the grotesque vocabulary of the Nazi period, was the term for persons who had been baptized as infants and not later on. I cannot help finding these words and concepts funny today; it is really impossible to think about them in a wholly serious way. But we must not forget what deadly signficance all that had for people in my country not much more than twenty years ago! I might add that in my own childhood and youth these things did not affect me at all. On Sundays Grandfather Goldschmidt, a Protestant churchwarden, betook himself with his prayerbook to the new Church of Christ—one of the few buildings in Mainz spared by the bombs of the Second World War—could it be because it was so especially ugly? Until my twelfth year I knew nothing of their 'non-Aryan' descent. This family matter was never mentioned; they had changed their faith with full conviction, wished to be assimilated into the nation to which they felt they belonged, and their fellow citizens also ignored the matter, as far as I know. Anti-Semitism found no soil in my native region. It existed there, as everywhere in the world, but as the obsession of a small group and the subject of a certain kind of gutter humor which was more rhetorical than serious. Socially it scarcely played any part, owing to the frequency of conversions and mixed marriages. The ghettos had vanished in Hesse sooner than elsewhere, probably under the influence of the French occupation during the Revolution and the Napoleonic era. There was no Jewish quarter, and even religiously minded Jews did not live apart. The openness of a riparian and frontier area as well as the easygoing, adaptable temperament of the populace no doubt helped bring this about. Certainly anti-Semitism based on 'race,' on the religion and origin of ancestors or some branch of the family, was wholly unknown. Neither in school nor in the army was any notice taken of it. When the racial delusions became a state religion among us, I knew what category I fell into, but even that could not shake my sense of my own being. The concept of 'mongrelism,' as the Nazis called it, is sheer lunacy among people of the same culture, language, and skin color; it is an invention of raving blind men. And any German exile of no matter what religion, descent, or political opinions could, in the Nazi period, regard himself as a Jew *honoris causa*, since like everyone who possessed the most elementary degree of humanity he condemned with anger, shame, and indignation the mass pogrom in our country, and unreservedly stood on the side of the persecuted. But I had no other religious or traditional tie to Judaism, and therefore always felt myself to be what I was and am by nature, language, and education: a German from the 'southwest corner' of our country, a region always inclined towards European internationalism.

My two sets of grandparents were so utterly different that it might be said to have been a case of polarity. This had nothing to do with their 'race,' but only with their personal qualities. I felt more drawn to the old Zuckmayers, or rather to my father's mother. She was, I believe to this day, the most beautiful old lady I have ever seen. Silvery white hair parted in the middle, eyes deep blue, of a more intense color than blue eyes usually have, which gave her glance a special radiance—she always looked as if she were glad about something. Even in old age and illness her features had a delicate symmetry. Her cheerful and generous piety, her intimacy with the church and the clergy, had nothing fanatical about it. Rather, her religiousness was a natural supplement to the realism of her daily life, a naïve, unsentimental relatedness to the transcendental, as tolerant and humanitarian as it was devout. There was no trace of bitterness or fadedness about her, such as is usually associated with the idea of a pious old grandmother. She was happy when we children stuffed ourselves with jam doughnuts or biscuits at her coffee table, but without making a fuss about it she always gave us a bag of sweets to be handed out to the children around the corner on the somewhat proletarian Pfaffengasse, where poor people lived—a bit of practical instruction in social-minded conduct, without sociological commentary, but also without sentimentality. The older and sicker she became—she died painfully of cancer after an unsuccessful operation—the more she tried not to let us children notice, and above all never to present an ugly and disturbing appearance. There was also a lovable element of feminine vanity in that. It was said that in her youth she had been the most beautiful girl in Mainz, and in dying she wanted to preserve for us an image of a comely old woman. Whenever we visited we were not allowed to come until she had made herself up on her bed of pain, combed her hair, and had the room aired. Then she lay, propped up on pillows, with a lace jacket around her shoulders, surrounded by vivid balls of silk yarn, for she was embroidering an altar cloth for her favorite chapel in the cathedral, the chapel of the Madonna in the Rose Hedge. That was how I saw her for the last time, when I was granted a brief furlough from my military training. She held my hand, looked at me for a long time, as if trying to discern something in my face, then she nodded and said: 'Nothing will happen to you.' She was unable to say any more, and I had to go. She also said to my parents, who were present at her last moments: 'Carl will come back.' Since my brother had not yet been accepted for service, I was the first of her grandsons to go to war.

She died in the autumn of 1914, shortly before I was sent to the front. The image of this old woman who had mastered all her suffering and died with the comfort of the Sacraments; the great stillness on her pale but unchanged face, with the violet hood over her white hair and dressed in burial clothes which she herself had carefully selected; the tart fragrance of the autumn flowers and the gentle submission of her hands clasped over her chest—this sight of death in its 'mildest form,' this dissolution of a fulfilled life lived to its very end, accompanied me like invisible music (there is no other way to put it), like a voice that could never be lost though never fully understood, through all the terrible years of the war and through everything that was to come afterwards.

I have no reason to glorify her husband, the white-haired judge with his neat Vandyke beard and his paunch. I liked him well enough, but our contact remained one of friendly aloofness. He had a certain dignified 'old-man' quality, but also something apathetic. I think he was not especially interested in children. What I particularly remember is my admiration for how much he could eat, and how after an enormous meal he would lean back and say, licking his lips: 'I could still manage a partridge.' For him a partridge was the quintessence of culinary minuteness, a *petit-rien*.

'Your Grandfather Z.,' a ninety-eight-year-old aunt (who alas did not reach her hundreth year) wrote to me recently, 'was of very lively disposition as a young man; he liked to dance and he also loved the theater. He was especially partial to the summer theater, in which there were such pretty girls.' Here I see traces of inheritance.

Of course I already knew a good deal about him in my boyhood. Children know everything and understand precisely the things their elders think they don't understand. I soon deduced what was meant by *Schaumgutsje* or *Schaumkonfekt*—words that cropped up in family conversations which would suddenly be cut short by a glance at the children or the phrase '*Regardez les enfants!*' These words did not refer to the dainties called by that name in Mainz, but to a particularly pretty and dainty maid for whom the old gentleman had only invented these pet names, but upon whom he had also bestowed an infant. The care of the child was a family problem, since Grandmother had to be shielded from knowledge of its paternity. I think she never learned the truth, which suggests as much tact on the part of the dainty maid as on the part of the family At any rate, no disturbance of connubial harmony was ever apparent. The old people lived amiably and patiently together; there prevailed in their house, until their years of illness, a muted, contented serenity. Evenings they played sixty-six, and there was always a pleasant smell in their rooms, quite aside from the enticing odors from the kitchen—of flowers in summer, and in winter of a peculiar lacquer that was put on the iron door of the stove.

In the home of my maternal grandparents, however, there was always a certain air of tension, sometimes of open discord; I can recall flare-ups that still have the power to shake me. These had nothing to do with sexual misbehavior, for this grandfather would have allowed himself such things only in his daydreams, but were due to the contrast of their natures. Grandmother's father had been an enthusiast about everything French, and in his old age he had translated Hippolyte Taine's *Histoire de la Grande Révolution*. Grandmother excelled, the older she became, in a rather childlike loquacity, an almost Tarasconese delight in story-telling and flights of the imagination. She could not stop telling stories and fairy tales, and repeating poetry, and I never tired of listening to her. She worshipped certain heroes, for reasons largely indiscernible, whom she extolled whenever her husband was not present. Foremost among these were William II, 'our glorious emperor upon his charger,' Count Zeppelin, the inventor of the rigid dirigible, and Émile Zola. Her enthusiams included the poetry of Schiller and all of opera, especially Puccini's *Madame Butterfly*, Wagner's *Tristan* and Leoncavallo's *I Pagliacci*. Other favorites were *Der Freischütz, Undine, Martha,* and *Il Trovatore,* whose melodies she sang, not quite accurately, but with all the greater delight. It was she who took me to the theater for the first time, an experience which for a child who had no television screen, no radio, no school plays, was a thrill almost inconceivable today. The interior of the theater, with its plush seats, boxes, and galleries, seemed enormous, and everything I saw—it was a Christmas pantomime—was real, the fairies, dwarfs, witches, the princes and princesses, the magic, and the angels who at the end descended from the flies along with a Christmas tree.

But her own performances at home were no less exciting. With flushed cheeks I listened when she told me the story of Émile Zola, how he courageously fought to prove the innocence of Capitaine Dreyfus, who had been wickedly banished to Devil's Island. As she spoke she often fell into French. Again and again I wanted to hear the story: how Zola cried: '*La vérité est en marche!*' or how the savage whipped-up mob in Paris reviled the great writer on the street: '*Crachez sur Zola! Conspuez Zola!*' (she shouted this in her highest falsetto), and how after the injustice had been exposed, all France burst out in enthusiastic cheers: '*Vive Zola! Vive notre grand Zola!*'

Her husband often came home when she was in the midst of such tales, and his only comment would be '*Bosse!*' (nonsense). That was not meant unkindly in Mainz; it was simply the term for everything irrational, exaggerated, unrealistic, or childish. But other, harsher words followed. He considered such stories the epitome of misdirected education, corruption of youth—for stories seduced young people into 'dreaming.' He called his wife a fool and railed against her father, the old fool, from whom all such things came. Apparently he had found his father-in-law insufferable, whereas she was passionately attached to the memory of her father. She would retort; soon the two would be shouting; she burst into tears and I left, unhappy and crying myself.

In my childhood I naturally feared this man and his ruthless pedagogy, although with his rough humor he often made us laugh. I blamed him for darkening her last years, when she was evidently failing, by ending her subscription to the opera and after a while denying her every kind of pleasure that he regarded as a '*Bosse.*' I had no comprehension of the stern law that governed his life. I did not understand his drive towards achievement, his high standards with regard to character and intelligence, his uncompromising nature, his loneliness, and his emotional starvation. Only later did I begin to perceive that behind his contemptous rejection of everything light-minded and easygoing lay a mandate towards rationality, clarity, importance. Thereafter I observed him, whose whole nature was so different from mine, with a detached but more sympathetic interest.

His life had run along a harsh, straight line. An epidemic had taken the lives of both his parents and he had been left, the eldest of many brothers and sisters, with no resources and staggering responsibilities. That was why the word 'duty' occurred most frequently and most stubbornly in his fairly limited vocabulary. At fifteen he was sent to relatives in America. He underwent a long and storm-ridden crossing in the steerage of a rickety emigrant ship, and upon his arrival was given a cool reception and little help. After a few hard years his homesickness and nationalistic feeling—for Germany was beginning to unify—caused him to return home. He arrived as penniless as when he left. From then on he moved steadily upwards by unrelenting work, self-education, and endless striving. Step by step he rose, and thanks to the general economic expansion of Germany after the war of 1870, he reached a position of prestige and prosperity. As director and joint-owner of the first trade journal for the wine trade, the principal business in our region, he carved out for himself a rather important place in the national economy. At the time he married he converted to Christianity—a step entirely consistent with his view of life and with the views of his times.

When I was a bit older and learned he was a convert, I was inclined to look down on him, especially in view of his sarcastic rejection of everything Jewish. But gradually I realized how naïve and shallow it was to take this attitude toward the 'apostate.' I learned to understand the human and historical causes for his choice. He had broken away from a differentiation and an outsider's position which necessarily struck him as outmoded and peculiar, and which was founded largely on religious traditions which to him as a rationalist and a Bismarckian meant virtually nothing. He believed that as a German of no matter what descent, he must belong to the people as a whole, must identify with the nation, and he confirmed this conviction by his whole life. I scarcely dare to think what an abyss of perplexity and despair this man would have confronted if he had lived to see later developments in his Fatherland (the word is the very one he would have used), and I thank God that he was spared it.

When in 1918 a French aerial bomb—one of the few dropped

upon German cities in the First World War—struck this grandfather's house, he went unscathed but his two young servant girls
were blown to bits. The horror did not fully reach him. Ever since
he had been widowed and no longer had anyone to quarrel with,
he had vegetated in a twilight world. But to the hour of his death he
remained, in his every utterance, faithful to the basic principles of
his nature and his character. The goal of his life was not wealth and
power, but honor and prestige—in a bourgeois, mercantile, legal,
and national sense. Possessing money seemed to him only a means
to this ambition, which he placed above all else. For me, however,
no other influence of my youth inspired so much opposition and
antipathy as did this man of rigid honor. I also think that the
deterrent effect of his spartan thrift (which I only belatedly understood as the consequence of his harsh youth), the warning example
of a man who failed to enjoy the fruits of his tremendous efforts,
has contributed to my laxity in financial matters and my dislike of
savings banks and insurance companies. I must add, though, that
the experiences of the war and the postwar inflation did their part—
but even then these catastrophes were rendered particularly vivid for
me by the way the wealth so hard won and joylessly guarded by my
grandfather melted away like snowballs, for it was invested in shares
of the German Berlin-to-Bagdad railroad and in war bonds. . . .

The times press. Time presses. I hear it pounding in my chest, in
my temples, in my head. One begins a book never knowing whether
one will complete it. Whoever begins to live, consciously to live,
and begins to think: 'I am living . . .'—whoever wakes up at night
and cannot help thinking: 'I am—I was—I will be . . .'—feels himself dragged into a current so strong that it cannot be breasted by
any swimmer, any more than the waves of the Rhine can flow back,
flow upstream, uphill, back to their source. Thus I feel the later
years of youth, before the outbreak of the war rudely ended or
transformed it—those few years between thirteen and seventeen—as
a continual rush and tumble of events filled with a tension and
excitement almost inconceivable to my older self. Something was
happening every moment; the elements had only to be shaken up,
like the bits of colored glass in the black cylinder of a kaleido-
scope, and figures were sure to form. At times it is hard for me to
distinguish whether things happened to me or to others.

A school friend who had lost his father discovered that a certain gentleman regularly visited his mother during the latter part of the long, noon hour. The pair would lock themselves into her bedroom. Soon the keyhole and the crack in the door no longer satisfied her son, who must have been a born voyeur. Over the bed was a slanting wooden ceiling, with an attic above. The zealous son bored peepholes into this ceiling and then rented them out to curious fellows for an entrance fee—stamps, or cash, anywhere from ten pfennigs to a mark; the boy charged what the traffic would bear and doled out the observation period according to the payment. I never attended one of these performances, although the others assured me they were really something to see. I suspect that what kept me from going was less shame at the show than disgust with the son's mercantile bent. Perhaps I was also instinctively sparing my imagination, which did not want to be burdened with such naked facts.

My erotic fantasies preferred to circle around clothed ladies. There was the daughter of an army officer, a few years older than us schoolboys, who liked to stroll about in riding habit, with black stockings and laced boots, whip in hand, flanked by a fierce German shepherd dog. She struck us as very sexy. We watched her from a distance, and none of us would have dared to approach her, although she knew some of us because her younger brothers and sisters were in our classes.

The high point of the year, apart from the Carnival, was the Mainz *Messe*—the great Fair that went on for a week in spring and fall, with all its alluring booths, with Ahua the Fishwife, Lionel the Lion Man, Wallenda's Wolf Circus, exhibitions of boxing, the tattooed beauties of the Orient (for adults only!), with the whimper of the old barrel organ, the blare of the carrousel music, the cries of the barkers, the balloons, the swingboats, the lanterns and torches smoldering at night. The site of the Fair was Halleplatz, the square opposite Town Hall. There was a so-called Sugar Lane where crowded stands to right and left sold freshly baked waffles, Turkish honey, poisonous green and scarlet lollipops, and other sweets. We were in the habit of sauntering along this Sugar Lane in the late afternoon and making worldly comments about passing women and girls. Suddenly, one sultry May afternoon, the sexy officer's daughter appeared in her riding habit, this time without the dog, and presumably because she was bored picked me of all people to take the Magic Tunnel ride with her. My triumph was complete. Gallantly, I let her precede me onto the two-seated padded bench and haughtily ignored my envious and grinning friends. Then we were whisked into the darkness of the tunnel and out into the light again—and as soon as we appeared in the light I was the perfect cavalier, bent over my lady's hand or holding her arm. But the moment we entered the darkness again, I sat stiff and abashed, not daring to move. On the last round in the tunnel, she quickly drew me close to her and let me feel the mounds under her tight blouse, then dismissed me with a light pat on the cheek. I responded to the cynical questions that awaited me at the exit with a discreet smile. But back home I wrote in my diary, which I have to this day, the sentence:

'To a man between thirteen and thirty, no woman is unattainable.'

Sometime later—this was when we were already secretly reading Nietzsche—my parents were pleasantly surprised to see that Fränzje Klum, one of my fellow rebels, and I had suddenly grown extremely pious again. Every Sunday the two of us had to go to Mass and then to a class in doctrine, which went on to rather late in the afternoon.

In reality we were pooling our pocket money and buying the cheapest tickets to the theater; the Sunday afternoon program was usually an operetta. There we saw a blonde young soubrette whom the whole city was raving about. Everyone in Mainz had fallen in love with her; there were even tea cosies made with her head in porcelain. An uncle of mine owned one and used to give her a moist kiss every time he lifted the cosy to pour another cup. She was Käthe Dorsch, then on her first engagement. I could not guess that some time in the future she would play the leading role in a play of mine, and that my meeting and friendship with her would be one of the significant events of my life.

Aside from such escapades, I gave myself during these years to a poetically more fruitful *tristesse*. *The Birth of Tragedy from the Spirit of Music* made a deep impression upon me. I wrote a series of short stories which I called 'Pessimistic Tales.' Almost all of them ended in murder or suicide. Schopenhauer and Otto Weininger, whose *Sex and Character* had just been published, were also beginning to haunt my writing. My models were Thomas Mann's early volume of stories, *Der kleine Herr Friedemann*, and Hermann Bang's *Exzentrische Novellen*. I found such reading in my parents' carefully locked bookcase; both my parents differed from the rest of their families in their taste for the 'moderns,' who were then thought rather eccentric. They also had the Collected Works of Ibsen and Björnson, and the plays of Gerhart Hauptmann, Schnitzler, and Wedekind.

All of a sudden, some time between 1911 and 1913, there began appearing in the window of Wilcken's Bookstore on Schillerplatz a series of books in a novel and uniform format, with the imprint 'Kurt Wolff Verlag.' The authors bore such unfamiliar names as Werfel and Kafka, and they had about them a revolutionary *élan* missing from the writings we had previously regarded as 'modern.' All those writings which were later to be covered by the blanket term 'Expressionism' came upon me with the impact of a storm. At the time I felt no connection between this literature and politics, and in fact these writers probably were not consciously seeking any such connection. At about the same time I went to Frankfurt alone, without my parents, and saw the paintings of Franz Marc, August Macke, Kandinski, Chagall, which grownups all dismissed as sheerest nonsense. I also saw some of the Italian Futurists. I remember a wild painting by Severini, and bought Marinetti's leaflet, 'Futurist Manifesto.' Previously, in the course of a summer trip to Amsterdam, I had discovered Van Gogh. I could not have defined what all this was about that had laid so strong a spell on me, why I felt this art to be a revelation or an illumination—but it was *our* time, *our* world, *our* sense of life that came rushing upon me, falling upon me, and suddenly I awakened to a consciousness of a new generation, a consciousness that even the most intelligent, most aware and unbiased parents could not share.

It was much the same with that other 'breakthrough' into the woods, into the open, into nature, which manifested itself in the *Wandervögel*. At first this had nothing in it of the nebulous or tempestuous ideology that later permeated the youth movement. It was a primitive urge towards freedom and independence that sent the youth of Germany off on hikes with maps, saucepans, and guitars. I was among the first to participate—never in a sizable group, only with a few friends. And although my parents themselves loved nature and liked to go walking in the countryside, these hikes with young people of my own age were something different. There was a spirit of adventure about them, and it was on such jaunts that I saw for the first time the more rarely visited forest areas of my native region. Probably for the first time in the bourgeois period, or even since the days of the wandering scholars, young people were determined to go their own ways, to venture alone into the open air, away from an atmosphere which in spite of all liberality we felt to be stale, confining, and sequestered. Perhaps we were feeling the distant tremors of approaching earthquakes. Perhaps we simply wanted to live after our own fashion, though we had no words and no program to define that fashion. Some of us might show enthusiasm for the first aviators, some about the new poetry, but the temper of the age had seized us all. We had pushed open a door; we were on our way; and we could no longer turn back.

The decisive first steps in the conquest of the air took place at this same time, and stirred us tremendously—were far more stirring to us, I imagine, than the conquest of space in the present day, although the consequences of the latter may be far more momentous. But flying came as unexpectedly to the majority of people as Columbus's discovery of America. Columbus, too, after all, did not know *what* he had discovered. Flying similarly stirred the imagination, the urge for adventure, the longing to participate in the new development at least as a spectator if no other way offered. And the city of Mainz afforded special opportunities for such participation to its citizens, and especially to me. For the classmate who shared my school bench was named Beppo Goedecker—another of my friends who is no longer living. The name Goedecker means nothing to people today. But my friend's elder brother was one of the first aeroplane manufacturers in Germany. This Goedecker had built his hangars on the Great Sands, the remains of what had once been an inlet in the tertiary epoch. It was a large expanse covered with fine white sand—our local Sahara or Baltic Sea beach—where later on as army recruits we were subjected to merciless drill. There were no houses or streets within miles. Here Goedecker made his first experimental flights in wide-winged monoplanes. We called his machines 'the grasshoppers' because they rose above the ground in brief hops, only to touch down again—without turning over, if the pilot was lucky.

The subsequently world-famous Dutchman Anthony Fokker began his work as a business partner of Goedecker. I remember him very well, for he went to the same bathing establishment as we schoolboys and at the same time, at noon—a slight, blond, very youthful-looking swimmer in red trunks. No one would have dreamed that his aeroplanes were destined to be the novel weapon of a world war—for during the war of 1914–18 he placed his talents at the disposal of the German army, and his planes were flown by the most famous of the aces.

I met him through my friend Beppo, and was allowed to stand around in the hangar and later in the fenced-off airfield when the 'grasshoppers' rose above the tops of the low pines and circled in bold, unsteady curves over our heads. The propellers were still started by hand, and at the landings the mechanics, including Beppo and myself, ran frantically after the plane as it hopped over the sand dunes, in order to hang on to both wings and forestall its tipping over. Pilots wore leather suits and crash helmets, and carried in their pockets a small comic amulet, not a St Anthony medal but a god called Billiken. Presumably it had been introduced by Fokker; it was a fat black idol, and to fly without it was courting certain death.

This was the only time in my life when I took an interest in technology. Thank God the impulse never returned, and it left no traces. But it was a truly world-shaking sensation when all the pilots in the Reich participated in the Prince Heinrich Flight in 1912. The Flight moved from place to place throughout Germany, a flock of more than a hundred fragile, fine-wired aeroplanes. At long intervals, one or another plane would stop on the Great Sands, where we sat with watch in hand beside Goedecker's telegraph set checking the details of the air review: who had taken off where, who had crashed where, who was still in the air! What excitement when the great Louis Blériot, the first man to fly across the English Channel, appeared overhead in person, landing on a curve with such precision that the days of grasshoppers and crashing crates seemed something from the distant past; and when the first flying acrobat, the Frenchman Pégoud, demonstrated dives and loops over the Frankfurt airfield—he who before climbing into his plane had nonchalantly urinated, regardless of the photographers and thousands of spectators.

That sort of thing is a lesson for life. Don't let anything embarrass you when your neck is at stake. Relieve yourself before you undertake a daring action. Go calmly, without tension and without superfluous burdens, into danger, and if possible win your race. Afterwards you can get drunk.

That was the conquest of the air. And we, in whose childhood years the horse-drawn cars rattled through Mainz, we who had seen the first automobiles and the first electric streetcars, we were taking part in it.

It seems to me that in those days any young man who was prepared to experience the unusual would have his chance. Whether that is still so today, or whether what life offers is felt by contemporary young people to be less exciting, more ordinary, I cannot say.

The current of music flowed through my youth strongly, gently, and passionately as the Rhine between its peopled banks. As a formative element it had more influence on my lifework than any literary impressions. This was largely due to my brother. Eduard, some six years older than myself, played an almost fabulous part in my life, something very rare among growing boys. The first human face I distinctly recall is not that of my mother or father, but his round, curly-headed boyish face—to my eyes as large as the full moon—bending with an expression of infinite tenderness and admiration over my baby carriage. Quite without cause, for I was surely no different from other infants, he admired me—presumably because the arrival of a little brother in the depths of winter had seemed to him a miracle. His solicitous affection provided me with an immense amount of stimulus and experience, and engendered in me the utmost trust. He never tired of sharing or enriching the imaginative games of a child so much younger than himself, and he was never ashamed, like other boys, of being followed around by his little brother.

I think that his was the first suggestion for the 'potato comedies' with which for years we entertained ourselves and a few friends better than other children with purchased puppet theaters. For it was all homemade, from the stage to the plays and the actors.

In the cellar of our house there were always sizable heaps of various kinds of potatoes kept for the winter. We picked our actors from these stores, casting them strictly according to their shapes. We used all kinds of borrowed and filched materials—scraps from the sewing room, bits of hemp, pebbles, little pieces of coal, carrots (excellent for noses), tinfoil or wax paper—and 'modelled' our earth-stained tubers into an array of characters, who would then perform on the top of an empty crate. We had potato kings, potato heroes, potato princes and princesses, potato villains and fools. The plots were sometimes borrowed from the Punch-and-Judy shows we saw at the Fair, sometimes based on well-known fairy tales, or other stories, 'restructured' for our special purposes. I am using terms from Bertolt Brecht's vocabulary, for the performances we gave were certainly 'epic theater' with a strong Elizabethan accent. There was a great deal of dying and killing; death and the devil came to claim their victims; and there was likewise a great deal of laughter. Ludwig Berger, who was my brother's age and who later staged my first play in Berlin, sometimes served as an audience and recollects that the effect was always a bit weird.

My brother had the somewhat disturbing fate of being a model pupil, always at the top of his class. He grasped the subjects with ease, and was by nature ambitious and hard-working, so that he was often held up to me as an example. That fact never caused any quarrels between us, however; I was not even irritated about it, but reacted to such references with a smiling indifference that brought my teachers to the boiling point. What raised my brother far above the level of model boy, as far as I was concerned, was his musical talent. While still a child he had graduated beyond the pianistic instruction of the village organist, and before long the excellent music teacher in Mainz, too, could no longer show him anything; for instead of the virtuoso pieces by Chopin or Schumann favored by this spinster, he had discovered on his own *The Well-Tempered Clavier* and regarded Bach as the crowning glory and guiding star of music—a verdict by no means taken for granted at the turn of the century. I undertook my first efforts at writing amid the strict and systematic strains of his keyboard exercises; and my brother was the first person who took my writing seriously. No other incidental sounds ever had so stimulating, calming, and at the same time such an arousing effect on my imagination, and to this day I love to have someone practising the piano in my house—practising it well, of course, and if possible repeating the same piece—while I work.

I was supposed to learn the piano too—playing a musical instrument was accepted as a matter of course among us. But I did not want to, for it was obvious that I could never catch up with my brother, or even come anywhere near him, and I did not like the piano teacher's system. 'Carl, the right wrist,' she would always say, and tap me on it with her pencil. I therefore chose the cello, and began with a quarter-size instrument under the instruction of Richard Vollrath, one of the kindest, most childlike, and wisest old men I have ever met. At the start I was a somewhat negligent and rebellious pupil in this field also. To my teacher, music, especially playing the cello, was a serious discipline. He wanted his pupils to practise and improve, not revel in the sensuousness of sound. But this is what I wanted to do from the start, before I had command of the instrument. I wanted to make it an object of my emotions, and to improvise by ear just as soon as I could handle the bow and manage a few finger positions. Above all I wanted to do what I heard concert musicians do: introduce the tremolo on all whole and half notes, in order to give expression to my feelings. But old Vollrath would fix his light-blue eyes upon me and say: 'First some technique. Then you can allow yourself feeling.'

I know of no better rule for the practice of every kind of art, and I wish I had always obeyed it in my own work!

There had never been any artists in our family, nor any writers or scholars; only practical men, millers, vintners, lawyers, businessmen, chemists, manufacturers. To my knowledge we had not even had a pastor or a teacher. The devil only knows what had got into my brother and me. But then I do know, too. Or I think I do. It must have been the union of this remarkable pair of parents whose mutual love never faded or gave way to indifference throughout sixty years of marriage, not even in times of utmost stress. Love is the strongest shaping power in our world. I am convinced that our parents' extraordinary capacity for love impelled the two of us to attempt the extraordinary.

For our parents art, literature, and music were things that aroused their interest or even their enthusiasm; but it would never have occurred to them that anyone of their sort, not to speak of their own children, could have the presumption to want to create or execute such things themselves. My mother had great funds of *joie de vivre*, sympathy and humor. My father was of a more somber disposition and tended towards brooding and dreaming, though he kept a tight rein on such tendencies. Both were musical, but they could never have imagined that they or their offspring would go beyond the kind of home music that was commonplace in cultivated middle-class families of those times.

What comprehensive musical knowledge I have, I owe to my brother. I remember especially Sunday afternoons, and sometimes winter evenings, when he played through the operatic literature in piano arrangements for me. I was permitted to turn the pages and sometimes try to sing one or another voice. As my brother grew up, talented musicians of different ages began coming to the house. They played chamber music, and when I reached a tolerable degree of skill on the cello they sometimes let me play along with them. I began with the lovely G-major Trio of Haydn, with its easy cello part, and moved on to Mozart and Brahms. Brahms was a kind of saint for music-loving Mainzers. The two Mainz conductors had been personal friends of his.

Our Mainz symphony orchestra gave weekly concerts and performed almost the entire body of classical music. In the decade before the First World War, modern trends were represented by the orchestral suites of Richard Strauss, whose *Eulenspiegel* I especially loved, and by the works of Gustav Mahler. Mahler's brand-new music, attempting to unite the popular element with new, bold instrumentation, exerted a tremendously stirring and inspiring effect upon us.

Thus the current of music that so gloriously poured through my childhood and youth was broad and variegated. A high point for me was the appearance in Mainz of the then little-known Spanish cellist Pablo Casals, who played a cycle of all Bach's solo suites for violoncello. I thought at the time: This settles it. I'll do nothing but play the cello and become a musician. But at my very next practice session I realized that I would never be able to summon up the required patience and industry. I have never possessed those qualities, but have, at best, learned them late out of sheer necessity.

I think that the greatest thrill of all for me was choral music. There was the Mainz cathedral choir, which sang Gregorian chants or Palestrina Masses on important feast days. But above all there was the Mainz Liedertafel, a private music group devoted to performances of the great oratorios, from Handel to Haydn, including the Bach Passions and the B-minor Mass.

A strange mood would possess me after such concerts, as we went home through the silent, nocturnal city. I could not speak, not to my parents, not to anyone else. Often I would go off by myself for an hour's walk. I would stand by the banks of the Rhine, or on one of the bridges, looking into the black water whose waves and currents seemed to repeat the music in a strange transfiguration.

Suddenly all of that was drowned out by the war, as if the music could no longer be heard for the loud beating of drums. Now there were no more questionings. Dreams and youth were over. Destiny had spoken—and we hailed it with pure rejoicing, as if it exempted us from doubts and decisions. We sang 'The Watch on the Rhine' as we—a long parade of youthful volunteers—rode across the old Mainz bridge one fair morning, bound for the front as replacements.

Four years later the few who survived returned in silence on a misty November day. But still we looked with hope upon the even flow of the Rhine where our native land awaited us, dimmed by the war, but scarcely damaged.

It is a blessing that life surprises us only with the events of the present and gives us no glimpse into the future. For less than thirty years later, once more after a dreadful war and a long, harsh exile, I rode slowly back into the devastated city over an emergency bridge. Of my childhood's bridge, only a few twisted girders protruded above the river. I walked through rubble in which I could no longer find the streets I had trodden on my way to school. I stood before the ashes of my father's house. But soon I again saw my parents, who had survived the bombs and the fires. And then I knew that although the iron pillars had been smashed and had sunk into the river like withered cabbage stalks, the bridge of my childhood was not gone. To this day a father's hand guides me, gently and firmly, over the unfathomable river.

1914-1918
I HAD A COMRADE

N EVER AGAIN IN THE HISTORY OF THE WORLD will a war break
out as in 1914. At least not within the realm of the Western
world as we know it. Whatever irrational vibrations, whatever latent potentialities for collective intoxications and enthusiasms
exist among the African or Asiatic peoples, lie outside our frames of
reference and may be discharged in other ways. But the old nations
of Europe as well as their descendants in the New World are now
considerably sobered—which is not to say that they have become
any more perceptive or prudent. Such a claim could be made only
for individuals, not for groups or nations. But people have learned
the meaning of fear. Even those born later, who have not themselves gone through any of the disastrous years, seem to have an
inherited memory, a prenatal trauma, which inclines them to
scepticism and rationality rather than naïve enthusiasm. Their unconscious has been politicized, as it were. Our unconscious was
romantically emotional and apolitical. The Second World War was
not greeted with such naïve enthusiasm in any of the participating
countries. But the First was so greeted in all.

Such an event, descending upon an unprepared world, upon
people who have not been exposed to propaganda and have not
succumbed to whipped-up hysteria, cannot be described like a
thunderstorm or a blizzard. What really happened in 1914, and
how it took place, can be reconstructed only from the experience of
an individual. Perhaps my own is especially illuminating because
we—my parents, my brother, and I—spent the last weeks of peace
not in Germany, but in Holland. Thus we did not gradually fall
prey to the war fever, as was the case inside the country, but had it
come upon us literally overnight, as a political explosion comparable
to the eruption of a cold volcano long thought extinct.

When the heir to the Austrian throne and his wife were assassinated in Sarajevo on June 28, 1914, I had other concerns. The event
excited me no more than any other killing or bombing anywhere in
the world, of the sort that were fairly common in Russia. It was not
even a general subject of conversation. We thought of it as a re-
grettable misfortune, one of those calamities common in the
Danubian monarchy with its multitude of unruly and antagonistic
peoples, whose mentality we found hard to understand in any case.

137

For me this was a period of crisis of extraordinary intensity, but for entirely different reasons. Shortly before the beginning of the summer holidays, which extended from July 1 to the second week in August, I was on the point of being expelled from school. I was then a senior with only half a year to go to the *Abitur*, the final examination which would permit me to enter the University, and now I was charged with having caused my class teacher to suffer a fainting fit—brought on, it was said, by my insubordinate attitude. The fact that this teacher was a sick and extremely nervous man saved my neck at the last moment—all the more so because he himself came to my defense. But I personally could not accept this fact as an extenuation—the less so because I personally respected and loved him as a scholar of distinction. I felt like a murderer, worse than the assassin of Sarajevo, who at least had killed on principle. For me, it had been purely high spirits, frivolity, defiance for the sake of defiance. After the incident, which set the whole school buzzing with excitement, I was taken home by the beadle and my parents were given a letter containing the *consilium abeundi*—the advice to withdraw voluntarily from the Gymnasium. Eventually, after a conference of the entire faculty, my suspension was lifted and I was received back on probation, with my only punishment several hours of detention in the school lockup. But during the days in which the matter hung in the balance, the atmosphere at home was fearfully sultry. My father was firmly determined that if I were actually expelled he would put me into a technical school as preparation for my entering his factory. From his point of view that was quite reasonable, for if a young man could not conduct himself in the Gymnasium, it scarcely boded well for his future years at the University. But for me exclusion from the University and the liberal arts course, and above all the threat of technical studies and the factory, would have meant a kind of life sentence, and I had made up my mind that if that awaited me I would run away from home and if necessary join the Foreign Legion. For in addition to the crisis at school there was an affair of the heart.

That was my first love, And, I was sure, my great love. The only one. The one that would endure forever, that could not be replaced or altered by anything in the world. The previous winter it had overwhelmed me and my partner in dancing class, a blonde, blue-eyed, bewitchingly pretty, bright, and cultivated girl named

138

Annemarie. At first our love was expressed in our common intellectual interests, which linked us far more strongly than a purely erotic attraction might have done. She was the daughter of a well-to-do Mainz family which played a considerable part in the cultural life of the city. She intended to study art history and already knew a good deal about the subject, which as far as I was concerned lifted her miles above the unimaginative, shallow daughters of the middle class, future mothers and housewives. To her, I was the 'young poet.' Although we saw each other every day, we daily exchanged immensely long letters concerning everything that moved us, and above all the future, which we could only conceive of as shared. Then came kisses, embraces, passion. And finally, just before my disaster at school, we were caught redhanded. For instead of bicycling to the tennis courts we gave ourselves to the games of love like Daphnis and Chloë in the Ingelheim Meadow, which in those days was still a lonely place.

In those days that was a scandalous affront to morality. The girl's parents put a prompt end to our connection. Her father, a man of great intelligence and solid scholarship in oriental art, regarded the affair as simple puppy love and decided that his daughter must be shielded from the possible consequences. We were forbidden to see each other or to correspond; she was stringently watched, and I felt that I had been cheated out of the best and noblest thing in my life. At the time our family started on our summer trip I was filled with a tragic *Weltschmerz* and bitterness towards 'society.'

Although notes were already being exchanged between Austria, Serbia, Russia, France, and Germany, my parents, like most other people, saw no reason to stay home or be anxious about the world situation. 'A war in our times is madness, atavism,' my father said. 'It would plunge the whole world into ruin. No one will go so far. By the time we come home it will all have blown over.' Yet we were in fact already conscious of what was impending.

I recall with great distinctness an evening walk with my brother amid the thistles and beach grass of the dunes. We gazed for a long time at a rusty sunset, followed by the swift spread of shadowy grays, and saw a ship, probably a fishing cutter, gliding silently and with ghostly slowness downstream, its russet sails set upon a pitch-black mast. Although it was a day in late July and nothing had really been decided yet, at this moment both of us knew that the war would come, that peace was lost and our youth ended. We took each other's hands, unable to speak in this moment of awareness, of sensing the inevitable; each of us, no doubt, felt a gathering fear for the other's life. We felt no stirrings of patriotism, nothing but horror and repugnance for something incomprehensible, for the senseless automatism of a rational world sliding into madness.

That night I wrote a series of poems which I later lost. It is one of the oddities of my life—I suppose such things happen to everybody, but most people scarcely notice them—that only recently, barely a year ago, these poems were returned to me. Along with a few of my letters and some other poems, they were found among the papers of a deceased friend, whom I had not been in touch with for forty years.

I am setting down the first and the last of these poems here because, more than any description, they throw light on the state of mind of a young person who had *not yet* been overpowered by the national frenzy.

First

First they hung
Like dark seaweed that the ocean spewed
Dully about the streets and squares
And each one's fear-tormented mind
Was full of pleading: Lord, avert it!
Lord, let it not be,
Do not thrust me into the grave!
The while each feels a monstrous pulsation
Of storms, plunging him into time,
And hears: music! A distant, swelling scream—
And suddenly there screamed
A man—a woman—
And soon thousands
Were screaming almost unaware
And singing, voices roaring
Toward the hard firmament like a chorale
Out of a flaming pyre's deathly pain
Which no one can escape.
That was, they told us then,
Enthusiasm. We want war, and victory!
Our weapons are loaded!
And now from all their mouths

Flaming fumes rose up
To deaf heaven.

One day

One day, when all is over,
Mothers will weep and brides will wail
And under the image of our Lord Jesus Christ
People will make the sign of the cross once more.
And they will say: you know it's all over now!
Let the dead mourn their dead!
But as for us, our hearts were broken
And all our lives we shall carry the shards.

I put these poems into an envelope and sent them special delivery
to the editor of the *Frankfurter Zeitung*.

On July 28 Austria declared war on Serbia and began advancing
on Belgrade. We read in the newspapers of a partial mobilization of
Russia against Austria. During the next two days my father made
several long-distance telephone calls. I assumed that he was calling
friends at home and the German consulate. On July 30 he emerged
from the telephone booth in a very grave mood. 'We must pack. A
state of acute emergency had been declared in Germany. All German
subjects abroad are instructed to return at once.' We left on July 31.

The hotel owner's wife asked me anxiously whether I might have
to go into the terrible war when I was only seventeen. 'Never,' I
said, 'I will not shoot at other people. I'd rather go to prison.'

Ours was the last train to cross the border before it was closed.
In Flushing, Germans who had come over on the ferry from
England got into our car. They said that anyone speaking German
on the streets and in restaurants in London was abused, even
threatened. They gave the impression of being distraught, per-
plexed. I suppose we seemed the same. That was the atmosphere at
the border station, late at night. But shortly after we crossed the
border everything incomprehensibly changed. It had begun with
the German customs men. Those ordinarily underdemonstrative
officials had greeted us with a joyful cordiality, as if we were relatives they had not seen for a long time. 'It's starting,' some of them
said. 'Tomorrow I have to join up.' There was an air of happy pride,
gay confidence, in these remarks, as if the men were setting out for
a rifle-club match or a wedding party.

The next station was already swarming with men in uniform. The train filled with soldiers on leave and reservists hurrying either to their companies or to a last visit home. Almost all of them were smiling; no one seemed saddened, thoughtful, or uncertain. 'We didn't want it,' many said, 'but now we have to defend our country.' Or: 'I hope my regiment is sent against the Russians. That's where the danger is greatest.'—'The Cossacks are already in East Prussia, they say.'—'We're Uhlans. We'll send them back where they came from!' People shook hands with the soldiers as if they were old friends. My father offered them Dutch cigars. (Even in this crisis he could not give up his little game of smuggling.)

In Cologne, towards morning, the serious aspect of the situation was driven home. The great railroad station boomed and thundered in a way we had never heard before. It was filled with the tramp of marching feet, the roar of vehicles, chorused songs, shouting, the clank of artillery being loaded onto freight cars, the whinnying of horses, the clatter of hoofs on the ramps. A regiment or more was on the move. A few officers entered our compartment in their new field-gray uniforms with shining leather straps and riding boots. A cavalry captain came into the car with his young wife. They stood in a close embrace, looking intently at each other, not saying a word until the signal for departure sounded. Then the woman tore herself away and ran out. 'Kiss the children for me!' he called after her, but she was already threading her way through the crowd, in tears. The officer lit a cigarette and smiled in embarrassment. 'Oh well,' someone said, 'for a married man . . .'

During our wait we had supplied ourselves with the latest editions of the newspapers. The mobilization was not yet official, war had not been declared yet. Strategic troop movements were in progress, that was all.

But no one thought of peace any longer. Morning dawned, leaden white and misty above the Rhine. The train rolled slowly on. Along the railroad embankments and bridges militia guards were patrolling, in civilian dress, with armbands, rifles slung over their shoulders. The cheerful enlisted men of the night before had left the train somewhere; the officers sat silent, quiet and composed, in our compartment. I had offered an elderly colonel my seat and was standing in the aisle, my forehead pressed against the windowpane. I remember precisely what I was feeling. With every mile we rode through German territory, something was entering into me—not like an infection, but rather like some form of radiation, like a completely novel, tingling current, as if I had placed my hand on the grip of an electrified machine. This new sensation dispelled the slight feeling of nausea caused by the unaccustomed night ride without breakfast, and the general excitement. It collected in the head like a bundle of bright flashing sparks which gradually, as the sun rose, set up a penetrating warmth in body and soul, a trance-like delight, an almost voluptuous pleasure in shared experience, in being a part of all this. I later felt such states of superillumination and euphoria once or twice more at the front, before moving forward for an attack; otherwise, never again. Every so often I surreptitiously glanced at the young officer who had bidden goodbye to his wife, and saw myself in his place (with my forbidden Annemarie). But I would also have liked to change places with him at once, or to march at his side. All this was not a matter of thinking, but of staccato associations. Yet it was decisive. His fate and that of all the many who might now be going to their deaths was my fate also, ours. There was no longer any separation, any distance. Nor was it any longer bad or terrible, since it was happening to all, and I was one among many, interchangeable with any other. The meaning of vicariousness, on which all human society is based, overpowered us all at the time, without reflection, with an almost religious force. It was an anticipation of what later was called, in a much-abused, stale, but highly meaningful word, 'comradeship.'

We got home to a house that had been closed for the summer. Everything was in mothballs, the upholstered furniture covered with dust sheets, for the maids were not yet back from their villages. In addition to the universal excitement, a special surprise was awaiting me. In the mailbox was a letter from the *Frankfurter Zeitung*— with a premonition that we would not be staying long in Holland I had given my home as the return address. The letter informed me of the acceptance of my 'highly gifted poems' whose spirit 'accorded fully' with the views of the editors. This was the event I had been hoping for, in my boldest dreams, since the age of fourteen. I had frequently submitted poems or prose pieces to newspapers and magazines, but these had always been returned with polite expressions of regret. Now the acceptance left me oddly cold; it rather disappointed me, certainly made me neither glad nor proud. Overnight, my own poems had become alien to me; I found them false, stupidly innocent, shameful. I had lost the feeling for truth that was

143

in them. Anyhow, the two-day-old letter had been overtaken by a special-delivery letter in which the editors rescinded their acceptance, or rather said that they would not be printing the poems, since the rush of events had made the editors' previous views obsolete. It was clearly essential to defend the ideal of a peaceful world with sword in hand, the second letter declared—words which struck me as utterly persuasive.

It was Saturday, the first of August. In our neighborhood, Mainz Neustadt, everything was silent. Not a person, not a vehicle was in the streets. The houses seemed lifeless. But from the center of the city we could hear the low roar of voices, indistinct and confused sounds of singing and military music. I ran towards it. The closer I came to Schillerplatz, where the headquarters of the garrison was located, the thicker grew the crowd. In normal times it was like this only during Carnival, when people massed to see the Monday before Lent procession. But the mood was different. Although there was a certain amount of hallooing, shouting, and laughter, one sensed a purposeful resolve in the tumult, and no suggestion of frivolity. It was as if everyone had something urgent to do there, something that could not be postponed. Small squads of the headquarters guard were marching about in the midst of the throng, putting up posters still damp from the press on all the street corners. In large letters easily legible at a distance were the words:

His Majesty, the Emperor and King, has ordered the mobilization of army and navy. The first day of mobilization is August 2.

Signed: Wilhelm, I. R.

That was all. Whoever was there at the time has never forgotten this text.

Here and there I met schoolmates or friends from the neighborhood. Part of the whole incomprehensible event, too, was that we scarcely talked to one another. We merely looked, nodded, smiled. There was nothing to discuss. There were no longer any questions or doubts. We would go along, all of us. Moreover, I can testify to this: there was no sense of coercion. It was not that we would have felt embarrassed to stay behind. Perhaps it was a kind of hypnosis, a mass decision, but there was no visible pressure, no thought control. Only two nights earlier I had said to a Dutchwoman that I

144

would never take part in war. Now there was no longer the slightest residue of any such feeling.

Broad Schillerplatz in front of military headquarters was black with people. They were probably awaiting some official proclamation, an address by the commandant or something of the sort. But nothing happened. The military band played the rousing old marches; here and there a few voices shouted hurrah, or began singing the national anthem; but these efforts quickly subsided. The atmosphere was somber and dignified, rather solemn, in spite of the ever-thickening crowd. Extras of the local newspapers were being hawked; we read that Russia, contrary to her explicit pledge, had mobilized her whole vast army, that the 'Russian steam roller' was thundering toward the German eastern border, that France had mobilized without warning and was threatening Germany on the west. All we talked of was which regiment we would prefer to serve in. One of our friends, the son of a high-ranking officer, informed us that declarations of war would be issued the next day, after which volunteers would probably be accepted everywhere. We were all burning to rush off to some barracks and not to go home at all. We had linked arms and formed a chain in order not to lose touch with one another in the crowd. To this day I remember the names of everyone who was with me then: Karl Gelius, Franz Klum, Leopold Wagner, Heinz Römheld, Geo Hamm, Richard Schuster, Ferdinand Pertzborn, Fritz Hahn. I see their seventeen-year-old faces as they were then, young and fresh. There is no other way I can see them, for they never aged. Everyone I have mentioned here is dead, killed in the war.

At the close of the evening the military band played, in slow tempo, the 'Song of the Good Comrade,' and we sang the words without suspecting the meaning of the stanza:

> *Eine Kugel kam geflogen;*
> *Gilt's mir oder gilt es dir?*
> *Es hat ihn weggerissen,*
> *Er liegt zu meinen Füssen*
> *Als wär's ein Stück von mir.**

* 'A bullet came a-flying;/Which of us will it meet?/It's he who now is dying,/Lies dying at my feet/As if he were part of me.' 'Der gute Kamerad,' a poem by Ludwig Uhland, has become a German folk song. The author has used the last line of this stanza for the German title of this book; it also carries the gently ironical sense of: 'As if it were a play by me.'—Translators' note.

Towards evening, just before darkness, the 117th marched out. This was the Grand Duchess's Own Regiment, the most popular Hessian infantry contingent, in which many well-known personages of the city had served. It was now being assigned to the mobile reserve. It paraded past our house, which was close to the railroad station, the higher officers of the regimental and battalion staffs mounted, the leaders of the smaller units, young lieutenants, marching on foot ten paces in front of their men, just as they preceded them later in battle and for that reason were mostly killed. They were dressed in field gray and wore the famous spiked helmets covered in gray cloth; steel helmets were introduced during the war. Almost all had bunches of flowers tucked into their caps, their knapsacks, or their rifle barrels. Many faces were flushed from the summer heat and wine, but most were calm and composed. Girls, fiancées, and sisters ran alongside the marching column waving to their loved ones. Some were crying. Our cook, too, stood beside us at the front door, weeping—her brother was a sergeant in the regiment, and when she saw him marching along with his group she rushed up to him and thrust a package into his pocket. He smiled and greeted us, a solid boy with a rugged, peasant face. A young soldier tossed his flowers as he marched past to a woman standing in front of another door. She pressed them to her heart; we knew she was his mother. He was still holding his hand raised as he disappeared around the corner. These little human details were what moved us more than the view of the whole, and they are what remain forever impressed on the memory. No bands played; the first regiments marched out quietly and without music. But from the railroad station we heard them singing as if with one voice.

The departure of the regular army, which at once was thrown against the enemy, had about it none of that war fever, mass hysteria, barbarism, or whatever else the world imagined to possess those German soldiers who were soon branded as Huns or Boches. These were disciplined, cool-headed, somberly resolute soldiers, many of whom were no doubt aware of the tragedy of what was happening. It was glorious, and at the same time terribly sad, to watch them. Fritz von Unruh, the later pacifist and radical opponent of war, has told me of his similar impression of his own regiment of uhlans: it was a fine contingent of men sound in body and unspoiled in mind, a promising, strong generation, truly the flower of the nation, who marched out to die. For only very few of those who were soldiers at the beginning of the war ever came back, and shortly afterwards the next generation followed them. Germany never entirely recovered from that loss. Just when she might have been on the point of recovering, her young men were once more herded into a war unleashed by criminal leaders and even more calamitous in its outcome. In those days, in 1914, we still believed that a war would bring about a true blossoming of the nation. Instead, everything withered.

My parents, too, were carried away by the power of the moment, deeply moved by the sight of the departing troops, and so shaken that I easily won their permission to volunteer. My brother, then twenty-four years old, had earlier been granted a postponement of his military service so that he could go on with his musical studies. He had been assigned to the Replacement Reserve and now had to wait for his call-up. Thus I was the first to go. My mother bravely tried to hide her anxiety, but she hoped that war would be over before my training was completed. At the time, almost everybody believed that, and when the Kaiser announced at a muster in Berlin, 'Before the leaves fall, you will be back home,' we took that as a guarantee. There was only one thing we young men were afraid of: that it would be over before we had our chance to participate. Next morning our first assault began—on the barracks. I wanted to join the cavalry because I thought of that as the boldest and noblest of the forces. But the regiment of dragoons in our city had already closed its doors after accepting a few sons of officers. The regiment did not have enough horses for training purposes. To be admitted you had to provide your own horse, and I only had a bicycle. Mounted on this, I pedaled at top speed, along with two boys of my own age, to the barracks of Field Artillery Regiment No. 27 in Gonsenheim. In this regiment, too, one was certain to have a chance to ride. After hours of waiting in an endless line of volunteers, I was actually accepted and sent along home with my mustering certificate with orders to report next day for medical examination. That consisted in a brief stethoscopic examination of the chest, an even briefer few pats on the back and under the kneecap, and I was a soldier.

Joining the army, having to put in that required year of service, had always been a baneful notion to me during my school days. It meant standing at attention, keeping your mouth shut, obedience, subordination—the loss of all freedom. Now it was just the opposite:

147

liberation. Liberation from the pettiness and narrowness of middle-class life, from school and cramming, from doubts about the choice of a career, from everything which consciously or unconsciously we felt to be the stultification of our world—all that we had already revolted against in the *Wandervögel* movement. Now that revolt was no longer limited to weekends and holidays; it was all serious, deadly, sacredly serious; and at the same time it was a tremendous, intoxicating adventure. For such excitement we were willing to put up with a little discipline and military drill. We shouted 'freedom' as we rushed into the strait-jacket of the Prussian uniform. It sounds absurd. But at one blow we had become 'men,' were confronting the unknown, danger, life in the raw. The threat of an early death seemed to us insignificant compared to this. It was in fact a kind of intoxication, a craving for immolation in blood, that swept a good deal of the world at that time. I do not think that Clemenceau's famous remark about the 'Germans' infatuation with death' was valid. I heard later that the same mood prevailed in France, in England, and by and by even in America.

We saw the meaning of the war in this inner liberation of the whole nation from its obsolete conventions, in this 'breakthrough' into the unknown, into some heroic venture, no matter whom it devoured. This was what fired our enthusiasm. Aims of conquest, considerations of power—these did not matter to us. When we cried 'freedom' we certainly meant the word in the primitive, nationalistic sense; we thought our nation should be freed from the threat to its existence (along with all the countries at war, we were convinced of that threat), freed also from the curbs which the world placed on the free unfolding of our country's energies. But we meant more. What animated the barracks and the encampments of volunteers and recruits in 1914 was by no means a 'militaristic' spirit. It was revolutionary. The youngest among us came, like myself, straight from the school bench; many came from the universities of the vicinity, Heidelberg, Marburg, Giessen, and from the technical schools. But aside from these intellectuals, there were young workers, apprentices, businessmen, farmers, artists, a cross-section of all classes and social strata. Beside me on the straw mattress snored an actor from the Mainz city theater. On my other side was a young mechanic whose father was a machine-operator in my father's factory. Now, and later at the front, the strongest ties formed particularly with members of the working classes whom we had hitherto scarcely known,

148

or known only superficially, and if we were wise we placed our trust in them. They had the advantage over us, the sons of the cultivated middle class, in their sense of reality; they were more competent, more skillful, hardier than us. And we were proud that there were no distinctions in treatment and in conditions between us, such as there ordinarily were between the one-year volunteers and the enlisted men. This breakdown of the caste spirit was not tainted by the element of 'racial community' decreed from above, as in the Nazi period. It was not based on any material interests or ideological dogmas. It arose, as it were, by itself, there was a natural elemental quality about it. Or so we young people believed and experienced it. Actually, it was the best and most constructive by-product of all the upheavals we were about to face.

Until the training staffs could be organized, we were kept busy transporting horses and cleaning stables, with riding lessons, artillery practice, marching drill. Interspersed were inspections, roll calls, and the endless waiting around. But dead tired though we were at the end of the day, we still spent half the night debating in those hastily built tar-papered barracks or gyms or eating huts where up to fifty and a hundred of us had been crowded together because of the lack of space in the regular barracks. I can still hear the hoarse, drunken bass voice of a fat Heidelberg student, who had gone through endless semesters without ever taking his degree, as he explained the spirit of the age to us and repeatedly burst out into prophecy: just as the war of 1870 had brought unity to Germany, the war of 1914 would bring her justice and freedom. Our victory (which no one doubted) would mean a new Europe, united culturally and politically under the aegis of the German spirit. Only then would true reconciliation among nations arise, and that in turn would open up a new horizon for all of us. Berlin would not be able to deny to the returning people's army free, universal suffrage and the secret ballot. (More freedom than that, we could not imagine.) The Kaiser, to whom we had sworn allegiance, was for us the man who had said on August 4: 'I no longer recognize parties, I recognize only Germans!' His Reichstag, including the Social Democrats, had acclaimed him enthusiastically for those words. To us they were a pledge, and we supposed that one of the war aims was a reformed, constitutional monarchy, an essentially democratic government.

The debates raged in all directions, incorporating religion, sociology, the spirit of Greece, the idealism of Kant and Schiller,

Goethe's view of the forces of nature, until the harsh voice of a drayman or Rhine sailor would shout, 'Quiet!' because he rightly considered sleep more important. I do not remember much about myself in this period, nor what I wrote during my leisure hours. I remember only that I had become a different person, one I had not known before. Everyone else had become different, and it was as if we all were meeting ourselves and each other for the first time.

Among the volunteers of this first period were not only the young, the inexperienced, the anonymous. Famous names, great men in cultural life and politics, were represented; we read about them in the newspapers and felt confirmed in our own decisions.

Romain Rolland, the great-hearted Germanophile, called for an international league of men of culture to counter national antagonisms. His appeal, launched from Switzerland, where the war had caught him by surprise, was ignored in his own country and sharply rebuffed by the Germans. Thomas Mann was one of the group of German scholars and writers who published a strong repudiation of the intellectuals of the 'West' and a profession of unconditional adherence to the aims of the national war. How did all this come about? Only narrow-minded fanatics can imagine that such eminent representatives of German cultural life were each and every one nothing but cowardly opportunists, that as 'lackeys of the ruling class' they blew the trumpets of war against their better knowledge, in order to assure the safety of their large editions or their royalties. They were neither craven nor opportunistic, but they were *profoundly unpolitical*. That was true even of those whose works were inspired by deep social feelings. Possibly they had learned to think in terms of social criticism, but critical responsibility for world politics or the politics of the day was alien to them and lay outside their cultural métier. Hence they were overwhelmed by the ecstatic credulity of patriotic intoxication. They went along blindly with the frenzy of the whole country. How could we members of the intellectual middle class, especially those of us who were young and belonged to a circle that had never been required to do any political thinking— how could we have been more critical or more temperate? Perhaps the fault or the failure of the older generation, from whom we derived our ideas, can be seen here. But I am rather inclined to think that our elders could not have been any different from what they were, not in their time. Historians will debate this and presumably never agree. The whole problem of the course of events remains unclarified. It is cheap and easy to speak of destiny. It is frivolous and dubious to decide that the guilt lay all on one side. But we, as individuals, would have had need of some almost inhuman traits to draw back from the destiny that confronted us.

There were exceptions, of which we knew nothing at the time. In Austria, the great poet Georg Trakl, who served as a medical aid in a field hospital, killed himself out of despair over the war. The extinction of our cultural and artistic future had begun, and it reached a peak during those four years. The same happened, no doubt, on the side of the English, the French, and the Russians.

In Paris, at the outbreak of the war, Jean Jaurès, one of the most prominent leaders of the Socialist International, had been assassinated by chauvinists. In Germany, the only opponent of war credits and proponent of the International, Karl Liebknecht, was locked up for a time, then put in a labor battalion. The public scarcely took notice, and we young people never even heard of the matter (only during the later years of the war did the names of Liebknecht and Rosa Luxemburg become meaningful to us). For we were filled with a love that made us deaf and blind to everything else. That is a fact, we marched off to this war like young lovers, and like lovers we had no notion of what was awaiting us. Like lovers who did not know the reality of love, who knew nothing of its bent for domination, its cruelty, and its power. So we plunged in: ardent, impetuous, intemperate, exalted. And again like lovers we were intoxicated with ourselves and our fancied irresistibility.

During the second week of August, when school began after the summer holidays, all seniors who had volunteered were given half a day's leave from their companies. Once more we found ourselves in the school auditorium, from which I had been so ignominiously banished a few weeks before, to take a special final examination, the 'emergency *Abitur*,' as it was called. Almost all of us were already in uniform, and the few who were not because of some physical defect, or because they were attending a theological seminary and could only go into the medical service, felt thoroughly unhappy and envied us. For us the whole affair was a great joke. The uniform gave even the worst student an air of manly dignity which the teachers could not contend with. No teacher could fail a young soldier, who was prepared to sacrifice his life for the Fatherland, merely because he was shaky on Greek grammar. Only the easiest questions were asked us; no one could possibly fail.

151

The *Abitur*, that dread final examination that had haunted so many years of our youth, became a family party. The principal called us all young heroes and vigorously shook the hand of every boy in uniform, even mine, his black sheep. We were delighted and felt we had bypassed one of the great terrors of our lives. For our minds could not yet conceive the greater terror. Fear of death was something we still had to learn. It had not been in the school curriculum.

Whether it is the mood at the outbreak of a war or a revolution, the kind of euphoria that prevailed during those early August days cannot persist for long without degenerating, without becoming a succession of empty phrases and senseless violence. Soon the war hysteria boiled up out of the gutters and took the form of a hunt for alleged spies. Supposed enemy agents were hounded on the streets on the flimsiest pretext. Woe to the man who had a 'foreign' look. Near my parents' house a person with an olive complexion and black hair was cornered by an ever-growing crowd, berated, beaten with canes and umbrellas wielded by old women. The rumor had spread that he was trying to poison the fountain (which was scarcely used any more and was in no way connected with the city water supply). Finally he was taken into custody by the police, then it turned out that he was the representative of a Spanish cork factory and had business relations with my father. He had aroused suspicion by trying to flee, it was then said in extenuation. Of course the man had tried to run away after he had been so careless as to throw a cigar stub into the fountain drain and saw people advancing savagely upon him.

This popular amusement quickly subsided. But now the home-front soldiers, flag wavers, orators, and armchair strategists took up their posts. The patriotism of the outbreak of the war became debased into jingoism. Palsied old men panted for enemy blood and apostrophized the German economy; paunchy citizens greeted one another loudly with the slogan '*Gott strafe England*' (God punish England)—as, presumably, twenty years later those of them who were still around said, 'Heil Hitler!' And the editorial writers of the newspapers added their mite.

We young soldiers, who were soon to be sent to the front, were not affected by any of this. We had more important things to do, more serious matters on our minds. We dismissed the noise and bombast of our heroic fathers (mine was not one of that brand) with sardonic grins. But we all believed the proclamations. It did not occur to us to doubt the official version, let alone to imagine that a victory communiqué had been exaggerated. The enthusiasm with which we had rushed into the services did not subside, in spite of the crosses inseparable from army life. Our conviction that this war was in a just cause, that we were defending our native land, grew with every communiqué, along with our admiration for the courage of the fighting troops, of which we were soon hearing from eye-witnesses, the wounded returned from the first battles. We were perpetually in a state of slight euphoric fever. There was something mystical in the air. When the bells rang for a victory, it was as if they were sounding of their own accord.

In the beginning there was a victory to be hailed almost daily: the fall of Liège and the great Belgian fortresses; the capture of Rheims, Lille, and Antwerp; the advance of the whole Western Front. And when the front came to a halt on the Marne and the Germany army had to accept its first great defeat, this setback was represented only as a strategic halt. We hailed this too, for it gave us our chance to participate in the final assault on Paris. Moreover, when the victories in France grew fewer, stout-hearted Hindenburg provided us with new ones to celebrate in his battles in East Prussia and Poland.

Of course we believed that Sir Edward Grey, England's Foreign Secretary, had plotted the whole war against us, for that was what we read. And we believed the 'German fairytale' that we had not violated the neutrality of Belgium by our invasion, thus provoking England's declaration of war. Rather, treacherous Belgium had invited the French to march through her territory, even providing them with transport for an attack on Germany, so that our invasion was only an act of self-defense.

Every nation believed at the time, of course, that everything its government was doing against the enemy was in self-defense. No nation thought it was fighting for purely material ends or the aims of power (though I must say again that the Russian mentality remains obscure and unknown to us). They had all taken up arms to defend their homeland; every nation was also defending the greatest good of humanity; and this faith was initially a real thing, not a product of propaganda. But as time went on the press in all countries drummed away on this theme and used it to whip up hatred, extreme nationalism, ruthlessness.

It is remarkable how swiftly in such times a difference between generations develops, and how deep a gulf forms between groups only a year or two apart in age. Everything that I am relating here applies only to that first contingent who became soldiers and went to the front in 1914. It is no longer applicable to those who were a year and a half or two years younger, so that at the outbreak of the war they were below military age, exposed to the jingoism of their schoolmasters and the freezing of the battle fronts, the degeneration of the initial advance into a war of attrition, into a universal, systematic mass slaughter. Erich Maria Remarque and his age group belonged to that generation. The heroic gesture of the volunteers was barred to them; they had to sweat out their normal time in school and then be unwillingly drafted, drilled, and harassed, and they went into the field without illusions, for they had some inkling of the horrors that awaited them there. For us the brief training period was a strenuous but also an amusing transition, a great joke, much as if we were playing parts in a highly realistic military comedy. The unaccustomed rigors, the major and minor privations and discomforts, were just what gave the experience its zest. From one day to the next we adjusted to sleeping on straw mattresses under scratchy woolen blankets along with a crowd of men whose effluvia and education were not the best. We sang incessantly, even when we staggered back to our quarters half dead from the strains of drill or marching. We had not previously known these war songs, some old, some new, and I cannot recall learning them; we somehow absorbed them.

It is a curious thing about war songs: they preserve the atmosphere of such a time and reflect its temper like nothing else. In the First World War we had our sentimental 'Annemarie,' and later the sad 'Argonnerwald bei finstrer Nacht.' The French had their bold, lighthearted 'Madelon,' the English their 'Tipperary,' the Americans 'Mademoiselle from Armentières.' In the Second World War the radio made 'Lili Marlene' the beloved song of all the combatants. Would a third world war have its song or songs? It is scarcely conceivable. Singing stopped, moreover, in those great battles of annihilation at Verdun, on the Somme, and in Flanders. After a year of the war no one went over the top with the 'Deutschlandlied' or 'Marseillaise' on his lips. Only behind the front, in rest camps, did a melancholy accordion and a few rough voices still continue to make music now and then.

But then, in our late-summer springtime of war, we still all sang and laughed away whatever secret fears and anxieties might be troubling us. We took the riding of certain corporals with humor rather than despair. Most of the noncommissioned officers who trained us were middle-aged men, decent people who for all their strictness had no tendencies towards brutality and sadism. They manifested a kind of avuncular good nature towards us. But here and there were incipient specimens of the later concentration camp guards: little men given total power over others who behave all the more savagely towards their underlings the more they sense their qualitative or moral superiority. But we were determined to show these mini-Caesars that they could not get us down.

One thing can be said for those barrack-room tyrants of the old days: they had the somewhat sympathetic trait of being corruptible. And they drank. Over a case of beer or a few bottles of wine, a temporary good will prevailed. They would become jovial, let it be known that they were 'also human' and kept after us only for our own good. But then they would abruptly return to their roles of supermen and barracks fiends.

I myself had discovered a difference between the 'military' aspect of our life, drill, goose step, petty harassments, and the 'soldierly' aspect, by which I understood manly discipline, rational obedience, weapons practice—the sort of thing we would need at the front. I despised the first and was persuaded of the ethical value of the second.

My first mild doubts of the beauty, truth, and goodness of our German soldierliness arose when I witnessed the treatment of the Alsatians among us. Alsace-Lorraine was regarded as an unreliable district. All available military classes there had been called up promptly at the outbreak of the war, removed from their native soil, and distributed among contingents from western and southern Germany. Although they were not very far, among us in Mainz, from Strasbourg, Colmar, or the Vosges, they felt as if they were in a foreign country. Our training staff treated them like second-class human beings, set them to all the filthy jobs, and harassed them in every way possible. They were mostly decent young peasants; you could hardly blame these sons of a border population, many of whose kinsfolk might be living on the other side, if they were not exactly delighted to be marching to war against France. They accepted it as inevitable and tried to do their duty. Towards us, their young comrades who were so enthusiastic about the war, they were pleasant and helpful. I became particularly close to one of them, perhaps because he was subjected to more than the usual amount of mistreatment. One night I was on stable guard with him. A horse broke loose and galloped, kicking wildly, down the corridor between the boxes. While I stood to one side, arms outspread, to frighten the animal back, my Alsatian friend tried to approach him from the rear to grip his halter. In the attempt he was struck in the head by one of the flailing hoofs. I held his bleeding head in my lap until the medical aides came. He died before dawn. He was the first war victim I had seen, and I wept and mourned for him.

Our training period passed quickly. It was summer. Autumn came; it was still warm. On our free evenings we sat around in the gardens of taverns, laughing, drinking, and waving at the girls who walked in pairs down the village street. In those days of intensified masculinity and bands of men gathered everywhere, the girls were in a permanent state of excitement and compliance.

When at roll call there was the sudden announcement: 'Twenty replacements needed; who volunteers?' we all rushed forward in a wild stampede, tried to push each other away to get taken first, and were deeply disappointed when we failed.

One day we were informed that a complete mounted battery was being assembled for the Hessian Field Artillery Regiment No. 61 in Darmstadt, for immediate assignment to the front. A new squad was still needed there, and we were asked who was prepared to be transferred. Again everyone volunteered, but I was chosen along with a few others because I had proved to be a good rider.

In Darmstadt we went through another two or three weeks of training. We were drilled to ride up at a brisk gallop with our light field howitzers and take positions. Throughout the entire war, during which we chiefly crawled through mud and swamp, this particular exercise was not used a single time. But we felt grand while we were practising it. We were so proud of our riding breeches and spurs.

And then suddenly the moment had come. We were to be ready to march in two days. I was not allowed to bid goodbye to my Annemarie in Mainz; the sanctions against our relations had been strengthened rather than relaxed by the war. But my parents were understanding, and so on an off-duty Sunday I had been able to see her in our small music parlor. We pledged faithfulness and resumed writing to one another every day under covering addresses. On my last evening, when we were all given leave, my parents came to Darmstadt from Mainz. We went to dinner and my father ordered the finest food and drinks, to give me pleasure, but none of us had much appetite. I could not help myself; there was a lump in my throat. Once, when I had to go outside for a moment and from the door saw the two of them sitting somewhat bowed at their table, I fought back tears. But next morning all that emotion had faded. We marched to the station with flowers in our helmets, our step light and springy. From all the barracks other young replacements joined us. Girls stood at the windows and threw flowers, cigarettes, and chocolates to us. Many of us must have looked like children with toy carbines and bayonets. The regimental band of the Cavalry Guards drew us along. We were singing so loudly as we boarded the train that the horses shied. The whole train rang with cheers and songs as the wheels began to move. A day later, shaken from the ride and weary from lack of sleep, we heard a strange, continuous rumbling, still far away. It made the windows of our compartment in the train rattle gently. That was the front.

I have not written a war book and have told no war stories. It seems to me impossible to communicate the experience, futile to attempt to reproduce the reality either in a transfigured, a heroic, or a critical way, or in the form of objective reportage. I have also almost never spoken about the war, and especially not with people who were not in it. With the others, a phrase sufficed: 'Somme, 1916.' 'Flanders, July '17.' After that we preferred to fall silent. In the few stories I have written that are set in the war period, the battles are at most touched on as background.

In the half century that has since passed, I have very rarely dreamed of the war. Only at first, when the war was barely over and I could scarcely grasp that I had actually survived, did I frequently find myself lying at night buried alive in a dugout, unable to cry out or move, until I awakened with a shriek that terrified me. Or else I heard a heavy shell whistling, moaning with inexorable slowness, and then with a sudden rise in pitch come down upon me, with the knowledge: Now! Now it's come! And I would find myself, as a chair or night table overturned with a crash, lying, dripping with sweat, beside my bed. Many men experienced this kind of war neurosis after having lived for years in trenches, facing gas attacks, under barrages.

157

In the Mainz hospital where I spent some time in 1918 recovering from concussion, I shared a room with another young officer who was always leaping out of bed screaming: 'They're coming—they're coming—they're coming!'

He saw figures climbing out of trenches for the assault and moving forward in smoke and fumes. Then, with contorted face, arms held convulsively in front of him as if clasping a bayonet, he would stand with his back to a corner of the room. He would not recognize me when I tried to calm him, would strike out wildly in all directions, and would have to be brought back to bed by two medical orderlies. In bed, he would slowly calm down, often sobbing.

In me these states soon passed, and the war and its fears vanished from my sleep, and also from my thoughts, as if I had to shake it off, bury it for a time, in order to let it go on living within me.

But the memory is alive.

It is inside me in as physical a sense as a component of my own body, a scar, a chemical substance in my glands. Yet at the same time it is separate from me, as if all that had been experienced by someone else. For it is no longer my personal possession. It is the consciousness of a generation sentenced to death, of whom only a remnant survived.

During the war years we often quoted the saying of Nietzsche's, a dangerous saying, but one that proved its validity for a good many of us. Later it helped my friend Carlo Mierendorff withstand five agonizing years in concentration camp: '*What doesn't kill me, makes me stronger.*'

But then he was killed after all by an aerial bomb during the Second World War. Otherwise, Hitler's hangmen would have done the job.

In February 1915 we were on a relatively quiet sector of the front and had just finished firing a barrage during an insignificant patrol skirmish. The skirmish had taken place towards evening, and just before dark I was relieved. For no special reason I began pacing up and down one of the communication trenches leading to the forward lines—probably I just wanted to be alone for a while. Down the trench, from the infantry position ahead of us, came two medical aides carrying a stretcher. It was a sultry evening; both were panting under the burden. For a moment they put the stretcher down to wipe the sweat from their foreheads.

'They get heavier when they're dead,' one of the aides said to me.

'But he isn't dead yet,' the other one said.

'What do you mean?' the first said. 'Shot right through the head.'

I had stepped closer without curiosity. In the sallow face, with blood running from the forehead, I recognized the features of my schoolmate Ferdinand Pertzborn, who had linked arms with us on the day the war was declared, and who had taken the special final examination along with me. As I bent over him, he suddenly opened his eyes and for a second looked directly into mine. I think he recognized me; something like an effort at a smile passed over his face. Then his eyes seemed to stop seeing, though they did not close. 'Now it's over,' one bearer said. 'Let's go.' They picked up the stretcher and tramped on. Only after they were gone did it occur to me that I ought to have closed his eyes.

A few days later another schoolmate, Karl Gelius, paid me a visit. He was already a lieutenant, promoted for bravery, and this was his eighteenth birthday. I opened a bottle of wine that my father had sent me and that had actually arrived unbroken. We wanted to celebrate, but he was not cheerful and scarcely drank anything.

'I only wanted to see you once more,' he said. 'I know I won't be going home again.'

I tried to get him out of this mood, reminding him of jolly times we had had during our schooldays. He only looked dolefully at me. 'We didn't know what it was like,' he said. He was killed a few weeks later.

If I reckon up my time at war, deducting all furloughs, I spent 1213 days at the front. During that period, between my eighteenth and my twenty-second year—which under normal circumstances I would have spent in university towns, among students and professors, in a thoroughly familiar environment—during that period I met people in all walks of life, of every type, from every region of Germany. I knew them in closest intimacy, with all their peculiarities, dialects, characteristics, and in the literal sense I knew how they lived and died. Traveling salesmen, acrobats, textile manufacturers, pharmacists, lumber dealers, pimps, paterfamilias, transvestites, miners, farmers big and small, engineers, mechanics, glaziers, theology professors, postal clerks, innkeepers, cod fishermen, butchers, railroad men, newspaper publishers, printers, brewers, precision machinists, music teachers, district attorneys, mental-hospital attendants, chimney sweeps, gigolos, doctors, canary breeders, educationists—the list could go on and on.

I loved Valentin, who came from the Palatinate—a ruffian, a vagabond, totally amoral, with a police record of fourteen convictions. Yet I could not help liking him. He was not a refined person. And he was a wretched soldier. This was deliberate. When we had to drag an artillery piece out of the mud by pulling on ropes, he was the one who would shout loudest, 'All together!' and would not move a muscle or lose a drop of sweat. There was a technique to it; he knew how to hold his breath so that his face flushed and everyone would have sworn he was pulling with all his might. He was a master at taking it easy, sparing himself effort, and yet he was a robust, muscular fellow. He hated danger and had an invincible distaste for dying heroically. As soon as we entered a dangerous position, or whenever an offensive was about to start, he contrived to make an old case of gonorrhea flare up again, or at least its symptoms—how, was his medical secret. Then he would have to be sent back to the nearest rear-echelon hospital. Once the battle was over and we were assigned to rest up in reserve positions, he reappeared and at once began stealing. But he never stole from his friends. Anyone he liked, or anyone who was decent to him, could trust Valentin with his money without bothering to count it. He stole for sport, because he liked stealing, not out of any 'neurotic tendency.' And he took pleasure in giving his loot away. Once he deserted the company. It seemed he had had a child by a lonely miner's wife in the coal district behind the Arras front, and on impulse he decided to visit the child and take it a bar of chocolate which he had filched. That was the way he was, very tenderhearted. I was his immediate superior and managed to hush up the matter. Otherwise it would have gone hard for him. His devotion to me was fabulous.

I met him again after the war at the Dürkheim Sausage Market, a famous fair in the Palatinate, where he had a job running the swingboats. We threw our arms around each other. In a rather classically pagan way of demonstrating his affection, he instantly called his girl, a pretty, strapping lass who ran the shooting gallery, and ordered her in the heartiest tone of voice to sleep with me. She seemed quite prepared to do so at once. But certain recollections prompted me to renounce the pleasure, which obviously displeased him. It took all my tact to get around the matter.

In general, the attitude of front-line soldiers towards groups of prisoners who were taken through the lines towards the rear was one of friendly sympathy mingled with a touch of envy, the thought: The war is over for them. You never knew whether you yourself might not be in the same situation tomorrow, and you wondered how you would be treated. If we had the chance we slipped a few cigarettes to them, and sometimes received a black Caporal or an English Players in return. Hatred for the 'enemy' in the other trenches had long since faded. For all of us the enemy was the war, not the soldier in blue or khaki who had to endure what we were enduring. Fraternization began very early. As early as Christmas 1914 the soldiers themselves in the trenches west of Roye stopped the nocturnal barrages that were standard even on quiet fronts. The trenches were close together here, and instead of hand grenades they threw packages of sausage or chocolate over the barbed-wire entanglements. A German patrol from one Hessian regiment fell into conversation with a French patrol; they shook hands and invited each other to their dugouts. The Germans brought beer or schnapps, the French brought wine. Of course these things happened without the knowledge of the officers, until one night a young lieutenant checking the dugout of a German platoon found a couple of Frenchmen gaily enjoying a meal; they had unbuckled their rifles and stowed them in the corner. His sense of correctness outraged, the officer had them seized and taken away as prisoners. That was the end of the brief period of fraternization.

On my trips to London for film work during those last years we spent in Austria, I liked to travel by one of the pleasant luxury trains (the Arlberg or Orient Express) which ran almost nonstop from Vienna to Calais. I would usually be seated in the dining car for breakfast when the train traversed a particular stretch of country. I would stare spellbound through the glass and read the names of the stations gliding past, each of them flashing through me like an electric shock: Hallu. Chilly. Chaulnes. Vermandovillers. Estrès-Deniécourt. Insignificant places south of the Somme, fairly close to Péronne. To other people there was nothing special about them. A fairly flat district in northern France, where small woods, farmhouses and church steeples had long since reappeared. But for me it was a lunar landscape, wild and deserted, without a tree or shrub, without the memory of any human habitation, torn up by craterlike shell holes, slashed by trenches, overgrown not with grass or grain but with rusty barbed wire, the whole swathed in a sallow, sulfurous mist.

Right by this railroad embankment, on which the train rushed along while the French waiter served fresh rolls, at the age of nineteen I had lain on my belly for a whole night, my rifle clutched in clammy fingers, not fifty yards from the enemy assault troops who had taken our front lines. If they had known that we were only a handful of men left, our cannons destroyed or out of ammunition, that our exhausted little band were the only guards on this embankment, they could have dispatched us like baby rabbits. But they did not know. They thought there were still occupied positions at the back of the railroad embankment, and luckily for us they had reached the goal for their present operation. They were very close; we could distinctly hear them talking and calling to one another as they dragged their machine guns forward; and the sounds they made were strange and disturbing, different from those of the ordinary *poilus*. These were Senegalese, the black auxiliary troops who were said never to take prisoners but to use their long knives to slit open the bellies of soldiers whom they overpowered. Later I saw such Senegalese infantrymen among the occupation troops in Mainz, and talked to them. I could never have imagined that these harmless, childlike fellows who were so fond of laughing and dicing were the same men we had feared like devils. But in certain situations there are no harmless people. You never know of what men are capable. Nor is it any consolation to anyone if it turns out afterwards that they meant no harm. That night I may have killed a few of them. I meant no harm either. I was afraid. Anyone who feels no fear is not brave, only stupid. In those years we learned that you can never become habituated to fear. It keeps coming back, like perspiration or digestion. You develop a certain technique for handling your fear, that is all. For that you receive medals for bravery.

The train has long passed, has already crossed the Somme bridge to Albert. The waiter asks whether I would like another cup of café-au-lait. But I am still lying on the railroad embankment. An endless, terrible night. . . .

It was the fourth of September 1916. Damp and frosty. There

were no longer any tracks on the embankment, nothing but crushed stone ground fine by shells, into which I pressed my half-frozen body. When I heard a noise, or saw a glimmer of light, I fired a single rifle shot towards it. My heart was fluttering, but my hands were calm. Again and again I counted my remaining cartridges, but could not keep the number in my head. Finally I had only a few hand grenades left. We had learned to pull the pin, count twenty-one, twenty-two, and throw them accurately at twenty-three. Our next guard was thirty yards away; neither of us could see the other. I was alone. By the time morning approached my fear had almost vanished. I felt nothing but a horrible, urgent need to relieve myself, and a deadly weariness. For this night had been preceded by a whole week without food and sleep under maximum artillery bombardment and gas attacks. Now the artillery was firing over our heads, bombarding the rear positions. When daylight came, our fate seemed sealed, but by then I was indifferent to everything. I crawled down from the railroad embankment and took care of my need. Then I crawled back up, my knees giving way under me. I lay on my face, from time to time raising my rifle. But my instinct for self-defense was fading out. I wanted only to sleep. To cease to be. I wanted extinction.

Then, before the sun rose, relief came. Silesian infantry had been brought up from a rear position and thrown into the breach. Young men, old men. On the way they had been issued schnapps to fight the nocturnal cold and the dysentery that was going the rounds, and since they had had no time to make coffee, they had drunk their liquor on empty stomachs. A good many of them had swollen red faces. Their clumsy gray figures appeared out of the ground mist in a widely dispersed row, jumping, reeling, stumbling over shell holes and trenches.

We few wrecks on the embankment simply let ourselves roll down from the top, and crawled on our bellies towards our liberators. Then a command rang out, and they began running over the railroad embankment towards the enemy, some screaming hoarsely to themselves, others with clenched teeth, a few waving their bayonets and howling from fear and drunkenness, at the pace of an assault run, which looks so alarmingly like flight, except that it is forward. ... From the other side, hesitantly at first, then with a kind of astonished and ever more violent unison, came the barking of the machine guns.

We knew that now several of them would fall stiffly forward on their faces. Others would whirl around before they fell, screaming. Others would run on and on. We no longer looked. We staggered back, back to somewhere where we could sleep.

Three days later the remnants of our battery were quartered in a rear-zone town to wait for new guns and replacements. We were washed and shaved, slept in a bed, saw women on the street; the evenings we sat in an *estaminet* and drank up our pay. At that time, in the brief rest after those worst weeks of the Battle of the Somme, I learned how quickly human beings forget. Among the men who had survived there was already the mood of a kind of war veterans' club, although in a matter of days they would be lying in the same muck. They no longer remembered that is was muck. What a terrific show that was! Not a word of their description of the 'show' coincided with their experience. They no longer knew themselves; they were different people from the men who had been in the battle, and they would be different again in the next battle. Their language had changed, too. They used bombastic terms which they avoided at the front. I never heard any high-flown talk when a man went out to bring back a wounded comrade. Then they used the familiar vulgarities. That was honest, and more modest.

In the midst of the dreary racket we were making and the intense physical sense of breathing, living, being, what I myself remembered of the battle was its tremendous loneliness. Whenever you faced the ultimate, you were alone. That night on the railroad embankment. That time I ran, breathless, dripping with sweat, across the trenches to reach a shot-up position in order to bring back a periscope and other instruments. Shells burst like meteors fallen from the sky. Earth spurted up; the air was one massive roar—and yet deathly still. Not a soul was in sight; everyone had crawled into a hole, hidden, buried himself. The loneliness was horrifying.

It was worst of all in the half-buried dugout into which I had to crawl through the air shaft. A single man had been left behind there as a sentinel. His name was Andrea and he was a Westphalian miner with strange watery-blue eyes. He was a member of a spiritistic sect and a teetotaler who wept when we drank, cursed, or made coarse jokes. Up to an hour before, we had heard his voice over the telephone line; then it had ceased. The line was in shreds. I had to go there to fetch whatever could be fetched of him and the instruments.

I called his name as I groped my way in the darkness. I shouted, bellowed: Andrea! My voice broke in the tunnel, which smelled of ecrasite and sulfur—and of death. It was like going into a grave. Outside, the shells howled and burst. But there it was quiet—incomprehensibly quiet.

Andrea was dead. He lay crushed between some splintered beams. I brought back the periscope.

Later we received strange disturbing letters from his wife, who also belonged to the sect. The letters disturbed us too. Her husband had appeared to her, she wrote; he kept coming back and talking with her. Back home in Westphalia he had told her about the hour of his death. He had died all alone in an abandoned dugout. No one had remained at his side; his comrades had fled, leaving him to breathe his last in his own grave.

The letters always ended with a torrent of charges and reproaches. But how could she have possibly known how he died? She had received only the usual official communication, nothing more. No one had written to her or told her about it.

But his lonely death was no more so than that of anyone else, than life itself during this period. The whole war remains in my memory as one great, inhuman loneliness—even when I was in the midst of people and longing to be alone.

During the four years of the war I went home on furlough five times. Three of those I was ordered back by telegram before my leave was up. That meant: attack, offensive, change of position, trouble. Those days at home, even when they passed undisturbed, without being cut short, were a compound of sadness and ecstasy. I kept the sadness to myself. It was impossible to communicate. Even at home the solitude was not relieved. I tried, we all tried, to cheer up our parents by telling jolly stories of life as a soldier. The stories were untrue, at least in the way we told them, and our parents sensed this. The truth remained blocked. Departure was in the air from the day of arrival.

Ecstasy: art, music. A concert. An evening at the theater. Visits to my older friend Ludwig Berger, to whom I could read aloud my first efforts at play-writing, from whom I gathered my first insights into the mysteries of the theater; model stage sets, sketches of scenery and costumes, theatrical criticism—the world I was trying to reach. Hours in Wilckens' bookshop on Schillerplatz, where we could find not only the exciting Expressionist authors whom we now regarded as a flame of rebellion—Heinrich Mann, Alfred Döblin, Fritz von Unruh, Kasimir Edschmid—but also the banned pacifist writers whose books were imported from Switzerland and sold under the counter: Leonhard Frank, Henri Barbusse, Henri Guilbaux.

Ecstasy: the brief meetings at my home with my beloved, as wonderful as ever and still barred to me.

But the sadness outweighed all that—sadness and an element of discomfort. Our country, apart from certain intimate aspects of it, was a source of embarrassment and irritation to us. It was confused and fretful, full of inflated gabble about 'holding on,' rife with the slogans of the new Fatherland Party, such as 'Peace with victory' and 'Not a step backward.' On the other hand there was a great deal of ill-tempered hoarding mentality. We too, during the last years of the war, subsisted at the front chiefly on swedes, old potatoes, dehydrated vegetables, stale bread, and poor-quality marmalade. But we joked or made up mocking songs about the food. At home everyone constantly complained about the rationing, though at the same time everyone contributed 'gold for iron,' hammering nails into the wooden 'Hindenburg' that stood in the market place in every town, each nail representing a mark for the war loan. For my part, I felt more comfortable during the rest days we occasionally had between battles at the front. Since I had become an officer I no longer had to spend them en masse and could wander around some French or Belgian town behind the lines, visiting churches and museums, and studying unconventional varieties of love.

During this period, perhaps like many of my fellows, I was living a strangely divided life. The two phases of it knew nothing of one another and did not touch. My sweetheart at home remained the only one, the pure, great love to which I never thought I was being unfaithful. At the same time I was attracted, with a force that was more than merely 'instinctual,' to a kind of female underworld in which the problem of fidelity or infidelity never crossed the threshold of consciousness: a world of vague, nocturnal, lewd, and nymphomaniac creatures who were often but not always whores, the fashionable cocottes of Brussels, the officers' girls of Lille, Ghent, or Douai. Some prostituted themselves out of necessity or vocation. Some were simply women hungry for love in a country that had been under occupation for years and where men were scarce. And what I experienced was not only venality and corruption, not only the abandon of women who had nothing to lose, but also warmth, tenderness, and sudden passion, made the more intense by the awareness of limited time. In a sense I was seeking to drown myself in the oddness of it all, for these encounters sometimes banished loneliness more effectively, and imposed fewer burdens, than 'true love' back home could possibly have done.

I watched from afar, abashed or repelled, the vulgar crudity with which the authorities ministered to the sexual needs of the enlisted men, the hordes of men who were resting or in reserve behind the front. I saw them standing in line in front of the military brothels like people queuing up in front of a butcher's shop in times of shortages. I heard the rude jokes they made as they shoved their way in and out, received and discharged by a medical aide who provided hygienic treatment after a period of 'pleasure' controlled by the clock. Five men per woman per hour was the accepted figure. I did not meet any of the women who offered this sort of service.

The others, whom we met in restaurants and night clubs identified by a sign, 'For Officers Only' (the Café Léonidas in Ghent, the Gaité in Brussels), or with whom we struck up acquaintance on park benches and boulevards such as the rue Nationale in Lille, were the prey of all, but they could still choose their men or refuse them; they themselves governed their own time; to that extent they were their own mistresses.

I felt a mysterious kinship with such women, and if they radiated the slightest humanity, I would be transported into a boyishly exalted mood. They were confronting a void just as we were confronting death. They were marked just like ourselves. Someday they would be driven naked through the streets, with shaved heads. But now they were giving a little pleasure to those who might be covered with earth on the morrow. Like us they were living as if nothing else existed besides this one night, these few hours, this utter absorption. To me, the fact that they were French, or Belgian, members of the 'enemy nation,' gave them a quality all their own, unlike their counterparts at home, whom I shunned. They felt that. They called me Charles or Charlie and regarded this young, responsive German officer as a kind of ally in a no man's land.

Once, during this period, I had the experience of having died, having been translated to another world. That was in the summer of 1917, during the worst phase of the Battle of Flanders. I had been granted a three-day relief from my observation post in Houtholst

Forest, which had long since been turned into a landscape of trenches and shell holes filllled with water or mud. For those three days I had obtained a furlough and quarters pass to Bruges, the city of Memling, the Venice of the North with its dark canals, which I had not yet visited. The furlough train was stalled for a few hours; somewhere up ahead the tracks had been blasted or bombed. The result was that I arrived in Bruges in the middle of the night. Scarcely anyone else left the train there. The officers' hotel close to the railroad station, where my quarters pass entitled me to a room, was closed. No one heard my knocking; probably the soldier on guard had fallen fast asleep.

Suddenly I became aware of the brilliant moonlight and started walking into town. In a little while the street came to an end. I found myself standing on the edge of a canal in which the black water flowed slowly, oily and glinting in the moonlight. A few steps led down to the canal, and there lay a small rowing boat, tied to a post. White painted letters identified it as a wherry belonging to a German naval division. I looked around; there was not a sentinel or a soul in sight anywhere. The inhabitants of the city were under curfew. The naval units were asleep. I went down the steps, loosened the rope, and with slow, almost noiseless strokes began rowing in towards the city. Actually I did not know in which direction it lay. I was drawn by the moon and the water, and I followed. No sound from the front could be heard here. Apart from the drops which sometimes splashed from my oars, the stillness was absolute. I must have passed the Béguinage, the hospital of St Jean, the well-known churches, but I could not tell. The boat carried me under low, narrow bridges, under the crowns of old willows whose branches grazed the water, past gables and walls of houses which seemed ghostly white and transparent in the moonlight. The moonlight constantly floated like a glowing, slowly rocking disk before me. All sense of my existence, of this world, of reality, vanished completely. I thought I was no longer alive, that I had fallen in battle. I do not know whether I fell asleep or lost consciousness. When I returned to reality dawn was already breaking. The cool of morning wakened me; I realized that I was still living and that the inflowing tide had carried me back to the starting point of my voyage.

My awakening came at this same period. My head cleared. I began to think sharply, logically, soberly, without illusions or self-deceptions. The whole experience of the war, including the days of 1914, now seemed to me like a murky dream. Now I thought I saw through the whole thing. This war was not some destiny that had fallen upon us out of the clouds. It was the failure of a world, our world, the world of nation-states that had been in existence for some two hundred years. It was a universal suicide, a world's end. I despised myself for my previous intoxication, while at the same time there was already growing within me the new chiliastic intoxication, belief in the 'war to end all wars' in the coming springtime of nations, in a changed and better world.

Along with this I had been seized by another kind of intoxication, an unquenchable thirst for knowledge, culture, insight, learning and understanding. I tried to make up for all that I had missed by immoderate reading, by devouring, plowing through all sorts of material. I spent a large part of my lieutenant's pay on books which I had sent from Germany, even though I kept losing most of them during attacks or in changing positions. Still, I read like a man obsessed. I wanted to know everything—and I think that most of what I still know today derives from that period, for the intellectual fever was combined with an impulse towards thoroughness and a capacity for retention which I myself did not understand. Older friends at home gave me some guidance in their letters. I did not care whether I would be taking all this knowledge into the realm of the shades with me, whether it was destined to be buried in some collapsing dugout as so many of my books were, or whether it was intended for some future life. No matter, I wanted to have it there and then. What I was experiencing was like a furious retort to the stupefaction which was our real task and our natural lot in the everyday activities of the war. I had always despised the apathetic stupidity of the average officers. Now I refused to play skat in the evenings; reading fanatically, I stuffed cotton into my ears in order not to hear their empty chatter.

The intellectual nourishment I devoured, along with contemporary novels, poems, and plays, cannot be listed. But for all my greediness, I was not blindly and pointlessly stuffing my mind. I went about my reading systematically. I really wanted to outwit the inanity and the loss of time the war was causing. So I drew up a strategic plan of what I thought could be learned without lecturers and seminars. I began with art history, for which the cities of Belgium and northern France offered visual instruction. Then I went on to economics, studying the classical liberals, Adam Smith and Ricardo, and going on through Louis Blanc and Lassalle to Hegel, Feuerbach, Proudhon, and Marx and Engels, finally reaching Max Weber. I read all the French books I could pick up in bookshops or from peddlers' carts, and discovered for myself Rimbaud—then hardly known in Germany—and Charles-Louis Philippe. I read Verlaine, Montaigne, and the great novels, above all Flaubert. I devoured Strindberg, Swift, Dickens, Tolstoy, Dostoevsky, Hamsun. Eschatology attracted me, and theologians and philosophers: St Augustine, Thomas Aquinas, Descartes, St Francis, as well as the mystics: Eckhart, Suso, Tauler, and Mechthild. Then there were the Silesian Pietists, and the defiant Humanists and Reformers: Hutten, Erasmus, Luther and his opponents, the fanatics and militants of the Peasant Wars—the world from which I drew the materials for my first play. I studied, pencil and notebook in hand, a history of philosophy from Thales to Plato, from the Stoa to Schopenhauer. I was insatiable. Buddha and Lao-tse, the Vedanta, the Upanishads, and the Bible were consolations in the frightful darkness all around me, the eclipse of hope, the continual threat to life, the fear of excruciating pain, against which in the end, however, no books or wisdom would be of avail.

Soon I acquired the nickname of 'the reading lieutenant.' Even mounted, when we were changing positions or advancing slowly on jammed roads, I would open a book. At times I would also be called 'Lieutenant Trotsky,' for this exponent of the Bolshevist revolutionary government who was building a red defensive army out of the remnants of the dispersed Tsarist forces fired my imagination, and I made my feelings vocal, to the horror of the officers' mess.

At an army bookshop behind the front, where I tied my horse one day when my unit was enjoying a brief period of relief, I was introduced to the works of Bakunin, Alexander Herzen, Peter Kropotkin, and Max Stirner. In the same army bookshop I found all the revolutionary pamphlets and magazines of this period. The literary and artistic liberality of the German Imperial regime is somewhat staggering from today's viewpoint. Presumably this side of public life was simply not taken seriously. The authorities could not imagine that such literature could have any effect upon a normal citizen of the Reich. They must have regarded such ideas as the preposterous notions of madmen, for otherwise there is no explaining the fact that the wildest revolutionaries were permitted to wield their pens relatively uncurbed, and that little attention was paid to the influx of antiwar writings from abroad. The leaders of the mutinous sailors of Kiel were put up against the wall, strike leaders were arrested. But Franz Pfemfert's magazine *Aktion*, which was sheer dynamite directed against the political order of the period, and full of innuendoes against the war and 'the ruling class,' was banned only once or twice by the Berlin commissioner, though some issues might appear with a few lines blocked out by the censors. Folios of drawings by George Grosz, brilliant in line, seditious in content, a slap in the face to every right-thinking patriot, could be published and admiringly reviewed in the major newspapers. For the rebels personally these were not easy times. Every effort was made to force them into uniforms; they tried by every means to escape. It was a catch-as-catch-can wrestling match, but on the whole the weaker men won. Even when drafted, they were sooner or later discharged, as was George Grosz, after a period of painful examinations and hospitalization, as cases of 'psychopathic unfitness.'

The military preferred not to burden the army with such men. Their convictions were regarded as the product of feeble-mindedness, and they were not taken seriously as dangerous. Since the arrival of totalitarian systems and contemporary dictatorships, a lenient attitude of this sort is no longer conceivable.

One day in 1917 I sent a letter by army post to Franz Pfemfert, the publisher and sole editor of *Aktion*, of which I had long been a subscriber. (The army post office had been faithfully delivering my copies every week.) I expressed my agreement with his literary, artistic, and political aims, and enclosed two poems as a sample of my own efforts. To my surprise, they appeared in the next issue of *Aktion*, without Pfemfert having sent a word in response. For the first time I was a writer in print, and thereafter I became a regular contributor to *Aktion*. In brief and unguarded letters Pfemfert encouraged me to send him more, and above all not to falter in my new belief: that this war and all wars must be ended, and that a reconciliation of all nations must be effected. This correspondence, too, resulted in a curiously double life. I led my men into positions, I did my war service as it had been imposed upon me, unstintingly. But my ideas and feelings, my beliefs and hopes, were with the 'International of all liberated peoples' such as was preached in *Aktion*, and my verse and first prose pieces appeared in that periodical.

The thinking of the young writers who felt united under that banner was still nonpolitical. There was an element of idealistic enthusiasm in our work. We dreamed of a 'spiritual revolution' to be initiated by cultural Germany and carried on by the leading minds of all nations. In spite of my reading of the *Communist Manifesto*, the *Political Economy*, and *Capital*, I could not imagine what a revolution, a political, economic, and social upheaval, really meant. As at the outbreak of the war, we were not prepared for reality. Basically, our feelings were once again romantic, idealistic, heroic, although with reversed colors. The events in Russia naturally stirred us—as they did all those who had begun to question the meaning and justification of the universal slaughter. The world would have to be changed so that such crimes against life, against nature, against all humanity and human dignity, could never recur. How could we help but see the uprising of a whole people as the first manifestation of the new era? How could we help but echo the old slogan, '*Ex Oriente lux!*' What really happened when the Social Revolutionaries and Mensheviks were isolated and destroyed by the Bolsheviks (with German assistance, for Ludendorff had dispatched Lenin to Russia in the famous sealed train) was a closed book to us at the time. It would take long, hard study before we could learn to open it and understand its contents. At this time a religious element entered into our belief in the necessity of 'the Revolution.' We regarded the preachers of a new social order as prophets, martyrs, and saints. We dreamed of the future as a realm of universal love and humanitarianism, beyond time and place.

After all our anti-assault guns had been shot up and we had lost half our men, our battery had received new artillery of an entirely different kind; heavy, 15-cm. long-barreled guns of great range. As far as my job was concerned, this did not change anything; I remained an observer. But then my duties took an interesting turn. First I was detailed to a special training course for long-distance and air observation. I soon became familiar with the nasty feeling of seasickness in being in the basket of a captive balloon which twirled constantly around its own axis under the great, swollen sausage of the balloon, while I had to try to observe firings and hits with my telescope. I also learned aeroplane observation, sitting in the flimsy seats of the 'crates,' crash helmet buckled to my head and sending radio messages to the ground in Morse code. For this purpose I spent a few days with the Richthofen fighter squadron, whose later commander, Hermann Göring, happened to be on leave. There I met a small, wiry, fidgety, peppery, and extraordinarily witty Air Force lieutenant who had already won the Pour le Mérite: Ernst Udet. We took a liking to each other after our first few words, drank our first bottle of cognac together, and until shortly before the Second World War never lost touch with each other.

Fortunately for me, air and balloon observation for artillery was soon abandoned because of its total inaccuracy. We were eighty percent less effective in the air. If a squadron of four to six planes rose on the German side, some twenty to thirty new planes with better armament promptly rose to meet them from the other side. To one of our balloons in the sky there were a dozen or more behind the enemy front. The proportions of artillery and ammunition supplies were similar; and now came the Americans with their fresh troops and their fearsome tanks, which crawled like giant steel beetles over trenches and barbed-wire entanglements. The war was lost and we knew it. But we still had to carry on for more than a year, in a hopeless situation.

Instead of growing apathetic, I became clairvoyant. It was a parapsychological phenomenon that was hard to bear.

I knew in advance, when we went into position, who would be killed.

The thing began during a railroad journey from front to front which lasted a day and a night. At night I was sitting in the second-class officers' compartment, eyes closed, drifting between sleep and waking.

Suddenly my orderly, one of our old soldiers who had been in the war from the start, called my name with a strange urgency. It was like a whisper on the stage, but it also had the tone of a smothered cry for help. I stood up, went out to the aisle, and looked around. I thought I had just seen him before me. But he was located several compartments further down, sound asleep, and when I asked his fellows about him I was told that he had not left his seat for hours. At that moment I knew. Sure enough, next day he was killed, as soon as we came under fire.

The year 1918 was the worst of all on the Western Front. The German army command tried, by stupendous efforts, to turn the tide in our favor. One offensive after the other was launched. Then came the terrible counter-offensives that destroyed us.

173

If I had not previously sensed the hopelessness of our position (though my comrades and I still believed we could wrest at least an 'honorable' armistice by continuing the struggle), my personal encounter with the Kaiser would have made me see the light. The encounter, I might add, was all on my side. Shortly before the spring offensive of 1918, I had to present three men of our formation to him for the award of the Iron Cross, First Class.

Several hundred men of various units were drawn up on a former exercise ground of the French army, to be presented their medals by His Majesty. The group of men in light-gray coats approached almost without a sound, like so many marionettes. I stepped forward and said my piece. The Kaiser nodded almost imperceptibly, and raised his sound hand to his helmet (his left arm was withered). Then an adjutant stepped forward and pinned the Cross to the soldiers' chests, while the Kaiser was already walking on.

During the brief moment while I had spoken I had seen the Kaiser's face from a distance of three paces, and it shocked me. It was frozen, gray of complexion, his mustache seemingly affixed to it by glue. His eyes were wide but sightless. They looked right through me. At what? At fatality, at an inescapable doom; that was my feeling. I retained the memory of a tragic mask.

My friend Carlo Mierendorff, the socialist, who received his Iron Cross from Kaiser Wilhelm in the summer of 1918, later agreed with my impression. He, too, had seen a man who knew himself and his nation to be finished. Why, then, did he not call a halt to the slaughter? Perhaps it no longer lay in his power to do so.

At the end of April 1918, when we were committed to the offensive against Armentières and were advancing upon the city, I had an experience that comes back like some frightful dream. The only Portuguese division that fought against Germany in this war had been overrun by our troops. A number of mules formed part of our booty.

All day long, down the same road on which we were pressing forward with great effort, streams of Portuguese prisoners were marched past us, all of them small men still looking distraught and frightened from the shock of the battle. Clinging to the arm of one corporal was a young Frenchwoman carrying an infant. She was allowed to follow along as if she would be able to accompany the man to his prison camp. Towards evening I received orders to ride ahead and set up quarters for our formation in a certain suburb of

Armentières. I was accompanied only by an elderly groom named Rupprecht. We had been told that there were still houses standing in the suburb, which I was to take over. When I arrived, I found only a single house intact; that had previously been the Portuguese canteen. Through the shattered windows I could hear screeches, singing, and bawling that did not sound human. I had Rupprecht hold my horse and went in. A number of German infantrymen, their nerves shattered by the battle, had taken possession of a keg of heavy Portuguese red wine. They were filling their mess kits with it and gulping it down. Two men, totally drunk, were sitting on the dead body of a Portuguese soldier, leaning back against the wall and roaring filthy songs. Another was throwing up in a corner. They had placed a dead Portuguese astride the wine keg as if he were on a mule; his mouth had sagged wide open, and a drunken lance corporal was pouring wine into it, shouting: 'Prost, Camarade!' The wine ran in streams down the yellow, whiskery chin.

When I tried to command their attention and make them clear out of the building, they shouted curses at me and laughed in my face. That was the first and only time, including the days of the November Revolution, that I encountered such behavior from German soldiers, otherwise so disciplined and obedient. It could only be explained by their total drunkenness. When I repeated my order in a sharper tone, one man came at me with his bayonet. 'I'll slit your belly open, you lousy bastard of an officer,' he snarled at me. 'You're no better than our drunk Portuguese!' He was bleeding from the shoulder, and I later learned that in the course of the day he had run a Portuguese through with his bayonet, and had himself been wounded by the dying man. 'You lousy bastard!' he kept repeating. I had no choice but to draw my revolver and release the safety catch. In his half-insane condition he might well have killed me if I had not fired two shots into the ceiling, then aimed the gun at him. That sobered him. The lance corporal came swaying up to me with a mess kit full of wine, as if he were going to throw it into my face. I put away my revolver and said loudly and distinctly: 'You can all kiss my arse!'

A burst of laughter. The lance corporal held the filthy mess kit out to me and said: 'Have a swig!' I drank. That was another thing the war had taught me. I knew that I could take a whole mess kit full without collapsing. Suddenly I realized that Rupprecht had tied the horses outside and was standing behind me with his rifle at the ready. Peace was assured. We shook hands; I took possession of the quarters and saw to it that the drunken men had a bed in a nearby stable.

One spring day a few years ago I was strolling along the Champs Élysées in Paris. Suddenly the traffic stopped, people stood still, and all the men removed their hats. I heard rhythmic drumbeats approaching and saw a band of civilians marching in the roadway, headed toward the Étoile and the Arc de Triomphe. I asked a man beside me what the parade was about.

'*Les vieux combattants,*' he replied, '*de la grande guerre.*' He meant, of course, the war of 1914–18. The veterans of that war. . . .

I too removed my hat; I would have done so even if the others had not.

The flag-bearer in the van was a bald-headed man with a white mustache. He had weary, sagging shoulders and was bracing the pole of the tricolor on his paunch. Then, in rows of four, marching briskly with blue, white, and red cockades in their buttonholes and the Croix de Guerre on their chests, came the sort of amiable people to be seen in every bistro, in every Métro station, in every cinema. I thought I recognized one of them as the owner of a Provençal restaurant. They were tall and squat, thin and fat; some sported mustaches, some were smooth-shaven. They looked like family men, dwellers in small apartments with flowerpots on the balcony, like post-office workers, tobacconists, jewelers, like progenitors of children and grandchildren. Many of them struck me as terribly old—they must have been about my age. . . . I had the feeling that I should be with them, marching along with them to the Tomb of the Unknown Soldier—that shattered, blasted, atomized Nobody who has become the symbol of our times. I had the feeling that I should go up to them and embrace them, all these big and little citizens, pensioners and workmen, that I ought to say to them: 'Here I am, the man who shot at you, whose life you had to try to take.' I had the feeling that I belonged to them more than to anyone else in this world. For they were the 'enemy.' I began to weep.

How the war ended for me is quickly told. At the end of July 1918 I was at the coal mines near Lens. A forty-foot-high elevator tower, which I was using as an observation post, was struck by a direct hit, and I was left lying for dead. After some time—I don't know how long—I was found unconscious but alive with concussion and a gash from a shell splinter above my left eye. After a week in the hospital a brisk captain of the Medical Corps sent me back to the front: 'You have headaches? Spells of dizziness? Vomiting? No reason for shirking. You're healthy enough to get yourself killed, and that's what we need young officers for now.'

I reported back to my post, but my battery chief recognized my condition and sent me home on a two-week furlough. There I collapsed. And I had the luck to be sent to a quiet hospital in an old monastery. Sleep. Rest. Catholic nuns. The one who tended me was young and named Sister Ambrosia; she had the eyes of my grandmother, who had died at the beginning of the war: deep blue and serene. Whenever she looked at me, I knew that I was safe. I sat in the little cloister garden, writing. Then came a convalescent leave which I spent all alone in Hirschhorn on the Neckar, staying in the old Gasthof zum Naturalisten. The trees were turning color; the smell of autumn was in the air. It was the beginning of October. I sat on benches in the woods and wrote. During this period my brother, who was serving as infantry officer on the collapsing Western Front, was severely wounded. We knew nothing about it; communications had broken down.

Once more I had to return to the front, after a wild night in Strasbourg, the headquarters of our replacement regiment. A former sergeant from our battery had opened a small tavern. It was the beginning of November, cold and foggy. I spent the night there. We drank tremendously. Two girls, whom he called his daughters although he had not begotten them, served us. He urged me not to return to the front; the girls would hide me, he said. But my head remained just clear enough for me to refuse the offer. I didn't want to be stuck here; I wanted to go home, and the way to do that was to join my unit. Next morning I rode a forage wagon into the Vosges, to the battery to which I had been assigned. There I found a number of men from our former battery; they had come here by the same route as myself, by way of a replacement regiment after being wounded. These men knew me. They told me that they were about to form a soldiers' soviet and would elect me to it. The top officers threatened to have us shot. They were merely laughed at. Next day they packed themselves into a divisional car and left the 'mutinous troops,' who were as tame as a herd of sheep which had lost their shepherd. I stayed: the 'revolutionary' men wanted to have an officer. These men sang, '*In der Heimat . . . in der Heimat . . .*' just as they had done at the beginning of the war—unlike the muddy *poilus* who climbed out of their trenches on the Chemin des Dames singing the 'Internationale.'

My men left me my epaulets and medals, tied a red armband around my sleeve, and handed the command over to me. Mounted on a tired nag for whom I pilfered oats in the villages between Colmar and Strasbourg, I led the remnant of our company across the Rhine bridge at Kehl. The Alsatians gave us hostile glares. We kept our eyes straight ahead, looking to neither right nor left. None of these soldiers imagined in the least that we had lost the war because of a 'stab in the back.' That was an idea that was talked into people later. We knew that we had been defeated. But we also did not imagine that the governments of the victorious nations were any 'better.' Starving, beaten, but with our weapons, we marched back home.

1918-1920
SEASON OF FRIENDSHIP

D ID WE EXPERIENCE a revolution in 1918? What I saw was a collapse that only briefly bore revolutionary features and whose aftermath continued for five years—until the end of 1923.

The fall of the German Empire found the German people, in spite of the preceding years of bloodshed and hardships, as unprepared as they had been at the outbreak of the war.

At best there was a quality of elemental revolt in the uprising of the navy, when the sailors forcibly prevented the fleet from sailing from port in a senseless suicide operation. Then they sent their messengers into the German cities to form soldiers' soviets, but on the whole they found only irresolute, bewildered men and officers who stood aside in vexation. Here and there, in garrisons and behind the lines, the men ripped off the officers' epaulets and decorations. Nothing of the sort happened to me because I was protected and vouched for by the men who were returning home with me.

In Berlin the Republic was proclaimed. It was represented by old Social Democrats like Friedrich Ebert, men who were not revolutionaries but who were trying to preserve the nation from chaos and impoverishment, to save whatever could be saved.

What took place was the shifting of a militarily and economically ruined nation from its historical order into a democratic order adapted to the present age. The venture proved a tragic one. Influential figures who backed the new Republic were in a sorry plight. Falling between two stools, they were ridiculed by the right and derided by the left.

There were radical leftist groups whose slogan was 'All power to the workers' and soldiers' soviets.' They could look to the example of the Russian Revolution, but they had neither a leadership trained for long years in conspiratorial methods nor the support of the masses—not even in Berlin or in the industrial regions. The majority of the proletariat clung to its seasoned Social Democratic and union leaders. Only comparatively small groups joined the Spartakus Bund inspired by Karl Liebknecht and Rosa Luxemburg, from which the Communist Party of Germany later emerged. Not even the formation of a leftist faction of the Social Democratic

181

Party, the Independent Socialist Party, changed anything fundamentally.

The people were exhausted, disillusioned, and the majority of them were not at all in a revolutionary mood. Demonstrations took place, but the words on the placards were 'Peace and Bread.' The word 'freedom' likewise appeared, but everyone ascribed a different meaning to it, and for the majority it might equally well have been replaced by 'Leave us alone.'

The Kaiser had fled to Holland, but he was not in flight from his own people. The Germans would never have treated him as the Russians treated Tsar Nicholas and his family. But there was reason to think that the victors would have made it one of the conditions of the Armistice, which amounted to total surrender, that the Kaiser be turned over to them. By Wilhelm's crossing to neutral territory, the newborn Republic was spared a difficult conflict that might have led to open civil war.

No civil war erupted in the exhausted country, which had already been bled white. There were only scattered uprisings which were swiftly crushed, and a succession of extremist acts of violence and vigilante murders—portents of the later catastrophe.

The Revolution did not lay hands on the ruling houses, the kings and grand dukes in the various German states. They were deposed and relieved of the burden of government, for which some of them may even have been grateful, but the populace bore them no grudge. On the other hand, there were certain district magistrates and regional governors whom the people would gladly have seen hanged, but these personages managed to be not at home at the right moment, and turned up again later—as regional governors and district magistrates.

Our own Grand Duke Ernst Ludwig of Hesse could rest assured of his popularity with his countrymen, even with the radical intellectuals and revolutionary workers. He was a polished, highly cultivated man who even before the war had encouraged modern art, to the horror of the conservative bourgeoisie, and who during the war had eschewed jingoism. Before the war he had shown his liberal temper in the case of the writer Fritz von Unruh, who was also an officer of the Guards. Von Unruh's pacifist drama, *Officers*, produced by Reinhardt, had brought the writer into serious disfavor with the German Crown Prince. But our Grand Duke invited von Unruh to his court as tutor to his son. Rumor had it that during the early years of the war Ernst Ludwig had paid a secret visit to Moscow, to try to persuade Tsar Nicholas II, who was his brother-in-law, to make peace quickly.

During my school days I often saw him in his box at the concert hall, a slender figure in a dark suit, with a narrow face and fine features. He would come to Mainz for a special concert and would respond to the audience's ovation with a charmingly modest gesture, obviously somewhat embarrassed.

Now, with all the politeness of a cabinet change in Britain, he was replaced by the similarly polished and likable socialist leader of Mainz, Adelung, who thereafter ruled Hesse with a mild, perhaps too mild a hand, without incident until the incursion of the brown tyranny.

Although the years after the First World War cannot be compared with the wretchedness of the second postwar period, the times were still bad enough. Food shortages bordered on famine conditions. Transport was chaotic; essentials like electricity and coal were often unavailable; the country was racked by strikes, dissension, and uncertainty. The prevailing mood was one of gloom and vexation.

For me, however, and for a number of young people who shared my feelings, these were inspiring years. We who had escaped death in the war felt life as a powerful reality, a current carrying us forward. We were glad to throw the ballast of the past behind us. Away with it! A new age was dawning!

Time, we believed, was on our side—few though we were. The future, we thought, would belong to us and to the alive, awakened souls throughout the world. There sprang up those great friendships which were based not only on the camaraderie natural to the young but also on common convictions. And those friendships have endured ever since, defying separation and death.

A few days after I had returned to Mainz we heard from a distant relative in Bremen that my brother was in hospital there, and that his condition was critical. We had had no news from him for many weeks. We wondered how he could have been shipped to Bremen from the Western Front, for Mainz was much nearer to Belgium and France.

My mother decided at once to go with me to Bremen; my father, already half blind by then, would not have been capable of such a journey. For it was a journey full of uncertainties and under the most difficult circumstances. Normal traveling time would have been ten hours. Now it took us three days and three nights.

I had talked the Supreme Soldiers' Soviet in Mainz into giving me a certificate recommending me to all local soldiers' soviets and permitting us to travel in military transport trains. During these weeks no other kind of passenger traffic was permitted; the ticket windows were closed and there were no train schedules. We had to wait on refuse-strewn platforms until some incredibly overcrowded train came heading in the desired direction, then we had try to squeeze aboard it. That was not always possible, for even the running boards would be occupied by soldiers, and hordes of others kept pouring into the cold, drafty stations, a good many of which had been shot up during the revolutionary skirmishes. In some of the larger stations a mobile field kitchen might be steaming away on the platform, presided over by nurses who ladled out a watery substance called either coffee or soup. If you were lucky and patient enough to obtain half a cupful to warm yourself, someone would surely shout that a train was coming. Then you rushed, spilling the warm brew on your trousers, in a wild stampede towards the cars, around which a ruthless hand-to-hand struggle began. In one such tumult I hoisted my mother onto my back and pushed her through a broken window into the toilet. I myself hung with a cluster of other men on the platform of the coal tender during the first day. At night we worked our way into a compartment intended for eight persons and now occupied by at least twenty. As for my mother, she was lifted into the baggage net where she was couched between knapsacks, steel helmets, gas masks, and assorted weapons, covered with pages of the revolutionary newspapers *Rote Fahne* and *Vorwärts*.

At first the enlisted men threw angry and suspicious glances at the officer's uniform which I was still wearing; but the red armband with the stamp of the soldiers' soviet won me respect, and these hardened brutalized men at once became gentle and helpful when they realized that a woman wanted to join her severely wounded son. From her bed above their heads my mother talked with them about their homes and their family concerns.

There were broken axles, damaged tracks, spells when no coal was to be had, endless stops along the way, near collisions, but we finally arrived.

It was a frosty morning. Bremen was in the grip of a general strike. There were no cabs, restaurants were closed, the streetcar employees were marching about the city with banners and placards, and the police were harrying the demonstrators instead of giving directions to strangers. And so we wandered on empty stomachs up and down an almost deserted suburb, until we found the bare school building that was serving as an emergency hospital.

At the end of a large hall full of severely wounded soldiers, mute or groaning, my brother lay on a wire framework that was supposed to be a bed, covered by a rough woolen blanket. He was bearded, emaciated, hollow-eyed as a ghost. He was still alive, but he could not move and could scarcely speak.

I found out what he had been through. During the retreat in northern France, in the last days of the war, he had been hit by a bullet that shattered his lowest vertebra and ischium, so that splinters had penetrated into the intestines.

He had lain helpless between the German and English lines, but his men had come in search of him, and carried him back. There was no longer a regular field hospital. While the fighting still continued at the front, everything in the zone of communications was in a state of dissolution: marauding rear-echelon soldiers who feared the frustrated rage of the civilian population and wanted to get home as quickly as possible had robbed food and hospital trains or commandeered them for the homeward journey. The doctors and nurses who remained behind were unable to deal with the constantly swelling influx of severely wounded men. They received no new supplies of bandages and drugs, had no means of performing operations or undertaking treatment. The emergency barracks were under fire from the steadily advancing enemy artillery.

Feverish, horribly injured, and virtually untreated, my brother was laid on his face and squeezed into an open cattle car with dying men. En route the dead were lifted out of the cars and left on the railroad embankment—out of necessity, not brutality. For my brother, it was an added torment that this train, in the course of its snaillike journey, passed through our home city of Mainz. It even stopped there for a long time. Although but half alive, he recognized the railroad station, knew that he was only five minutes away from home, and begged the medical aides to unload him there and carry him home, or send word to his parents. But this could not be done, for there were no orders for it ... and the ghastly journey continued to a painfully remote Bremen.

Now, as we stood by his bed, he was, because of the nature of the wound, still lying on his belly. A meal was just being distributed from a huge caldron; it consisted of evil-smelling old sauerkraut and pieces of rancid bacon. He could not eat a morsel of it.

While my mother tried to find a doctor or a nurse, I went to the office of the 'hospital commandant.' He proved to be a truculent sergeant who snarled, when I pointed out my brother's condition and the impossibility of such food for him: 'There's nothing extra for officers now.' They'd had plenty long enough, he said. If my brother couldn't eat what was offered, he'd have to fast; that was healthy anyhow.

This was no doubt a fellow who had plagued his recruits and, since he could no longer do so, took his cue from the Revolution to vent his bullying on the officers. I had to show him my certificate from the soldiers' soviet, threaten to denounce him to the soldiers' council in Bremen, and rattle off the names of Party leaders to whom I promised to complain. Only then did he send for the doctor in charge, an overworked, overtired man who himself had no authority at all. He advised me to transfer my brother as quickly as possible to private care, for if he did not undergo an operation immediately—and there were no facilities for one in the hospital— and if he did not receive decent food, there was no hope for him.

My mother scurried indefatigably about the city. With an energy and tenacity no one would have credited to this frail-looking woman, she succeeded in locating a private room in a Protestant clinic, in finding an eminent surgeon who took the case in spite of his crowded schedule, and she also rounded up special food rationing cards—all things that were virtually unobtainable at the time. Meanwhile, I was battling to obtain my brother's release from that morgue of a hospital, and his discharge from the army.

My mother stayed on in Bremen to nurse him back to health. She brought him home months later.

I returned home, once more in overcrowded transport trains, obtained my discharge, took off my uniform, and immediately entered life—which in this case meant the University of Frankfurt.

The two decisive experiences for me in this dreary revolutionary winter in Frankfurt were my meeting with Carlo Mierendorff, and the theater.

The Frankfurt Schauspielhaus [Playhouse] was at that time one of the greatest centers of Expressionist theater, almost more so than the Berlin stages. A kind of high-principled, highly charged mode of stylization had grown up at the Schauspielhaus. Frankfurt Expressionism did not last very long; it could not compete with Reinhardt's art of character delineation. But during those years of explosive intellectual tensions and spiritual exaltation, it had its hour.

My own relationship to the theater was that of a gallery spectator, sometimes wildly enthusiastic, sometimes youthfully critical. Producers or actors were still virtually demigods to me, leading exciting lives in an as yet unattainable Parnassus, a legendary realm of untrammeled spirit and artistic intoxication.

Although this was a childlike and childish notion, it was true in essence; and with the audacity of youth I had no doubt that I would conquer this world someday, and possess it.

Instead of attending the unspeakably boring lectures on Roman law and classical political economy—my father had insisted on my beginning with this course of study, as a sound foundation for whatever career I might follow—I worked away in my small, poorly heated room on dramatic experiments whose subjects were as overweening as they were unperformable. I was going to write a new *Theatrum Mundi*, a cycle of tragedies and comedies that would begin with Prometheus and end with Lenin. I stormed and shouted around that tiny room—especially when a friend came to visit and I could read aloud to him—so that my landlady became seriously concerned about my mental health. I actually succeeded in completing a *Prometheus*, that favorite motif of youthful idealists. In fact the basic notion was not bad. In bringing fire to men, Prometheus wanted to bestow not only warmth and light, but the greater blessing of peace. In the first act he went to the men of the valley, in the second act to the men of the mountains. But both groups, long-standing enemies of each other, after receiving Prometheus' gift, drove him away with mockery. In the third act he had to look on helplessly while they used fire to make war upon one another and was then condemned to eternal suffering by the cold majesty of the gods. The epilogue enjoined men to unite and overthrow all gods and altars, in order to establish their own kingdom of peace on earth.

A boyhood friend of mine who was later to have an international career as a theatrical and operatic producer sent a copy of the play to our idol of noble manliness, the actor Carl Ebert. Unexpectedly,

I received a postcard from this gentleman asking me to come to his house for a talk; another person would have fed the manuscript into the stove. I had unmistakable talent, he told me, but certain things showed immaturity and lack of experience. However, he went on, he had arranged for me to meet the play-reader of the Frankfurt Schauspielhaus, Dr. Plotke, who at the moment was in the hospital, severely ill with pulmonary influenza, but was continuing to operate from there.

In this way I met one of the most remarkable, and also typical, personalities of those days, unfortunately shortly before his death. Plotke, an advocate of political theater, and a leading member of the Independent Socialist Party, lay in bed glistening with sweat and flushed with fever, talking hoarsely to several people. For hours, interrupted by fits of coughing, he dictated the texts of appeals and proclamations. It is said that he continued this until the hour of his death, despite the doctors and nurses. A young man of the leftist press took down a stenographic record, and even after his death fanatical editorials by him continued to appear.

He did not discuss my *Prometheus* at all, but proposed that I write a *Spartacus* for the Schauspielhaus. The play must take place in a modern factory and must represent the proletariat's struggle to win full power. During the intermissions armed sailors would read to the audience the texts of Karl Liebnecht's and Rosa Luxemburg's *Spartacus Letters*. He himself read aloud from some of those letters, and became so impassioned that it seemed as if he would make his final exit at any moment. In fact he died a few days later.

I never wrote *Spartacus*, never even attempted it. I soon discovered that my talents and my sensibility pointed in an entirely different direction, not towards the theater of political propaganda and proclamations. But politics had now become our destiny, and it has never since surrendered its hold upon me. Rather, in many respects it has determined the paths of our lives.

I was still associated with *Aktion*, whose editor, Franz Pfemfert, had plunged into a more and more immoderate radicalism. By this time he was already several miles to the left of the Russian Communists. Radical magazines were springing up like mushrooms in those days. They resembled one another to the point of indistinguishability in format, contents, and contributors. The really important ones were still only René Schickele's *Weisse Blätter*, Herwarth Walden's *Sturm*, Wieland Herzfelde's *Malik*, and Pfemfert's

Aktion. But suddenly, in nearby Darmstadt, a periodical appeared that had its own character and tone. It was, moreover, actually published and edited by young, very young, people, instead of by middle-aged and semi-illustrious writers. Its name was *Das Tribunal*, and it had a remarkable background.

A few years before the war a group of secondary-school students had formed in Darmstadt, young people who were passionately interested in modern art and modern literature. They talked about starting a magazine. August 1914 sent the older members of the group—the seventeen- and eighteen-year-olds—into the ranks of volunteers, just as it did me. For years they were scattered over the various fronts, but they did not lose contact with one another or their sense of inner community. Then, in the middle of the war, in 1915, a group of juniors born in 1900 carried out the plan. The dynamo of this undertaking was a boy named Joseph Würth, then fifteen. Not creative himself, he was an enthusiastic lover of the arts. At the same time he had a cool, critical mind, a fiery spirit, a clear intellect, and reckless energy. In other words, he was a born publisher. Since the first meeting at which the bold project was launched took place in the attic of Würth's home, it was dubbed *Die Dachstube* ['the attic']. The first publications of *Die Dachstube* were leaflets and were hand-written and multiplied by hectograph. Soon the boys saved up enough pocket-money to buy a hand printing press. With their primitive equipment they issued literary works in a typographical form that is still regarded as a significant achievement. They also published woodcuttings and graphic works by young Darmstadt artists. And they prevailed on booksellers to distribute their products. Darmstadt provided favorable soil for such a venture. Thanks to the Hessian Grand Duke's active encouragement of the arts, a group of modern painters, sculptors, craftsmen, and writers had gathered in the city. There was the *Sezession* group, with such artists as Max Beckmann, Ludwig Meidner, Paul Klee, and Frans Masereel, who exhibited their works, then scarcely known or noticed. Many of this group supported *Die Dachstube* by contributing jacket drawings and illustrations without a fee. Until the end of the war the magazine continued to be run by Gymnasium students, but there was nothing amateurish or schoolboyish about their work, though also nothing of 'precocity in a sophisticated sense. This was rather the expression of a tremendous intellectual energy seething under the surface apathy of the war, of a remarkable new spirit on the part of talented young people who boldly confronted the coming new age.

In November 1918 the following leaflet appeared. I have kept the original. It read:

To the readers of Die Dachstube

Die Dachstube is closing. It has collected, sifted, trained. That work is done. Now more is needed; now the outlines of the new world must be sketched, must be fought for. Silence is betrayal. A new audience is marching onstage. The times command us to envisage greater goals. We are establishing

Das Tribunal [The Tribunal]

Early in 1919 I received a brief note from Carlo Mierendorff. It was addressed to the Revolutionary Student Council of the University of Frankfurt, to which I belonged. He wrote that he had read pieces of mine in *Aktion* and learned that I was studying in Frankfurt, as he too was doing. *Das Tribunal* needed contributors as well as editorial help. Would I let him know whether I would be interested in meeting him?

I replied at once, and there took place a meeting like few others in my life, rich in encounters though it has been.

Oddly enough, we had arranged to meet not at either of our rooms or in some café—though I can no longer explain why—but at a mass demonstration in the gigantic Frankfurt Saalbau, where even twin brothers would have had a hard time spotting each other. We agreed that we would meet at a certain entrance. As identification Carlo was to carry an issue of *Das Tribunal* and I the latest issue of *Aktion;* these we were to hold up against our chests like posters.

That was one of the most agitated, wild mass meetings Frankfurt had seen during that wild year. It had been called subsequent to the assassination of Liebknecht and Rosa Luxemburg, which had taken place only a few days before. Among the thousands of people pouring into the hall, colliding, pressing forward, or being pushed by ushers and marshals, amid the stream of wet winter coats and in the dim light of the lobby, we actually found each other. Both of us, prone to anecdotal hyperbole, later used to recount that we had each forgotten our magazines, but that we had recognized each other anyhow, merely by the 'smell of the personality.' A nice fictional touch, it was nevertheless basically true. We sniffed at one another like dogs or wolves of the same litter.

So far, those students I had come to know at the University had struck me as by and large a wretched lot. I mistrusted the members of the Revolutionary Student Council and of the Socialist Workers Group, whom I could already see as future party bosses, careerists, bureaucrats with an eye to their pensions. To me they were mediocre, petit-bourgeois without a spark of artistic feeling, desiccated discussion machines, lacking élan and imagination, overfond of bringing up a 'point of order.' At best they were ideologists without adequately grounded ideologies. Their aim was not freedom and self-development, but realistic politics, and in their various groups they behaved like officials, parliamentarians or narrow-minded commissars, not like young people seeking fresh ways to shape their lives.

Yet even these were the exceptions, for the majority of the students consisted of a sluggish sulky horde, contemptuous and hostile towards the new Republic and any social progress, lamenting the lost lustre of their caste and the superior troughs at which they had formerly fed.

Now, I knew at a glance, I had found the man I needed. We stood jammed in that crowd, taking each other's measure out of the corners of our eyes. Amid the roar and turbulence of the mass meeting, with the exchange of a few hasty phrases, we struck up our alliance.

The meeting ended in uproar. The police cleared the hall, the crowds scattered—but we stayed together, stayed together all night, engaged in arduous discussion. It was raining, the night was misty, damp, and cold, our rooms were unheated, the taverns were all shut. We broke our last cheap cigarette in two and walked each other home, back and forth, for hours, from one quarter of the city to another, because we simply could not finish. That night was the first of many, countless nights in which we repeatedly walked each other home and conducted the same emotional, never-flagging conversation that circled around the same subjects, the major themes of our lives.

But we would also begin, without transition, to provoke and tease each other. We kept this up throughout all our years of friendship; this sort of thing helps to preserve brotherly feelings from sentimentality or excessive emotionalism, and also keeps them fresh. We quickly discovered that we had both served in the field artillery, at times even in the same regiment. It is characteristic of this generation that we, who were so opposed to war, felt that the common experience of war had forged a special link between us.

I became a contributor to *Das Tribunal* and also worked on the editorial staff. I no longer remember or possess the things I published in the magazine, rarely under my own name; usually, like others, I used some collective pseudonym.

Carlo Mierendorff, radical in his thought, original and independent in his opinions, had a moderating influence upon my own radical views, which at the time were still far too much caught up in illusions.

He had, to be sure, nothing in common with those nonentities and future bureaucrats who seemed already old and had never been young, and whom we both depised. His initial interests had been literary and artistic; politics were his passion, not yet his profession. But his thinking was clear, rational, a far cry from weak sentimentalism. In his precise, sardonic way he could at once distinguish truly valuable and creative ideas from well-intentioned ideological and humanitarian rhetoric of the kind that was current in those days, both in art and in politics. Soon we became reciprocally our own toughest critics, and by our criticism we encouraged and helped each other. I needed and loved his feeling for moderation, his sense of precision, proportion, and authenticity. Things were not always entirely peaceable between us. But we fought out of affection and sympathy, out of gaiety, enthusiasm, love of life. We had disagreements, but these never had a tinge of misunderstanding or real dissension about them.

We also fought physically, without any perceptible reason or provocation. Sometimes we fell upon one another like crazy savages, from an urge to measure our strength. These fights were not matters of jealousy or anything of the sort—if such feelings arose, we took care of them humorously. More mysterious rituals were involved. And since we were usually in about the same form, these were tough battles; they did not end until one of us had the other pinned to the ground.

We were already mature men that time in our Henndorf house when my wife bit Carlo like a dog in his bare calf (he was wearing leather shorts) because he had got a stranglehold on me in an unfair wrestling match. He hopped around the room clutching his wound and giving vent to exaggerated screams, while I berated my wife.

When I look at his picture today, I realize that he was beautiful. At the time such a word would never have entered my head. We thought women alone were beautiful, if they were; men were likable or disgusting. But Carlo's head, with his wide forehead under very thick blond hair, with his bright eyes in which temperament and gaiety covered a premonitory sadness, with his strong but finely chiseled cheekbones, nose, and chin, *was* beautiful. Not too beautiful. He had, in the best, simple, and modest sense, a German face. That face could have belonged to no other nationality. In appearance and nature Carlo was a German—the kind of German personality that can be loved, wished for, and hoped for.

He was of medium build, like me, broad-shouldered and strong. We could trade suits and shirts, a fact that lent some amusing twists to our association. During the first year of our friendship we had only one dark suit with striped trousers between us, my own, and on certain occasions we had to cast lots to decide who would go. Later I became too fat for the suits, and Carlo had provided his own; but our shirts were still exchangeable. We loved the checked cotton shirts such as American farmers and woodcutters wear, the kind that have become the rage nowadays because of American influence. In those days they were still unusual. There was a certain 'cowboy shirt' we kept stealing from one another for years; it had dark-red horizontal stripes, and Carlo maintained that it had been 'soaked in buffalo blood.' When he vanished into the dungeons of tyranny, that shirt stayed with me. I continued to wear it across the ocean, on my American farm, until it fell to pieces. That was after his death.

I still keep dreaming of him. Scarcely ever of other friends. Frequently, I wake up in the morning—now, more than twenty years after his death—and know that he was with me again. It is always the same dream: he suddenly emerges, laughing, from a group of people, and at first I start, for to me he is still in concentration camp, and I want to greet him with wild delight: You're out! You're here! He comes towards me, calls my name. In the morning I no longer remember the rest of the dream. It fades, mists over. But every time it leaves me with a sense of deep uneasiness.

Perhaps a feeling of guilt is involved. While he was being dragged like a galley slave from camp to camp for five long years, while he was suffering and excluded from life, I still had a country I could call home, and in spite of all my grief for lost Germany and all my knowledge of what hung over us, I was living through a fulfilled, vital period. There was nothing I could do to change his fate. It would not have helped him if I had been compelled to share it with him. I could not even send him a book, a few cigars, or a letter; at most I could impart a rare greeting indirectly, through a mutual friend. I had been warned, as had all his other friends, that any package or message from abroad—let alone from one who was himself exiled—could only have worsened Carlo's lot. Nearly a century had passed since the days when Carl Schurz rescued the poet Gottfried Kinkel from the Spandau Fortress and galloped with him through the night across the nearest frontier. I could do nothing at all for Carlo, and he knew it. Later, after his release, when I had already lost my home in Henndorf, he sent me his regards. Even then I was forced to respond to them indirectly, through my parents. I cannot reproach myself for any fault towards him. And yet, unconsciously I feel guilty—because I did not undergo the same things. Perhaps because I am alive.

Twice, during that winter, we saw aspects of inferno. In a poorly lit square in the old part of the city and in the adjoining narrow streets was the black market, where everything could be had that was unobtainable or banned: foreign money, foreign cigarettes, food, shoes, clothing, guns, medicines, probably also narcotics—cocaine or morphine. The black market began after dark, and there was always a bustle of men and women in groups or slinking singly along the streets. Prostitutes and pimps also formed part of these crowds.

One rainy night in February (in memory it seems to me that it was rainy, drizzling, or foggy all through that winter in Frankfurt) we were on our way home from the theater when we heard shouts, brawling, and a few isolated shots in this district. Out of curiosity we went towards the noise.

A dreadful riot was in progress. That night the police had sent in a few men to stop the trading in contraband wares or the sale of stolen goods. The intention was certainly not to prevent housewives or the heads of families from buying the bacon or the pound of white flour they could not otherwise obtain. The object, as we later learned, was to arrest an organized gang of thieves for whom warrants were out. But the appearance of men in uniform unleashed a blind fury in the mob. One of the policemen, attacked by superior numbers, had probably fired a warning shot into the air. The man was separated from the others, who had to defend themselves and could not go to his aid. Amid frightful screeches that had a note of orgiastic frenzy or insanity, the policeman was dragged to the nearest bridge. We were close by and saw how the man was beaten upon his already bleeding mouth and eyes as soon as he attempted to say something or to cry for help. When he stumbled, the mob kicked him and trampled upon him. He was hauled up on the railing of the bridge and, badly injured as he was, thrown into the river. Then he was bombarded with paving stones while struggling for his life, until he helplessly drowned. It was impossible to intervene; no words would have brought this mob to reason; we would have been lynched ourselves. Nor was it possible to distinguish any individuals; the mob was a compressed, faceless horde. The women behaved worst of all; their voices screeched through the night like the gabble of apes; they raged and foamed at the mouth.

La crapule. La canaille. Was this what 'the people' were like, the people for whom we wished to fight?

We knew that we couldn't generalize. But we had now seen the horror that was different from the war—the horror of the unleashed masses. Later on we were both to see that in even more appalling forms. Next day the newspapers reported that the dead policeman had been a member of the Independent Socialists, married and the father of two children. A few people were arrested and released again for lack of evidence. There was no one on whom the guilt could be pinned.

Towards spring, strikes and riots erupted in several towns and industrial centers. Here and there battles were fought between demonstrating or locked-out workers and units of the army which seemed to be too weak to suppress the disturbances. In the universities appeals were posted—not only by rightist organizations but also by the Defense Ministry—calling upon the students to offer their services as 'temporary volunteers' in order to support the troops against the rioters, since the army was kept very small by the conditions of the Armistice. The Rector of the University of Frankfurt convoked a student assembly in the main auditorium. The place was packed with students from all the faculties. Carlo and I had missed each other and came in through different entrances. First the appeal for volunteers was read aloud, and was greeted by a

195

thunder of stamping feet, the traditional expression of enthusiasm. Then the Rector delivered an address which differed not a whit from the well-remembered balderdash of the worst period of the war. He called the striking workers and their leaders 'unpatriotic rabble' and, supported by the loud stamping of the students, went on to speak unctuously about sacrifices and duties. Those who would volunteer to participate in these struggles—against their own countrymen—were promised full credit for their lost study time as well as all possible consideration in their future exams.

I was boiling with rage and could not control myself. Although I knew that I stood almost alone against the overwhelming majority, that I would be talking to deaf ears and closed minds, I demanded the floor and protested at the top of my voice.

'The workers who are striking today,' I shouted from my seat, 'are our comrades of yesterday. Anyone who goes out and fires at them is not a patriot, but an enemy of his people and a scoundrel.'

At once all the students, with a jerky, mechanical simultaneity, jumped to their feet and roared in furious unison: 'Out! Kill him! Criminal! Agent! Pig! Out! Out!'

From all sides they rushed at me, cheesy faces with bared teeth. I was seized by many hands, blows rained down on me, and I was pushed down the aisle—all I could do was protect my face with my arms. Then I flew out the door, propelled by kicks, and tumbled down the broad stone steps.

Just before they seized me I had caught a glimpse of Carlo at the other end of the hall being beaten in the same way and heard his loud clear voice as he tried to second my protest.

We found each other out in the street, one of us with a bruised knee, the other with a sprained wrist, and discovered that aside from these injuries nothing serious had happened to either of us.

We had already decided, some time earlier, to go to Heidelberg in the spring, together with Theo Haubach. Now, limping, we turned our backs on the inhospitable University of Frankfurt.

Whenever I recall the first year in Heidelberg, it appears to me in an everlasting flow of morning light and sun, of cheerful serenity, illumination, exuberance and intellectual excitement.

There was no bad weather there, even when it poured or the heat hung sultrily over the roofs.

Nor was there anything gradual and deliberate about the ties that formed here. Just as the fruit trees burst into blossom all up and down the Neckar Valley, so alliances among young people flowered overnight in Heidelberg. Most of us had not known one another previously, but the sympathies among us developed rapidly and often became friendships for life.

While still in Frankfurt I had occasionally accompanied Carlo to Darmstadt for editorial meetings of *Das Tribunal*, and I had met his friends there—above all Theodor Haubach, who had been close to Carlo from the time when they were schoolboys together. Even in those days they were already called the Dioscuri. Later, in the secret councils of the German Resistance movement against Hitler, and in those other plans conceived in the remoteness of exile, the name of Mierendorff was seldom mentioned apart from the name of Haubach.

My own friendship with Haubach, who in contrast to Carlo was a rather cool and reserved fellow, came about all of a sudden, in the course of a trip in a third-class compartment from Darmstadt to Heidelberg, where we wanted to look for rooms shortly before the beginning of the semester. On boarding the train we were still distant and rather wary; by the time we arrived, barely two hours later, we were intimate friends and imagined we knew a good many things about each other that in fact were revealed only later on, in the course of long nocturnal walks.

Haubach loved the night. Often we would take a late cog-wheel rail car up to the Königstuhl, then tramp back home by the light of flashlights along roundabout paths through the woods. Or else we would set out at about midnight, leaving the lights of the city behind us, and tramp for hours along the river and then back. At such times, when we could scarcely make out each other's faces, Theo would become open-hearted and confiding. He would weave a fabric of audacious ideas, or would begin to sing in his rather harsh, jagged voice. His favorite piece was the marching motif from Gustav Mahler's Third Symphony (Entrance of Summer).

He was of slender build, almost gaunt, dark-haired, with a narrow face shaped by divergent tensions, and a manner that concealed the soft and gentle side of his personality behind a deliberately stressed vigor. Intellectual distinction was united in his features, his language, and his bearing with soldierly discipline, a readiness to serve and command—a rare combination. Even in the periods of his political activity he had none of the commonplace shallowness of the ordinary activist. He used no propaganda clichés in his speeches and his

197

writings. Even at the very beginning of his political activity, he despised all trite formulations, all vague, unexamined phraseology.

Like Carlo, his original interests had been literary and artistic. But for him poetry and music (with which he was thoroughly familiar) were not means for personal release or emotional intensification, but objects of sober, searching investigation.

When he decided to dedicate himself to politics, which in the end were to devour him, he did so with misgivings. But he realized how imperiled the new Germany was, and thought he must help defend her.

At first there were three of us, Carlo, Theo, and myself, who matriculated on the same day and at once joined the Veterans' Association. Soon others joined who thought and felt as we did, wanted to live as we did, and with whom overnight we became close friends and political allies. Although a few of us took part in the Socialist Students' League and in the Sociologists' Club, we did not form a 'group.' We were a circle drawn together by an affinity, a small orchestra of friends in which each played his own voice, united by the new key which we sensed and sought in art, society, and culture, united also by a boundless pleasure in life, laughter, games, and amicable mutual mockery, always rather adventurous in spirit, wide open to everything bold and original, to all the creative tinder of those times.

I am unable to recall how first meetings with individuals came about. We tracked one another down by scent, recognized one another without introductions. Henry Goverts, the future publisher, was one of the first to join our crowd. With his Hamburgian and English descent and education he brought into our somewhat rough-and-tumble, somewhat anarchic and disreputable society, a touch of civilization, the manners of a gentleman, but he participated at once in our improvised entertainments, outdoing us all in highly imaginative performances.

At the time most of us had no money, or very little. We had to get along on scanty allowances from our war-impoverished families, and somehow earn extra money on the side. It was the same for me.

My father's factory had with difficulty complied with war-production rulings and shifted to the manufacture of shell fuses. Now it was nearly bankrupt, like the wine trade itself, the chief industry of our area, and was slow in recovering. My father, afflicted with eye trouble, had had to retire prematurely. His pension and investments suffered fatally from the rapid devaluation of the currency, and the war bonds he had patriotically bought were good only for papering walls. From 1917 on we had been undernourished. We suffered from a wild hunger, a physiological greediness for sweets. If any ever came our way, we devoured them like gypsy children. We craved for alcohol in the same way. Sometimes we received condensed milk in packages from abroad. We ate the sticky, viscous, heavily sweetened stuff with spoons. A can of corned beef was the very height of nutritional longing. We drank sour wine of the cheapest sort, or 'monopoly schnapps' made from potato peel and sold by the government distilleries, until our heads smoked. Our suits had been cut out of the remnants of gray-green cloth left over from the manufacture of uniforms. Our shabby overcoats dated back to our prewar school days. Professional prospects seemed as meager as the lunches in the university dining hall. But none of this could cloud our gaiety, none of it sour our humor.

It was the 'fifth spring,' as Brecht has called it in his 'Ballad of the Dead Soldier,' the first spring and summer after four years of war, the first time in four years that we were able to live freely and safely. We woke in the morning and were happy that no one would be shooting at us this day. We went to sleep with the reassuring thought that no alarms would wrench us from our beds. The dreary, uncertain winter lay behind us. We were alive and we wanted to use life and taste it to the full, with all our stored-up strength. Of course we had lost four years of study, but we felt more mature, more experienced, surer of ourselves and our goals than other students who were just coming out of school to the university. Here in Heidelberg, the most progressive and intellectually most demanding university in Germany, we had our chance.

If our crowd really was a magic circle, as I suspect, its center and its centripetal force were concentrated in a true magus, as eccentric as he was remarkable, who was ahead of all the rest of us in universal knowledge, intellectual alacrity, and the fact that his personality was fully formed. That was the unforgettable Dr Wilhelm Fraenger.

He must have been about thirty then. Director of the Institute of Art History, he had the vast intellectual background with which to deal with all the artistic tendencies that were proliferating at the time. The bizarre, rare, and mysterious elements in the arts, and above all in ethnology and folklore, were his favourite areas of research, in which he delved with great erudition, inspired intuitiveness, and a brilliant power of expression. But he was also a teacher and he exercised, in the Socratic sense, considerable influence over his younger friends, not by the way of dry didacticism but by the use of lively dialogue. Some of the best talk occurred during banquets—symposiums—or on walks, outings, and at artistic events.

His appearance was as unusual as his mind and his imagination. In that academic environment his looks, too, had the mark of sterling originality. Not very tall, rather thickset and compact, with an early tendency to a small paunch, with something opaque and devious but also enticing and gracious in his features, he looked when he laughed or sang to the accompaniment of a guitar, or when he was engaged in animated conversation, rather like a faun-eyed, worldly preacher, a sensual anchorite. When he came walking down the street, slightly dragging his left foot, which was misshapen from a childhood injury, wearing his black, broad-brimmed hat, or when he received us in his study, wearing a loose velvet jacket or long dressing gown, you did not think of a modern scholar or of a contemporary bohemian, but rather of an alchemist, a secret Freemason, a sharp-tongued arch-rogue, or a monk who had shed his cowl, a Reformer or Anabaptist. But he also reminded you of a hardheaded, eloquent disciplinarian of society and culture like Jan Amos Comenius, the great educational reformer and one of his favorite writers, from whom he quoted frequently.

Even before I went to Heidelberg I had called on Fraenger and struck up a friendship with him. For me he was one of the strongest attractions in this city of so many brilliant thinkers. My girl friend had brought us together—she was still the same sweetheart from Mainz whose parents had barred her from me for so long that a marriage became inevitable. When I went to Heidelberg, her family promptly transferred her to Frankfurt. That made my *vita amorosa* in Heidelberg rather more colorful but did not in the least detract from my constant love. During the last years of the war she had studied art history in Heidelberg, and had had the experience of a Rembrandt seminar with Fraenger. She knew what such a scintillating and extraordinarily versatile personality would mean to me, and had therefore introduced us.

Now I brought my Darmstadt friends to Fraenger. He welcomed them warmly, for an enterprise like *Das Tribunal* perfectly suited his taste, as he delighted in youthful boldness and artistic experiment. A character like Mierendorff's, full of high spirits and high ambition, was bound to appeal to him at once.

Fraenger himself had fathered an avante-garde movement in Heidelberg. This did not center around a magazine but rather around an intellectual association, which was meant to serve as a counterpoise to the traditional timidity and routine grind of the university. Fraenger wanted the dynamic potentialities of modern art, of the new provocative literature, of current research and irtellectual re-evaluations, to explode academicism sky-high. He wanted to put an end to the old-fashioned professorial jogtrot and replace it with a 'pedagogical province' (to use Goethe's and Hermann Hesse's phrase) more in keeping with our contemporary sense, inspired by the spirit of social criticism and social revolution.

Among traditional academics he was regarded as the devil incarnate, or at any rate the devil's Mephistophelean and, worse still, his Bolshevistic emissary. There were those who would gladly have indicted him for corruption of the youth—'*quod juventutem corrumperet.*' But a few progressive-minded yet reputable academicians were on his side—among them Karl Jaspers, then still a lesser-known philosophy teacher, and Hans Prinzhorn, the physician and psychologist, who had just published his epoch-making *Die Bildnerei der Geisteskranken*, a fundamental contribution to modern aesthetics as well as to psychoanalysis.

We came just in time to provide a sound and vital basis for the 'Community,' as Fraenger had baptized his group. We served as both audience and participants, the disciples and assistants at his 'productions,' which ranged from shows of slides and private seminars to poetry readings and theatrical performances. The plays might be brand-new, or else old favorites that had been rewritten or rearranged. These performances usually took place on summer evenings in the Wolfsbrunnen, an old tavern on the left bank of the Neckar, at about the same height as the Heidelberg Schloss. It was situated at the edge of the woods, had a large garden and a spacious public room, and took its name from the fountain at its entrance whose waters splashed from two stone wolf heads. The trout served at the restaurant were fresh-fished out of the fountain pool. And the wine was excellent. This romantic spot was less than an hour's walk from the Schloss. We announced evenings of the Community by posters and handbills, and soon had large bands of young and old people coming to our performances. They were even willing to pay a small entrance fee. Fraenger had obtained a municipal license for 'public performances with and without music.' Our expenses were small, since we did almost everything ourselves; but the take usually proved just enough for some rounds of drinks at the 'symposium' that finished off these evenings. If costumes were required, we borrowed them from the municipal theater. We used no curtains, and provided the musical accompaniment ourselves.

The quality of our productions was far above the level of ordinary amateur dramatics or student skits. Fraenger, moreover, always stressed the intellectual and intercultural aspects of our work.

I recall one evening when Prinzhorn, a towering figure in a Burgundy-colored frock coat, together with a young soprano, gave a recital of the old French text of *Aucassin and Nicolette*. Prinzhorn himself had a fine, trained baritone. Meanwhile the rest of us filled in the background of the poem by pantomime.

One performance that was a complete success in spite of wild improvisation—so much so that it became a veritable legend among cultured Heidelbergers—was a Bellman Evening. Together with Fraenger, I had written a general outline for the thing, merely sketching in the scenes, with a few suggestions for the dialogue.

Karl Michael Bellman, the Anacreon of Scandinavian rococo, poet, composer, instrumentalist, favorite author of King Gustavus III, a hard-drinking genius who died young, is to this day well known in Sweden. I had earlier discovered him for myself, and Fraenger, who to his own guitar accompaniment gave masterly recitations of his *Songs* and *Epistles,* had made him familiar and indispensable to our whole circle. We adopted the first bars of his finest melody, 'Linger by this spring,' as our group whistle; at any time of the day or night we would use it to lure each other from his room, and years afterwards, wherever we met, to identify one another at a distance.

Bellman was then almost unknown in Germany. Now we introduced him to the Community's audience with a series of dramatic sketches of his life. Apart from the texts of those magnificent Bellman songs, which were accompanied by guitar, harp, oboe, cello, and French horn, we did not memorize any lines, but let the dialogue grow of its own accord. It also grew out of the spirit of the moment and out of wine, for we had only had a single rehearsal, and that had taken place that very afternoon, in the course of which we had already become fairly tipsy. As Bellman himself used to do in the taverns around Stockholm, we had set up a small stage in the center of the tavern garden. It was little more than a largish platform: boards laid on empty barrels. Here stood a narrow bench for the love scenes and a few folding chairs for the musicians. For dances we jumped down and performed our polkas and minuets amidst the close-packed audience. Our leading actress was an artists' model and a friend of poets and painters named Mimi. She came from Karlsruhe, in Baden; we called her 'the Badic Aspasia.' For the first and probably only time in her life she wore a hoop skirt, and every time she sat down it tipped up, to the delight of the audience. Under it she wore nothing but her lovely legs.

The tavernkeeper made a good deal of money out of us, for such performances were always followed by a bacchanalian feast of trout and crayfish. At our rehearsals, therefore, he provided us with free beer and a bottle of kirschwasser. By the time the audience arrived at dusk, we were already afire with inspiration. Moreover, on the stage we did not use colored water or cold tea, but only genuine beverages, in the style of Bellman. Toward the end of the Bellman performance Fraenger and I, acting out a brawl, were so little in control that we rolled off the stage and under the surrounding tables. We then dragged each other out by the legs. The audience found that bit of business highly effective. But even in the advanced stages of intoxication we rendered the songs, the poems, and the music with artistic accuracy. We were, to put it humorlessy, faithful to our work.

Dawn was almost always breaking with dew on the ground by the time we tramped back to the city after such nocturnal festivals, blissful, tipsy, and eager for new things.

Fraenger offered us such novelties in plenty, and always in the shape of a desirable adventure. The outings we took with him, in groups of three or four, were far more to us than 'educational experiences.' They were journeys into the unknown and miraculous, voyages of discovery and dowsing expeditions. The people we met on the way, in trains, restaurants, buses, and on the street, were as much part of the course and the purpose of the excursion as examining a Carolingian building, Gothic cloisters, a baroque staircase, or the medieval women's baths under the synagogue at Worms.

The Café Wachter in Heidelberg was an attractive place, though of somewhat ill repute at the time, where you could drink at any hour of the night, provided you went in through the back door. It was the meeting place of those enterprising businessmen who 'stopped up the hole in the west': that is, who took advantage of the murky customs and trade relationships with the occupied Rhineland to make large profits in export and import deals of dubious legality. The dirty café tabletops were their account books, the marble densely scrawled with columns of numerals among which, in moments of reverie or relaxation, the traders drew obscene figures. Their cryptic additions ran diagonally across a bosom or a pair of spread thighs. Sometimes they left half-smoked Camels or Lucky Strikes lying in the ashtrays. American cigarettes were out of reach for those who had less flair for business enterprises. We would put the butts into a cigarette holder and puff away, thinking: This is how the great world smells.

But on the top floor of that same building was the apartment and sanctuary of our own Dr Wilhelm Fraenger. Here he lived with his many books and pictures in a semi-enchanted palace open only to initiates. His housekeeping was managed by his 'excellent Gustel,' a girl whom he had known since his youth in Franconia, and whom he continued to refer to as 'my cousin' until he ultimately married her. Perhaps she was actually his cousin, for in many respects she looked like him. She was an adorable woman who knew how to hide her light under a bushel. Those who did not know her well would fail to notice her extraordinary intelligence. And she also had a precious trait for a man like Fraenger: whenever he wanted to be alone with his work, his friends, or himself, she knew how to vanish as if she had never existed.

On narrow Krämergasse, right around the corner, I had found an attic room that suited me perfectly. I could reach it directly by a steep staircase, without having to pass by any other apartment.

At night, if there was still a light showing in Fraenger's windows, his close friends would announce themselves from the street with the Bellman whistle. Then, if he felt disposed for company, we could spend a few hours together. It did not bother him to have visitors when he was in the midst of work on one of his lectures or articles. He would sit at his long refectory table, which was heaped high with quarto sheets covered with his fine, clear handwriting— teapot and spirit stove at his right, chamber pot under the table at his left, for while he worked he drank immense amounts of tea and considered trips to the toilet a waste of time. Frequently he read aloud to us from the pages he had just written, and let us participate in his problems of style—in his struggle for precise expression without renouncing wealth of imagery, in his efforts to bend prose rhythm and grammar, syntax and tone to the given subject and to let the implications of his words shine through with perfect clarity.

The writers whom he invited to come to Heidelberg to give readings generously did so without compensation, since the audiences were students, but Fraenger used the small entry fees to provide these guests with overnight accommodations. Among them was Klabund, a frail-looking lover of mankind, suffering from then incurable tuberculosis. Another was Theodor Däubler, a Tuscan tower of a man whose gigantic frame would not fit into any normal bed—a bearded Oceanus with a deep organ bass who sent his verse rolling endlessly forth like the billows of the sea. He, too, had been promised free board, and Fraenger—who was responsible for the finances—was much dismayed when he consumed three dinners in one night at the hotel. Moreover, Däubler also had to be given a room with a double bed, since he did not fit into a single one.

Still another writer was Hans Schiebelhuth, with a circular head like a seal's and round, somewhat protruding eyes filled with a look of infinite kindliness, sagacity, and humanity. Right from the start we got on so well together that he spent the night on a wicker chair in my attic room, and stayed on for some time afterwards. For sleeping we took turns at using the bed and chair, which had been softened by the weight of many tenants and their visitors. Our affection for each other—for it was more than friendship—never stopped; he became a third son to my parents, a playmate to our daughters, a virtual member of the household in Henndorff, and a comfort in exile, where he was almost the only person with whom I could talk about Germany and know that my feelings would be understood.

Paul Hindemith came also. I had already met him through my brother, and all of us were in the habit of going to Frankfurt for performances of his provocative one-act operas. In Heidelberg he gave a concert, first playing old music on the viola d'amore, his favorite instrument. There was no hostility, and the applause was loud. But when he went on to perform a composition of his own on the viola, an uproar began; there was whistling, laughter, boos, which we countered by vigorous ovations for this master and pioneer of modernist music. Later we carried the small, good-humored musician on our shoulders through the city to our favorite café, a smoke-stained place with wooden tables and benches where Heidelberg porters and draymen in addition to undemanding artists and intellectuals drank their beers. In the corner stood a battered piano on which Hindemith demonstrated the 'seal's piano': using his palms like flippers, and without striking individual keys, he banged out delightful parodies of well-known tunes. As he played, he himself looked for all the world like a trained seal. Liszt, Chopin, and Wagner played with flippers certainly proved more amusing than when played with fingers.

Fraenger's lectures and exhibitions, which for the most part had to consist of reproductions of the originals, familiarized us with modern and classical works of art: the half-forgotten contemporary of Rembrandt, Hercules Seghers, whose sickly larch tree hung on Fraenger's wall; the sculpture of Barlach, Lehmbruck, and Archipenko; the paintings and drawings of Meidner, Grosz, Purrmann, Dix, Beckmann, and the *Blaue Reiter* group, which for us had already become classical.

But our god was Oskar Kokoschka, and Fraenger was his prophet. To me Kokoschka still seems, more than half a century later, the greatest among the many great artists of this time. The poet Else Lasker-Schüler coined the phrase which still seems to me the definitive pronouncement on him: 'A latter-day old master.' If we stand before his very early portraits (who in our time has painted hands as he did!), we understand this verdict. But for us he was even more than that. In his masterliness there never was (and never will be if he lives to be a hundred, which he may well do) anything academic. That masterliness never traveled well-worn paths; it erupted from a volcano whose fiery torrents were drawn from Hephaestian forges, from apocalyptic depths, from the supreme laws of life itself. We felt the same message in his highly individual poetry, which in later years was followed by a completely personal and unmistakable prose. Whatever so tremendously excited us in that poetry and in his dramatic sketches cannot be logically explained, even though his writings were logically enough developed from their basic concept. I suppose it was the coexistence of rational forces with something archetypal, the boldness and vast reach of his ideas and their terse, eruptive expression, that made us respond to this writing as to a sacred cause. Here, we felt, was a creative mind which could illuminate the darkest riddles of the human psyche.

A high point in this summer of overwhelming abundance was the Kokoschka matinee inspired by Fraenger, which took place on a Sunday morning in the Frankfurt Neues Theater, with the actor Heinrich George participating. Fraenger had left Heidelberg to sit in on the rehearsals for several days beforehand. We joined him on a Saturday. He met us at the station and informed us that the great Heinrich George himself, after a performance in the Schauspielhaus, would be expecting us in his apartment.

There, towards midnight, we were confronted with an astounding sight.

Amid half-emptied glasses and bottles, George stood on the table stark naked in his baroque corpulence, playing a violin in drunken rapture. The instrument looked like a child's toy in his mighty hands and against his bull's neck. Only naked man, he bellowed in greeting to us, only naked man could function as an artist; that was ecstasy, everything else nothing but stale bourgeois fraud. Tear artists' clothes off to see if they're authentic! He was sweating like a horse. It was rather alarming to think that his slogan might reach into the concert halls.

Lying on the bed, listening peacefully, was his present mistress, who at least had a kimono on. At a sign from him she stood up and filled huge water glasses with cognac for all of us. I noticed Fraenger, who had to speak in the morning, secretly emptying his glass under the table. We others held out our glasses to be filled whenever the naked centaur commanded, and he emptied his with each of us. Finally he fell off the table, gathered himself up, and tramping over several broken glasses went unconcernedly to bed with bleeding feet. But he had first carefully placed the violin in its case. Next morning, correctly attired, he stood punctually on the stage, and delivered his difficult text without missing a word.

Before the curtain rose, and after the lights had been dimmed, Fraenger addressed the audience from a box. Wearing a black coat buttoned high, he spoke in his solemn preacher's voice about Oskar Kokoschka and his work. The audience listened politely, with an air of faint embarrassment. But an uproar broke out when the drama, *Job*, was presented. Kokoschka's stage directions state that 'Life' is to appear to the lamenting Job in the form of a naked young woman. Under George's influence this instruction was taken literally at the Frankfurt performance. Since no actress wanted the part, probably less out of prudery than from a concern for professional status (she would have only a single brief sentence to say), a shapely lady from a Frankfurt night-club had been enlisted. With a good deal of effort the sentence, 'Good day, my friend, life smiles at you,' had been drummed into her. But she hardly had the chance to speak it. Indignant catcalls—'Curtain!' 'Stop it!' 'Shame!'—interrupted her. We managed to get through the matinee, but there were many disturbances and at the end we put up a fight, for Kokoschka and the theater, against indignant stalwarts who stormed the stage with the intention of thrashing the actors. In fine fettle from this skirmish in the war for Art, we returned from ignorant Boeotia to Arcadian Heidelberg.

Heidelberg was then inhabited by gods and demigods, prophets and fools, fauns, bacchantes, and Eroses, Dionysians and Peripatetics, with a goodly sprinkling of nymphs, hetaerae, and vestals. Even the incubus was not missing; the evil, limping dwarf in the form of Joseph Goebbels, who had missed out on his share in the war because of a clubfoot and who directed his envy and hatred particularly against us, who had returned home transformed and full of new drive. Later we would be the first objects of his persecutions. In those days he was fairly unnoticeable among the crowd who attended the lectures of Friedrich Gundolf (who was Jewish). This was the summer of 1919, when Gundolf was giving his famous lectures on Romanticism. The hall was always jammed; our group, too, made a point of being there. But the lectures came at an unfortunate time, those hot hours between two and four in the afternoon when a normal person, whether he has dined well or not, feels a healthy sleepiness keyed to that time of day. Moreover, Gundolf lectured with the monotonous intensity customary in the Stefan George circle, and which required the utmost concentration from listeners, and to those who were not particularly receptive sometimes sounded like the wail of a howling dervish. I missed none of his lectures but slept through most of them and learned what Gundolf said only after they came out in print.

Even in the intellectually rarefied atmosphere of Heidelberg, the group I have been speaking of constituted a minority. The work of the great majority of the students, who in terms of those times seemed to be overcrowding the University, consisted of the same crammers and grinds which you found everywhere. But our group, the outsiders and rebels, were in good favor with the important professors and associated with them in private life—even I, who somehow could not stick it out for long in any faculty. In contrast to my friends, who from the start were working toward a specific goal, I no longer had the patience for systematic study. Moreover, my goal was different. I wanted to devour all the culture and ideas I could without having to settle on any specific branch of study. A single seminar with the leading professor of literature, a Baron von Waldberg, sufficed to make me avoid the history of literature like the measles. 'A bit of good luck,' Gundolf later said to me. 'Otherwise you would never have become a writer.'

At times Fraenger tried to urge me to do my dissertation in the field of art history. He suggested that I work with Carl Neumann, the old Rembrandt specialist and a highly intelligent, stimulating scholar, on the subject of 'Rembrandt as a director.' That was surely a congenial theme for an up-and-coming man of the theater; but here, too, I lacked the patience for systematic work. Sociology, which most of my friends regarded as the crucial field, was interesting to me only as an expression of the spirit of the age. I was deeply impressed by the scientist Hans Driesch, a small, stocky man with a heavy-nosed, Socratic-looking head, and soon I switched to zoology, biology, and botany. For a time I sat stooped over the microscope in the beginners' class. But I soon found out that the sciences were not my vocation, merely one field of interest among others. 'Learn to see, learn to read, learn to write,' Schiebelhuth said to me. 'You need no more.' And that is what I did. In my second year at Heidelberg the acceptance of my play, *Crossroad*, called me to Berlin, and that was the end of my university studies.

During this whole period, I took a lively part in the demonstrations, debates, and struggles of my friends, who were determined to engage in politics. At first these activities were still colored by the chiliastic faith in 'humanity' of the early postwar period. From Brussels came Paul Colin, who had put out a magazine called *Clarté* and was attempting to found an international society of the same name. When he spoke in the auditorium on international understanding and the overcoming of nationalism he was booed by nationalist and racist students—they were even then calling themselves *völkisch* and were already in the majority. During the discussion period these students came at him with ugly insults. But the reactionary students had no speakers of any stature to oppose to

209

our small group. We took the floor one after the other and turned the meeting into a triumph for the Belgian champion of peace.

Our opponents knew precisely who they were—and we knew them. We had been in the war long enough to understand the kind of resentment felt by men who had arrived at the front too late to be promoted to the rank of officer or to win any of the more important decorations. We also knew those who would have loved to go on playing the reserve officer all their lives, pretending to a heroism that no longer meant anything to us.

They could not accuse us of being shirkers or cowards. Mierendorff had received his Iron Cross from the Kaiser after rescuing several pieces of artillery from under the bullets of enemy infantry. Lieutenant Haubach had been mentioned several times in the orders of the day for intrepid patrols. Hans Schiebelhuth had volunteered for the chasseurs, had been wounded several times in battles against the Italians in southern Tyrol, and could boast of a number of medals. Egon Wertheimer was among the first Austrian military pilots and had twice escaped from a burning balloon by parachute. Henry Goverts had been a front-line officer from the beginning of the war. Anyone who tried to call us 'unpatriotic scoundrels' because we advocated a world of peace and social justice merely made himself ridiculous in the eyes of reasonable human beings.

We went a step further: we took fencing lessons with heavy swords in order to meet the bullies on what they regarded as their own ground. But they did not challenge us. Now and then they tried waylaying us at night to beat us up, but we were prepared for that sort of thing and stuck together like shock troopers, so that they got the worst of it.

It is an interesting sideline that we were on the best of terms with the members of the most exclusive Heidelberg fraternity, the Saxoborussians. These aristocratic young men, whose First Officer at the time was a Baron von Waldhausen, attended our performances, had a club of their own for furthering modern music, and were even interested in our political views in a distant and strictly intellectual fashion. These circles had a sense of culture and quality that kept them aloof from the roughnecks and loudmouths of the '*völkisch*' clique. Later on, too, few of them went over to the Nazis. Even if they were not exactly philosophers, they were not benighted race fanatics. The ones who made the biggest fuss about 'race' were always those who were devoid of breeding.

As far as politics went, we had no reason for optimism. The new age we were hoping to build, the age of German democracy, had begun with disappointments and setbacks.

Most discouraging of all was the feebleness with which the leaders of the new German state used their newly gained freedom. They manifested the groping uncertainty of people who have so long lived in darkness that they do not know how to live in full daylight.

Most embittering were the killings of defenseless prisoners under the eyes of the democratic government, killings committed by a brutish soldiery who called themselves the guardians of the new state.

Painful were the ineffectual and confused uprisings, such as that in Munich, followed by brutal suppression which trampled turbulently over everything progressive. In Munich the troops of General von Epp had clubbed to death, among many others, Gustav Landauer, the Shakespearean scholar, a well-meaning idealist.

Painful and disappointing was the failure of President Wilson's mission. For we Germans had been much impressed by his Fourteen Points proclaiming equal rights for free peoples—only to be met with the harshness of the victors, who made the conditions for the German Republic so hard and thereby gave aid and comfort to its domestic enemies.

Embittering was the special position of the reactionary Free Corps, which emerged from those German troops whom the victorious Allies had allowed to remain under arms in order to combat Bolshevism in the Baltic regions, and which now turned against the Republic.

Depressing and lamentable was the apathy of the German middle classes and the rise of unscrupulous speculators who made use of the emergency to create their own industrial and financial enclaves, while the German economy and currency foundered.

We did not deceive ourselves about that situation. We were well aware that the Weimar Republic had begun unpromisingly. But with a certain pride bordering on arrogance, we believed that if only we could take our turn at the helm we would turn it by a hundred and eighty degrees and steer through every storm.

My friends, and chiefly Haubach and Mierendorff, arrived at a difficult and important decision in the course of that year. After serious thought and thorough analysis of the ideological and factual premises, they decided to renounce radicalism, even though the

211

radical attitude was more in keeping with their youthful temperament. They came to the conclusion that Communism, as it was represented by the Communist Party of Germany, was bound to lead not to any progressive development, but to destruction, which would also spell the end of socialist endeavors. Carlo Mierendorff wrote his doctoral thesis on the economic policies of the Communist Party of Germany. In a paper that took him more than three years of research he went to the roots of the matter. When my friends decided to join the Social Democratic Party, they were well aware of the price they would pay. They realized that they would be involved in a two-sided struggle against right and left, and in addition would be faced with authoritarianism and hostility to youth within the ranks of the Party itself. They took this step not in order to pour new wine into old bottles, but because they were convinced that the great organization of the old party and of the trade unions was still viable, although very much in need of revitalization, and that this organism alone was capable of leading and preserving German democracy.

Never, however, did they veer into demagogic anti-Communism. To them the Soviet Union was a fact, a necessary fact for the future co-operation of nations, a state whose full right to existence had to be understood and acknowledged. Marcel Cachin, the French Communist leader, a man of high intellectual caliber, was one of their friends and advisers; they turned to him repeatedly for guidance in matters of foreign policy. But such connections did not affect their firm attitude where German politics were concerned.

Alas, there were too few of them. They were a small, though strong, brave, and brilliantly equipped, vanguard. And so during the coming fateful years they more and more became a forlorn hope.

Das Tribunal had continued merrily on its way during our first year in Heidelberg. But its founders, above all Mierendorff himself, had the wisdom to dissolve it before it had lost its fresh and original character and degenerated into a mere oppositional sheet existing solely for the sake of opposition. We marked the end of *Das Tribunal* in the Café Oper in Darmstadt; it was a celebration, for we felt no sadness, but looked forward to new and greater tasks.

Three years later—by then I already had an exciting period in the theater behind me, after my first Berlin flop—I paid a summer visit for a few weeks to my friends in Heidelberg, where most of them were preparing for their examinations. In this period there occurred an event that deeply affected us.

On June 24, 1922, Walther Rathenau, the German Foreign Minister, was assassinated by some ignorant young men who considered themselves idealists of the 'Nationalist Movement.'

Up to the end of the war Rathenau had devoted all the force of his personality to working for a German victory, or at least for an honorable peace. He had then placed his great intellectual abilities at the disposal of the German Republic, in order to restore prestige and prosperity to his country in spite of the harsh peace treaties. He was in the best and truest sense of the word a patriot, and a man whose voice also carried weight abroad.

He was murdered because he was a Jew.

The government proclaimed the day of his funeral a day of public mourning. Heidelberg University closed for the morning. The Rector's office had ordered the black, red, and gold flag of the Republic to be flown at half mast from all University buildings. While a solemn procession of democratic citizens and workers was moving through the town to lay a wreath for the dead statesman, word went around that the Institute of Physics had neither closed nor flown a flag. Professor Lenard, a nationalist, had refused to observe the period of mourning. He was not going to let his students be idle on account of a dead Jew, he said.

With a troop of working people, Carlo Mierendorff went to the Institute and in the name of the Republic and the University took the obstinate professor into protective custody. The Institute was then closed in keeping with the general order from the Rector. There was no violence, and the professor was released after a few hours. Aside from his brief period in custody, nothing happened to him.

But this incident, which preserved the dignity of the occasion and the authority of the University, created a tremendous stir among the opponents of the Republic. Carlo was indicted for 'breach of the peace' and threatened with dismissal from the University just before he was to receive his degree. But his brilliant defense and the support of the entire body of liberal professors won him unconditional acquittal.

On the evening of that day of mourning our group of friends met in the Golden Pike. We wanted to celebrate Carlo's courage and decisiveness, but we were in a despondent rather than a festive mood.

Outside, troops of fraternity men and other rowdies were marching around. For the first time we heard one of those choruses which later, when Hitler's brown gangs staged the 'national rising,' were to reverberate through the cities of Germany:

> *Verreckt ist Walther Rathenau,*
> *Die gottverdamte Judensau!*

> (Rathenau's croaked, that's fine,
> The goddamn bloody Jewish swine.)

We sat together—a small, sober, determined group. We were listening to the voices of the murderers.

1920-1933
'WHY SHOULD I CRY...?'

BERLIN was worth more than a Mass.

This city devoured talents and human energies with a ravenous appetite, grinding them small, digesting them, or rapidly spitting them out again. It sucked into itself with hurricane force all the ambitious in Germany, the true and the false, the nonentities and the prize winners, and, after it had swallowed them, ignored them. People discussed Berlin only if its spheres of influence remained impregnable to their advances, as if the city were a highly desirable woman whose coldness and capriciousness were well known: the less chance anyone had to win her, the more they decried her.

We called her proud, snobbish, *nouveau riche*, uncultured, crude. But secretly everyone looked upon her as the goal of their desires. Some saw her as hefty, full-breasted, in lace underwear, others as a mere wisp of a thing, with boyish legs in black silk stockings. The daring saw both aspects, and her very reputation for cruelty made them the more aggressive. All wanted to have her; she enticed all; and her first reaction was to slam the door in the face of every suitor. Yet the foolish, the charlatans, the purveyors of froth, were more likely to slip in through a crack and temporarily insinuate themselves into her graces—only to go flying out through the back door into the rubbish heap when their hollowness and impotence were revealed.

The others, who brought with them some genuine substance, had a harder time of it at first. They encountered her scepticism, her skittishness and disdain; usually they were rudely rejected several times before they could make good their claim to her attentions.

But once they had done so, their triumph might be absolute.

To conquer Berlin was to conquer the world.

The only thing was—and this was the everlasting spur—that you had to take all the hurdles again and again, had to break through the goal again and again in order to maintain your position. The roaring cheers of today were no guarantee against the oblivion of tomorrow.

After a success you had to change your telephone number in order to enjoy a moment's peace; after a flop the great silence settled down that same evening, and you were stranded, drifting in icy darkness. But it was always possible to make the Pole by a fresh assault, and breakfast in the sunlight.

Anyone who has lived in Berlin, especially in its theatrical world, knows why the word 'breakfast' comes to me so readily. The image calls to mind that lucid, shimmering early morning after a wakeful, wild, drunken opening night; or the mornings in the overcrowded train, when you were still half dazed from nocturnal adventures and on your way to another rehearsal, trying to catch up on a bit of sleep standing up.

There was no easy credit, no resting on cheap laurels, no way of sinking back and putting on fat. The air was always brisk, as if it were peppered, like New York's in the late autumn; you needed little sleep and never seemed tired. Nowhere else did you fail in such good form; nowhere else could you be knocked on the chin time and time again without being counted out. And if you were lucky, all this coincided with a time in your life in which every crack on the head, every blow to the solar plexus, made you the more lively and keen.

Berlin at the time still bore the imprint of the lost war. People were nervous and ill-humored. The streets were dirty and thronged with beggars, war-blinded and legless men; in passing them those shod in oxfords and spats slightly quickened their pace; George Grosz and Otto Dix have depicted such scenes.

There were black-marketeers with wide 'tango trousers' and nipped-in jackets in garish colors and loud checks; the jumpy confidence men; the winners on the stock exchange and in the literary sweepstakes, resplendent in black horn-rimmed glasses and sporting what was called the 'Bolshevik' haircut, hair brushed back flat, the nape of the neck ruthlessly shaved and thickly powdered—it was these who filled the cafés and set the tone. It was one of conscious cynicism, snotty, casual—putting a brave front on permanent insecurity. The women wore their shapeless sack dresses above the knee, their bobbed hair cut too short at the back, so that by morning a black stubble showed.

> Why should I cry when the time comes to part?
> Around the next corner there's another sweetheart

went the most popular song of the day, boastfully warbled out in every *Diele* (that was the name for those little bars with small shows that could be found on every street corner). People quivered with hysteria when the latest quotation on the dollar came out, and fired a bullet into their heads at the first quarrel with a girl friend.

Nevertheless, you could already sense something of that incomparable intensity, that stormy upsurge which within a few years made Berlin the most interesting and exciting city in Europe. That particular temper made its first appearance in cultural life, especially in the theater. The theaters outdid one another in brilliant, sensational, daring performances. A generation of extraordinary actors and directors was at work, and in spite of a flood of incompetence and sheer bluff, talent and ability were to continue to triumph.

The press was cruel, merciless, full of savage irony, yet not discouraging. For behind its cutting tone it still maintained principles, a desire for quality, a readiness to make discoveries and to further new talent. The most scathing notice, the most scornful rejection, though it might be shattering at the moment, still left open the possibility of returning to the fray with new work, of forcing a hearing, of winning out after all. The critics, like most of the literature of this period, were not conformist. Decrees on the part of one would be challenged by contrary opinions from another, and there were enough good minds among the critics to balance one another out. The game was grueling but the rules were fair.

The audiences, too, played a part in the game. The battles of wit and the juicy theatrical scandals had as much excitement as a boxing match or a six-day bicycle race. But the public also had a desire for strength, potency, potential, and were ready, after the first hoots of indignation and the jeering whistles, to be convinced and even carried away. Audiences were still to be reckoned with because they possessed both tradition and curiosity about novelty; they were a dangerous, unpredictable power which could not easily be fooled or led by apron strings.

Berlin smacked of the future. For the sake of that you were willing to brave the cold, the filth, the ill-treatment.

In January 1920 I had married my old sweetheart. The marriage was an attempt to retrace our way back to the world of childhood, from which we had been so rudely driven by the outbreak of the war.

The attempt was foredoomed. I was trying to realize again the wishes of a purer, unclouded time, although these impulses were no longer nourished by the same blood—for the old adage tells us that our blood is renewed every seven years. I was trying to cling to everything savoring of home, that was dear and familiar and hallowed by memory; the very things that do not grow along with us and that we can only truly possess again after we have eradicated the past entirely from our hearts.

My new wife and I spent the summer in Heidelberg as if we were living a sweet dream under Brecht's 'white cloud,' in the delicious delusion that everything would be this way forever: in a moonlit bliss that gave me the serenity and the strength to write a play, not just toss off the sketch of one, as I had done hitherto, but to finish one in all its incompleteness and imperfections.

It was not a good play. The original title was *Ultimate Crossroad*, which was later simplified to *Crossroad*. It was a muddled, chaotic affair, without a trace of theatrical technique. But in the spectrum of those times it seemed exciting and hopeful, and some sort of magic must have issued from its lyrical tone and its bursts of drama, for otherwise it would not have made its way to the stage and to publication, which in those days was much more difficult a feat than today.

Although it could still be classed under the vague heading of Expressionism, the influences at work were not so much the current German dramatists such as Unruh, Toller, Hasenclever, Kornfeld, Kaiser, and Sternheim. The gloriously eloquent plays of Paul Claudel, the secular 'prayers' of Francis Jammes, the animal paintings of Franz Marc, had godfathered the play, as well as—though I was quite unconscious of this—those mythic, earthy, lowly, universal characters created by Gerhart Hauptmann, who in this respect was one of my ancestors.

I sent the play to Ludwig Berger, who was making his first splash as a director in Berlin. He undertook to read the main scenes to Leopold Jessner, the manager of the Berlin National Theater. Next day I received a triumphant telegram from Berger and a second from Jessner, confirming acceptance of my play for performance in the big theater on Gendarmenmarkt. A few days later a charming letter from Kurt Wolff arrived, informing me that the play had 'made the strongest and most gratifying impression' upon him and that he would like to bring it out as a book. A contract accompanied the letter. That was in October 1920.

Jessner had taken over the former Royal Prussian Playhouse and within a year, owing to his vigorous staging in a new, monumental style, by creating an ensemble of talented young actors, and by a bold choice of plays, he had made it the most important theater in the German-speaking countries. Kurt Wolff was still the leading publisher of the younger generation, the preceptor of all modern, progressive literature. And I was not yet twenty-four. I knew that thousands of plays were submitted without being given a hearing. The repertories were dominated by a group of playwrights who had already arrived, and their production during this period was enormous. Wedekind and Strindberg, too, had only just attained full recognition; Hauptmann was regarded as old hat, but he had not been dropped by the theaters. Bernard Shaw led all the rest. It was a rarity for an unknown young author to be accepted and performed —even Brecht had to wait for years to see his brilliant early dramas staged.

It was a tremendously lucky break for me. Naturally, it carried no guarantee of success, but at the moment that was irrelevant. It was the springboard, the stirrup, the open door, admittance into a closed realm of stringent customs; it meant being 'in' the theater, part of literature. It also meant a first advance and a ticket to Berlin.

'We are happy,' the telegram had read, 'to put on your promising work as the first offering of this season, and are expecting you for the rehearsals.'

I went alone; my young wife stayed in Heidelberg for the time being, waiting until I found suitable quarters. I sat through the journey suffused with a sense of power like that of an uncrowned king secretly entering his kingdom. My fellow passengers cursed the unheated train and the government. I felt warm and wonderful.

It was a cold, nasty winter morning when I left the Anhalter Station in Berlin, carrying my suitcase. The wet streets were filled with people with turned-up collars, hastening to their offices. I was bumped, pushed, snarled at. 'Hey, watch your step or you'll be ordering a car from Grieneisen.' The full charm of this remark dawned on me only after I repeatedly saw the name 'Grieneisen' on billboards, along with a picture of a coffin. It was the largest Berlin funeral home. But I liked everything: the noise in the streets, the throngs at the streetcar stops, the sight of the cab drivers lounging over their wheels in their leather coats, taking sips from their thermos bottles and exchanging quips on the news of the day. This was the big city, and to me it was sensational and stimulating.

I had been told to go straight to the office of the management of the National Theater on Dorotheenstrasse. There I was sourly scrutinized by many officials in many anterooms, until at last a man who looked as though his job was to distribute medals to forgotten veterans of the Franco-Prussian War handed me a pass which entitled me to visit the dress rehearsal of the latest production. I was told that the rehearsal had already begun. Still dragging my suitcase after having snatched a hasty breakfast of sausages and brandy at a bar, I rushed to the theater on Gendarmenmarkt and entered through the stage door as if I were passing into the sacristy of a cathedral.

There was, of course, no sign of a dress rehearsal. But as I stole on tiptoe into the orchestra, a roar like that of a tiger rang out from the stage, so that I thought a performance was going on, for the vocabulary was that of Shakespearean curses and oaths.

'Villainous slaves! Varlets'—and so on. But it was only a quarrel and, as I soon discovered, hardly an unusual one in theatrical life. Fritz Kortner, the actor, was registering a complaint about a shaky step or a rickety landing on a staircase, and since he was in the costume and spirit of Richard III, the language of the play naturally rose to his lips.

He was raging so fearfully up there that I was utterly agog, as if beholding a madman. In the semidarkness of the orchestra distracted groups were standing around, whispering timidly, and on the stage, with the swaying tread of a circus elephant, a strangely disproportionate figure, looking larger than life, paced back and forth, now and then raising his hands placatingly and then, with a gesture of helplessness, dropping one hand to the hairless back of his head, the other to his backside. This was the famous producer Leopold Jessner.

'Gentlemen,' he began during a momentary lull in the imprecations, and in a tempered, parliamentary tone: but he said nothing further, once more lifted his hands as if in blessing, and in a flash had left the stage. A measure of calm descended, though only temporarily and only seemingly. For rows are part of the essence of theater; they are absolutely essential for letting off steam, because the theater is always functioning under excessive pressure.

At the time I knew nothing of this. But I soaked up the highly charged atmosphere and surrendered wholly to the spellbinding proceedings on the stage. This was, in fact, a production destined to make theatrical history. For the first time a play of Shakespeare was being given without change of scenery. The set consisted only of a gigantic staircase painted in tones of gray and reaching almost to the height of the proscenium, interrupted only by landings at different heights as functional planes for the different scenes and supplemented by a forestage extending beyond the footlights. There was no other décor. The play depended entirely on expressiveness of language and gesture, precision and passion. Kortner stood on the forestage speaking the prologue, with bowed head he confronted his victim's widow to court her, at the head of a few men he marched limping into battle, keeping time with dull, staccato drumbeats. When at the end, beaten, in flight, he appeared on the highest step of the stairway and with his shout, 'A horse! a horse!' he galloped as if clubfooted down the entire stairway, himself like a harried nag—then the scene crackled and sparked and the audience was in the grip of a totally realized histrionic art.

During breaks in the rehearsal I followed after the producer. Finally I was able to speak to him. He greeted me like the envoy of a foreign power, and since he could not remember my name he respectfully introduced me to all his people as 'our author,' so that I almost began to imagine I had written *Richard III.*

He beckoned to a young actress who looked enchanting in the black velvet costume of a prince, a gleaming strand of blonde hair falling over her forehead, and told her that she would be playing the lead in my play. She was Annemarie Seidel, who had made a great reputation in Munich. She, too, was new to Berlin, and this part in *Crossroad* was to be her first major role at the National Theater.

Annemarie Seidel stood very straight, with an imperious smile, neck curved back as if in unconscious self-defense. The boy's costume of doublet and hose brought out her graceful femininity. As she spoke her lines she kept her arm slightly bowed, one hand on her hip, the other resting easily on her chest. Her voice had a somewhat roughened, cracked note; early death was implied in it and in her wide-open eyes that glittered as from fever.

After the scene she came down into the orchestra. We sat side by side and covertly observed one another in the dim light. We exchanged

223

no more than a few words; once our hands touched as if by chance. At that moment, without knowing or guessing or even wanting it, my youthful marriage was over.

The rehearsal went on until late in the afternoon. At the end I asked her whether she had any plans for the evening, and she told me to wait at the stage door until she changed. She reappeared wearing a somewhat shabby camel-hair coat and a very smart little hat on her silken hair, now arranged prettily in curls. We walked together down Friedrichstrasse to Unter den Linden, she leading the way since I did not know Berlin, and into Habel's comfortable pub with its scoured wooden tables. We began drinking wine. We drank a great deal. I had money for the first month in my pocket, and did not care how much of it I left in Habel's cash register. We sat in a corner and forgot there was anyone else in the tavern. Soon I was reciting some of my poems to her. The winter dusk descended upon the roofs. Then it turned dark outside, the lights of the city went on, and we were still sitting there when they went out again after what seemed no time at all.

That night was a bitterly cold one in Berlin. The wet streets iced over, and toward morning when I attempted to find the small boarding-house in the West End where I had reserved a room, I staggered and reeled like a burlesque dancer on streets that could have been safely traversed only with ice skates. To make matters worse, I was still carrying my suitcase. Never since have I known such sheer slipperiness in any city. You had to grope your way along the walls of buildings and cling to lampposts; otherwise you kept falling on your face.

On one street corner a knot of shrieking, laughing people, evidently likewise not entirely sober, were slithering about, trying to help each other up and continually falling down again. Some, who had given up, crawled on all fours back into the café from which they had come—a well-known artists' café. Being a stranger, I wanted to balance my way elegantly past the group, but a man on his knees, holding his hat between his teeth, grabbed my leg for support so that I fell on top of him. While we rolled over and over, like wrestlers in catch-as-catch-can, in vain efforts to get to our feet again, the stranger thought it proper to introduce himself formally. He turned out to be a well-known actor who by chance was to have a role in my play; in fact, he had just received the script. Having established all this, after repeated efforts to prop ourselves up, we lost all hope of ever standing on two legs again and remained sitting on the sidewalk. We had cognac brought to us from the café, and discussed drama and the theater until the seats of our trousers froze to the pavement.

When the morning sun thawed the ice and turned the city back into a swamp, Berlin seemed to me a conquered province, and I fell into bed in glorious exhaustion.

Six weeks later the first catastrophe took place.

It was the opening of my play. I sat in the producer's box, solemnly dressed in black, and felt as if I were at a funeral—quite rightly. Outside, it was snowing; cars made slow progress; the theater filled falteringly.

From the box I could closely watch the second row from the front, where the critics were seated. It was a chilling sight. I hardly think they were all so old as they seemed to me at the time. The best known of them were probably in their fifties. To me it looked like a dismal jury of old men. Some of them seemed to have risen directly out of their graves, bearded and in evening dress, solely for the purpose of muttering some terrible curse. Far to the right, with impenetrable mask and ironically tilted snout, sat Alfred Kerr, that sinister figure whose raised or lowered thumb decided life or death for a new playwright. All the way over to the left, eyes sparkling hectically, and wearing an invisible Jacobin's cap among his moderate colleagues, sat Herbert Ihering, only thirty years old, the champion and expounder of modern drama. These two lived and wrote their criticism in closest enmity. They rent each other's favorites till the feathers flew. We unknowns, at any rate, were the plucked fowl; praise could come only from one of the two. You were sure to be scalped by the other, and since at the time Ihering was backing me, Kerr's damnation was a certainty.

Nemesis took its course. Annemarie Seidel, for whom that evening was a triumph, and the others gave their best. Ludwig Berger's staging was inventive and vigorous. His brother Rudolf had created a striking set, framed and sustained by lowering trunks of leafless beeches. But all that—and this was clearer to me from scene to scene—could not save the play. In the box with me was Else Lasker-Schüler, whose poetry I admired and loved. Ludwig Berger had told me that she had leafed through the script and come across a passage in which I spoke of the 'azure tide' of the sky. 'Ugh,' she had said, 'a poet doesn't say azure. A poet says blue.' In the meantime, however, she had read the whole play, attended a rehearsal, and become my strongest advocate. From that time on, until the last time we saw each other in Zurich in 1938, she did not miss a single one of my openings.

That evening, grateful though I was for her belief in me, she became something of a menace. The drearier the mood became, the more zealously, with growing solicitude, she stuffed chocolates into my mouth; she kept fetching them up with a loud crackling of paper from an old-fashioned reticule. Sweets disagreed with me; the chocolates were making me feel nauseous, but I could not refuse her ministrations. A single shot of whisky would have been more to the point.

Somewhere in the audience my parents and several friends were hidden. They had taken the long journey for the privilege of attending their son's disgrace. They had been seated, of all places, in the row reserved for members of the former Royal Prussian theater administration. These worthies were not the ideal audience for my play, and expressed themselves by catcalls, hisses, and, at passages intended seriously, laughter.

One lady turned to my mother and remarked: 'An unfortunate madman must have written this.'

My father left Berlin next day, confirmed in his old fear that I was a hopeless case.

The play was a total flop. The insistent applause of a few youthful enthusiasts in no way affected the icy and sometimes vocal disdain of the majority. At the end I was called to the stage by a few isolated partisans, among them Carlo Mierendorff. I stood there defiantly rigid, the target of shrill whistles and a few scattered bravos, and nodded my head several times, briefly and jerkily. In spite of everything, that was a great moment.

Next day, suffering from an infernal hangover, I read the notices. They were disastrous, with the exception of the few modernists of Ihering's persuasion, of Maximilian Harden, who was always in the opposition, and of Siegfried Jacobsohn. These few predicted that the sun would rise for me.

But for the time being the darkness was extreme.

'This incurable lyric poet,' Alfred Kerr wrote, 'who occasionally hits off a few good lines of verse, will never produce a sentence that is speakable on the stage.'

After three performances, the last two of which played only to a few spectators who had wandered in by mistake, the play vanished from the boards and was never seen again.

I felt, after that enormous forward dash and all the excitement, as if I had bounced from a high trampoline for master gymnasts head over heels into a garbage can. But the painful impact numbed neither my self-confidence nor my zest. I had no intention of giving up. Failure—that was how we felt in those days—was in itself a kind of accolade. An easy success would have been suspect. A flop was more honorable than a hit. A young playwright had to be the center of controversy; otherwise he was worthless. At least I had attained that. And I had decided that the theater was my element.

I stayed in Berlin, without money, without a job, without fame, and Berlin began to have its way with me.

I cannot possibly set down all the ways in which I tried in the next few years to earn a livelihood.

I became acquainted with Berlin from below, from the perspective of a basement, from the point of view of ugly tenements and gloomy airshafts.

My student allowance from home had ceased. I no longer wanted to attend the University: it would be a waste of time, I thought. Altogether, I had no desire to enter any of those fields which my father would have considered reasonable; therefore I could no longer live on him. That seemed to me perfectly obvious, all the more so since I knew that after his retirement from business to have continued supporting me would have involved sacrifices on his part. He, moreover, thought it his duty to discontinue assisting my foolishness. As he saw it, a man had first to establish the basis of a livelihood before he could involve himself in uncertain literary ventures, and given his premises he was perfectly right.

My point of view was different. I wanted to make my way in the theater however dark my chances seemed at the moment. I wanted to learn the craft of the theater, to live in the theater's magic circle. I wanted to be a writer, not—which might have been practicable—a journalist for some newspaper, but someone who expressed his own thoughts, come what may. I had the firm conviction that this was the right course for me and that it would turn out well. But I had no way to prove that. Therefore I had to draw the logical conclusions.

This was done without dramatic scenes, without anger and rejection, without the conflict between father and son which in those

227

days was obligatory to every aspiring young writer. This despite my father's habit of repeating—especially at meal-time, when I would be home after a long absence—'You are nothing, have nothing, can do nothing, will be nothing, and now you know it.' A little formula that was not exactly encouraging.

Even during the years of my vagabond life I had never quarreled or broken with my parents. We had merely come to a decision. I wanted to lead my own life, without any curbs on my freedom. Therefore I had to manage for myself.

That was not easy. I was able to help out as assistant director now and then at the National Theater, under Berger and Jessner, and later Fehling; but only as a volunteer. All salaried positions were taken, and the theaters in those days were not rolling in money. I could not even earn a bit as an extra because there was a union of extras and I did not qualify for admission.

In those days there did not yet exist those other fields like radio and television in which a reasonably able young writer can make a living or even do quite well for himself. Luckily for me, I venture to say. For I was spared the conflict and the temptation, after the first check for a successful radio play, to write a second and then a third, and finally to bog myself prosperously down in that branch of writing, content with a car and a nice apartment.

Those who thought they had talent for playwriting had to play for the highest stake. Their only chance was the theater. It should be obvious that in saying this I am not denigrating the importance and the artistic potentialities of radio and television. I am commenting only on their effect upon the development of young playwrights, and hence of the theater.

To be sure, there were the movies, which in those days were largely poor-quality and gangster movies. But if you were not part of the clique it was almost impossible to break into script writing. The superstition prevailed that to write a movie script you had to be acquainted with certain mysterious laws of motion pictures, laws which of course didn't exist or which any intelligent person grasped after he had been to the movies three times. Supposedly, only certain pharmacists could mix these potions. And the pharmacists did not admit newcomers because then their bosses might realize that they themselves were not indispensable. For subjects or stories, successful magazine fiction was bought or classics were appropriated. For movies on a higher level, such as Erich Pommer and others were already trying to produce, the well-known writers were sought after. I wrote at least half a dozen silent-movie scripts, of unusual or unconventional content, but was not able to place a single one.

There remained one other small branch of the metropolitan entertainment industry: the literary cabaret. But there were already several people of great talent dominating the scene in Berlin. Moreover, the ironically aggressive tone that cabaret calls for did not come naturally to me, and I was not witty enough for the devastating Berlin tone. If I did ultimately succeed in writing a ballad-like *chanson*, and placing it somewhere, the fee scarcely paid the costs of production—that is, the price for my coffee and drinks that I owed to a patient waiter, along with his tip.

I worked concurrently on two plays, a comedy in verse and a drama about the Anabaptists. The first I threw into the stove after it was finished, when I decided that it was wretched theater. The second was doomed by the subject matter. But its wild prose scenes did have some trace of theatrical craft and language. Friends, actors, and directors encouraged me, and I obstinately stuck at a task that seemed beyond my powers. I had long since used up Kurt Wolff's advances; though he never asked for repayment, I could not impose any longer on his generosity.

Now and then a poem, a small prose piece, or a playlet of mine was printed in a newspaper or magazine. The fees did not suffice to pay the rent for the furnished rooms from which I kept moving, expedited by angry landladies, into cheaper and cheaper ones, until I finally found refuge in the house in which Annemarie Seidel and her friend Lily Donnecker occupied a large apartment. The house had an unheated attic room which was not in use. I seldom used it. I lived in desperate circumstances, but I was not alone.

The parting from the sweetheart of my youth, breaking a tie and a marriage which we had both believed would be lasting, had not been easy. A good deal more went to pieces than a naïve student liaison. But for me the step was healthy, necessary, inevitable—inevitable if I were to 'grow up'—and for her this dissolution of our marriage at so early a time, after only a summer together, was more bearable than a later rift, after considerable pain and disappointment, would have been. What had come between us could no more be resisted than a natural fate. Its name was Mirl.

That was the nickname by which Annemarie Seidel was known to all her friends. In the world of the theater she also went by that name, and young Berlin intellectuals, the bold and aspiring poets and many already successful celebrities, regarded it as a distinction to belong to the 'Mirl circle.'

Although she came from a family of literati, Mirl herself did not write; she began to only in her last years. She was a far cry from a bluestocking; she was entirely and remarkably a woman. An amalgam of intellect and imagination, levity and dreaminess, soundness and strong passions, she seemed almost too singular to be real, yet gave the impression of a perfect naturalness. For grace and sophistication I have never known her equal.

Our living together began with infatuation and imaginative games, grew into a close inner communion which—even though it could not lead to marriage—lasted for a lifetime, and almost ended in tragedy, on the very brink of death. The way we lived during those two years from 1920 to 1922 was, seen from today's perspective, the essence of Berlin bohemianism. But we did not think of it that way at the time, for we had no inclination to glamorize ourselves and our life.

Mirl, too, was no financial genius, and her salary at the National Theater remained pegged at the level of a beginner. Her efforts to make a little extra by appearances in cabaret failed, in spite of her close ties with the performers, poets, and composers of this 'minor art,' for though she had a great feeling for music she simply could not carry a tune. Moreover, even then she was troubled by a recurrent dry cough which made it hard for her to last through long parts, such as that of Ariel in *The Tempest*. When she was acting in the evening, I sat in a bar opposite the National Theater and waited for her. A fatherly waiter let me run up my checks until one or another of my sporadic sources of income enabled me to settle the bill. I met quite a few such fatherly waiters and tavernkeepers in a Berlin so often decried as tough and unfeeling, and I have never forgotten them.

When she had time off, we wandered like gypsies around the big city, or sat long nights in her apartment with our group of friends.

The dearest of these was Walter Mehring. Born and brought up in Berlin, he epitomized in his early writing the *élan vital* of the city and its highly charged intellectuality. His chansons, which at once shocked and enraptured the cabaret audience—especially when he delivered them himself in his sharp, somewhat nasal voice—were the quintessence of Berlin. They dealt with every aspect of the city, all its strata and classes, with strong emphasis on the seamy side of things, yet suffused with poetry and brilliance. His verses had an elegance of language such as is ordinarily found only among the French. Even before Mehring became half Parisian, he was a Parisian Berliner in his poetry. He looked like one, too: very small, thin as a comma, with a delicate face and a nose sharpened to a very fine point.

Sometimes we were invited, or merely tagged along, to one of those rowdy Berlin parties where there was no special need to know the host, who would come from the world of high finance, or would be a stockbroker or a movie-director. Ordinarily the great man did not know half of his visitors. He was content if they were artists, or thought they were, ate up his platters of cold meat, and drained his innumerable bottles. These affairs were a mixture of sport, snobbery, showing off, and generosity. You could go to the homes of such princes and patrons and drink yourself senseless, but you could not borrow from them; they wanted to have something and see something for their money, even if it was only a bathroom splashed with vomit, or a pair of prominent lovers who had passed out in the host's own bedroom. We aspirants shuffled along on the edges. Towards morning, if we had not had enough of it all and left early, we were swept out by servants and cleaning women.

The most interesting and attractive Russian restaurant in the Berlin West End was a Ukrainian-Caucasian place called, after a national folk song, 'Allaverdi.' If you were known there and had a free spender with you, you could stay after the official closing hour. When the upstairs restaurant was closed, you descended a winding staircase behind the bar into the cellar, where, as in the speakeasies of New York during Prohibition, small tables and folding chairs had been set up among the racks of bottles and the kegs of beer. These tables were occupied until daylight. Drinks were mostly champagne, brandy, and whisky, at high prices. To make these strong beverages go down more easily, platters of smoked salmon and sturgeon, Russian pickles and marinated mushrooms were handed around. A single gypsy violinist played softly to the accompaniment of a bass balalaika. One night, when we were there with a patron, a curiously excited whispering and buzzing arose among the Russians. It passed from table to table. Then there was a sudden silence, and many of the men stood up to bow in the direction of a small sofa in one corner. There sat an inconspicuously dressed woman with a silk shawl over her head. It was Pavlova. She was obviously in no way annoyed by this classless homage. On the contrary, she suddenly rose and with an expressive gesture removed her shawl and the jacket of her suit, under which she was wearing a sleeveless white blouse. In a moment all the table and chairs had been whisked into an adjacent cellar. Everyone crowded against the walls and bottle racks. Pavlova whispered briefly with the violinist, who began the melody of *The Dying Swan*, and for five minutes she floated about that narrow space like a phantom, then with a deep bow of her whole body sank to the stone floor. The cheers that burst out seemed on the point of shattering the vaulted ceiling, but she silenced them with another gesture of her lovely arms, then returned to the small sofa and her companions. Thereafter, no one looked in her direction.

Berlin was much intrigued by the various types of Russians who added special nuances to its rich spectrum—the exiles who lived on what diamonds they had smuggled out, or earned their keep as waiters, peddlers, decorators, and gigolos; the Bolsheviks, who had just come to power; and the other assorted revolutionaries still fighting for power, all of whom appeared to us in a thoroughly romantic light. The anarchistic, adventurous note of the period of exile and conspiracy was still alive among the early Russian Communists. Although they lived only for their political work and did not avail themselves of the proclaimed 'sexual freedom' and the 'right of every human being to his own body,' they were far removed from the later type of respectable moralistic Party regular, the patriotic model Comsomol all head and no private parts who seems to consider instinctual life, unless it takes place along the quiet Don, a manifestation of late-capitalist decadence. Many members of the foreign missions lived quite freely with the female members of their staff in those days. Karl Radek coined the witticism, 'First came the matriarchate, then the patriarchate, now we have the secretariat. . . .'

We read the ultra-liberal book by lovely Madame Kollontai, *Love in the New Russia*. We were impressed—far more than by our own drab leaders—when a Berlin première was attended by the Soviet Minister of Education, Lunacharsky, the creator of the 'Prolet Cult,' with his elegant wife, usually dressed in the products of Parisian *haute couture*.

During those years Stanislavsky came to Berlin with his unsurpassable company to give performances of Tolstoy, Gogol, and

Gorki and dramatizations of the great Dostoevsky novels. The plays and the characters were familiar to us; one did not need to know Russian to perceive the artistic quality of his staging and his actors. Tairov came with his 'Unleashed Theater'; the Meyerhold troupe came; the Yiddish Theater came and the Habimah with its unforgettable performance of *The Dibbuk*. Somewhere later there was a Russian cabaret in Berlin, The Bluebird. Every night it put on its show in German spoken with a Slavic singsong. The place was always jam-packed, the costumes and turns were colorful and fantastic and stamped by the particular genius of the *conférencier* Nyushny.

Then there was the new Russian movie, which for a time seemed to promise that the proletarian revolution, combined with the originality and artistic drive of the Russian people, would revolutionize all the modes of artistic expression and usher in a new kind of cultural and intellectual freedom. We saw Eisenstein's *Potemkin* and Pudovkin's early movies, and were overpowered at once by the mythic simplicity of their content and by their artistic quality and inventiveness. For the things they showed had never before been known to the screen. There were evenings when an unknown young writer like myself could sit at a table with writers and directors of the stamp of Eisenstein and Pudovkin—for they all visited Berlin—and listen worshipfully to their talk. I also met Ilya Ehrenburg in Berlin at that time. He was just back from a trip to South America, and I shall never forget that he gave me a huge black Danneman Brazil cigar—the first one I had ever smoked.

Thus there was the everlasting influence of the Eastern Russian temperament upon Berlin's cultural life, and that influence was more productive, more stimulating, than most of the things that came out of the West at the time. There was also the Russian Tearoom on Nürnberger Strasse, where—to our astonishment and delight—the sugar stood on all the tables in large bowls, to be used freely, and when you ordered a glass of tea, pastries were presented too in a large basket, to be enjoyed freely as well. Thus Russian grandeur invaded a Prussian world that was narrow by tradition, and narrower still under the present conditions of economic want. We never knew or cared whether the invasion was one of Tsarist *noblesse* or Bolshevist libertarianism. We loved the Russians and felt a kinship with them in our intellectual and moral aspirations, and in our own libertinage. As yet we knew nothing about the

233

despairing suicides of the two men whom we regarded as the leading poets of the new Russia, Mayakovsky and Esenin.

Such heady experiences were only moments in a long, cold winter when for the first time sheer economic distress gripped me by the throat. The fact that I was not living alone kept me from feeling misery or futility, but it sharpened my awareness of material need. For of course I wanted to be the one who would rescue us from our predicament. I still did not know what further extremities awaited me.

Toward spring Mirl's cough had grown so much worse that the doctor ordered her to take a prolonged vacation from the theater and, if possible, to seek out sea air. I had unexpectedly come into a small inheritance consisting of some valuables left me by my grandmother, who had died during the war. They had been lying in a safe deposit box in Mainz, and I had completely forgotten that I had reached my majority and could ask for them to be turned over to me. Never was an inheritance spent more quickly or more necessarily.

The doctor had recommended the Baltic—lacking foreign currencies, Germans could not even think of the Mediterranean in those days. In rain and snow we traveled to the Kurische Nehrung, that string of lovely sandbars along the Baltic coast. We had been told of the fishing village of Nidden. Since there were no steamers yet, with the ice only beginning to break up, we traveled the last part of the way in a horse-drawn wagon which served the isolated villages along the Nehrung. For many hours we rode through woods and bumped over sandy paths across the dunes. It was a ride into a primeval world. Once we had to make a longish stop when a bull elk stood in the way eyeing us, its great palmate antlers lowered. The driver considered it prudent to stay where we were until the animal became bored. Towards evening we saw the moon rising above the tall dune which is said to have covered an entire village, one that lost all its inhabitants at the time of the plague. The changing countryside, beach and forest, quicksands and moors, confirmed our rapturous feeling of having come to the right place.

Spring burst forth almost with our arrival—a spring of the sort that occurs perhaps once in a decade. This was to be the famous vintage year of 1921. The sky arched in cloudless blue over all of Europe. For months not a cloud was seen.

We could not have led a life of such precious, paradisiacal solitude on an island in the South Seas. From the end of March to the
end of June we were the only guests in the village. Outsiders came
there only during the summer holidays, in July or August. It was
considered to be too cold there in the spring. But this spring the sun
blazed. We could bathe naked in the Baltic, for we reached our
solitary beach by way of a disused path through the woods, and not
another soul went down to the beach at this time. The fishing season
began then, with the young eels passing through the Haff. In the
evenings we would see the fires that were used for smoking the day's
catch. The village consisted of wooden houses roofed with thatch,
many of them painted in bright colors, their gables decorated with
carved elk or horse heads. There was also a wooden village church.
The inn was glorious; it always smelled of grog or the pure, strong
aquavit of the district which was called, simply enough, *Klares*—
'clear.' In the evenings we drank with the innkeeper, who, when
he had tanked up sufficiently, became very much of a freethinker
and regaled us with his less-well-known versions of East Prussian
songs. For breakfast there were huge plates of bacon and homemade
sausages. Everything was very cheap. We would have liked to stay
on forever. In the evenings, I worked on my Anabaptist play; by
day I lay in the sun with Mirl. But her vacation was unpaid, and my
'inheritance,' the proceeds of my grandmother's rings which I had
sold in Berlin, melted away. Mirl's cough vanished and she became
as tanned as a fisherman's daughter. When summer came, we took
the ship across the Haff and watched the coast of the Nehrung
vanish. I have never seen it again.

Berlin was noisy, hot, and dusty. We were planning to marry but
had no money. Mirl had a few more evenings of performances. At
the last performance of *The Tempest*, during which she had to dash
up and down steep iron steps behind the stage in order to appear
at a height at one moment, down on the floor at another, her winged
shoe caught in the iron bars of a step. She fell from a considerable
height to the stage floor. Since she had no external injury and had
broken no bones, she went on to the end of the play, half stunned.
That night she lost the child that had been conceived in the spring.
She was sick and miserable. The theaters closed in July; although
she had a contract to resume in September, there was no pay for the
intervening period. She had to give up the apartment, which was too

235

expensive to keep through the summer months. I still had my wedding ring, and my divorced wife, with whom I have remained friendly to this day, sent me hers because she knew that I needed things to pawn. Gold fetched a good price in those days. The amount I received from the pawnshop just sufficed for tickets to Munich. There things would be better.

Mirl's mother was a fragile, lovable old lady—or what we then considered old. She was one of those women who, having lost their husbands early in life, give the impression that they are still in communication with them. Sometimes she smiled absently as if she were seeing or hearing someone whom others did not notice.

She lived on a modest pension in a fine, spacious Munich apartment. Again and again I have observed that people in reduced circumstances prefer to give up everything imaginable rather than their apartments or their houses, even though they no longer have anyone to serve in the dining room and can only boil an egg in the spotless kitchen. A house, an apartment, is a psychic shell, a magical web, that keeps woe and pity at a distance and helps a person maintain his pride.

Mirl was able to crawl off for a few weeks into the room which she had occupied as a child and look after her health. Her only winter coat, which she now did not need, and a few valuable first editions which she owned, went off to the pawnshop, only to be redeemed out of her first autumn pay-packet.

I could not live there, of course, but only visit. We were seriously thinking of getting married in Berlin as soon as *The Anabaptists* was put on, for we had no doubts that it would be done and would be a success. But we did not want to agitate her mother with such premature prospects.

I stayed with Lotte Pritzel, Mirl's best friend. She was a brilliant maker of dolls, creations which inspired a good many articles and essays at the time. They were delicate things of wax and cloth, marked by subtle elegance and a touch of childlike depravity, like some of Beardsley's figures—though not at all obscene—and because of that singular note all the more attractive, even to solid, middle-class buyers. But she could not or would not commercialize her curious art, and so she lived her bohemian life on Clemens-Strasse, in Schwabing, with a man named Dr Pagel who looked half like a pirate captain, half like a Dostoevsky character (but without a beard). In his earlier years, it was said, he had been a brilliant physician and scientist. Now he used his medical license chiefly to write out prescriptions for cocaine and morphine—above all for him and his doll queen. During the nights, when I sat in her studio with my manuscript spread out on her sewing table among pretty snippets of silk and batiste, or when I tried to sleep on a mattress that had been laid on the floor for me, I could hear the two of them in the adjoining room in that state of hyper-lucidity, that state of mind which makes the white powder so irresistible to addicts. They would be talking, murmuring, quarreling for the fun of it. Sometimes there would be an outcry: 'I'm going! I've had enough!' Then the door would slam, then another door slammed; there would be a noisy tugging and pulling on the stairway, which would pass into a purring murmur, and the whole game would start over again. In time I learned to sleep quite well in spite of it. By day they looked sallow and had inflamed nostrils, but seemed perfectly happy.

'Coking' was a great fad in Schwabing in those days, and also in some of the Berlin circles on the fringes of the arts. It was regarded as an interesting vice, the vice of geniuses; and some of those who succumbed were destroyed by the drug. Addicts are missionaries, always out to capture the souls of others; they would like to make everyone believe that their church alone brings salvation. They have to be fended off. Although I was thrown in with people who sniffed cocaine in great quantities, I myself never indulged in it. The whole idea was repulsive to me, if only on account of the inflamed nostrils. Mirl, too, never touched so much as a pinch. Drinking was enough for us; in her it led to a lucid abstractedness, in me only very rarely to a hangover. I could always take alcohol, have remained faithful to it, and so far as I know it has never done me any harm.

Soon the summer in Munich was over. Before we returned to Berlin, Mirl and I spent a few days at Kochel Lake. From there I wrote a letter to Ludwig Berger, a letter I saw again only recently, when he published it on the occasion of my sixtieth birthday. I wrote: 'I have certainly kicked over all the traces, but I am glad because I feel that only this way can I make progress. There is no track at all, no path, no model, no Gogol's overcoat, no laws . . . there is only prodigality, the thousand-armed godhead who reappears in ever new avatars. There is nothing at all absolute, only self-discipline, which everyone must have in the proportions that are right for himself. Basically it doesn't matter a damn to me whether I shall someday be pounding stones or be a play-reader. The essential thing is elsewhere.'

Matthäi-Kirch-Strasse in Berlin was then a quiet, substantial residential area (a few years ago it was in ruins; I don't know what its condition is today), actually rather an oblong plaza with solid old houses, at the end of which stood the brick church of St Matthew from which it got its name.

In house No. 4 on this street we found an amazingly cheap apartment, for it was in the basement, below the concierge's booth. It consisted of one large room, whose barred windows extended only halfway up above the front garden, so that the place was always in twilight. Mirl had a few good pieces of Biedermeier furniture with which we furnished it quite comfortably. We borrowed a rug. I had a windowless cubicle, with a bare bulb suspended from the ceiling, next to the coal bin. The furnace room radiated just enough warmth to take the edge off the cold if we left the door open. In this furnace room stood an old tin tub into which we could pour hot and cold water. After bathing we had to tip it into a sink and scrub it out. Adjacent was a toilet which was also used by the concierge's family. Someone had lent us an electric stove, but out of thrift we rarely used it. In this apartment, which we regarded as a wonderfully lucky find, we spent Christmas and headed for the gloomy early spring of 1922.

I now devoted my time and energy to earning our basic livelihood. For a few weeks I had something almost like a job—a dispiriting episode. An acquaintance put me in the way of some miserably paid work in an unknown editorial office maintained by some obscure men. It was called ITA, that is, International Telegraph Agency. I never found out what its real business was. The 'office' was situated in the attic of a tenement in the remotest North End of Berlin; every morning I had to set out on a global tour to reach it. There was no elevator, of course, and the stairs were in such a state that the banisters were missing from the upper stories. Only the sure-footed could risk the climb. I sat there with a narrow-lipped woman secretary who looked and smelled sour. We had large pastepots and shears, and our job was to clip from all imaginable international newspapers every item referring to the foreign or domestic trade of the Baltic nations which had won their independence after the war. A swarthy gentleman came twice a week, and under his supervision we would work up highly dubious 'world telegrams': reports and articles with statistical documentation in which a few zeros more or less apparently did not matter. I suspected that they were being used for anti-Polish propaganda purposes. I became more and more allergic to the whole thing. One day the swarthy man informed me that ITA was to be temporarily closed at the end of the current week. Breathing easier, and unemployed, I went down those perilous flights for the last time. The stairs had at any rate given me the idea for a murder movie which I dashed off in a single night. It would have been so easy to lure someone up there on some pretext, knock him down the stairs, and escape over the roof. But the script was rejected on the grounds of improbability.

Once Albert Steinrück, the actor, a grand personality of the great days of the theater, found a job for me as an extra at UFA, which was then doing a movie (silent, of course) on Frederick the Great. My sole qualification was my command of military horsemanship. I became a soldier again, but this time in a past century; I helped an old Prussian cavalry regiment win the Battle of Leuthen.

There was almost more waiting than in the real army.

The whole affair would have been pure comedy if it had not taken place under financial pressure. Later, after I had written *The Captain of Köpenick*, I was asked how it was that I, a Rhinelander, had been able to imitate Berlin jargon and humor so credibly. Those three days in the dressing room, the canteen, and on the 'battlefield' with Berlin horse-cab drivers, garbage men, stableboys, and discharged jockeys—who made up the army in the Frederick the Great movie— would have provisioned me for a dozen Berlin comedies.

At the height of the campaign it turned out, after a costume historian inspected the scenes already filmed, that we were wearing the wrong breeches, a kind that had been adopted half a century later, so we had to fight the whole battle once more in the correct breeches and repeat the great parade, and therefore we had more pay-days.

When the Seven Years' War was over I sat around the movie exchange for days, trying to hire myself out as cowboy, mounted messenger, or postilion, but the competition was too great, the prospects were too meager, and I had to abandon the attempt.

Another enterprise, financially the most promising one, came to nothing—thank God, for otherwise I would probably not be around to tell the tale. I met an acquaintance of mine from the war named Egon Steger who had been an aviator and who was now a mail pilot flying one of the old crates which were still left in Germany and which only an insane optimist could call airworthy. The manufacture of new planes was still forbidden to Germany by the terms of the Treaty of Versailles. This man had come across the idea of staging parachute jumps at the Tempelhof airfield on Sunday afternoons, using a parachute which he had designed and made himself. He found a 'manager' who was prepared to advance the fuel and advertising costs. He proposed that I go into partnership with him—that is, for half of the net profit I would jump several times from the crate which he was piloting, and entertain people by the prospect of smashing myself to pieces. On the first trials, which we undertook with a dummy, the parachute opened twice and twice did not open, but my friend insisted that trouble lay with the way the dummy jumped. I was so desperate that I almost consented—behind Mirl's back. But then there occurred a little incident that saved me. In order to make me feel secure in the air, the pilot took me along on a mail flight to Hanover. On the way back we ran into a thunderstorm that tossed the fragile machine around like an orange peel in the ocean surf. I was strapped into the auxiliary seat. The motor gave out; my friend made an emergency landing on a potato field. We capsized and climbed out of the plane, badly shaken but unhurt. Cursing horribly, my friend tried to repair the plane, and soon we were almost at loggerheads since I am completely inept mechanically and could not distinguish between the large nut and the small monkey wrench. Fortunately, he himself had to give up soon; German aviation had one plane and one pilot less, for immediately after this potato-field incident Steger turned his talents to insurance and our parachute project came to nothing.

Towards the end of the winter Mirl played again in the National Theater. But she could barely get through the rehearsals, in which I frequently took part, and she managed the opening night only by taking large quantities of codeine and other drugs that the theater's doctor urged on her. The nasty cough had appeared again, in a worse form than in the previous year; it was accompanied by bouts of fever and acute chest pains. By now even a spell on the Baltic seacoast would not have sufficed to restore her to health.

Among our acquaintances was a young doctor who did not

ask for money and presumably was not very competent, for he diagnosed severe bronchial catarrh, which he said could be cured by resting in bed and compresses. He obtained an inhalation apparatus for her, and prescribed various syrups and herbal teas. We thought that hot red wine with rum would set her up. But her condition did not improve, nor was it helped by a drive in a horse carriage owned by a fellow I knew from 'Frederick the Great's army' and who took us out gratis.

That was our last happy day. A pallid March afternoon sun was shining. Mirl, in a soaring euphoria, let herself be driven out to Grunewald Lake. We ate in the Hundekehle restaurant and spent far too much money. I bought her violets from a flower seller prowling around the restaurant. We let our driver drink as much beer as he could hold. For half a day we were princes. Mirl's cough seemed to have vanished after a bottle of Burgundy. At night it came back, much worse. She had to ask the theater for sick leave, first for a week, then for longer. The theaters paid only a month's salary in case of illness; then there was no further income. She had no insurance—people did not think of such things in those days, or perhaps it was we who did not. She lay in bed, in the feeble light of a floor lamp, and grew steadily weaker. I would carry her into the furnace room for her bath; then she had me bring her cosmetics to the bed and made up. Every night she would begin to shiver with fever. I no longer believed the diagnosis of bronchial catarrh. I wanted to send her to her mother or her sister, but she did not want to leave our happy home and remained convinced that she would be able to return to the stage in a week or so.

I made desperate efforts to raise money, but could not find enough for a good doctor and proper care. I would have stolen or robbed a bank if I had been able to. The young doctor came often, drank the last of our whisky, and said that she was getting better. The March rain dripped into the front yard, the concierge no longer kept the furnace running very high, and the room became damp. The young doctor said that damp air was good for the bronchia.

When I returned one day after vainly going around to editorial offices and movie studios, she was gone, along with some of her clothing and her suitcase—the bed was empty. There was a note on the pillow that I was to call the Hotel Prinz Friedrich-Karl on Dorotheenstrasse and ask for a Herr van Hoboken. The note was in an unfamiliar handwriting.

I had heard about this man from her. He was the son of a Dutch millionaire, in his mid-thirties, who had rented a villa in Munich and liked to play host to Schwabing artists. But there was more to him than that. He studied music, and since he himself was neither instrumentalist nor conductor nor composer, he devoted his life and part of his fortune to musical research, to reconstructing the lost 'original line' in classical music, using the original scores of the great masters, or their writings, to rescue the music from nineteenth-century 'interpretations.' His books on Joseph Haydn and his Haydn Archive, the product of much earnest labor, are still regarded by professionals as indispensable, a significant contribution to the musical history of the eighteenth century. At that time we did not know anything of this work, however. We regarded him as a rich amateur and a charming host who spent his countless gulden on colorful revels.

He had admired Annemarie Seidel since her appearances in the Munich theater, and treated her with a courteous fondness to which she responded in kind.

When I finally reached him at his hotel, after innumerable calls, I heard what had happened. He had come to Berlin for a brief visit and wanted to call on her. The management of the National Theater informed him that she was sick, and gave him her address. When he appeared there in the morning with a bouquet of flowers, he saw at once how seriously ill she was. In half an hour he had brought the greatest specialist in Berlin to her bedside. The specialist declared that she must be removed to a hospital at once, that she had a grave case of pneumonia and pleurisy, perhaps something worse, and that not a moment was to be lost. With utter selflessness, without even realizing the nature of his feelings for her, Hoboken undertook the necessary steps.

An ambulance carried her to the best and most expensive hospital in Berlin. There is no doubt that by acting swiftly he saved her life. Thereafter I met Hoboken almost every night. He had me to dinner and kept me informed of her condition. He had been warned against me, and told that I was a kind of gypsy or semi-Indian, carried a long knife, and was murderously jealous.

But now we both shared the same anxiety. We became friends.

Mirl was not allowed to have visitors. The puncture treatment of the pleurisy put a fearful strain on her; her life was in constant danger. Moreover, a 'moist spot' had been discovered in her lungs,

242

and I knew what that meant. Only a long, thorough cure, complete rest, change of climate, a stay in Davos or in the south, could save her from tuberculosis, according to the medical ideas of the time. I could not offer her these things, and she herself could not afford them. It was the end.

But I wanted to remain near her as long as she was in danger, and perhaps see her once more. After a few weeks had passed, I was able to visit her in the fine hospital in the West End—but only once, for her fever was rising. We were gay at this meeting. Towards the end, we recalled the verses from Shakespeare's *Julius Caesar*, where Brutus parts from Cassius:

> If we do meet again, why, we shall smile;
> If not, why then this parting was well made.

Over the decades we have repeated these lines again and again, whenever we have met somewhere and parted once more.

Even while she was still sick, I had turned to a new source of livelihood which was to bring me into graver danger than the parachute jumping. That, too, was proposed to me by a war comrade I had run into by chance. A former officer, he was now dressed with suspicious elegance. It turned out that he had become the manager of several illegal gambling casinos and night clubs.

In my desperation I was eager enough when he held out the prospect of earning good money in Berlin night life. I became a tout for those night clubs in Friedrichstadt which were run illegally in private homes after the official closing time. At the hour when the better restaurants had just closed, I had to lurk in the area between Kranzler Ecke and Potsdamer Platz accosting the kind of men who looked as if they were willing and able to pay for this kind of entertainment and conduct them to these secret places. There were two things to avoid: the competition of other touts, which could take a brutal turn, and the attentions of the police. It did not require much psychological awareness to recognize suitable customers. The best of them were provincials, businessmen or gentlemen farmers, occasionally Reichstag deputies who were staying in Berlin for a short time and wanted a taste of metropolitan pleasures. The amusements offered by the night clubs were distinctly modest and entirely disproportionate to the price or the risk of being picked up in a police raid. Ordinarily the establishment was situated in a ground-floor apartment facing a courtyard rather than the street, and the place was changed weekly. You identified yourself by a special knock at the door or window, then passed down darkened corridors and stumbled over unexpected steps. The whole mood was adventurous; the patron felt like the hero of a detective story, which stimulated the consumption of champagne. A muted phonograph whined nasally, and a few girls of indeterminate age and origin (you could not tell whether they were janitors' or generals' daughters) wearily and unimaginatively performed 'nude dances'—sufficiently covered by veils of cheap cloth to keep the men company at their tables and inspire them to larger orders. The whole thing might easily have been considered as a social-welfare association. With the exception of certain mistakes in addition on the check, nothing criminal went on, and I had no need to feel myself a member of the underworld when I whispered to the men in their heavy ulsters: 'How about another nice little night club tonight? Intimate show, reasonable prices...'

Then I had to put up with their contemptible indecision, and afterwards the painful procedure of accepting the tip. It was not exactly what I had in mind as a vocation for life. If I stuck at it, that was more a reflection of my raging desperation, which in turn came from deeper, more dangerous sources than sheer lack of money.

One night my boss suddenly transferred me—perhaps in order to let me work my way into a higher income bracket, perhaps because I was not especially gifted as a tout—to Berlin's West End. He himself took me there in a cab and filled my pockets with several packets of cigarettes and cigars, but above all with small folded squares of white paper, like the usual headache powder packets which were sold in chemists' in those days.

He gave me brief, hasty instructions on how I was to act. I was to walk slowly up and down the street, just like a streetwalker, calling out softly, 'Tssigars, tssigarettes'—with a sharp, hissing *s* sound. That, he told me, was the signal for the customers who would identify themselves by sniffing loudly through their noses. When they did, and paid a considerable sum, I was to press one of the paper squares into their hands along with the cigars or cigarettes. When I asked what was in them, he said 'Snow,' but added reassuringly that in reality the stuff was only salt mixed with crushed aspirin, therefore hardly illegal—but all the same I should keep a sharp eye out for the police and if neccessary assert that I had found the packets in a cab. Nothing could happen to me then, and if anything did he would compensate me accordingly, provided I did not mention his name. Then he jumped into the waiting cab and was gone.

The whole business worried me extremely. I knew quite well what was meant by 'snow' or 'coke.' There was no way of telling whether he was really engaged in a double deception and fooling the cocaine-starved buyers with salt, or whether he had told me that to quieten my fears.

Touting for the night clubs had seemed relatively innocent. What was it to me if some tipsy provincial awoke next morning with a throbbing head and an empty wallet? But now I asked myself whether I was not really committing an unjustifiable act, ignoring a boundary that should not be crossed, not only legally, but morally and ethically. But I needed money; perhaps if I were solvent I could still save what seemed to me more precious than life—though this thing had in fact already run its course and had no future. It was senseless, but at such times one clings to senselessness, to madness and last desperate schemes. Moreover, there was no turning back now. I should have thought the business over sooner. But everything had happened too swiftly.

'Tssigars, tssigarettes,' I hissed under my breath, rehearsing, as I squeezed my way past the lifeless, unlighted shop windows of the Kaufhaus des Westens, the great Berlin department store. Suddenly a slim, black-haired young woman confronted me. Her face, heavily made up and thickly powdered, looked like a mask in the glow from the street lamp. She was swinging her pocketbook and letting it slap against her brief skirt in what seemed to me a hostile, provocative manner. The eyes in her mask scrutinized me closely. 'What are you doing here?' she asked in a faintly Slavic accent.

'What's that to you?' I said in a carefully rehearsed imitation of the Berlin night-life manner.

She shrugged.

'Watch how you go, sonny boy,' she said. 'The police are pretty sharp around here. I suppose you're new to the business?'

I turned my back on her and walked in the opposite direction. I'm quitting, I thought. I'll give the stuff back and call it quits. If I only knew where the boss is now. . . .

Then I noticed that a broad-shouldered man in a light trench coat, who had been standing in one of the entrances of the closed

245

department store, was watching me and slowly beginning to follow me.

I felt hot under the collar. If only I didn't have that damned stuff in my pocket. I walked faster, passing several strollers. The man in the trench coat did the same. Suddenly the girl was at my side again. 'Take my arm,' she whispered, 'and act like you're one of my tricks. Come on, hurry up!' she snapped, her voice still low.

Without fully grasping the situation, I did as she said. Taking her arm, I began chattering loudly with her and laughing.

We sauntered across Wittenbergplatz and down a few more streets. The man in the trench coat watched us irritably until we vanished from his view.

Then the girl drew me into the entry of a building.

'You know,' she said, 'you must be the biggest dope that ever walked. Did you really think you could get away with it?'

'I don't know what you mean,' I said, still mistrustful.

'That one over there knows,' she said grinning. 'He's from the plain-clothes squad. Nothing he can do to me because I'm registered. But he had his eye on you right along; he would have picked you up first thing.'

'What for?' I asked obstinately, although by now I was convinced that the woman really wanted to help me.

'Come on, quit fooling about,' she said, lighting a cigarette. 'You aren't that good an actor. So happens I know Gustav, the fairy that was with you in the cab. I guess your lamp's run out of oil, eh?'

She tapped the region where I carried my wallet.

'Sure, sure,' she said, 'nobody can see at night. Let's have a look at your stuff,' she commanded in an abrupt, matter-of-fact tone.

Since I realized that she knew the whole story anyhow and that I was at her mercy if she wanted to inform on me, I took the little packets from my pocket—glad to get rid of them.

She began counting them, her eyes assuming a greedy expression. 'How much is your boss asking for a shot?'

I told her.

'Wait here,' she said hastily. 'I won't run out on you. I have a connection over there in the Femina Café; he'll take the whole lot.'

I remained standing in the dark entry, and lit one of my 'tssigarettes.'

Half an hour later she came back. She seemed in excellent humor and smelled of brandy.

'I bamboozled him,' she said. 'He was high already and didn't even count.'

She pressed the money into my hand—more than I was supposed to deliver.

'Forget it,' she said when I started to thank her.

I shook her hand.

'Where are you going now?' she asked.

I shrugged. I really didn't know. I didn't want to go 'home' to the cellar apartment on the Matthäi-Kirch-Strasse where Mirl's bed still stood and a few of her things were hanging. I had already spent a few nights in a cheap hotel near the Potsdam Station.

'You can come with me,' she said. 'I live in this house—it's got central heating. I've finished work for the night.'

She saw me hesitating.

'Don't worry,' she said, laughing. 'It won't cost you a thing. I don't like staying alone.'

'I know how you feel,' I said.

The room was no better and no worse than all the others in this neighborhood. Beat-up, formerly respectable furniture, a brass bed with lace coverlet, several wretched oil paintings on the walls. I recall that the wallpaper had a pattern rather like the clubs in a deck of playing cards, dark against light brown. I could not stop counting them.

'My name is Lyuba,' she said, tossing off her jacket. 'My family came from Warsaw, but I won't tell you they were Polish nobles.' She continued undressing and took a bright-colored kimono from her closet.

'You don't have to come on all that fast,' she said when I sat down on a chair without going near her. 'Don't you like my looks?'

She had swiftly removed the paint from her face and I could see that she was quite pretty and far from old.

'I do,' I said, 'but I've got another girl on my mind.'

'And it's all over with her,' she said, taking something from her pocket. I saw that it was one of the packets she had evidently kept for herself.

'Don't you "coke"?' she asked.

I shook my head.

She took a sniff; her eyes darkened.

'That's good stuff,' she said. 'Makes you forget everything. Try it.'

247

'I don't want to forget anything,' I said.

She took two glasses and a rectangular bottle from the closet. It was Polnischer Reiterschnaps, a strong, bitter herbal liqueur. I recall the picture of a cavalryman on the label.

I tossed down one glass, then another.

'What made you think it was over?' I asked.

She laughed.

'Teach me something about men! If you were happy, you'd be treating me different. Then you feel like gods; one more or less don't matter. Then you tell yourselves you're not cheating on anyone, you're just spreading some joy around. But when it's over you discover all of a sudden that she was the only one.'

Yes, it was over. She was so right and had read the situation better than I could.

She refilled the glasses and suddenly gripped my shoulders.

'Give up,' she said. 'Clear out. What do you want with that fairy Gustav and all his rackets? You'll only go to the dogs. It would be a shame. You could do something with yourself, you're still young.'

She sniffed the drug once more; it made her still more talkative. I soon ceased listening. We drank the liqueur until she nodded off. I carried her to the bed, covered her up, and lay down on the tattered sofa.

Next day I sent her flowers. I thought that would give her a kick.

I returned to Mainz. It was an admission that I had failed in Berlin. But at home I could rest up for a few days. Then I would see.

After asking Mirl's mother for her daughter's hand, with all due ceremony, Hoboken took Mirl to Davos.

I stayed one or two weeks in Mainz, and there I had the luck that had eluded me in Berlin. I was offered a paid position, an engagement with a contract.

The Chief Director of the Mainz Stadttheater, Dr Kurt Elwenspoek, whom I had met earlier, had just been appointed general manager of the Municipal Theaters in Kiel. He offered me the job of 'dramaturgist' there—a post that involved the reading and recommending of plays, and some duties as general assistant. But the contract also promised me the right to stage a few plays of my own choice. I could also be drawn upon to act in small, smaller, or the smallest parts. Pay: the minimum.

All this accorded perfectly with my desires—most of all the

prospect of directing. Hardly anyone else would have offered that to me, a beginner without any demonstrable stage experience.

Kurt Elwenspoek was a remarkable man. He used a small mustache to conceal the softness of his mouth and a reckless consumption of alcohol to cover the soft and unstable features of his character. He was that idealistic brand of person who makes life difficult for himself but decidedly easier for the people around him, and especially for his subordinates. He could never believe, or even imagine, that other people were not just as liberal, generous, kind, honest, and decent as himself. He met the world with a childlike trustfulness, and in the final analysis it did not disappoint him, for if someone let him down, someone else helped him out; his credulous friendliness was irresistible. He had the inclinations of a *grand seigneur*, and really needed the income of an American movie star or modern German tycoon to carry out his concepts of hospitality, generosity, and cosmopolitan style of life. The result was that he was always living beyond his means, which endeared him the more to me.

He loved the stage more than he was able to control it, but he knew something about theater and had a boundless admiration, with no trace of envy, for people with theatrical talent. As manager of a provincial theater of moderate importance, he possessed a rare quality which his young protégés valued higher than the Theater Commission and the municipal officials to whom he was accountable; he was wholly receptive to everything new, bold, venturesome, and unusual, and was always ready to risk the experimental, without regard to financial loss.

There were not many general managers like that at the time, especially outside of Berlin. Moreover, they were under various restrictions. Nowadays the worst that can befall them is to be sneered at if they fail to produce new and provocative works. In those days it took considerable courage to venture beyond the standard programs or to foster an experimental style beyond the ken of provincial audiences. Kurt Elwenspoek had a great deal of that kind of courage, and I owe it to his open-mindedness and intrepid character that I took my first leap into *active* theatrical life. As it turned out, that leap was to be a double somersault: forward and backward.

It was spring, and the season would not open until September. I had no fears about the forthcoming summer. There was only myself to take care of now, and I knew I could manage somehow. A few newspaper contributions now and then would provide for my needs. In the circumstances I did the best thing I could have done to bring a breath of fresh air into my life and dispel bad dreams and nocturnal brooding: I went on a walking tour with my friend Schiebelhuth. Sometimes we worked for farmers who needed help with the haymaking, in exchange for bread and soup. We slept in barns and stables, or on benches in the parks of old castles, among jasmine bushes and yew hedges.

There was little motor traffic in those days; moreover, we preferred dirt tracks where at most we would meet an occasional farm wagon. We walked along the embankments and towpaths beside the rivers, and did nothing that we did not enjoy. My knapsack was stocked with a large assortment of the dramatic works of world literature, in the paperback Reclam editions, and whenever we stopped for a rest I would tinker with these scripts, making cuts, sketching the outlines of scenes, positions, walk-ons, and so forth—for fun and for practice.

In Heidelberg I had known a Norwegian student named Erik Hunter, who was a member of Mierendorff's circle. His father owned rich sulfur deposits in Lapland as well as shares in other mines. He had made it a policy to be host to a German student for the summer holidays, ordinarily someone from the technical academies who was preparing for a career in mining. The student would be provided with free passage on a freighter, some valuable work experience and pocket money, and a taste of Norway. Now young Erik was able to persuade his father to invite an aspiring writer rather than an engineer, with the idea that I might write something on Norway. I obtained a commission from the *Frankfurter Zeitung*, which had already published a few small prose pieces of mine, to do some articles.

For me it was a tremendous opportunity: to see a bit of the world, and to get away from Germany, which was almost impossible for young people in those days because of the currency situation. Moreover, it would get me through the difficult summer. I felt I simply had to go. But I needed a Norwegian visa. I sent my passport to the Norwegian legation in Berlin and was informed that I must deposit the equivalent of ten Norwegian crowns. Given the rapidly advancing devaluation of the mark, that was a vast sum which I did not have and could not raise. Still, I could not bear to give up the chance.

Without my passport, which was still in Berlin, and without a visa, I set out for Brake on the Weser, where the Norwegian ore steamer *Blaamyra*—on which I was to have a passage—was just unloading its cargo and preparing to put to sea again.

By the cheapest route, in fourth-class local trains, I reached Brake on the eve of the vessel's departure. I had exactly half a mark left to my name. My passport, which I had asked to be sent to general delivery at Brake, had not arrived. I went to the captain, showed him my letter of recommendation from Narvik, and asked him to take me along anyhow, perhaps as a stowaway. He couldn't do that, he said; he would simply put me down on his crew list; the crew passed the border control as a group, without individual checks. But I would have to do some work on board to justify my rating.

This captain, who had formerly sailed the seas of the Far East, was a delightful man with a ruddy complexion which I quickly suspected came less from sea air and salt water than from internal liquidity. How right I was about this guess I discovered the very night before embarkation. For my first participation in the life of the ship, he taught me the 'whisky organ.' What you did was first pour a finger of whisky into a glass and fill the rest of the glass with water. This was followed up by a drink consisting of two fingers of whisky, and so on until the glass held only one finger of water. I don't know whether it was this game, or the game the North Sea was playing, that made me feel so awful next morning. I had to leave the incredible breakfast of bacon and eggs, ham and smoked fish untouched; I regret that to this day. The captain ordered me onto the upper deck. A summer storm was blowing up. 'Good for sobering up,' he said, and advised me to take as secure a stance as I could with my face to the wind and let my knees respond to the movement of the ship. By noon I was well; I made up for what I had missed at breakfast, and ever since then I have never missed a meal on a sea voyage. My work was easy; I had to keep order in the radioman's cabin, where I also slept, and occasionally sweep out the galley or dump a pail of refuse overboard. In return I was fattened up as if I were going to be slaughtered in Lapland. It was a glorious voyage, a whole week of it along the Norwegian coast, in ideal summer weather.

We arrived just in time for me to see the midnight sun, the northern horizon bathed in a fiery glow into which the dully gleaming globe dipped and rose again. Then came the white nights with

251

their strange sallow light that casts no shadows and lies chill and evenly over mountains and fjords. Darkness never falls. You lose all sense of time. When it is clouded or misty and the sun does not shine, it might just as well be midnight as noon, and the people feel sleepless and exalted. Those are the nights, or days or evenings, when the girls go singing through the mountain forests to gather berries. You heard their voices far and near as if they came from brooks or birch groves or marshy pools or the cliffs of narrow, deep fjords. Alluring sounds; you felt like following them and losing yourself, never to return.

My friend's father employed me for a time in his mine, setting me an easy job that even with my technical incompetence I could handle. I had to help lay a new cable through the shafts and follow other cables, checking the insulation and the telephone connections. In the army I had been in a telephone squad. I learned the work quickly, picked up a few scraps of the language, and got to know the miners at work and in their barracklike dwellings near the small village, which consisted mainly of a store, a post office, and the wooden cottages of a few craftsmen. Beyond that the farmlands began, and then the wilderness. I was paid for this work and did not have to spend the money, for the hospitality was unlimited. I was always being invited to one house or another, for voyages far into the Atlantic, and taken along to cliffs where thousands of birds screeched and fluttered. I went on country outings. The Swedish steamer *Liljewacht* was anchored in Narvik, and I was invited to a dance aboard it that lasted two days and two nights. I also spent time in solitary hunting lodges beside glassy green mountain lakes; we fished for trout from the boat, and for the big salmon by casting in the cold, rushing streams.

In August I went as a porter on an expedition into the mountains and high moors of inner Lapland. By then I was strong enough to carry a considerable load on my back in a wooden frame, and to keep going for days over pathless slopes of scree and undergrowth. The purpose of the expedition was to survey the silver deposits that had been discovered near the Swedish-Norwegian border. Besides myself, the expedition consisted of a state geologist, two mining experts, and two Lapp guides with Iceland ponies. The ponies carried the tents and sleeping bags which we needed during the cold nights. We traversed a vast wasteland such as I had never seen before. On the way we met wandering Lapps with their herds of reindeer whose hooves crackled like sparks. I saw snow owls and lemmings. At night, when the gradually darkening sky was already taking on a bluish-green hue, the northern lights flashed and flickered. Then the first stars gleamed.

Setting a date for my return was a problem. Since I had no passport, I would have to sail back in a German ship: that seemed the likeliest way for me to slip back into the country without trouble at the border. A freighter on which my friends could obtain free passage for me was not leaving until the middle of September. But on September 1, when the theater season opened in Kiel, the ptarmigan season opened in Lapland. I had been invited to take part, and I wanted very much to.

I sent a telegram to Elwenspoek in Kiel explaining that I would have to report for duty three weeks late because I had contracted the Lapland sickness, which was very infectious. Anyone familiar with the north knows that the so-called sickness consists of fits of melancholy which drive a good many persons into manic depressions during the endless winter night.

I felt lighthearted. I had recovered from the bad spell in Berlin. I could still feel my grief like a scar that is not yet quite healed. But I knew that I was the stronger for it. A sharp wind had blown me out of a wrong and difficult situation. I was full of gratitude for everything I had experienced and full of fervor to begin anew.

The Norwegian crowns I had earned—for I had also been paid for my work as porter—provided me with a glorious entry to Kiel. In Germany the inflation was swelling; it had begun slowly but was inexorably quickening its pace. To possess even the tiniest sum in foreign currency made one temporarily a financial mogul. For the first few days, until I had found two small rooms, I stayed in the Hotel Holst, Kiel's finest, whose headwaiter had once served the Kaiser and ever since could only lisp out of sheer awe at himself. As long as I had crowns to change, I gave him such princely tips that I had credit there for the rest of the season.

But that was not important—only the theater counted. I now had to approach the whole thing in other terms, no longer as a young writer and volunteer assistant at rehearsals, but as an active collaborator who had a voice and actual influence. The only aspect of the work that interested me was the actual staging and the choice of program. Office work bored me, and I had a physical abhorrence of files. My successor must have cursed when he had to clean out the

Augean stables of my desk drawers, into which I had stuffed the 'current correspondence,' answered or not. But the office stationery was perfect for setting down dialogue and drafting verse. My boss did not care. He himself was no bureaucrat and gladly let me overwhelm and infect him with the 'storm-and-stress' atmosphere and the brilliant follies that I showered upon the solid, respectable city on the Baltic.

He accepted my suggestions with regard to the program: Büchner and Barlach, Lenz, Grabbe, Strindberg, Wedekind, hardly a digestible lot for the Kiel of those days. But almost at once we were off to a good start. Something astonishing happened, similar to what had previously happened in Heidelberg. Out of the blue a group of friends sprang up, people who had not known one another previously but immediately took to each other. It was all due to the perceptiveness of General Manager Elwenspoek, who had gathered a group of talented beginners from among the best acting schools of Berlin, Frankfurt, and Dresden. With the support of Elwenspoek, we mounted an attack on the petrified, superannuated, to our minds dying, or dead, routines of the older theater people, who seemed to think only of their prospective pensions. We called these well-established directors and actors 'art bureaucrats' and felt enormously superior to them. For their part they were in the majority and were horrified by the antics of us 'snotnoses' who were ruining the theater, they thought. Opposing fronts formed rapidly, and the hostility hardened the more our 'Young Circle' (as we called ourselves) developed momentum and brought the general manager over to our side. The struggle was waged obstinately and unfairly by both parties—by ours with the intolerance and radicalism of youth, by the others with the rigidity and incomprehension of a generation that had been thrown off balance by social change and felt that everything novel or in any way revolutionary was a danger to its very existence. What was more, we, and especially I, were suspected of political leftism, and when I went around with a Chasseurs d'Alpins cap I had bought in Mainz (in those days the beret was not yet part of the literary man's headwear), Kiel's reactionary fraternity students decided that I was a 'Frenchified German' who ought to be horsewhipped out of Schleswig-Holstein.

Within a short time we were well known, or notorious, throughout the city. The first plays we produced—straight out of the classical repertory, but in adaptations that made them unrecognizable to

secondary-school teachers—seemed scandalous and outrageous. Subscriptions were canceled, fierce letters from readers appeared in the
newspapers. The critics attacked us too. To make matters worse,
the Social Democratic newspaper came out in our praise, and long
discussions of the 'new theater' in Kiel appeared in Berlin and
Hamburg journals.

This opposition did not discourage us. On the contrary, it had a
stimulating effect. Aside from our enormous pleasure in the performances themselves, we enjoyed provocation and rebellion, and the
sense of a mission. Starting from Kiel, we intended to renovate the
theater, and starting from the theater, the world. We were still
living under the aegis of the chiliastic postwar ecstasy. But Kiel was
the worst imaginable soil for such an undertaking. It was the city of
pompous imperial regattas; the revolutionary sailors of the naval
base had long since vanished. Only their embittered, pensioned
superiors remained. The Skagerrak League of former naval officers
and a dyed-in-the-wool conservative, intellectually constipated
merchant bourgeoisie set the tone and the thinking of the city.

We, however, looked for support from the few and to the idealism
of our general manager. When the Theater Commission refused us
the money we needed for mounting a new production, we made
everything ourselves. Our actresses sewed the costumes and we men
refurbished old sets. We dug up talent wherever we found it. A few
young people with only the scantiest previous experience played
their first parts in our performances. They were by no means the
worst; some of them subsequently made great names in the theater.

In front of me there is a letter I wrote to my friend Hans
Schiebelhuth, returned to me from among his posthumous papers.
It is on substantial rag paper; the printed letterhead reads:

United Municipal Theaters of Kiel
Office of the General Manager
Stadttheater, Neumarkt

October 22, 1922

Dearest brother in the Lord, in my heart, and on the road—since
Allah in his inscrutable wisdom has sped me from the North Cape
and Sahara to Kiel, in the last-named place I sit daily, what a
shame, in an office for almost two hours, the chair padded with
manuscripts, and by a harsh manner (especially on questions of
advances) further the illusion of being indispensable. . . .

In this capacity, my older and wiser brother, I am writing to you. Behold, such power is given unto me over life and death.

Vraiment: couldn't you put a few weeks in between your walking sticks and write a play? I'll give it its opening here *at once*. There's not a thing; all this Expressionism turns my stomach. . . .

Yours,

Zuck

I really was sick and tired of Expressionism. The newer plays of the successful Expressionists seemed to me more and more strained, more and more alienated from life. I began to suspect that in the theater, too, man is the measure of all things, and that it is essential to restore the creaturely nexus, to create anew the tension between individual, society, and the riddle of the universe which has always been the heart of drama.

In the course of this winter typewritten stage scripts from the Gustav Kiepenheuer publishing house reached me. They were *Drums in the Night*, *Baal*, and *In the Thicket* by an author hitherto unknown to me: Bertolt Brecht.

I rushed to Elwenspoek. 'Here's a writer! A new tone! A power of language and form that sweeps away all this stale Expressionism. We must have him!'

I made an arrangement with Kiepenheuer to produce *Baal*, which had not yet been performed, in Kiel. I wrote to the author that I was planning to stage the play, and asked whether he could not come to the rehearsals. After a while I received a postcard from him typed entirely without capitals, in which he expressed himself willing to come to Kiel and take part in the rehearsals if the theater would pay his expenses and a director's salary; the amount he suggested was unusually high.

There the matter ended, as far as Kiel was concerned. The Theater Commission did not approve; the contract signed by Elwenspoek and me remained our legacy to the theater, which probably had to pay a fine for nonfulfillment.

There may still be a few old people in Kiel who remember that theatrical season of 1922–23, which was marked by uproar, creative chaos, and bankruptcy.

For all of us in the Young Circle, and particularly for me, it was

256

a tremendous period. The more we dared, the more we got ourselves talked about, the more plainly the coming debacle loomed on
the misty horizon over the Bay of Kiel. But we had some glorious
moments. I gave a lecture series: 'Elements of the Theater: the
Sources of Its Revitalization.' One matinee in the series bore the
'hard sell' title: 'On the Circus, Carrousel, and Country Fair,
Swingboat Men, Jugglers, and Vagabonds.' It preceded my production of Molnár's *Liliom*. (My lecture was printed by Siegfried
Jacobsohn in the *Weltbühne*.) The last sentence, after which several
of our actors appeared on the stage to recite various 'folk texts,'
read:

'You are going to hear rough, vulgar, unprintable language! The
long dead, anonymous authors do not apologize!'

Those so-called 'folk texts' had all been created at my desk a
few nights earlier; the Kiel play-reader was hiding behind deceased,
anonymous authors. Among the texts were a tightrope walker's
song, street urchins' rhymes, and the conversations of prostitutes
spoken in the Hessian and Palatinate dialect. I had had a young
actress translate one of these pieces, which was especially raw, into
Low German, so that the people of Kiel would understand it exactly.

The *pièce de résistance* was a 'Mainz Ballad of Schinderhannes,'*
in fifteen stanzas. For each stanza a lurid poster painted on cardboard was shown. These pictures were of my design; I still have the
preliminary sketches in pen and colored pencil. They were recollections of a Schinderhannes ballad I had heard as a child. Hans Alva,
the actor, dressed in a red shirt, recited the ballad. A young actress
attired in rags changed the pictures. The whole Young Circle sang
the refrains, as a chorus of stupid onlookers. I alternately played the
guitar and, between stanzas, the accordion.

We had enormous fun, and so did some of the audience. The best
joke of all was a reviewer's writing a serious essay about these
specimens of 'genuine folk poetry.'

But these productions were increasingly stirring up the wasp's nest
of public indignation, both among the theatergoers and among the
older actors, who were furious when we assigned a lead role to a
beginner, or had the part of an aged man played by a beginner. I
did Wedekind's *Marquis of Keith* with a punching bag near the

---

* Schinderhannes, an eighteenth-century German Robin Hood whose real
name was Hans Bückler, was beheaded in Mainz in 1803, and soon became
the subject of numerous ballads.

footlights at which the Marquis practised to the rhythm of his sentences. Moreover, all the characters were in deliberately exaggerated make-up. When we put on *The Magic Flute*, not in the usual pseudo-Egyptian décor, but with the stage framed in colored glass, in modern dress, and with the performers making rhythmic movements, there was considerable commotion in the audience. Many people walked out in protest. Even some of the singers carried on as if they had been raped.

Nowadays no one would fuss about such experiments or even more radical ones. If people were doubtful, they would look on, shrug, and say: 'I suppose it's modern.' But today I am proud of good old Kiel, whose provinciality I then derided in satires and polemics. For I regard it as a noble feeling that people became excited, defended a position, applied a standard, even when that standard was narrow or superannuated. I think it good that we were able to stir up feeling, indignation, disputation, that we were required to fight, to risk our own standing in order to establish the new standard, more in tune with our time.

It was fairly obvious that we were doomed to defeat in this battle.

Receipts dropped rapidly. More and more subscriptions were canceled. Elwenspoek had serious run-ins with the Theater Commission, and could have saved his position only by firing his troublesome young associates and dropping me from the staff. He did not dream of doing this. He stood by us and by his convictions, even after ugly pamphlets charging (not without justice) the Young Circle with licentiousness and alcoholism were distributed at the University and among the members of a Protestant youth organization.

Behind his back the older actors and directors circulated a petition against the general manager himself and his 'youthful clique.' It was signed by the entire staff, except for us, of course, and two of the sopranos of the opera company who were on our side. The document was presented to the municipal government and would alone have sealed our fate had we not taken matters into our own hands. For I had launched us on an escapade that was guaranteed to cause a storm. The general manager let us go ahead, agreeing that we might as well depart not with a whimper but a bang. On a retreat, it is proper to blow up your stronghold, in this case the theater, at least symbolically.

In less than a week I worked up an adaptation of *The Eunuch* by

Terence, a brilliantly constructed farce dating from the most lavish and lascivious period of Roman theater. The motifs of the play were tried and true elements of Greek and Roman comedy.

As I noted in my prologue:

Terence borrowed it from Plautus, who took it from Menander—
The fact that classic writers thieved is truth, it isn't slander.

For my part, all I borrowed from the play was the outline of the plot and the cast of characters. I rewrote it entirely in the brashest German of the postwar era, stuffing it with all the blunt political and other truths we wanted to hurl at the people of Kiel, and transforming the Saturnalian eroticism of the original, which centers around the great whore Thais and her lovers, into sheer obscenity.

It was a mixture of braggadocio and deliberate challenge, containing some spontaneous highly theatrical scenes and some linguistically startling, even poetic, dialogues which would abruptly trail off into farce and uproar.

Elwenspoek considered it a stroke of original genius, though not a finished work of art, and had no doubt that he was introducing a future playwright to the theater. For me it was a finger exercise, a trial of craftsmanship, and above all a prank. All the parts, down to personal details, were written to fit the actors of our company, including the ones who were our bitterest enemies and whom the general manager, by virtue of the authority he still possessed, forced to participate, under pain of dismissal for breach of contract —a price none of them was willing to pay. Moreover, every part was good, full of comic effects which, however outraged, an actor would not like to let slip. After all, they could always clear themselves afterwards on the ground that they were merely obeying orders.

We were already rehearsing before the last sentence was written. I directed, and thanks to the enthusiasm of the Young Circle—every member understood what was involved—the performance proved to be a brilliant one. The courageous general manager, who no longer had anything to lose, arranged the first night as a closed performance for invited guests, with the idea that the play would be shown to the public the following night. The leading figures in the municipal government, society, the University, the Skagerrak League, and the press were invited. Two free tickets had been provided for everyone, and almost all the men came with their wives. Elwenspoek delivered an introductory talk in which he proclaimed the discovery of a dramatic talent whose name would one day be world-famous. He concluded his address with a quotation from Goethe: 'And you will be able to say: We were present.'

The people of Kiel listened, sceptical and mute.

After the prologue, which as in the classical theater dealt with the symbol of the phallus as a metaphor for creative Eros, and ended in a eulogy of that noble member, no one dared breathe. Obviously, no one wanted to miss a single one of the frightful words that were being spoken, and no one left the theater before the last curtain buried all hopes that worse was still to come. Yet something even worse did come, according to the notions of the period. One of our young actresses who was totally without talent but enchantingly lovely was led across the stage in the guise of one of Thai's abducted virgins and slave girls. She was naked except for a veil around her waist; her breasts were daubed orange and around her navel was painted a sun with blue rays. Since her speech was marred by a lisp, I had given her only a part of a line to speak: at the end, when she was asked where she had been held during the period of her abduction, she replied: 'On Lesbos.'

The boastful general who lost every battle except the battle of the mattress, and his sly parasite, were played in masks suggestive of Hindenburg and Ludendorff (though the doughty old field marshal hardly deserved that, being indubitably more partial to the church than to the brothel) and used the language of military headquarters. And Kiel's pillars of society, especially the critics, present in the audience, were caricatured as the eunuchs.

A few young people to whom we had given free seats in the gallery—my matinee audience—laughed and applauded at the final curtain. The invited guests left the theater in ominous silence.

That very night a session of the Town Council was called and the general manager was asked to cancel the play at once, before there was a public scandal. Since he refused, the theater was closed by the police next day on grounds of 'gross misdemeanor.' The general manager and I were dismissed without notice, some members of the Young Circle were temporarily suspended from theatrical work, all our contracts for the next season were declared null and void. In the document stating my dismissal the reason given was 'Because of effrontery, insolence, and total artistic incompetence.'

With this diploma in hand, I left Kiel in the dead of night, for I felt that I could no longer safely appear on the streets. Elwenspoek found a temporary position in a bank. Next winter he moved to Munich and then to Stuttgart, where he resumed his work in the theater and lated turned to radio.

Munich was my destination, too. Our caprices in Kiel had made news in the world of the theater. Hermine Körner, the great actress, had taken over direction of the Munich Schauspielhaus that year. I had sent her a manuscript of my *Eunuch*, along with a recommendation from Elwenspoek, and offered my services as playreader and director. For I was after all 'free,' I was available, and after my glorious disaster in Kiel I was convinced that I was eagerly awaited and needed everywhere.

Hermine Körner replied that she had seldom laughed as much as when reading *The Eunuch*, and that she might possibly use the play in her theater. She asked me to call on her.

I reached Bavaria largely on foot, walking all the way from the far north to the far south of Germany. I could afford a train ticket only when I sold something en route to a newspaper or magazine. This was the summer of 1923; the inflation was nearing its climax, and we lived between millions, billions, and zero. I was always in the latter region. On the platform of a fourth-class train, chewing a crust of stale bread, I wrote a poem entitled: 'Food.' It was a hymn to the pleasures of ingestion. The poem was published and made something of a splash; no one saw it as being merely a delirium produced by the pangs of hunger.

The Eunuch was not performed in Munich. There was no Young Circle at the theater there, and on receiving the part scripts the ensemble of the Schauspielhaus flatly refused to speak such language. Hermine was wonderful; she not only continued to uphold the play but hired me out of sheer kindness, for she already had an assistant. I therefore became 'second play-reader,' without any definite functions, and received a minimum salary that became less every payday, for by now the dollar was worth billions of marks, and unless you rushed to the grocery with the freshly printed paper money in your hand, to convert it as fast as possible into some edibles, it was devalued again within a few hours. My marks usually sufficed for a package of spaghetti and two tomatoes; I was known in my lodgings as the Spaghetti Baron.

During the first period of my engagement Hermine Körner was

producing Schiller's *Maria Stuart*, mounting the play in the spirit of Reinhardt. She herself played Elizabeth. Her Maria was Tilly Wedekind, the widow of Franz Wedekind, who had died towards the end of the war. In the spring of 1966 Tilly Wedekind celebrated her eightieth birthday, so she must have been thirty-seven then. She was a woman of ravishing beauty, beauty which was enhanced by a touch of mystery, a shade of melancholy, an intimation of suppressed sadness. Her smile was gentle, of a quiet, delicate loveliness. Wedekind had restricted her mostly to parts in his plays, so that this was the first time in many years that she was once again playing a classical role.

During one of the rehearsals, in which she and Hermine were alone on the stage, I was asked to give the cues and indicate the positions of the other actors. But I kept looking at Tilly, whose breath-taking beauty distracted me, so that I often stumbled over the cues. Then I began stumbling for another reason. I had never seen *Maria Stuart* on the stage. I knew the play only from a hasty reading in school and had been on strike against it, so to speak, because of the sickening moralistic lessons our teachers drew from Schiller. Consequently, I had almost forgotten the play. Now, as the two ladies spoke their lines, I perceived for the first time the magnificent interlocking of scenes and themes, the smooth composition, the power of the language and the human portraiture in this work. Overwhelmed, I began reading the full text instead of the cues, and kept bursting out with exclamations like 'Wonderful! What a play!' and phrases of that sort.

'You really don't know the play?' Hermine asked, laughing. 'As a play-reader you certainly mustn't let on.'

'Why not?' I said. 'You must have realized by now that I'm a rotten play-reader, but I'm going to be a good dramatist.'

In saying that I won Madame Tilly's heart. I became a frequent visitor to Wedekind House, the handsome home on Äussere Prinzregentenstrasse where the brillant *épateur* of the bourgeoisie had spent his last years, and struck up a lively friendship with his two daughters. With Pamela, then sixteen, I sat around on the floor of her studio playing the guitar—she spoke and sang with the sharply pronounced diction of her father, whose death mask hung on the wall. With Kadidja, the twelve-year-old, I indulged in wild Indian games.

Through Pamela I also met the eldest pair of Mann children—

Thomas and Katja Mann having had their children in three pairs, a boy and a girl each time, not twins but so close in age that they almost seemed to be twins. That was especially the case with Erika and Klaus. She was a clever, dark-eyed schoolgirl, then in her senior year; he was a pallid young man, tormented by his talent, from an early age marked by a complex and difficult nature. They always tramped around the city together and made a game of pilfering small things from department stores. In other respects, too, they had an inclination for adventure and an ideal of the picaresque life, which was what I probably represented to them. We were fond of each other. But I was not a visitor at the Mann house, then in the throes of 'disorder and early sorrow.'

Most of my friends were actors, and it was at an after-theater party in someone's place that I met Bert Brecht. I can remember a few of the other people who were present at the time, but not distinctly. They are all vague; the only face I see clearly and sharply is his. And I can still hear his unique, unmistakable voice.

Brecht was then, along with Lion Feuchtwanger, who must be reckoned his real discoverer, the dramaturgist for Falckenberg's 'Munich Kammerspiele.' The previous year Falckenberg had performed a work of Brecht's for the first time, the drama *Drums in the Night.* Now he was receiving from the Theater, much as I was from Hermine Körner, a kind of writer's salary, without being tied down to any specific job.

I had read his early plays and seen a performance of *In the Thicket*, which—as was customary with unusual plays at that time—rapidly vanished from the boards again. But I was not yet acquainted with any of his poems, except for those used in the plays. I did not know his songs and ballads. And you did not really know them until you heard him sing them while playing the guitar. He was expert on the instrument and loved complicated chords difficult to finger: C-sharp minor or E-flat major chords. His singing was raw and abrasive, often with the crudity of a street singer or music-hall minstrel. An unmistakable Augsburg intonation underlay it. Sometimes he sang with something approaching beauty; his voice floated along with emotional vibratos, enunciating every syllable with great clarity. When he sang you could say of his voice what Herbert Ihering had written about the diction of his early works: 'It is brutally sensual and melancholically delicate. There is vulgarity in it, and abysses of sadness, savage wit, and plaintive lyricism.'

Whenever he took up the guitar, the babble of conversation stopped; the footbeat of the tango dancers shuffling about in murky corners came to a halt, and everyone gathered around him as if under a spell. That first evening I met him he sang his ballads and songs as I was to hear them many times afterwards, through the years. But this was the first time. Dazed, stirred, enchanted, I sat in a corner, and I was terribly embarrassed when one of my friends from Kiel who had also wandered to Munich and was there at the party spoke up: 'Now Zuck ought to sing. He can play the guitar, too. You've got to hear him.' Several of the others chimed in.

I did not want to. I wished I could slink away. But I did not want to seem the kind of person who modestly refuses and has to be coaxed. So I said nothing at all, hoping that the rest of the party would ignore the call and begin dancing again.

But my friend from Kiel persisted: 'Zuck, sing the Seidelbast song.'

Brecht stood up and with a look of disgust held out the guitar to me.

There was a silly ballad called 'Johann Gottlieb Seidelbast' which used to be sung at student drinking bouts. Probably Brecht thought that was what was meant. My own 'Seidelbast,' actually entitled 'Brandy in the Spring,' was a poem I had written a few years earlier while sitting in a tavern waiting for Annemarie Seidel. I had scribbled the lines on the backs of those damp beer coasters that bear the words 'Pilsner Urquell' on their faces. Toying with the disintegrating corpse of an alcoholic, the whole thing was a concealed love poem, each stanza ending with the refrain:

Aus meinem Herzen wächst der Seidelbast.

('Out of my heart the daphne grows.')

I had made a simple melody for it, supported only by a few chords.

I plucked away at the guitar for a bit, to give myself a feeling of security and to get used to the width of the frets. Then I sang as well and as boldly as I could. It was really more a recitation than a song.

When I had finished, Brecht came over to me, measuring me with an odd look, out of half-squinting eyes. It was impossible to say whether his look was wary, cool, or friendly.

'Hearr, hearr,' he said, with his hard *r*. 'That's not at all bad.'

In the course of that night he and I sang a good deal more; we took the guitar from each other's hands as if we had been doing so for years. In between we danced. I noticed that he danced with great precision and musical sense, very quietly, his face absorbed, his knees a little bent, wholly lost in the movement. When the party broke up, he asked me where I lived. I told him. He said we might as well walk part of the way together.

I can still see him trotting alongside me through the deserted streets, dressed in his loose leather jacket, under which in those days he liked to wear very fine white shirts, the guitar wrapped in a cloth and tucked under his arm, his leather cap pulled over his forehead, shoulders rounded and hunched, so that he seemed smaller than he was.

We were chewing on the stubs of cheap black cigars as we walked. Our conversation became so lively that suddenly we found ourselves not in front of my apartment but in front of his. It was on the ground floor in a corner house at the end of Ludwigstrasse, near the University, while mine was at the end of Maximilianstrasse, almost at the Isar. We walked the whole way back to my place, and then to his again, back and forth. It was a lovely night in mid-October, brilliant with stars, and smelling of fallen leaves.

'This fall of 1923,' Brecht said, 'is an extremely successful fall.'

This was his way of commenting on nature. Dawn was already breaking as he remarked that he had a bottle of beer at home, and some leftover whisky, and maybe his wife would make coffee for us; we might as well have a little more music.

His infant daughter was at that time still in her cradle in the back room. Even then she bore a remarkable resemblance to her father. Whenever I see her on the stage nowadays—she is the actress Hanne Hiob—I give a start, because I feel as if young Brecht were up there on the boards, disguised as a woman.

There followed a period in which we spent a great deal of time together. We often went for walks in the Englischer Garten or the Isar Woods, sometimes accompanied by Brecht's friend Caspar Neher, the stage designer, with whom he discussed all his projects. When he was at work Brecht needed listeners, including the kind who made suggestions or could give him advice. He then immediately seized on these proposals and worked them up, after his own fashion. This kind of partnership was altogether foreign to me—I could then and can to this day turn out something only when I am alone—but watching it fascinated me and gave me a vision of all kinds of possibilities. Once Brecht took the director Erich Engel and me to visit Lion Feuchtwanger, with whom he was about to do a version of Christopher Marlowe's *Edward II*. Feuchtwanger knew a great deal about the theater and was extremely well read and the two discussed the background, the construction, the order of scenes, the general thematic line. In such matters Brecht readily permitted others to advise him, and even guide him. But everything else, the shaping, the linguistic form, the atmosphere, the dialogue, came from himself, and in those realms he was the absolute sovereign. His poetic and scenic ideas were inexhaustible; he produced them with ease and might later reject them with equal ease. I recall that there was a particular scene which Engel and Feuchtwanger thought called for a soliloquy. In five minutes, with three persons sitting around him smoking and drinking coffee. Brecht had written the soliloquy. He read it aloud. In twenty lines of verse he conjured up a half-decaying, amphibious, algae-tangled underwater realm of the dead, in which a man foresees the inescapability of his fate. We thought the soliloquy magnificent and that it fitted the dramatic structure perfectly, but Brecht put the sheet of paper into his pocket. It was too lyrical for the theater, he said; he'd use it for a poem. And he wrote a new text. In no one else have I ever seen such fertility. It sprang up from every root yet was always controlled by critical reasoning.

I knew at our first encounter that I had met a genius, or at least a personality of a brilliance such as I had never previously been acquainted with. At that time I could not know the determination with which he would drive his talent on to greatness.

Herbert Ihering, who rapidly became almost lyrical in his enthusiasm for Brecht, summed up the quality of Brecht's genius in the essay he wrote on the occasion of Brecht's receiving the Kleist Prize. A great deal has subsequently been written about Brecht, but never anything more pertinent. Ihering wrote:

'A poet who would seem to portray decay and with this portrayal spreads light. Who would seem to be cynical, and with this cynicism moves our hearts. *Who is young and has already seen all depths.*'

That was it. Brecht was then twenty-five, yet all his friends felt this element, and so did he. But he was far from emphasizing it in any portentous manner. He despised the kind of writer who goes about as a prophet and seer, only too conscious of his 'mission.'

266

Brecht's view of the world was realistic, governed by scepticism and humor, as was his way of expressing himself privately. 'Now what did old Papa Brecht tell you?' I often heard him remarking when something startling happened in our circle. And he had in fact made a prediction almost every time, always being right.

I also realized from the very start that I would have to beware of him. For I was mindful of my own talent, was myself seeking a mode of expression, and unless I were careful I would succumb to his magnetism. Brecht was dangerous in many respects, as every genius probably is. He did not want admirers or disciples; but he did want collaborators who could co-operate with him and therefore subordinate themselves to him.

For all his seemingly conciliatory nature, he had a strong craving for power; not raw power, but the power of the mind, which does not command but guides.

In the late twenties, when the concept of literary and theatrical 'collectives' became fashionable, especially in Berlin, I once said to him: 'For you the collective is a group of intelligent people who contribute to what one person wants—that is, what you want.'

He admitted, with his peculiar sly smile, that I might not be so far wrong at that.

'Every man is the best man in his own skin,' he says in his play *Drums in the Night*, and although this sentence is also capable of a democratic interpretation, the conception of the strong man, the best man as the survivor, is firmly anchored in his work. 'For the strong man fights and the weak man dies . . .' I can hear him singing. The social-revolutionary element in young Brecht was not founded on humanitarianism or ideology. Rather, it sprang from an anarchic vitality in which elemental sadness, melancholia, and the harsh drums celebrating death and begetting merged musically. This young man Brecht enticed, enchanted, entangled, and enraptured everyone, above all by his overwhelming musicality, which continued to operate throughout all his future work. Of course the music of the *Threepenny Opera* is by Kurt Weill. But anyone who knew Brecht's intonation, anyone familiar with his own melodic diction (as it emerges, for example, in the song of the pamphlet seller in *The Life of Edward II*, a song for which he himself wrote the music), must realize that the famous organ-grinder bars of 'Mac the Knife' are due to his inspiration and his suggestions.

In those early days I often had the impression that in his gift for

language and music he was akin to a Hungarian or Slavic gypsy—
the kind who without formal training and without knowing the
notes can play any instrument with immediate mastery. Legend
has tried to turn young Brecht into a fiery idealist, a dark-eyed
archangel with flaming sword, or at least into a kind of potential
bomb-thrower. All that is literary fabrication. What he really seemed
to be was a pied piper, a musical arch-gypsy, with the features,
however, of a Jesuit seminarian, of a Black Forest vagabond, and of
a truck driver. In saying this I see a clear line between the bizarre
and devilish charm of his face as a young man and the Roman
handsomeness of his death mask.

I am flying in the face of standard criticism when I maintain that
in Brecht's youthful works there was a religious note—pagan, with
overtones of nature myth, as it were. He felt that there was something over and above man, something beyond man and his economic
conditons. There was the great heaven of *Baal,* the choral heaven by
no means to be understood merely as a physical phenomenon.
Rather, it is a contrapuntal countervoice to death and nemesis.

> Praise the tree which grows on carrion, grows
> >   jubilantly toward heaven!
> Praise the carrion,
> Praise the tree that devoured it,
> But praise heaven also.

Even though the next stanza extols this heaven's indifference,
its cold aloofness from the life and death of individuals and
the creatures of earth multiplying like infusoria—even so there is
no denying that in young Brecht's poetic vision and intellectual
vistas such a heaven existed as a power, as a mystery, at the least
as a radiance of incomprehensible beauty. At that time, in the
autumn of 1923, Brecht made me the gift of a typewritten manuscript of his play *In the Thicket* (later called *In the Thicket of the
Cities*) and for dedication wrote on the first page:

> It is right for a man
> To smoke
> And to struggle with metaphysics.

Words like 'changing the world' were not part of his vocabulary at the time. He despised the rhetoric of proclamation, as it was practised by the enthusiasts of Expressionism. Later on when he spoke of 'changing the world,' he meant a perfectly specific, concrete change for which he had provided an ideological substructure. But when I first met him he stood aloof from all ideologies, and from politics in general. We talked about these matters frequently and at length. In those days I was much more 'committed' politically; in time the proportions were reversed. I gave him Ernst Bloch and Lukács to read; he did not know them, and they did not arouse his interest. For his part, he gave me Kipling. You can learn from him, he told me. He used everything that he could learn from, from the Bible to the original farces of Karl Valentin, the comedian; everything from which he could extract a distillate for fresh starts. He would write new classics—after his own fashion. Schiller, Kleist, Hölderlin—these classic German writers could provide the linguistic substance with which to stamp a new classic out of the old ones. Shakespeare was something else again; with his 'artistic realism,' Shakespeare was political theater.

Like the character Kragler in his *Drums in the Night*, Brecht had turned away from the aborted revolution; he turned, however, not to the 'great white bed' but—for the present—entirely to the theater. Already he had in mind his concept of epic theater. Proclamations and even persuasive opinions make no sense, he said, unless you have the power to carry out your theories. To that end you need an instrument. Our instrument is the theater, that is all. It can be politically effectual only if it seizes firm hold of people and shakes them out of the sentimental daze too long associated with playgoing. He never sought the fame and glory of superficial success. What he was after was real influence.

There was something of Mac the Knife in Brecht. If someone were blocking his way, and if he met that person after dark in the vicinity of the Bastille or in the slums of London, he might have slid a blade between their ribs, gracefully and without a scruple. This, of course, must not be taken too literally. In the flesh Brecht was no Villon, no Rimbaud in personality, though he was so in spirit and in imagination. For he was saving himself for greater things, not squandering his strength as a libertine and adventurer. All that he put into his ballads.

The nights we spent drinking together, that time in Berlin, passed peacefully, in conversation and making music, sometimes in sizable groups, rarely with women. Women were for seeing alone. For him everything was a preliminary to fresh work. He liked to talk about taking it easy, but even when he was being lazy he was working. In general he lived quietly and without excesses.

Important boxing matches excited and fascinated him. So did automobiles. I recall how he bought his first small car on installments and at once took it out for a spin. This was at night, and when its motor died, another friend and I had to push it until it started again. But he was no speed demon, and always drove cautiously. Nor did he have any urge to travel to far lands. But when he had to go into exile he faced the unknown with the tranquility of a Chinese sage.

His political evolution is not properly part of this story, since I did not share it. He wanted firm doctrines, *ordo*, clear directives, and accepted the first set of rules that came along, which he decided was also the best and most humane. His artistic theories are also not germane to this book. I am speaking only of the man and writer as I knew him.

His canonization nowadays concerns me no more than did the rabid outcry against him in the past. What remains with me is memories of a friendship that was never wholly lost, even though our ways parted.

In those day politics was already reaching for our throats, but we did not feel the stranglehold or recognize the gravity of the danger. The convulsions of inflation had racked Germany. At the beginning of 1923 the Ruhr had been occupied by the French. In October a short-lived Rhenish Republic, partly the outcome of separatist tendencies, was proclaimed in the occupied territories. Concurrently there were bloody uprisings in Saxony, Thuringia, and Hamburg. The Reichswehr struck hard wherever there were disturbances among the suffering workingmen but did nothing about the growing strength of the illegal Black Reichswehr, the organization of vigilantes and terrorists which gained special prominence in Upper Silesia. Friedrich Ebert, the temperate President of the Reich, a man always ready to adjudicate differences, was forced to impose a state of emergency upon the whole of Germany, for the ugly atmosphere of mass impoverishment and profiteering drove many to extremism.

And in Bavaria Hitler's brown battalions marched for the first time. They were supported by the former Free Corps, which had been disbanded by law. These were people who had withdrawn to the Baltic regions, the last refuge of particularistic rebellion against the Republic.

Once when I was on an outing I happened to be in the vicinity of the Bavarian towns of Miesbach and Schliersee. The area resembled an army camp; everywhere troops were bivouacked and filling the taverns. I sat with them and talked to a good many. They were crude, limited, pigheaded men. We (meaning Germany) must become a military power again; the Jews and 'Marxists' (whom they imagined as superdiabolical bloodsuckers and monsters, as depicted in the propaganda with which they were fed) had to have their necks twisted. Some smaller groups were monarchists and sided with the Church; with them it was possible to argue. But not with the others. The only language they understood was that of the rifle butt and the long knife.

Among the leaders of the Free Corps were a few nationalistic idealists. Their underlings were rough soldiers who had not found their way back into civilian life. They recognized only one virtue: obedience. Trained killers prepared to do anything on orders, they could be used for any purpose.

Hitler's SA, the Storm Troopers, were recruited from among the discontented and the failures, men of all classes consumed by envy and hatred, trigger-happy and ripe for any kind of violence.

During this period I frequently attended Adolf Hitler's beer-hall meetings. I wanted to know just what the situation was. Once I succeeded in getting a seat so close to the speaker's platform that I could see the spittle spraying from under his mustache. For people like us the man was a howling dervish. But he knew how to whip up those crowds jammed closely in a dense cloud of cigarette smoke and würst vapors—not by arguments but by the fanaticism of his manner, the roaring and screeching, interlarded with middle-class oratory, and especially by the hypnotic power of his repetitions, delivered in a certain infectious rhythm. This was a technique he had developed himself, and it had a frightening, primitive force.

He would draw up a catalogue of existing evils and imaginary abuses, and after listing them in higher and higher crescendo he screamed the rhetorical question into the beer-hall crowd: 'And whose fault is it?'—following up with the sharply metrical reply:
'It's all/the fault/of the Jews!'

The beer mugs would swiftly take up the beat, crashing down on the wooden tables, and thousands of voices, shrill and female or beer-bellied basses, repeated the imbecilic line for a quarter of an hour. Anger that a mug of beer cost four hundred million marks added impetus to the pounding.

But there was more to it than that. Hitler was able to put people into a trance, like the medicine man of a savage tribe. Yet these people were no savages; they were merely distraught petit-bourgeois who, faced with the breakdown of long-established values, did not know where to turn. This development in Bavaria was a rehearsal of what was to be done with human beings. The performance itself was postponed for ten years. As for these beer-hall extras, they had their evening's session of hate and went their ways, and next morning the whole episode seemed rather unimportant.

On November 9 1923, when Hitler and his Storm Troopers, with the participation of General Ludendorff, marched through the streets in his abortive *Putsch* (he had proclaimed the overthrow of the Federal Government the night before), I was among the people on the street. I heard the rattle of shots as the troops of the Bavarian government fired at the rebels. In ten minutes the brown battalions were disarmed or dispersed. The people in the streets were motivated more by curiosity than by any revolutionary mood. I heard cursing, but no one seemed to know whom the curses were for. Whenever that was in doubt in Bavaria, the Prussians would do for targets. At any rate the majority of the Bavarians stood behind their government. In the course of that rainy day, in spite of the pools of blood near Preysing Palace, the whole affair turned into an entertainment. Everybody went out on the streets, not to demonstrate or to take sides, but simply to be there when something was going on. In the afternoon, when the police raised the barriers at Odeonsplatz, thousands streamed together from all sides. In front of the Feldherrnhalle a few machine guns had been set up. The guards stood on the steps with shouldered rifles, but did not stop a few apparently licensed speakers from attempting to address their followers.

One of these speakers was a well-known ranger named Escherich who had founded a nationalistic paramilitary organization called Orgesch (from ORGanization ESCHerich)—a middle-aged man in hunting costume with a substantial belly and beard; another was a spokesman for the student fraternities, a young man dressed to the hilt and whose face was a mass of dueling scars. They stood at different corners of the upper terrace, could not see one another because of the guards in between, and did not know that they were both talking simultaneously and equally inaudibly. Their voices were drowned by the noise; you could see only the motion of their mouths and their gestures, which ultimately led the people in the square to roar with laughter and applaud ironically, as if they were watching a comic duel between two barkers at a fair. The orators had to give up and go; the people continued laughing and finally went off to drink beer. That was the end of the famous Ludendorff-Hitler *Putsch.* In later years the participants were decorated with the so-called 'Order of Blood.'

Hitler, too, had to go—first to a hiding place and then, after a fairly amiable trial, to prison in the Landsberg Fortress where, twenty-five years later, the Americans hanged some Nazi doctors. . . . There he was given a great deal of patient paper and he composed *Mein Kampf*, which subsequently befuddled the mind of the nation. But no one gave much thought to him in those days. The nation was busy with consolidation and reconstruction. The magician Hjalmar Schacht had created the Rentenmark and paper money was no longer being printed in denominations of billions. Gustav Stresemann ran the government and launched a policy of reconciliation with the West, especially France. The inflation ceased, German currency returned to normal. For a few years modest prosperity reigned.

In the late autumn of that year, while staying with friends at Tegernsee, I had written a play in a single night, to the accompaniment of a howling foehn wind. Its title was *Kiktahan or The Backswoodsmen*, set in the Far West of a romanticized pioneer America. Brecht thought it was good—it was the only play I wrote under his influence. Since it was turned down by a reader at Kurt Wolff's publishing house—Wolff himself was away at the time—Brecht sent it to his publisher in Potsdam, Gustav Kiepenheuer, who, however, did not publish his plays either, but merely reproduced them for stage purposes. Kiepenheuer accepted it for his stage series, and even paid me an advance.

Brecht said we had to go to Berlin. That was where the theatrical battles were being fought, he said.

The fact that two of us got there was something we owed to the director Erich Engel. During this period in Munich I had become almost closer to him than to Brecht. He was a remarkable person, small, vigorous, prematurely bald, with a sharp-featured Gustav Mahler head. His was a skull that showed the fine modeling of late-Roman sculpture; if I survive him I would love to have that skull prepared by a taxidermist so that I could keep it on my desk. His eyes, behind his glasses, had the curiously alert look of a detached observer. Even in conversation, or when he was directing—even when he was making love, I suspect—he seemed really to be dealing with an epistemological problem.

(Shortly after I wrote the above sentences I heard news of his death. I am letting the passage stand unchanged, for the joke was meant as a loving tribute.)

This style of his stage managing corresponded to the incisiveness of his features and to his intellectual coolness, though it never became rigid or tense. Rather, his great contribution was to help us all throw off the yoke of Expressionist 'formalism' by means of a novel, intellectually heightened realistic technique. Engel prepared the way for the later 'Brecht style,' and developed it further in collaboration with Brecht. At the time I came to Munich he was the general manager of the Bavarian State Theater. Towards the end of 1923, he was appointed artistic director of the Deutsches Theater in Berlin. One of his first acts in this post was to offer Brecht and me similar contracts as play-readers—'dramaturgists'—at the theater. The contract would run for a year. This permitted me to go to Berlin, and so I did—this time to stay.

Berlin had spruced up its façades and done some repainting. The seedy crumbling look of many buildings in the early postwar period had vanished. Everything seemed brand-new—possibly a bit too new, as if bought fresh off the griddle, but gay and smart. Other aspects of the city, traffic, restaurants, street life, seemed less chaotic, less underhand and underground, also less adventurous. There was a new Kurfürstendamm society whose parties were more elaborate and select than those of the good old sharks of 1920 and who felt themselves entitled to an even crasser display of snobbish cynicism. At one such affair that I attended in February 1924 the walls were festooned with such maxims as: 'Love is the foolish overestimation of the minimal difference between one sexual object and another.' The girls hired to serve drinks went about naked, except for transparent panties embroidered with a silk fig leaf. They were not, like the 'bunnies' in modern American night clubs, there just for looks, but could be freely handled—that had been included in their pay.

All the shops were bright and shiny, crammed with silver, porcelain, crystal, furs, toiletries. The delicatessens were jammed. Amusements for the common people were also going full blast again. At the bock beer festivals there was not a seat to be had. In the spring huge crowds poured out to see the flowering trees in Werder, going by excursion steamer filled to capacity and complete with a brass band.

War and the immediate postwar period were forgotten. There was a burst of vitality and indeed recklessness. Moreover, the intellectual, artistic, cultural, and social life of Berlin was going through a boom that before long secured the city an exceptional position among the capitals of Europe and attracted to it an international elite. This boom was not merely a superficial phenomenon; it was generated by deep-seated creative forces. Support came from the truly aristocratic, truly open, truly cultivated Berlin society, those solid groups from the old West End who still exceeded the newly rich in numbers, standing, and influence, as well as from the young people of all classes, including the working class, temporarily secure because of the growth of large-scale industrial enterprise. The fine, big theater of the Freie Volksbühne on Bülowplatz (later to be called Karl Liebknecht Platz, still later Horst Wessel Platz, and today Rosa Luxemburg Platz) was filled to the last seat every night, for the most part by members of the labor unions, who applauded the ideologically and artistically bold productions of Erwin Piscator. All the theaters were flourishing; it was their finest hour. Money was plentiful, and thus a Berlin theater could afford to have two play-readers on its payroll, readers moreover who were far too busy writing plays themselves and therefore not especially eager to read the plays of other writers and look after the mail and the files. But that didn't matter so much, for the Deutsches Theater also had a chief dramaturgist and a 'dramaturgical editor' who kept things going. Brecht and I were considered ornamental additions of a progressive sort who would attach the younger generation to the triumphal chariot of the whole enterprise.

Brecht did not even make a pretense of working. Occasionally he turned up in the theater and demanded dictatorial powers. Above all he wanted the 'German Theater' to be renamed the 'Epic Smoking Theater,' with the whole operation devoted exclusively to his plays. In those days he cherished the theory that the theater audience should be able to smoke and drink as at a variety show, so that they would not fall into what he considered to be a false 'mood' or expectation of continuous suspense. Rather, they should be able to focus their attention as at a boxing match or track meet on the individual rounds or events, to be divided into epic segments. When all these suggestions were turned down and he was, to boot, not allowed to direct a Shakespeare performance, he vanished again and thereafter limited himself to coming in punctually to collect his salary.

In the wing of the theater overlooking the street, where the offices were situated, I was assigned a large room for my sole use. Every morning the famous theater attendant Zimmermann, possessor of a long, white, two-pronged beard, came in and deposited six or seven glistening black coal briquettes alongside the old-fashioned tile stove, to keep the room warm during the day. Some time later I arrived with an empty briefcase and the morning newspaper. After reading the newspaper I used it to wrap up the briquettes and stow them away in the briefcase. Then I left, seemingly heavily laden with manscripts, and made good use of the briquettes in the tiny stove of my small furnished room, where I was working on a new play. When Brecht was hard up for fuel, we shared the coal. We also shared the key to my office—which was at some distance from the other offices—for the purpose of certain appointments, for there was a very comfortable sofa there. Every so often I would actually read a play—I recall reading the manuscript of a comedy by Robert Musil. Since I was an admirer of Musil—sections of *The Man Without Qualities* had already been published in magazines—I started on the play with great respect, but found it involved and loquacious. I left the manuscript along with the key, which he happened to need, for Brecht, asking him his opinion. Next day I found it; he had scrawled in pencil across the envelope, 'Shit.' That was one of our formidable efforts as play-readers.

I participated in the rehearsals all the more assiduously. Erich Engel was at this time producing Büchner's *Danton's Death*, with Kortner as Danton. I assisted in the practical work, drilling the extras, supervising some rehearsals, taking my place on the stage with a Jacobin cap and stamping about in the *Carmagnole*. Once when an actor was sick I had to fill in at the end of the play in the role of the Second Executioner, who saunters across the stage after washing the guillotine. I was stripped to the waist and smeared with red ink. I myself was deeply impressed by my performance.

All these activities combined to develop in me a sense of theater, until I had it in my fingertips. I think that such training for the aspiring playwright is far more valuable than any seminar on stage-craft, let alone the kind of playwriting courses considered useful in America. That year Max Reinhardt staged Shaw's *St Joan* with Elisabeth Bergner—the German opening took place a few days earlier than the opening in London—and Pirandello's *Six Characters in Search of an Author*. Many of the great actors of Berlin were on the stage at that time, and I sat at the rehearsals excited and fascinated, watching Reinhardt spin his magic. I took in every minute phase in the transformation from the first concept of a part and a scene to its full realization. All this was particularly instructive because Reinhardt, before blocking, would dictate enormously comprehensive director's notes in which all the details of his production plan, down to the intonation and pantomime to accompany specific sentences, were entered in a language that some-times sounded borrowed from trashy novels: 'A woeful twitch of sorrow appears upon his face,' or 'Her hand darts involuntarily to her heart,' and so on.

Once he was standing on the stage with his actors, he would forget all that, would often let their natural reactions guide them to a totally opposite effect, would not say a word that was not pertinent, lucid, highly intelligent, and precise, and was often able to bring a barely rehearsed scene to a pitch of perfection by giving the tiniest of hints, by speaking a few lines himself, by changing a position, but above all by his unique gift for tense, stimulating listening.

Groups of actors, large and small, always stood around in the venerable paved courtyard between the Deutsches Theater and the Kammerspiel Theater, a courtyard separated from the street by a row of buildings. Among these actors were stars and beginners, the celebrities of yesterday and tomorrow, as well as accomplished or embryonic stage managers, stage designers, and playwrights. There was constant debate, quarreling, sneering, reviling, laughing, and the discussion of new plays. Here in this courtyard, and in the stablelike entrance (which also smelled like a stable) to the dressing rooms, was the concentrated theatrical atmosphere, a throwback to those itinerant troupes of mountebanks of olden days, upon whose arrival in town housewives hastily took the washing off the lines. Pretty women passed by; a good many love affairs started here, and a good many friendships were made. Here I first met the actor Heinz Hilpert with his jutting, impudent nose and the mouth cynically distorted in the Berlin fashion. In the courtyard of the Deutsches Theater I offered him a Havana freshly filched from a prosperous relative. We took turns smoking it, since I had no other—not yet suspecting that this was a cigar symbolic of brotherhood, one that would remain alight for a lifetime.

At a matinee in the Deutsches Theater one fine February day in the year 1925 I had my second Berlin opening. It was a version of *The Backwoodsmen,* that play I had written in Tegernsee. Heinz Hilpert directed. This was the first play of mine that he staged; there have been seven others since then. My play was put on by a special group called the 'Young Stage.' The rehearsals all took place at night or in the late afternoons because the actors were rehearsing for the regular programs in the mornings, and performing in the evenings. They had an enormous capacity and willingness for work, devoting whole nights to these projects. That was especially true of my dress rehearsal, which did not end until Sunday morning, a few hours before the curtain rose for the first performance. We were all completely wound up. As I watched the audience pouring into the theater everything flickered before my eyes, not only from excitement, but also from the quantities of black coffee and brandy I had been drinking to keep awake. We had a good house, an audience composed half of the intellectual elite, half of sensation seekers. The leaders of the Berlin intelligentsia and Berlin society appeared in the orchestra and in the boxes. I recall especially Albert Einstein and Gustav Stresemann, not to speak of Brecht and many others of my own generation. All the Berlin producers, managers, play-readers, and critics were present, and there were even some from provincial cities.

My heart sank, for I had long since ceased to believe in the play and had even tried to withdraw it shortly before the performance. On the other hand, the gamble was irresistible.

The performance itself almost turned into a disaster, the male lead having drunk himself into a stupor, from sheer excitement and exhaustion. He never knew which scene he had already played and which was still to come; we had to hold on to him in the wings to keep him from repeating the same entrance or drunkenly barging in

278

on the scenes of other actors. Nevertheless the play as performed turned out to be exactly what I had meant it to be: a wild battle, an open clash of opinions, a furious pro and contra, accompanied by loud applause and jeering whistles. In one scene the commotion rose to such a pitch that we were beginning to think we would have to stop. But Leopold Jessner, the general manager, who was sitting among the audience, rose to his full height, stretched out his arms in a priestly gesture, and intoned: 'Respect the work, please.' He was able to calm the turmoil; the lights, which had already been turned up, were dimmed again, the curtain remained up, and the play was performed to the end. Hilpert and I came out after the final curtain and bowed. We were greeted by some of those piercing whistles which people who could not manage with two fingers produced by whistling over large housekeys. Much to the delight of our friends and followers, we stuck out our tongues at the whistlers and booers.

I awaited the critical anathemas in a stoical spirit. The piece was uneven and murky, sketchy in plot, badly organized. Nevertheless it had good roles and a few highly dramatic scenes. That day marked the beginning of a director's career—on the basis of his staging, Hilpert received an important contract—and the triumph of a character actor: Rudolf Forster. He had played a ruined Austrian count who becomes a swindler in America. Forster played the part with such decadent charm and such a unique, wholly personal tone that after this performance he became one of the most celebrated and sought-after actors on the German stage.

As for myself, this performance and this whole theater season had given me something far more important than success and royalties: insight. For the first time I took fair measure of my own limitations. This had nothing to do with self-restriction or modesty: to recognize limitations is not the same thing as being limited. Within the boundaries drawn by one's own natural inclinations and talents one can achieve anything and everything.

I did not lower my sights. But I began to know or to have intimations of what I wanted and what I should and should not be doing. I had neither the gift nor the wish to inaugurate a new epoch in literature, a new theatrical style, a new artistic direction. But I knew that a new vitality in effects and in values could be achieved by certain artistic means that were essentially timeless, by a kind of humane art that can never be outmoded as long as human beings think of themselves as what they are. This was not a program; it was the outcome of a totally personal evolution. I was not looking for anything programmatic and had no theories about what I ought to be doing next, not even definite plans. I wanted to reach out to nature, life, the truth without divorcing myself from the demands of the hour, the burning questions of my own time. I managed to find my own tone in a few poems, though not in my prose writings. I must now manage to do that for the theater, whose essences I had been absorbing for five years.

Rarely had I been in such good spirits as in the period that followed. I was unemployed again; the contracts for Brecht and me had not been renewed at the end of the season. Apparently the Reinhardt theaters had to save on coal briquettes. But nothing worried me. There are times when you know in advance that you are going to be lucky, that whatever you lay a hand to will succeed. There are times when you can physically feel the benign influence of the stars. I must have been in such a vein at that time. I think that if I had gone to Monte Carlo that year I would have broken the bank.

A somewhat crazy woman who lived in my boardinghouse told my fortune from cards one evening and suddenly cried out: 'Money is close at hand. A blonde woman is approaching you. You are going to be married this year and become rich overnight.'

Naturally, I did not believe a word of it. Blonde women occassionally approached me, but not with marriage in mind, and there was certainly nothing like money in either of my hands. I owed my landlady, in whose parlor the oracle was pronounced, months of rent. But she was a dear old spinster who, aside from her toothless dog, loved only me and Hindenburg.

Hindenburg had been elected President of the Reich in May, upon the death of Friedrich Ebert. I was standing with Brecht near the Siegesallee amid a jubilant crowd when he made his official entry in a gray open car. Brecht said—I remember his exact words: 'At the end of the first quarter of the twentieth century of the Christian era they brought a man into the city and paid him the highest honors because he had never read a book.'

This was an allusion to an apocryphal or genuine remark of the old general to the effect that the only books he had ever read were the Bible and the Army Manual. But even his accession to the presidency could not dim my inner glow.

*

My mother's cousin, Dr Ernst Goldschmidt, of Mainz, who while I was still a boy had married a charming soubrette of the municipal Opera House and who had actually written opera librettos himself, had since those days become a very rich banker in Berlin. But he was still mad about the theater and was a sponsor of all the arts. For the summer he had invited me to be his guest in a palace he had rented at Wannsee.

It was an awful place, an imitation medieval castle, but it had a park fronting on the lake and a large octagonal tower room with a magnificent view. There, I resolved, I would be able to write my new play. I had two subjects in mind, one tragic and the other humorous. I thought of the latter as a 'lyrical comedy,' to be set in my native region.

I had to keep my host from suspecting my financial condition or realizing how much I needed his hospitality. For I knew too much about the psychology of the rich man to give my cousin the chance to regard himself as my benefactor and me as his dependant. On the contrary, I gave him the pleasure of my company, which he really enjoyed, and at the end of the week—after mulling over the alternatives of going to the Alps or to the seacoast—I was persuaded to prolong my stay. The cuisine and the wine cellar were excellent, the cigars were there for the taking, and my host was a charming person who moreover went into the city every morning and returned only toward evening.

Whenever I myself had to go into town, Goldschmidt's valet Paul lent me the fare. With the discernment of domestics, he had sized up my situation and—with equal prescience—counted on having his good deeds rewarded with interest in this rather than the next world. He also provided me with razor blades discarded by his master after only a single use, and with other necessary articles.

I worked with zest. In keeping with my mood, I had decided on the comedy, although I thought it had the slimmer chances for success. I wrote it in my native dialect, though dialect plays were considered old-hat. But I had to write it that way; there was no other choice. For the first time since the war years my mood was one of unclouded gaiety, and that mood was intimately linked with the landscape, the melody, and the whole world of my boyhood. Back home, I thought, back home in Mainz, Darmstadt, or Frankfurt the play may be put on and understood, for its moving spirit was love for the Rhenish Hessian atmosphere and it was saturated with the humors, in every sense, of that region. Comedies, it is said, are usually written with morose earnestness. That may be true. I laughed with every sentence I wrote.

In the midst of this work, precisely at the major intermission between the second and third acts, I met my wife.

Within a short time I had no doubt that she was and would remain my wife.

Our first meeting took place in a turbulent setting.

It was a party at the home of a young actor's mother. The whole company, who had just given a sensational performance of Wedekind's *Franziska,* as well as a large number of other Berlin artists, had been invited. Without either lasciviousness or cynicism, purely in a spirit of fun and *joie de vivre*, artists in those days dressed very scantily. Even then—though only among intimate friends—ladies who had something to show went 'topless.' Men sometimes appeared in bathing trunks, but with a formal bow tie.

My wife, however, appeared in a simple dress buttoned to the throat—and by that alone she fascinated me, as well as by her lovely, youthful face, although I really thought her much too thin. I showered attentions upon her at once; she did not condescend to the slightest intimacy. On the contrary. Since the general racket obviously bored her and, probably, because she was simply tired, she lay down on the sofa in a small room to rest. I was not able to rouse her, whatever jokes I made. She slept soundly.

But we met again, loved one another, and at once decided to marry. She was twenty-four, I just five years older.

This decision was not arrived at frivolously. Never had I been so serious about anything. I was filled with an awareness that my libertine life must come to an end and a proper, productive life begin. Wife and children belonged to such a proper life. And I could no longer imagine any other woman as my wife. She felt the same way. I was convinced that with the founding of a family my strength and my ability to master life's problems would grow. It was not necessary to have more than that. For both of us such a step had nothing to do with speculating on success and on the prospects before us.

We knew a simple fact: happiness had come to us and we had to hold on to it.

Her maiden name was Alice Henriette Alberta Herdan-Harris von Valbonne und Belmont—Alice von Herdan, for short. But now her name was simply Frau Frank. For she too had a premature youthful marriage behind her, with a man named Karl Frank. The survivors of the Vienna Youth Movement will remember him as one of their most inspiring leaders. He was extraordinarily handsome, of a dark, alpine type. He had been converted to Communism. Though he was later to break with the Party, at that time he lived more for Party work than for anything else. We still have friendly, almost familial relations with him. But the marriage had already gone to pieces, although the two had had a daughter, Michaela, then two years old.

I had not the slightest hesitation about 'marrying into' this combination of mother and child. Michaela grew up with us like my own daughter, who was born a year later. For me there was scarcely any difference, and to this day I regard her as my daughter, her husband as my son-in-law, her children as my grandchildren. She simply had two fathers, which is much better than none.

My wife had no father; he had died early after running through his fortune. Her mother, who came from a well-known North German family, was an actress at the Burgtheater in Vienna. There Alice, her only child, had grown up. More to earn her living than because of genuine inclination, she too had become an actress. I have never seen her on the stage; she did not want me to, even after we were finally living together. The exhibitionist trait which is an integral part of acting was alien to her nature. Her real desire, and her great hope, was to study medicine, in whose theoretic aspects she was especially interested.

Though I was bringing to our marriage nothing but my debts and she nothing but a lampshade—albeit a very large one—I promised that I would very soon make it possible for her to undertake such studies within the framework of a secure livelihood. Both of us were firmly convinced that everything would work out.

Perhaps that is why it did.

It occurs to me now that in addition to the lampshade she had a piece of property of extraordinary importance to me—an old typewriter, already distinctly rickety. On this machine I finished my comedy, which I had begun writing by hand, so that I would have it ready for submission as soon as it was done, although at the time I typed very laboriously, with one finger of each hand. I literally wrote the play with bleeding fingers, for the E and R keys were askew, and I bruised myself each time I hit them. Moreover, the shift key did not work, so that the whole manuscript looked like a solemn poem by Stefan George or e. e. cummings, with no capitals.

Thus it was that *Der fröhliche Weinberg* ('The Merry Vineyard') was written.

In the autumn of 1925 the play was rejected by all the Berlin theaters. None of the producers and hardly any of the directors, except for Hilpert—but he was working in Frankfurt—thought it had any chance. Some thought it too daring, others too rustic.

Although I now had a contract for a novel from Ullstein's Propyläen Verlag, and was receiving small monthly payments in advance, our financial situation was growing perilous and the prospects of a performance became slimmer and slimmer.

Then my play fell into the hands of 'old Elias.' It was sheer chance that I had not met Julius Elias, the patriarch of Berlin artistic life, earlier. But now it happened just at the right moment.

It is hardly possible to describe this man because nobody would believe the description. I do not imagine that any such phenomenon exists these days. At any rate I have never again met anyone who combined such a wealth of temperament, intelligence, knowledge, and cultivation with such unreserved helpfulness, such passion for discovering, supporting, and advancing talented young people, such perfect altruism, faith, and capacity for enthusiasm.

Small, flat-footed, with a Chaplinesque gait, thick, gray-streaked black hair, mustache, and eyebrows, eyes always flashing with zeal and zest, he would shoot toward you like a rocket as soon as you entered his office. His very manner of shaking your hand made you believe in yourself.

'Do you need money?' That was the question he shouted at me in greeting when I first called on him. And promptly answered it himself: 'Of course you need money. All young playwrights need money! But don't worry!' he went on, still at the top of his voice, although I had not yet said a word and was standing perfectly still, dumbfounded. 'Don't worry. Your play will make millions! Millions!' He threw his hands up to heaven like a biblical prophet, then let them drop on my shoulders. Looking up into my face paternally, he shook me vigorously. 'Don't let success go to your head,' he cautioned. 'Don't go buying a big house and a fancy car right away. You don't need those things. You can be really great if you stay reasonable and keep working. Buy your young wife pretty clothes, but not too much jewelery; otherwise she'll develop a passion for diamonds and throw your money out of the window.'

'For the present,' I said modestly, 'she has no winter coat and the play has been rejected everywhere.'

'Nonsense,' the old man overruled me. 'From today on you're a made man.'

I was not so sure. But when Julius Elias made predictions, you could rely on them, however fantastic they seemed.

He had experience. In the eighties and nineties he had helped found the Freie Bühne, where Gerhart Hauptmann began his rise to fame. He had helped edit and translate the first edition of Ibsen's collected dramas into German. He had organized the first exhibition of French Impressionists in the days when people still attacked those 'seditious' paintings with canes and umbrellas. The first monograph on the great German painter Max Liebermann had been written by him, and there was hardly a graphic artist of the new and newest generations for whom he had not been nursemaid and patron for a time.

Right now he was director of the Arkadia Verlag, a theatrical branch of the Ullstein firm, to which, incidentally, Brecht soon moved; this time I acted as intermediary.

A week after old Elias had assumed responsibility for my career, I heard that Saltenburg, who managed three large Berlin theaters, had accepted the play and that it would be put on before Christmas. Elias had achieved this by sheer blackmail.

Saltenburg, in order to keep his box office well in the black and his actors gainfully employed, needed the performance rights in Paris hits, the light boulevard comedies that were practically sure-fire. Almost all of these were in the hands of Julius Elias, who also translated some of them. The result was a kind of barter deal. Elias promised Saltenburg four sure-fire French plays that other Berlin producers were angling for, solely on condition that he put on *The Merry Vineyard*.

During this period I had to pass through a great, a diabolic, temptation. Elias suddenly telephoned me and asked me to come to his office at once. There was a difficult decision to make, and I alone could have the last word, he said.

There I found Dr Robert Klein, then Saltenburg's business manager. Later he took over the management of the Reinhardt theaters and ran them for several years with great success. This shrewd man, who already had had a great deal of theatrical experience, made me an offer. Saltenburg, he told me, had no real faith in the play. If he put it on at all, he would do it with second-class actors and run it in a second-class theater usually devoted to cheap musicals, scheduling it for a month at most. That meant that it would be declassed as far as Berlin was concerned, and would be ignored. He himself, he continued, had many doubts as to whether the play could be put over, but he was prepared to take the risk, because he was deeply concerned about my work and my future. But to put the play on successfully, he must be able to deal freely with it, which was impossible unless he had all the rights and, of course, some prospect of recouping his expenses.

He was offering me twenty thousand marks, cash outright, if I would sell the play to him and give him carte blanche in regard to its theatrical production. That would mean security for me, regardless of success or failure, while for him it would be a wild gamble. Perhaps he'd show the play in the provinces first, then rent a good Berlin theater and assemble a cast of stars. This way I might well make my breakthrough; in return he would net a bit of profit from the rights for future performances.

It was a frightful situation; I sweated from every pore in my body. For me twenty thousand marks was a fortune. It meant security for a long time to come. My advance from Ullstein amounted to three hundred a month and ran only to the end of the year. I had scarcely started on the novel. And I had twice had the experience of seeing how a Berlin performance, even with top-notch actors, could miss fire and close overnight without yielding me a penny. I was then living with my wife and Michaela in a furnished apartment whose rent alone devoured a third of my allowance from Ullstein. And what would happen when that allowance ran out?

With Robert Klein's money I would be able to live in the country for a year or two and work away freely. . . . All this passed through my mind in seconds, while I became almost nauseated from tension.

Dr Klein had asked Elias to let me talk to him alone, so that Elias could not influence my decision by signs, looks, and winks, as he would surely have tried to do. And Elias had said to me: 'I can't take the responsibility of giving you advice. There's too much money at stake.'

The tempter was already taking out his checkbook. At that moment I came to my senses. If this man is prepared to risk such a sum, I told myself, he must count on a profit of at least twice as much. And anyway I had been taking risks for many years now. I was not going to be deprived of this great possibility, this chance to stake everything on a large sum or on zero. Better to go through struggle and uncertainty a while longer.

I said no.

'You'll regret it,' Dr Klein said.

Elias was called in. He threw his arms around my neck and sent for a bottle of champagne.

When I went home, I was as battered and exhausted as I had been during the war after a six-day barrage.

A week later the play, not yet performed, received the Kleist Prize from Paul Fechter, a severe critic who was judge of the prize that year, and had hitherto been by no means well disposed towards me.

In those days there was not yet an inflation in literary prizes. Only two prizes of importance were given annually, the Kleist Prize in Berlin and the Georg Büchner Prize in Darmstadt. Then there was the Frankfurt Goethe Prize, which was given only at three-year intervals for a body of work such as that of Stefan George or Gerhart Hauptmann, and the state Schiller Prize, which came due only once in five years and because of its high standards was in fact almost never awarded.

The Kleist Prize was considered the highest literary distinction for young playwrights. Its purpose was to encourage preferably unknown beginners, and to make the public aware of them. Nomination of the prize winner was awaited every year with suspense. Brecht had received it two years before; earlier prize winners were Hans Henny Jahnn, Arnolt Bronnen, Fritz von Unruh, Ernst Toller, and Walter Hasenclever—all considered the hopefuls of the literary world. Seven years later, when I myself was asked by the foundation to decide the award, I gave it to Ödön von Horváth. In addition to an appreciation of the prize-winning work which appeared throughout the German press, it consisted in a sum of money: fifteen hundred marks. My wife and I were absolutely astonished; we were deluged by telephone calls after the news appeared in the morning papers. Old Elias—it was he, of course, who had made sure that the play reached the hands of the judge—had not let on. I had no suspicion that it was even under consideration.

At first we were numbed, as if struck by some tragedy. Then we began dancing with Michaela, hopping like three monkeys all around the apartment. With the ten o'clock mail a registered letter with the check arrived.

We cashed it at once, and with the money in our pockets we started out on a triumphant stroll and shopping spree through the city. We dressed ourselves in new clothes from head to foot: a cream-colored suit for me, a suit of the same color for my wife. Then we went to the most select ladies' shop for a dress, a dressing gown, and a silk nightgown for Alice. We went from shop to shop. We needed shoes, socks, stockings, coats. Michaela received a dress and toys. By nightfall we still had enough money left to go out for dinner. I decided to combine this with a grand gesture.

During the previous winter I had discovered an intimate, pleasant restaurant on a quiet side street of Berlin's West End. The food was delicious; and the owner, Herr Hacker, was a lover of theater and the arts. At that time I was still working as play-reader for the Reinhardt theaters, and the Young Stage had put on my play. In spite of the scandal, this play of mine had made a great impression on progressively minded Herr Hacker. I had returned to his restaurant again and again on special occasions, had brought friends with me, and Herr Hacker had time and again extended credit for the check without a grumble.

We decided to crown the day by going there, and I meant to use the rest of the prize money to pay my debts. That we were running through all the money in a single day seemed to us perfectly natural. Those fifteen hundred marks were a gift from heaven, not destined to be doled out thriftily and pettily; they were meant to be sacrificed to the gods.

In Hacker's restaurant we ordered everything we ordinarily denied ourselves: hors d'oeuvres, venison, fine wine, dessert. When we could eat no more, I asked the waiter for the check and for the total of what I owed the restaurant. Instead, Herr Hacker in person appeared at our table. Not a word had been said about the prize up to this point. But he bowed politely to my wife, then said to me: 'A man who wins the Kleist Prize has no debts.'

With that he tore up all the checks I had previously signed, including the one for the present evening.

In Saltenburg's eyes the award of the prize for the play did not improve its chances. On the contrary, as far as he was concerned the prize made success even more dubious. For it often happened that such advance laurels stirred the critics, who did not like to be told what to think and in any case lived by upsetting accepted opinion, to reject a work all the more forcefully. Among theatrical people there was a well-known saying of L'Arronge's:

'The prizer a play is, the flopper it flops.'

Even now the producer tried in every possible way to squirm out of the agreement, but Elias was adamant. He raged like a madman until the play was scheduled and, what is more, not in a second- or third-class theater (after the Kleist Prize, Saltenburg could no longer pull this trick) but in his best house: the Theater am Schiffbauerdamm.

Elias was drunk with victory. He formed the habit of stopping acquaintances on the street, seizing them by the top button of their coat, and shouting into their ear: 'Have you heard about Zuckmayer? Remember that name!' (Many a button was ripped right off.)

An operetta director was chosen to stage the play, a capable practical man of the theater and an affable person who, partly because the dialect was foreign to him, left me to handle the actors. The cast was uneven and by no means brilliant, but it had a few people who were uncommonly well cast.

Then something happened that filled experienced theater people with profound distrust: from the first to the last rehearsal everybody laughed.

The curious mirth began when instead of reading 'sample pages' I read the entire play to the assembled cast—a practice that usually does not go down very well in the theater. Every morning all the actors were as high as if they had drunk champagne. Without losing patience, they let me coach them endlessly in the exact pronunciation of the dialect. (There was not a single blowup.) In brief, everything that happened was of the sort that is regarded as a bad omen in the theater—even a brilliant dress rehearsal at which the laughter was continuous and the scenes were interrupted by applause. Everyone who was the slightest bit superstitious had to conclude that the play would be a disastrous flop, and Saltenburg was more convinced than ever that old Elias had put a flea in his bonnet that was going to keep him scratching. I sat behind him at the dress rehearsal and saw him twitch painfully at every laugh, at every handclap from the spectators. During the intermission I heard him say to his stage manager: 'Have the sets for the last play ready. We'll need them again in three days.'

It was three days before Christmas—and my mother was coming from Mainz for the opening. My father, remembering what had happened the last time, could not face it.

I paid a call at Ullstein's to ask for a small additional advance of a hundred marks with which to buy my mother a present. But I was turned away: I'd already had too many advances, I was told—I'd better call again the day after the opening.

To avoid all discussion, I had informed my parents of my marriage as a *fait accompli*, and of course they were hardly delighted that I had ventured on marriage in my situation, with, what is more, a divorced woman who was bringing a child with her. I did not have the funds for a trip to Mainz with my new family. The result was that my mother would be meeting Alice and Michaela for the first time. We were bracing ourselves for that moment with some anxiety.

But after I had met my mother with a bunch of violets at the Zoo Station in Berlin and taken her to my apartment, she simply embraced my wife and kissed Michaela.

When we rode to the opening in a cab, I said to my mother: 'If all goes well, you'll have a pair of overshoes with fur lining for Christmas.' I did not dare to imagine anything more munificent than that.

My wife was wearing a glorious evening dress and silver shoes, both borrowed from a friend. I had on my old black suit, brushed till it shone, and newly purchased patent-leather shoes that creaked like an oxcart on its first ride over the prairie.

Before the opening, when I peered through the well-known hole in the curtain, I saw the same baleful row of prominent critics sitting just as they had done at the time of my funeral in the National Theater five years before. Almost the whole band was there, save for a few who had meanwhile expired of old age.

This time I did not take a seat in a box. I was too overwrought, and besides I had work to do on the stage. Throughout the whole performance I stood in the wings and—so amused watchers later told me—repeated every word, moving my lips soundlessly.

Almost at once, after the first few sentences, there came a sound from the audience that alarmed me. It was like the growl of a hungry beast, and it suddenly swelled to a shrill, piercing neighing.

I had never heard such sounds before. Immediately afterward there was a clatter and crackling as though a hailstorm were suddenly descending on a tin roof.

Bruck, the stage manager, was suddenly standing beside me pinching my arm like a crab. 'Roars of laughter!' he whispered. 'Applause in the middle of scenes.'

I was icy cold. It was like coming under fire for the first time, again.

I cannot describe how that evening passed. It lives in my memory as a single hurricane of noise. I gave up watching the actors; I could hear from their voices that they were rising to greater and greater enjoyment in the performance and that everything was going better than during our rehearsals. Through a crack at the fireman's post, from which the audience is visible, I saw a tossing surf of heads, faces, shirt fronts; I saw shoulders shaking incessantly with laughter, mouths wide open, howling and screeching. It was like the outbreak of a contagious laughing sickness, an epidemic ecstasy of merriment, a medieval mass intoxication, and that was how the participants and even the critics described it afterwards.

In the midst of all those people who were laughing till the tears streamed down their faces and their dress shirts rumpled, while total strangers were banging each other on the shoulders, there were only two persons who sat there in dead seriousness, not so much as smiling: my wife and my mother.

For us it was no joke. For us it was a matter of life and death, the decisive battle.

The two women had only met that morning and had had no time to become close. But now a common anxiety had thrown them together. They sat pressed against one another like frightened chickens, and held each other's hands. Their seats were in the critics' row. Right beside my mother sat the fierce Kerr, who in the past had so frightfully savaged me.

When the intermission curtain fell, the applause thundered out so loud that I thought the chandeliers would come crashing down. I heard my name being shouted as if the archangels were summoning me to the Last Judgment.

I went out on the stage, dazzled and in a kind of trance. Again and again I went out and back, out and back—later I was told that I had been pale and funereally grave, and that my new shoes had netted a burst of laughter of their own by creaking so loudly.

My mother, too, when I met her for a minute behind the stage during the intermission, was numb and pale. She merely whispered with frozen lips: 'Kerr smiled twice.' It sounded like: The hangman is ill. The execution is being postponed.

During the last act I stood in the wings again and without noticing what I was about drank a bottle Nackenheimer '12 that the actors had given me.

Toward the end I had a 'part' myself. The act takes place at dawn, and at a certain point a cock is supposed to crow. Since our stage manager, a city boy, could not turn out the kind of genuine cockcrow that was needed, and since tape recordings did not yet exist, I had assumed responsibility for doing it myself, at least at the opening. In spite of the Nackenheimer I crowed on cue, and not badly, according to earwitnesses.

At the final curtain, the mood was like that at a bullfight. Ladies threw bouquets and handkerchiefs onto the stage; the curtain puller had a stiff arm; and I was embraced by so many actors that my old black suit was smudged incurably with grease-paint. But it could be pensioned off now.

Old Elias had tears of happiness in his eyes when he came back stage, but he was no longer capable of saying a word to me. He had shouted himself hoarse during the performance.

Suddenly, how it came about I don't know, there was an improvised celebration in full swing. It took place in the city apartment of my cousin, the Knight of Wannsee, in whose summer palace I had written the play. He had been at the opening, of course, but had practised prudence; he said nothing about a party until the intermission. As the evidence mounted that the play was a hit, he invited more and more people. That was not a problem in those days; there were caterers who in response to a telephone call at any hour of the evening could supply a cold buffet for any number of persons.

Now—it was already after midnight—the elite of Berlin were circulating through Goldschmidt's apartment. Everybody wanted to be there that night, and Paul—who had guessed so right in helping me out during the summer—handed around the champagne with beaming smiles. I was handed around too, and in my daze I could hardly grasp the resounding names that figured in the introductions. They were the names of higher powers who ordinarily sat enthroned high above the clouds and did not exist as normal living beings. These were not people—they were companies, enterprises, editions, publications. How would I, a young writer for Ullstein Verlag, ever have seen a living Ullstein? And there were three brothers of that name all assembled at once, Franz, Hermann, and Louis. These were not just names; they were the House of Ullstein. Every third figure in full dress, holding a plate of cold salmon or a glass of champagne in his hand, was named like a newspaper head or a publisher's imprint: an Ullstein, a Mosse, an S. Fischer, a Rowohlt, a Kiepenheuer. . . .

Old Elias whirled around in a grotesque dance, as though his legs were Chaplin's sandwiches in *The Gold Rush*, from one group of publishers and producers to the next, and since he was still unable to talk, he merely tossed all ten fingers into the air. Everybody understood what he meant. They talked about me as if I were a bundle of securities that only yesterday could have been bought cheaply and that now had suddenly shot up in price.

Later that night I saw my wife, completely tipsy, sitting between two Ullstein brothers and rapturously telling them that I would certainly never write the novel I should have delivered weeks before. I had to lead her away before she betrayed all my professional secrets in her blissful state.

But all that was really of the past. Now work could begin.

Next morning—it was December 23rd, a clear, sunny winter day— the same accountant of Ullstein Verlag who two days earlier had refused me a hundred marks informed me that he could give me any sum up to ten thousand. That limitation was imposed only because there was no more cash in the house, since it was just before the holidays, but of course he could place larger sums at my disposal. . . . More than a hundred theaters had already sent wires asking for production rights in the play.

Still slightly stunned, I thrust a bundle of bank notes into the hip pocket of my trousers.

Fortune. Success. But along with all my natural happiness, I felt threatened, as if I were facing a new and as yet unknown danger.

The Berlin notices were fantastic. The most grudging critics, however it may have gone against their grain, had to concede that something extraordinary had taken place that evening. Notoriously cool-headed judges like Alfred Polgar freely affirmed their pleasure in the play. Herbert Ihering ebulliently began his notice: 'Storms of applause from the orchestra to the galleries, from the galleries back to the orchestra. Writers develop, talents grow!'

Most incredible of all, even Kerr praised the play after his fashion. Whereas previously I had wandered between the fronts, attacked by both sides, now Greeks and Trojans alike raised me on their shields.

Reporters and photographers telephoned, the UFA newsreel came, foreign correspondents called. . . . Overnight I had become the man of the hour.

Producer Saltenburg stalked around like a cock that had not only mounted the hen but also laid the egg and hatched it himself. He was now firmly convinced that he had 'always known it' and had discovered me. The lines in front of the box office at the Schiffbauerdamm Theater wound all the way to the Friedrichstrasse Station, and by Christmas Day a sign had to be posted: Sold out until January 10th. By Saltenburg's reckoning, the play would run for a year. It ran two and a half.

But *The Merry Vineyard* had some odd vicissitudes.

In Frankfurt, too, where Heinz Hilpert opened with the play on the night after the Berlin opening, it was received with the same tempestuous enthusiasm. But as it began making its way through the provinces the 'healthy instincts of respectable people' stirred. In the course of the next year the play, which nowadays seems so innocuous, produced sixty-three theater riots—a careful record of which was kept by the House of Ullstein, because each one increased the number of performances and the sales of the printed book, in which people were already underlining 'those passages.' To this day I meet elderly ladies who tell me that as young girls they managed in spite of severe prohibitions to take a secret stroll in *The Merry Vineyard*. I feel as if I had educated a whole generation of well-bred young ladies in the facts of life.

But it was not so much the strong language and erotic passages that made the play a focal point of trouble. Rather, it was a political reaction, and one that I had expected, though I had not expected it to be so strong.

'Zuckmayer does not wield a lash,' Carlo Mierendorff wrote in a review of the play in January 1926. 'He contents himself with making certain contemporaries (immortally) ridiculous. But the victims are roaring with fury.'

Those roars resounded throughout Germany. Above all, they came from the National Socialists, who had found their voices again and were once more making themselves heard. They rightly felt that they had been portrayed in the comic characters of the play, into whose mouths I had put the old and new radical and anti-Semitic phrases. The *Völkischer Beobachter*, Hitler's newspaper, foamed. The Nazis were also outraged because the play took away from them something they thought they had a lease on: the German landscape and German folk life, but without any of the blood-and-soil nonsense.

More surprising was the reaction of the students, who identified themselves with Assessor Knuzius, shown in my play as a demoralized, down-at-heels dowry hunter who tries to impress simple people as an 'academic.' When he gets the tough innkeeper's daughter instead of the rich heiress of the vineyard, he makes a drunken final speech praising his own idiocy as the 'source of the regeneration of our nation in regard to its virtue, military capability, cleanliness, devotion to duty, and racial purity.' In creating this comic character I had not the slightest intention of pillorying academic youth as a whole, but those young people felt pilloried. Student corps demonstrated against the play, threw stink bombs, chanted denunciations. There were brawls and arrests in the theaters.

There was an endless list of other groups who felt that the play was aimed at them: innkeepers, pig breeders, veterans' organizations, wine dealers, bureaucrats, even the Jews. A bishop lashed out against it from the pulpit in language reminiscent of Luther: 'All the devils of indecency leap out of the wine keg,' he said. In Stuttgart schoolchildren were marched through the city bearing banners with the slogan: 'Parents, preserve your purity; don't go to *The Merry Vineyard*.' (Parents went in droves.)

At the opening in Munich, which I attended, the audience was spurred to redoubled applause by a few whistles and cries of protest. At the end a band of irate students gathered with sticks and clubs at the stage entrance, from which I would be leaving with the actors and Otto Falckenberg, the director. The cab drivers, who were waiting outside to drive us to a party, came in and offered to act as bodyguards; they had brass knuckles, which cabbies usually carried for self-defense. Surrounded by these tough Bavarians, I strode out into the street ready to fight, with the rest of the theater people following close behind. To our right and left our enemies stood like a guard of honor. But only after we had entered the cabs did a single thin falsetto voice shout: 'Boo!'

In Gera I staged the play myself at the invitation of Prince Heinrich XLV* von Reuss; that was at the beginning of January and was one of the first performances after Berlin and Frankfurt. The princely family had held on to a sizable fortune which it used chiefly to convert the pretty former court theater into a modern stage of major rank. Seldom have I worked in so good and productive a theatrical atmosphere; this was due above all to the influence of the prince, a cultivated patron of the arts. I stayed as a guest in the Palace of Osterstein, which overlooked the city. It was an ancient edifice, but equipped with all modern amenities. Every morning a resplendent carriage and team awaited me at the gate, the coachman in braided livery, to drive me to the rehearsal. It was waiting again at the stage entrance even if the rehearsals were prolonged into the afternoon, and drove me back to the palace at a brisk trot. There a servant had kept a warm lunch for me. In my rooms I always found two crystal carafes of wine, a chilled carafe of Moselle and one at room temperature of Bordeaux. No one disturbed me, and if I wished I could invite actors up for private rehearsals. I had never in my wildest dreams imagined such discretion and such truly princely hospitality. I felt as if I were being treated like Goethe at Weimar, in his days as Privy Councillor to the Duke. Sometimes, but always after the most delicate inquiries as to whether I might have other plans, I would be invited to tea or dinner with the aged princely couple. Those were animated, stimulating hours such as I might spend among highly cultivated people in Berlin. There was not the slightest trace of aristocratic pride or outmoded ceremonials. Soon I had established an easygoing, warm friendship with the prince.

But in this town, too, the nationalistic middle class and, above all, the students of the Institute of Technology were affronted by the play and by the racy performance—all the more so when drunken Knuzius sitting on the manure heap mentioned, among the damsels he had allegedly deflowered, the names of several princesses related to the House of Reuss-Gera. A few days before the opening incendiary articles appeared in the local newspapers and the word flew around of preparations for a riot. When the intermission curtain fell, an ominous silence ensued, and everybody looked up at the 'court box,' where the princely family had their seats. At this the old prince leaned far out over the railing and began to applaud loudly and

* All male descendants of the House of Reuss were, by immemorial custom, named Heinrich. Translators' note.

ostentatiously. The evening was saved, and ended with stormy applause.

In those days that theater gave performances of Brecht and other provocative young writers who were considered dangerous even in Berlin. It is one of the cruel and grotesque misunderstandings of our times that after the Second World War the hereditary prince, whose parents had died in the interval, was thrust into a camp by the Soviet occupation forces. He did not survive his treatment there.

The uproar against *The Merry Vineyard* proved worst of all in my native region of Rhenish Hesse, though I had thought I was composing a love song to my homeland. But I myself was partly to blame for the fuss. Authenticity in the very sounds of the language is essential to the poetic substance of reality. In my desire to come as close as possible to that reality I had unconcernedly used proper names that really existed, names I had heard in my childhood, of families who still lived in the region and were well known there. I myself knew none of them personally, knew nothing about their private lives, and had not the slightest intention of borrowing models from reality, describing actual events, or caricaturing living persons. Both the plot and the characters of the play had been invented.

But a name like 'Gunderloch' is not one you can invent. It was coined by the region; it seemed to me as unique and unmistakable as the hilly vineyards with their low walls and bumpy paths. I had often heard the name during my father's conversations about cork orders, and things of that nature. To me such names were no different from the folk songs of my homeland, which I also put in the play. I thought I had adequately concealed the locale by calling the tavern in which one act takes place *Zur Landskrone;* there is no 'Crown' tavern in my birthplace. A tavern by that name stood and still stands in Oppenheim.

The real Gunderloch was an honorable and highly respected vineyard owner in my home town of Nackenheim. He was at this time eighty years old. I myself imagined that in my fictional Gunderloch I had represented a man whom no German could object to having as a namesake. But from all sides people were telling the old man that he was being derided in a 'filthy play.' He heard it so often that he finally believed that it was so and brooded over the matter to the detriment of his health. I was sincerely sorry when I heard of this; I had never expected anything of the sort to happen, but there was nothing I could do about it now. I simply had to resign myself to the anger and outrage of my native region.

Thomas Mann, whom I met at this time when he came to Mainz for a reading, told me that this sort of thing happened to everyone who dared to represent his home town without embellishment. People like to see themselves not as they are, but as they wish they were, he said. He himself had been Lübeck's black sheep for twenty-five years, he remarked, but the day comes when they make one an honorary citizen.

That is what eventually happened.

But this early in the game, when the Mainz Municipal Theater ventured to put on the play, there were wild scenes. The Hessian vintners organized protest marches through the city. My innocent parents had to let down their shutters for fear of having their windows stoned. Many wine dealers canceled their orders with the cork factory, which still bore my father's name. There were rumors that the theater would be stormed, with the result that all streets leading to it were cordoned off by the police; only ticket holders were allowed to pass the lines. With a measure of pride the newspapers reported that such a massing of police in the streets had not been seen since the visit of the Tsar and Tsarina to Mainz in 1900.

In the theater itself, however, nothing happened but a brief scuffle between groups of people whose opinions differed. Yet for a while it was scarcely possible to open a morning newspaper without reading about a new 'row over Zuckmayer.' I was also indicted for blasphemy. The charge was leveled by a Protestant consistory on the basis of a poem of mine in some magazine. I came away from this suit with honors, however; the court acknowledged that 'the religious feeling in the author's nature poetry cannot be denied, and there can be no question of any intent to blaspheme.' George Grosz, who had been through numerous court actions on such charges, appointed me an honorary member of the 'Society of God-fearing Blasphemers.'

A new phase of life and work—and not the easiest—had begun. The hubbub over *The Merry Vineyard*, which to me seemed overdone, had upset rather than satisfied me. Now I had to prove, above all to myself, that my success had not been due to sheer chance, that my work was not ephemeral. And I knew that people stood ready with sharpened arrows, eager to shoot me down from the high perch to which I had flown. A young writer does not find the faring easy after a sensational success.

But it was not only a question of making my way in the theater and in literature. The fuss over *The Merry Vineyard* had unveiled the malignant, implacable grimace, the distorted face of vengeful, hate-filled reaction which was to cheat the German nation out of its best and most hopeful period, which was already digging the grave of Germany's civil liberties. The whole process was already in motion —camouflaged, hidden, but steadily undermining and incessantly spewing out its propaganda. We sensed, although at the time we did not clearly recognize and could not believe, that the good times before us were threatened and limited. Time was running out for the German Republic. The evil tide was already rising; one day soon it would be up to our necks. It was all the more urgent, therefore, to do well whatever we did now, and to find a firm place to stand before the ground was washed from under our feet. It was essential to make use of the favorable hour, to waste no time at all.

And so I worked on my next play for an entire year, although the outline and the first scenes had come to me easily, in one sudden rush. The good fortune that had thrown financial independence into my lap had to be earned anew. Saltenburg, who had an option on the new play, urged me to hurry. The publishers urged me to hurry. After such a breakthrough you had to strike while the iron was hot, they told me. But even if I had wanted to I simply could not produce anything quick and ready-made. To this day I do not know what 'routine work' is. With every new piece of writing I face a new beginning. Moreover, I was born under Capricorn; 'Capricorns' are said to be slow but stubborn—a good counterpoise to the frivolity I am also prone to. I chiseled away at the material of my *Schinderhannes* fully aware that, by turning to the 'popular' tone and to feeling as a basic theatrical ingredient, I had embarked on a dangerous direction. My path was running counter to all the literary tendencies held to be contemporary.

But there was no other path I could take, and I was profoundly convinced that for me it was the right one.

In the autumn of 1927 I saw people weeping during the closing scenes of *Schinderhannes* as they had laughed at the performance of *The Merry Vineyard*.

But these were not the sobs of sentimentality; it was deeply felt emotion called forth by the indescribably delicate, almost unearthly art, warm with the breath of life, of the actress Käthe Dorsch. Especially in her movements of silent expressiveness she transcended the artificialities of the stage.

This performance in Berlin's Lessing Theater, for which I had again taken over the directing, was aided by a supplementary attraction. Max Liebermann, then eighty, the dean of German painting, designed the sets, at the coaxing, of course, of old Elias. He did not worry about the technical problems, but painted water colors which were then transferred to large drops. One painting, *In the Cornfield*, which he had washed with golden brown and ocher yellow colors, held the very essence of a summer day, ripe with harvest.

My meetings and conferences with the great old man, sometimes in his country house at Wannsee, sometimes in his city apartment on Pariser Platz, are among my gayest memories. His Berlin wit and his bluntness of speech were proverbial. I was given some astonishing samples of it. Once, when I visited him in the morning, he offered me a bottle of heavy Burgundy and a gigantic Partagas cigar.

'You see,' he said in his thickest Berlin dialect, pouring me glass after glass without drinking a drop himself, 'I can't any more. I used to love to drink and smoke in the morning. But when you cross the eighty line, that's over. The only thing that still does its job right'—he slapped his trousers loudly—'is the old peter.'

I may have looked at him in some perplexity, for he added: 'Would you believe it, only yesterday in the studio. There was one of these dames who are crazy about art . . .'

Three months before the opening of *Schinderhannes* Julius Elias died of pneumonia. I received the news in Henndorf. I went to Berlin and spoke at his coffin before the cremation—that was the first funeral address I had to give. The whole of Berlin's art and cultural world was present, several generations of it, and many wept. All seemed to feel as if they had lost a father. I think I was the youngest of the mourners, and I was certainly one of those who had lost most.

In the meantime, in addition to the Wiesmühl in Henndorf, we had set up an apartment in Berlin. It provided us with all we needed: a studio for me, a small dining room, two tiny bedrooms like ship's cabins, connected by a hallway with closets, a nursery, kitchen, and bath. In addition there was a large roof garden which looked out over the whole city, from the radio tower to the dome of the cathedral. Our life was divided between Berlin, the Salzburg countryside, and occasional trips. Good years. Bad years. Imperiled years, years of life. As yet we were not aware of the future cataclysm. We had to meet our present, personal dangers. When I married at not quite twenty-nine, I thought myself a grown man. But who knows when he is grown up? I was ready for marriage, for domesticity, but I was not yet domesticated. I had learned a good deal, but still had just as much to learn. Among other things, that marriage is a thing of hazard like rope-dancing and writing plays, and that like both it is also work. It has remained so after more than forty years, and consequently has never become dull. And has proved its enduring qualities best when the weather was worst.

New friendships sprang up, with painters, writers, musicians, and other contemporaries. Moreover, some of the old Heidelberg circle, our 'clan,' had moved to Berlin—including Carlo Mierendorff.

In the late fall of 1928 a novel began appearing serially in the *Vossische Zeitung*, a work that had been accepted only after long difficulties. It was a kind of war diary that shook us and later millions of readers through the world: Erich Maria Remarque's *All Quiet on the Western Front*. I wrote the first review of the book for the *Berliner Illustrierte*, which then had the highest circulation of any German picture magazine. At the time I did not know Remarque, and knew nothing about him. Weeks later we had our first meeting, and there began an endless, inexhaustible round of nights together which continued through Austria and Switzerland and all the way to America. The amount of alcoholic beverages of all kinds that we put away would no doubt be equivalent to the stock in the cellars of a large international hotel. Perhaps that had something to do with the war, which we never alluded to in all our talks, the serious and the humorous ones, but whose oppressive, secret shadow was always present. We felt a sort of taboo about the subject, that is was better to drink the memories away. But we liked drinking, too, and it never occurred to us to put the blame for our plight on our fate as a 'lost' generation. Later it would be called 'defeated' generation. But such pompous phrases, which could conceal everything or nothing, supreme talent or supreme stupidity, were as repugnant to me then as they are today.

301

At a party in the home of Count Richthofen a man with the build of a second-rate boxer and a bald, spherical seal's head came up to me and said: 'You smell.'

'So do you,' I said without reflection, although there was no noticeable smell coming from him, and certainly not from me. We were all in evening dress, and I had bathed before coming.

'You smell,' the man repeated again and again, whenever he came my way amid the throng of guests.

Gradually, I began to wonder. I asked several of the ladies whether there was anything wrong with the way I smelled. Not at all, they said.

Suddenly this troll—by now I had realized that he was not human but some primitive creature imported directly from the wilderness—came up to me with a plate of lobster salad in one hand and a beer glass full of aquavit in the other. He said:

'You're younger than I am, but you couldn't pin me down.'

'Who knows,' I said.

He gripped my arm and felt the biceps.

'Nothing there,' he said. Then he turned around, pulled up the tails of his coat, and extended his backside towards me. 'Hit me,' he said.

It was like slamming my fist into a block of stone.

He turned around and grinned.

'You punch like a girl,' he said.

That was too much for me.

'Come outside,' I said.

'No holds barred?' he asked, his glistening troll's face beaming.

'If you like.'

'Let's go.'

I had already had quite a bit to drink; otherwise I might not have been so reckless. The troll had the strength of a bear.

On the front terrace we threw off our tail coats and after a few punches and gropings we were rolling on the ground. The waiters and maids formed a circle around us. We gripped each other by the nape, destroying our stiff collars and shirt fronts. We wrenched each other's legs out of their sockets, dug knees into each other's bellies, dragged each other the length of the terrace. In the course of all this we rolled against a pedestal from which something fell—there was a shriek of horror from the servants—and shattered to pieces. Later it turned out to be a genuine Chinese vase of the Ming period.

How it happened, I don't know—perhaps from sheer fury, for he was stronger than I—but suddenly I was kneeling on his chest and with all the force in my body pressing his shoulders down into the fragments of delicate porcelain. I was panting and sweating, but I stayed on top even though he got his knee between my legs.

A few of the guests had come out, and with the blood roaring in my ears I heard one them say:

'Olaf, give up, this is Zuck's round.'

Then I suddenly realized how I knew that troll's head. I had seen it in the magnificent self-caricatures that Olaf Gulbransson some-times published in *Simplizissimus;* I knew it also from the brilliant line drawings I'd seen in his shows. We pulled ourselves to our feet. I held out my hand, but Olaf gripped me by the ears and kissed me on both cheeks.

'I told you you smell,' he roared enthusiastically. 'You smell of talent.'

He tugged my ears affectionately till I thought they would come off entirely—and that is the way he always greeted me thereafter, for many years.

Other encounters began in a more civilized fashion. There were the Sunday afternoons in the home of Wilhelm Solf, former governor of the onetime German Pacific colony of Samoa and last German Foreign Minister before the end of the war. He had also been Ger-man Ambassador in Japan for many years and had become one of the greatest collectors and connoisseurs of Japanese art. As often happens to people who devote themselves to the study of a foreign culture, he took on its attributes. His thoroughly German grayish-blond head made one think of a samurai or of one of those poets painted by Hokusai. The Japanese quality was there in the line around his mouth when he smiled, in the curve of his high forehead, in the gleam of his thoughtful, intelligent eyes. On those Sundays, to which we were often invited, he and his wife Hanna assembled at teatime a special circle of diplomats, artists, writers, and scholars. Those were spirited hours, without the slightest touch of dull con-vention. The Solfs had the kind of salon we think of as typical of periods of high civilization—the sort of thing all too rare in Berlin in those days, although there were probably still salons in Rome or Paris. It was a circle, not a group, not a clique, not a set. People did not chat there, they talked—about art, literature, the theater, and politics as well. And the more menace and extremism began to distort the whole aspect of the period, the more serious those conversations became. But their very intellectual level gave them an encouraging character. Solf himself did not live to witness the disgrace of Germany, or only for a very short time, but the Solf circle continued to exist until it was broken up by the Gestapo and the bombs of the Second World War. Frau Hanna Solf and her daughter spent frightful years in the concentration camp of Ravensbrück until the end of the war brought their release.

In the Solfs' house I also met our dear friend 'Petrus,' or 'Uncle Friedrich,' as the children called Pastor Friedrich von Erxleben. He wore no cassock, only a dark suit and a high-buttoned vest. Nevertheless he would have looked like a Catholic priest even in shirt sleeves or a bathing suit, not because of any pronounced dignity or any trace of asceticism and renunciation (you only sensed those qualities when you knew him very well) but because of a sort of vital, gay, religious serenity—I can think of no other way to put it. He was probably not yet fifty at that time, but he seemed ageless and timeless: on the one hand he was like the portrait of a wise old abbot, on the other hand like a secular man full of youthful fire. His temperament and his way of living were equally dual, though not divided. I have never met a person in whom simple piety, genuine unswerving faith, was so closely linked with high intelligence and open-mindedness, but who yet in no way gave the impression of a divided soul. He came from Koblenz; the singing intonation of the Moselle country could be heard in his speech. In his youth he had been an opera singer and had performed as Tristan. What had prompted him to give up art and music—to which he remained passionately devoted—and to take holy orders was his personal secret.

That afternoon at Solf's he came over to me, a full wineglass in his hand, and said: 'So you wrote *The Merry Vineyard*. Some of my colleagues preached against it, but I maintain that so much *joie de vivre* is a proof of God's existence. It's a pious play!' No man of the cloth had ever told me that.

Earlier, he had lived in Rome as professor of classical languages at the Jesuit College. Now he had a one-story cottage in Berlin's North End, in a settlement that had been built by Frederick the Great for his retired army officers. There was a small Catholic church in the neighborhood. But Erxleben was not in charge of a parish; he lived there as a private scholar, while serving as chaplain for the Catholic members of the Berlin police force. This office later involved him in severe conflicts, in which he demonstrated great courage. For after 1933, in the early period of the Nazi tyranny, he had admission to police hospitals and infirmaries to which fearfully beaten victims of the Storm Troopers were taken. (Hitler's SA had been appointed an auxiliary police force.) Most of these victims were people who had been taken out of their beds at night without judicial process or legal warrant. He saw many of them in the condition in which they were delivered after 'interrogation'; he stood by many of them as they died painfully; and many decent policemen of the old force poured out their hearts to him.

It was self-evident that a man who knew so much, and refused to hold his tongue, would not be allowed to run loose in the long run. He too spent the last years of the war in the Ravensbrück concentration camp. Frau Solf later told me that every morning at reveille he sang the *Gloria* in a voice so loud that it could be heard through much of the camp. He went on doing so in defiance of the daily penalties and beatings meted out for it. He survived the camp, but afterwards he was a physically broken man. Spiritually, he remained unbroken in his faith, in his love of man and the world, in his religious serenity, to the day of his death, a decade after the collapse in 1945. For a time he administered a small parish in a Moselle village. I sometimes visited him there, together with the President of the Reich, Theodor Heuss, who was a close friend of his. Then he retired to spend his old age in the home of friends by the Rhine. I spent New Year's Eve of 1954–55 alone with him in his quiet, pleasant room. He cooked for both of us; we drank, smoked, and talked away the night. At one point in the evening he turned on the radio and we heard a graceful Mozart piece conducted by Bruno Walter. 'No,' he said after a few minutes, 'that makes me too sad. Mozart always makes me think of death.' He put Chopin's piano concerto in E minor on the phonograph. 'A professional melancholic like Chopin always cheers me up again,' he said.

A week later he was found dead, sitting on the edge of his bed; the cigar had fallen from his mouth and gone out; his old dachshund Seppel was asleep at his feet.

Courage, endurance, serenity—that was his legacy.

In 1928, when I wrote my play *Katharina Knie*, which I subtitled 'The Tightrope Dancer,' I was again drawing on memories of my youth. And once again I ran into trouble over a name. This time the clash took place before opening night.

For me the name 'Knie' was as timeless and abstract as, say, Till Eulenspiegel. In the villages of Hesse when a troupe of tightrope dancers appeared to stretch their rope from the gable of the town hall to the church steeple, the children ran after the little caravan shouting: 'The Knies are coming,' no matter what name was inscribed on the leader's wagon. 'Knie' simply stood for tightrope dancer or acrobat. To us they were all Knies. As a boy I myself had seen white-bearded 'old Knie,' who had made this name so popular as he performed his feats in the traditional costume of the tightrope dancer: pumps, blue satin doublet, and plumed beret. I had watched him by smoking torchlights scramble up the ladder: an acrobatic King Lear! 'Pull hard, pull hard!' I had heard him shout, in the voice like that of a captain of a three-master in a hurricane, to the peasant boys who hung in clusters from the hawsers, trying to tauten the rope. That resounding command and then the sudden silence of the musicians, followed by a slowly swelling drum-roll—it was all breath-taking, as every true artistic production should be. And it was one hundred percent genuine right up to the danger of his breaking his neck. Among his bravura stunts was cooking an apple pancake on an alcohol stove in the middle of the rope. As the climax he rode his grandmother across the span in a wheelbarrow. Then, after a loud dispute between two voices—for he was also a ventriloquist—with the grandmother constantly contradicting him, he seized her by the collar in a pretended fit of rage and hurled her into the market square. And although everyone knew that the figure was a lifelike stuffed doll, the audience would give vent to a ritual cry of horror as she whirled through the night air with flying skirts.

Such was 'Papa Knie,' who traveled the German countryside between Basel and Koblenz, up and down the Rhine, who was said to have produced sixteen children, all of whom followed in his footsteps, and who was respected as no television personality is today. Albert Bassermann, the greatest actor of the older generation, in his late fifties, had seen Papa Knie in his youth. He accepted the part enthusiastically—with the more eagerness since I had written it in the dialect of the Rhenish Palatinate, which was also his own native dialect.

So far, all was going well. The play was finished, and the other parts were also happily cast. The rehearsals had begun; the first night was set for December 22nd.

Suddenly I received a letter from a Zurich lawyer who brusquely identified himself as the legal counsel for the Swiss National Circus and the 'Knie dynasty.' He protested the use of the name 'Knie' in a theatrical production, and what is more by an author who was considered 'morally not unimpeachable.' The dynasty feared its reputation would be impaired, the lawyer wrote, and warned that legal measures might be taken to halt the production.

I felt as if I had been clubbed. I had had no idea that the real ancestor of the 'dynasty,' Friedrich Knie, the son of Maria Theresa's personal physician, had performed before Napoleon, doing a backward somersault over nine saddled horses, nor that he had afterwards moved to Switzerland, nor that his sons had long since established the Swiss National Circus and become rich men. Simply to replace the name of Knie by Hand, Fuss, Kopf, or Steiss* seemed to me impossible. And a trial or injunction just before the opening night would be a catastrophe. It would mean removing the play from the boards, probably permanently.

Along with the lawyer's threatening letter, however, was a brief note written by the press agent for the Knie Circus. His employers, he wrote, were really not such ferocious people; I ought to get in touch with them personally over the lawyer's head, but please not betray the fact that he, the press agent, had given me this tip.

I therefore wrote a most polite letter to the owners of the Swiss National Circus. I did not want to send them a manuscript of the play, since some passages might be construed wrongly. But I asked whether one of them might not be able to come to Berlin in person, attend a rehearsal, and convince himself that the play would do no harm to their name and status, but on the contrary might well do them honor. I awaited the reply in a state of extreme nervousness.

Instead of a letter there came a telephone call: the Knie brothers had come, all four of them, and were expecting me for 'negotiations' next morning at ten in the Hotel Central, the favorite hostelry for acrobats and circus managers. I went. In one corner of the lobby, squeezed tightly into huge leather easy chairs, was a fearsome sight.

They looked to me not like four men, but like four Goliaths, giants in well-tailored suits. Although at that time I myself, in my

* Hand, Foot, Head, Rump.

early thirties, weighed a good 210 pounds, I felt in their presence like a puny page at the court of a rococo sovereign. There was massive Frédéric, his hair combed far down over his broad forehead, wearing the small gold earring that used to be the mark of the guild. He was in charge of the tigers and polar bears at the circus. There were his equally spectacular brothers, Charles (elephants), Rudolf (horses and acrobatics), Eugène (business). In their youth they had all worked under the open sky, as acrobats, trapeze artists, tightrope dancers, trampoline jumpers, and human pyramids. Now they wore rings on many fingers and had heavy gold watch chains, with expensive amulets appended to them, over their swelling vests.

They looked hard and disparagingly at me, as if I were a new number not yet ready for the arena, and to put me in my place hardly rose to greet me. But they finally agreed, chiefly out of consideration for the great name of Bassermann, to attend a rehearsal of the play the following day.

A 'run-through rehearsal,' with no interruptions and the play performed as if for an audience, was very welcome to both the director and the actors at the present stage. I begged the actors, who were already fairly sure of their lines, to improvise the sense of a sentence if they could not exactly remember it at the moment, rather than drop it, so that the whole play would be heard in one swoop. Of course there were no sets and no costumes yet, but neither were there any at morning rehearsals in a circus. In fact, I rather think that the empty house and the empty stage, with just a few indicated props, made a favorable impression on the Knie brothers. It must have seemed more natural and reminded them of the way things were done in their profession.

Politely, we led the four massive men into one of the front rows of the orchestra. The director and I withdrew to the back of the darkened house and left the actors to their fate.

During the first act, in which the poverty and hard life of the small troupe of acrobats is described and in which the owner's daughter, young Katharina, steals three sacks of oats for her starving donkey, there was a heavy, foreboding silence up front, where the four Knie brothers sat. (Circus people, with their traditional honesty, are rather oversensitive to such matters.) But in the second act there is a strong dose of sentiment, though not of a kind that professional circus people would find romantic or unrealistic. When Father Knie bids goodbye to his daughter, so that she will have a better life and better food on a farm, and in the third act in which, after her return, he climbs to the high wire for the last time before he lies down to die ('A real high-wire man dies in bed'), strange noises could be heard from the row in which those Goliaths sat. It sounded like the snorting of sea elephants, like sperm whales blowing, or like the death rattles of the last saurians.

They were not just weeping. They were wailing. A gigantic sobbing and snorting had broken out, and they gave themselves to it like children, loudly and without restraint. Some of the time they draped their arms over the seats in front and pressed their cheeks against the plush backrests, some of the time they clasped each other for comfort. And again and again I could hear one or the other of them cry out in a breaking voice:

'It's Pappy! It's Pappy, living and breathing!'

At the end they pressed my hands so that they ached for three days, and with mystic reverence these eminent men let me introduce them to Bassermann. They could scarcely believe that the actor had not known their father, whose portrait he had summoned up for them with such accuracy even of intonation and gesture. Their last objection, that the Knieses had long since ceased to be such poor people as they were represented here, we settled at a breakfast in the Hotel Prinz Friedrich Karl. We assured them that the program would lead off by mentioning their present status and the importance of the National Circus.

The play was saved. We became friends—and how many a good hour I have since spent in one of their trailers, which are equipped with mahogany furniture and oriental rugs. We celebrated New Year's Eve of the next year, 1930, with the whole Knie family in Vienna, where their circus was giving guest performances in the Prater. At midnight Charles led me to the elephant stall. It smelled pleasantly of hay and pachyderm droppings there under the canvas. Except for an occasional jingle of chains or the thud of a great foot stamping, the tent had that almost solemn stillness that emanates from sleeping or resting animals. Only Rosa seemed restless. She was said to be a particularly teachable elephant female, but not very friendly, especially toward strangers. Her small eyes sparkled watchfully. And she was the one I was supposed to go up behind. I was to pull one of the long wiry hairs out of her tail, then lean backward quickly, since she would instantly swing her powerful trunk back at me, Charles said. And so she did, but I had been nimble enough.

Such an elephant hair, pulled out at the moment the new year begins, is said to bring luck. I have it to this day.

Six years later, at an anniversary of the Knie Circus, my *Katharina Knie* was staged under the big top at Bellevueplatz in Zurich. It was given right in the middle of the arena, before a tremendous crowd, once more with Albert Bassermann in the lead role. During the intermissions there was a performance by the then youngest members of the 'dynasty.' Freddy is now the director, but he was then nine years old, with long blond curls, and an accomplished equestrian. His cousin, Eliane Knie, still younger, walked with elfin grace on the 'slack wire.' When the final applause simply refused to die down, I was called into the arena. Charles Knie appeared in the maharajah costume in which he usually showed his elephants, accompanied by Rosa, whom I had already met. At his command she knelt on her forelegs and raised that dangerous trunk in a cradle-like arc.

'Don't worry,' Charles whispered to me, 'she's good as gold when she's working.'

He locked his hands to form a stirrup. I set my foot in it and swung up onto the trunk. 'Just grip the stirrup across her forehead and wave with your other arm,' he told me as Rosa calmly rose to her full height. I hardly think any other playwright has ever appeared before the public on an elephant's trunk.

The theatrical fate of the play was amazing, too. In spite of a tumultuous success on opening night, the entire Berlin press attacked it, including my previous well-wishers. The one exception was Kerr, who of course had to put himself in opposition to the others. He pointed out, with some justice, I must say, that such a brilliant part as Bassermann's did not write itself. Otherwise, the hounds barked in unison and the horns sounded the mort. The merciless notices were reprinted in many provincial newspapers.

But now something happened that would scarcely be possible to such an extent, if at all, nowadays: despite the verdict of the critics, the play made its way triumphantly through the theaters of Germany. In Berlin it ran for a hundred performances. Nobody except the critics remembered that it was judged to be a flop. In the large provincial cities, and in Vienna too (where Bassermann also took the lead), it had a far better press, and it remained in the repertory of all the many German theaters. At that time we had several hundred independent municipal and state theaters with their own ensembles, something that has never existed in any other country. Plainly, if what you wrote was good theater, even the powerful critics could not kill it. But this only spurred my ambition to do better.

Next summer I received the Georg Büchner Prize and the Dramatic Prize of the Heidelberg Festival.

In those days there was no plethora of festivals any more than of literary prizes. There was Bayreuth, and there was Salzburg. Otherwise, ruined castles and church portals were still left in peace. Only Heidelberg had fostered a number of summer festivals in the late twenties. The emphasis there had been on avant-garde and quality work. But since suitable new plays were lacking, the sponsors of the Heidelberg Festival offered a rather sizable prize to encourage the writing of new dramatic works. The prize carried no obligation, but it was hoped that the prize winner would write a play suitable for performance at the Festival.

I seriously intended to fulfill that hope on the part of the generous donors. What I had in mind was an 'Eulenspiegel,' which I conceived of as a poetic Punch-and-Judy comedy in verse. For a year I slaved over this notion, while at the same time I wrote a children's play, *Cockadoo-Cockadoo*, an adaptation for Erwin Piscator of the American war play, *What Price Glory?*, by Anderson and Stallings, and the film script for *The Blue Angel* for Erich Pommer, the pacemaker of UFA and best of the German movie producers. But I could not master the material. The children's play was cheered for weeks by Berlin school children; the American war play was produced under the title of *Rivalen; The Blue Angel* (the scenario and dialogue were entirely my own, while Friedrich Holländer wrote his unforgettable songs for it) displayed Jannings at his height as an actor and made Marlene Dietrich, under Josef von Sternberg's direction, a world star. But all these things were pieces of craftsmanship, finger exercises, études. Still the *Eulenspiegel*, which I regarded as my major dramatic effort, would not move. It came to grief, as it was bound to, on the discrepancy between the outlines of the old chapbook, to which I tried to adhere, and the modernity and the living reality I was striving for. I was about ready to throw the whole thing up, in any case, when I received a suggestion for a subject I had not previously considered: *The Captain of Köpenick*. The suggestion came from my old friend Fritz Kortner.

All I knew about the 'Captain of Köpenick' was the anecdote concerning his stroke of genius, his masterly impersonation in the Köpenick town hall.* I knew also that after a brief prison term he had been pardoned by the Kaiser and had traveled through the cities of Germany selling autographed picture postcards of himself in uniform. I had seen him peddling these cards at a Mainz Carnival in 1910. Still uncertain, I asked my publishers to obtain the old newspaper clippings and the trial record of the convict shoemaker Wilhelm Voigt. And suddenly it struck me that *he* was my Eulenspiegel—a poor devil whose eyes had been opened through necessity and who became an exemplar of the truth for an age and a nation.

For although the story was more than twenty years old, it was highly pertinent at this very moment, in the year 1930, when the Nazis were entering the Reichstag as the second-strongest party and thrusting the nation into a new craze for uniforms. The story was an image, a farcical mirror image, of the evils and dangers that were growing in Germany, but also of the hope that they could be overcome as the shoemaker had overcome his difficulties by native wit and humane insight.

Determined to write the play, I fended off various offers of collaboration. I have never really liked team work in any case. Moreover, I realized that I could handle the subject only in my own fashion, not as a tract but as a portrait of a man. I withdrew to work in rural Henndorf. What remained of the original Eulenspiegel idea was the concept of a fairy tale. To tell the story like a fairy tale, though in the tone of a comedy, seemed to me the way to give it a timeless truthfulness beyond the immediate occasion. In the course of long walks I worked out the order of the scenes. But at the beginning of September, when I spent an evening with Max Reinhardt and Helene Thimig at Leopoldskron Palace, not a single word of the play had yet been written down. During the night Reinhardt asked me what I was working on, and suddenly I began to recite the play. Or rather, I acted it out, for hours, with all the scenes and characters, often astonished at my own inspirations. For I conceived still unplanned situations, dialogues, and curtain scenes—the play was already there. Reinhardt was a hypnotist: merely by his way of listening he could send people into a trance of creativity, and all that was still nebulous for me had taken concrete form.

* An impostor in military uniform had presented himself at Köpenick city hall and demanded delivery of the cash box, which, of course, was handed to him.

Next day Reinhardt's head office in Berlin, to which he had telephoned, sent me a telegram: would I please send the manuscript at once. They wanted to stage the play as soon as possible. I wired back that I had to write it first. . . .

I did that without haste, but also without faltering at any point, in the course of the next two months. I was alone in autumnal Henndorf; my family had preceded me to Berlin. In November I followed with the finished manuscript.

The performance of Heinz Hilpert's masterly production was threatened by a near disaster at the last moment. The opening night had been set for March 5, 1931. On the eve of the opening the National Theater was conscripted for a dress rehearsal to which the families of the actors—in this case a sizable number—as well as colleagues and professional theater people were invited. Such previews have their good and bad sides. They allow the actors to experience an audience reaction, but the audience is, after all, not an ordinary one. Moreover the crowd of colleagues includes not only friends but also gossips and slanderers, and you never know what kind of rumors will go racing through the city and rob the opening-night performance of its virginity.

This preview came within a hair of not taking place. An hour before curtain time Hilpert received a despairing telephone call from Werner Krauss's wife. The call came from the Ratskeller in Köpenick. Krauss was playing the lead, and he had worked up the role of Wilhelm Voigt with marvelous discipline and pleasure in his part. That afternoon, his wife said, he had hit on the idea of going to Köpenick to inhale some of the 'atmosphere' on the spot.

Hilpert realized at once what that meant. He dashed into a cab and raced to Köpenick. There he found Krauss in the hands of an aged waiter who a quarter of a century earlier had served the genuine impostor half a bottle of wine while he was waiting for the delivery of the cashbox. Krauss had not limited himself to a half. He was in a state of temporary blackout, induced partly by the drink, partly by his strong response to the locale, partly by that morbid fear of first nights which sometimes seizes actors, especially the great ones, like a fit of madness. He didn't need any dress rehearsal, he said thickly; he'd be there for the opening tomorrow, but until then he meant to stay in Köpenick with the wine. He proposed that Hilpert do the same; let that bunch carry on with their dress rehearsal alone.

313

Somehow Hilpert managed to get him out of the Ratskeller, into the cab, and back to the theater. In the green room he was doused with cold water and filled with hot coffee until he actually donned his costume and mask and appeared on the stage. And now something weird and terrifying took place. He played the enormous part, more than three hours long, like a living marionette. It was as if he himself were not there at all, merely the role. He did not miss a single entrance, a single position, a single cue or sentence; but obviously he did not know what he was doing or saying. He acted as we imagine a zombie must—utterly unconscious of what he was doing. A sense of numbness spread among the spectators, as if a ghost were moving about the stage.

Hilpert was shattered. Oddly enough, I myself felt totally unconcerned. Not for a moment did I doubt that after this insane display Werner Krauss would come to himself and make up for everything on opening night.

When, after sparse applause that sounded like mockery, the audience left, I persuaded Hilpert to join us with Krauss in the green room. We must not leave him alone now and let him become discouraged, I said. Unwillingly, with compressed lips, and long nose quivering with anger, Hilpert went along. 'Be nice to him,' I said outside the door. But as soon as we were inside, he rushed at Krauss, who was still slightly stunned, and snapped at him: 'I'll never speak to you again!' Then he ran out. (For two years he actually did not speak to him.) But Krauss had not even noticed Hilpert. He was sitting with my mother, whom we had earlier brought in because she wanted to clasp the great actor's hand. She had been so excited, and so enthusiastic over my play and the whole performance, that she had not noticed his condition. Krauss fell in love with her at first sight. 'Zuck's mother!' he said again and again, in ecstasy. In trying to rise politely from his chair to greet her, he seized her hand in such an iron grip that it took all her self-control not to cry out in pain. For days afterwards she had a red spot on her skin, the impress of a ring that he had squeezed into her flesh while clinging to her hand.

The following night he acted with a sureness, a precision, a magnetism, such as I have scarcely ever seen in any other actor. That part proved to be one of the greatest triumphs of his career. When I paid a brief call on him during the intermission I found him sitting in his dressing room, now completely calm and sober. He merely asked: 'Am I good?'

Then he told me that he had slept all day and toward evening—
an hour before curtain time—had taken two sleeping pills!
'So I won't overdo it,' he said.

The effect of *The Captain of Köpenick* was deeper and more lasting than that of *The Merry Vineyard*. Friend and foe alike understood the play as the political act it was meant to be. And so far my
friends, at least in that part of the population who went to the
theater at all, or who read plays, were still in the majority. The very
fact that here too the 'other side,' above all the military, was not
simply castigated but represented with an attempt at justice, lent a
special force to the play and its ideas, without the distrust and nasty
aftertaste that a one-sided view, or propaganda, always inspires.
There were no riots in the theaters, although the Nazi press waxed
rabid over the play, especially the Berlin *Angriff*. Referring to one
scene in prison, that paper—edited by Goebbels—predicted that I
would soon have the opportunity to become acquainted with a Prussian prison from the inside. I was even then threatened, in anticipation of the coming seizure of power, with expatriation, exile, or
simply the hangman. Defamatory letters arrived. I threw them into
the waste paper basket and chose to believe the others, the letters of
approbation and encouragement. 'The best comedy in world literature since Gogol's *The Inspector General*,' Thomas Mann said in a
letter written under the immediate impact of the play. For us his
was still the voice of Germany—not the rantings of the agitators in
the Sportpalast.

The play ran in theaters throughout Germany for almost two
years, until the end of January 1933, when the Nazis came to power.
When you heard the laughter and applause of the audiences in the
sold-out houses, you could almost forget what was happening outside
in the streets. For there was nothing more to laugh about in the
Reich. Throughout Berlin, but especially in the eastern and northern
parts of the city, long lines of men could be seen waiting in ragged
clothing, their faces pale and swollen, unhealthy, undernourished.
These were the unemployed, whose numbers increased steadily,
whose appearance grew more and more pitiable. They were waiting
in front of the employment bureau where their relief certificates
would be stamped. Then they would receive their dole—from re-
venue the government had managed to raise by increased taxes,
cutting officials' salaries, and other unpopular measures. The

315

allowance never quite reached the minimum that a man, let alone a family, needed to exist. The unemployed stood in those lines summer and winter, in rain and cold, the collars of their old jackets turned up, their clammy hands clenched in the pockets.

These were hapless groups. Along with the disappearance of margarine and coal from their lives, they had long since lost their 'Berlin humor.' They could scarcely muster the strength to complain or start a row when one of the bureaus closed early because it could not handle the crowds, or when word went around that the price of potatoes had risen again while they were waiting for their starvation handout.

Those scenes in Berlin could be duplicated throughout Germany: lines in front of the employment bureaus, the welfare windows, the grocery stores, the factories (which could employ only a fraction of their former numbers), and the closed mines. In 1931–33 more than six million persons stood around that way in Germany, without jobs, condemned to idleness and waiting, and gradually slipping into hopelessness, disgust with everything, with the world in which they lived, with the government that was barely keeping them alive, with themselves and their own patience.

The German Republic's period of prosperity and boom had lasted barely four years, until the influx of foreign capital came to a sudden end. Its source had been chiefly the United States and it ceased with the American Depression, which drew all of Europe along in its wake. In Germany, along with an industrial standstill, an agricultural crisis ensued. The large landowners were heavily in debt and tried to use the public purse in their own interests, while the small farmers opposed the authority of the hated 'government' by passive resistance or revolts against the ' tax squeeze.' All the anger, the hatred, the sense of outrage were directed against this 'government' which the rightists denounced as 'the Jews' republic' and the leftists as 'the capitalist state.' The emergency ordinances with which the administration tried to curb extremism from both directions achieved the opposite effect. Open warfare broke out between the Communists and the Nazis; hardly a night passed without bloody skirmishes with clubs and guns. But the most fateful development of all was the impoverishment of the lower middle class. In spite of the boom that had begun after the inflation and had for a time produced the illusion of general prosperity, there had never been a revaluation of the pensions, insurance policies, and savings accounts which had melted

316

away during the period when marks were printed in denominations of billions. The 'little people' who had been fairly well off under the Kaiser had had no share in the boom. Embittered, they hated everyone 'on top': the leaders of the dominant parties that represented German democracy, and the financiers who were still living in luxury and lulling their secret terror by hopes of a new wave of prosperity. Middle-class to the core, these people who did not want to be proletarianized and would have felt it a disgrace to become 'red Socialists' provided the vast hordes of Party members and fellow travelers for brown National Socialism.

In mid-July 1931, when I returned to Berlin from Henndorf for a few days and went to my bank to draw some money, I found the bank closed and the building surrounded by excited, cursing, or wailing people fearful for their savings. No wonder that Nazi slogans such as 'breaking the thralldom of interest rates' were eagerly hailed. The average German felt himself abandoned by all sides. No wonder he mistook the lust for power of the Nazi leaders for something healthy and vigorous, promising a gleam of hope for better times to come. He did not realize that he would be falling prey to a new and still worse deception, that instead of honest though feeble efforts to deal with the crisis, all would be staked on a vicious gamble.

In the meantime, all went on for us as before: life, work. With Heinz Hilpert I did a dramatization of Ernest Hemingway's *A Farewell to Arms*, mostly because Käthe Dorsch wanted to play Catherine. Hilpert and I had a jolly spell of work in my Henndorf house. We proceeded cautiously, like instrument makers, taking all the dialogue and in fact almost every word from the novel. The play was given in the Deutsches Theater; Hemingway came to the opening from Paris, where he was then staying. He was drunk by the time he arrived. He had a hip flask of whisky in his coat pocket, and from time to time would raise it to his mouth, screwing up his eyes as if taking aim; then he would look around, half absently, half daringly. Hilpert took him to the Hotel Eden, where he promptly went to the bar and ordered champagne. He brought the hip flask to the performance, and whenever he was not taking a nip from it he seemed to be dozing. He understood no German, and it was not clear whether the scenes he saw on the stage reminded him of anything in his book, or of anything at all. During the intermission he was taken to the dressing room to see Käthe Dorsch. He squeezed her hand and asked loudly and clearly how much 'this girl' charged for a night. Since she understood no English, she thought he had paid her a compliment on her performance. She smiled and gave him a gracious nod. Thereupon he offered her a swallow from the hip flask, which she refused by sign language. We managed to persuade him to leave the dressing room after he had made a firm offer of 'a hundred dollars and not a cent more.' Fortunately, she did not understand that either. Hemingway was well aware, of course, that you cannot buy an actress for a night, but was having fun playing the American hillbilly. At the end of the evening, which proved a great theatrical hit, the hip flask was empty and Hemingway had to be taken home in a cab. He spent the rest of the night drinking at the Eden Hotel, then took the train back to Paris in the same state in which he had arrived.

Hemingway was a man who looked handsome when he was drunk, perhaps even more so then, though with none of that air of super-masculinity which he struck in his stories. He was handsome like a river god who had not yet fully awakened. Massive, with his thick eyelashes, determined to throw himself into the stream of life, but in his awakening already close, very close, to that other sleep.

During those last years before the end of the Weimar Republic most of us lived like peasants who mow hay or cut the wheat while the clouds of a coming storm are piling up on the horizon. The air is still. There is no knowing whether the storm will descend or pass over. And so one goes on mowing until the first gust of wind howls.

But a political movement that threatens the existence of a state is not a matter of the weather. It is made by men and can be fought by men. In the period before the power to act was taken from us, did we do enough to avert what was coming? I don't think so.

'Too little and too late,' people in America were saying at the beginning of the Second World War about the efforts of the Western Powers to check Hitler. It seems to me that what we German intellectuals did during that period was also too little and too late. Granted, my political friends, especially Haubach and Mierendorff, wore themselves out during the last years of the Republic in an incessant battle against Hitlerism, a struggle that left them not an hour for a private life, scarcely time for sleep. The Nazis later settled scores with them for that. But when Carlo Mierendorff invented the

318

emblem of the three arrows, with which young socialists painted over the swastika at night, it was already too late; the arrows no longer stood for those large parts of the population who for years had felt cast out from the political process. The masses of the unemployed did not give a damn about words and emblems; what mattered was the hot soup distributed by the Storm Troopers. They did not consider or did not know that the money for that soup came from the same big industrialists who had closed the factory gates and left them all to starve.

We intellectuals contented ourselves far too long with laughing at Hitler, the housepainter and paperhanger. We ridiculed him, maintaining that he looked like a barber, or the type of confidence man who preyed on women. Yet millions of German women and youngsters who had the vote in this 'freest of republics' thought he looked like a nobleman, or even a movie star—that being the very height of glamour at the time. We made fun of his poor German, his bombastic style, and were convinced that such a half-educated fool could never be taken seriously in Germany, a nation of scholars and professors, let alone have the faintest chance of achieving leadership. Millions of leaderless Germans did take him seriously; they heard him speak a language they understood. And when he came to power the scholars and professors, with some praiseworthy but not very numerous exceptions, were ready to adjust to him and to translate his vulgar gibberish into their own academic, high-flown, mystagogic jargon.

Although the Nazi movement in its beginnings was sustained by ugly, vindictive elements lusting for nothing but power, it would be unfair altogether, altogether wrong and misguided, to issue a wholesale condemnation of the large number of Germans who poured into the Nazi movement at the beginning of the thirties. For at this time the hopeless were joined by the hopeful, the idealists, the believers who in their wishful thinking imagined that something ethical and decent underlay this allegedly spontaneous popular movement. (In reality it was not spontaneous at all, but the product of clever organization.) The chief failing of such people consisted in their being unpolitical—as the nation had been in 1914 when it entered the war. Politically unprepared as they were, the collapse of 1918 and the Revolution had taken them by surprise. Not educated to thinking politically and not willing to learn how, a great many Germans succumbed to quackery and tyranny. They were only too ready to imagine that the 'national rising' represented a true rebirth even in the realm of public ethics; that it meant the end of partisan bickering, equality of opportunity, a return to upright ways of living and forms of social organization. A slogan such as 'The Third Reich' sounded a mythical note to which we Germans are all too susceptible. It sounded like a prophetic promise. Many young people, some of whom later gave their lives to resisting the tyranny, first entered the Hitler Youth in good faith, out of the sense that there was something rotten in the state and that our public life needed a cleansing. I knew a number of young army officers who had spent some time in Russia, in the course of training exchanges that were customary under the Weimar Republic. They developed leanings toward the 'ethical commitment' of Communism and then came to feel—most of them only temporarily—that National Socialism offered the opportunity for fulfilling such obligations in a form appropriate to the German tradition: by the interaction between the elite and society. Many persons imagined that Christian principles would prevail in the Third Reich, including love of neighbor; that materialism would be given an ethical cast. Hardly anyone thought that the threats against the Jews were meant seriously. Even many Jews considered the savage anti-Semitic rantings of the Nazis merely a propaganda device, a line the Nazis would drop as soon as they won governmental power and were entrusted with public responsibilities.

All this excuses nothing—neither the self-deceptions, the looking the other way, nor the deliberate blindness when the worst came to the worst. But what I am saying here should serve as an explanation for the way a large part of the nation drifted into uncritical acceptance and irrationality—a drift that is so hard for other nations, and for later generations of Germans as well, to understand.

We, those of us whose mission it was to offer timely opposition, hesitated too long to burden ourselves with the crassness of everyday politics. We lived far too much in the 'splendid isolation' of culture and the arts. And so we too, even though we became victims of violence or were exiled from our native land, share like all other Germans in that collective shame—to use the term that Theodor Heuss deliberately pitted against the senseless anathema of 'collective guilt.'

*

The faces of people, and especially of German youth, changed during those last years before the end of the Republic. They no longer resembled the faces I had seen during my early days in Berlin. The extremists on both sides developed their own physical type. You could recognize them physiognomically.

Many of the youthful nationalists had eyes deep-set and close together, a well-shaped but somewhat too narrow forehead with hollow temples, and around chin and cheeks a certain softness which was screened by a forced look of tension. The radicals of the left were distinguished by lips permanently curled in ironic disdain— they knew perfectly well how things were likely to turn out, and could not be persuaded otherwise even if the opposite happened. The radicals of the right, however, proclaimed by their firmly compressed lips, their resolutely jutting chins, and the vertical furrows in their brows, that they were fully determined to annihilate their enemies. Ironclad dogmas and theories seemed to have driven laughter from these faces. Gaiety was banished and enjoyment of life sentenced to death for high treason. Nothing made these people so dangerous, so forbidding, so self-destructive, as their total lack of humor.

Among the older generation of the upper class the prevailing type was more and more that of the 'Jockey Club' member, as represented by Franz von Papen and his circle: elegant 'gentlemen riders' who seemed to imply, by their real or pretended nonchalance, that they were politically and personally superior to the chaos of partisanship and the turmoil of events, and would contrive to turn things their way at the proper moment. They surely believed that, and tried it too. But they were painfully surprised when Hitler, after they had lifted him into the saddle, rode them down without a qualm.

We ourselves went on hoping for the best up to the last moment, and even then we did not want to believe the trend was irreversible. For us, that last moment was the Berlin Press Ball on January 29, 1933.

The Press Ball was the most important social event of the Berlin winter season, and although I personally had no particular liking for balls and official occasions (the best part of them, for my taste, was the aftermath, going with a few friends to a cab drivers' café in the small hours of morning), my wife and I regularly attended them as guests of my publisher, who sent us the expensive tickets and invited his authors to a special box for honored guests. All the theater, movie, and press people went; we met many acquaintances there, beautiful women, interesting people of all sorts. And when I did not happen to be having a first night it offered my wife the chance to wear a new evening dress, and me to make her the present of one.

We set out fairly late, after dining in a good restaurant, and were determined in spite of evening clothes to have a good time. My mother accompanied us, for she was visiting us for a week. She had never attended a ball in Berlin and was very excited. She too wore a new dress I had given her for Christmas—silver-gray with lace insets.

The mood in the crowded ballrooms that evening was the strangest I had ever experienced. Everyone sensed what was in the air, but no one wanted to admit it fully.

That afternoon the Schleicher Cabinet had resigned. The formation of a new government was in full swing—that was all anybody knew. People indulged in a macabre blend of somberness and hectic gaiety.

In the Ullstein box, which adjoined the government box, we met our friends the aviator Ernst Udet and the novelist Bruno Frank. Others came and went. None of the Ullstein brothers had appeared; Emil Herz, the firm's managing director, did the honors. He was forever refilling our glasses, saying each time: 'Drink up, go ahead— who knows when you'll again be drinking champagne in an Ullstein box.'

At the bottom of our hearts all of us were feeling: Never again.

Udet and I, who took brandy between the glasses of champagne, were soon in that condition in which one no longer guards one's tongue.

'Look at the tinware,' Udet said to me, pointing around the hall. 'They've all got their gew-gaws out of the mothballs. A year ago no one would have been caught dead with the stuff.'

Sure enough, on many lapels and dinner jackets you saw the ribbons and crosses of war decorations which in the past no one would have dreamed of wearing at the Berlin Press Ball. Udet took his Pour-le-Mérite from his neck—he always wore it under his white tie with evening dress—and put it into his pocket.

'You know what,' he proposed to me, 'let's take our pants down and dangle our bare backsides over the railings of the box.'

To worry my wife, who thought us quite capable of carrying out such a stunt, we went so far as to loosen our suspenders. In reality neither of us was feeling in a jocular mood.

The government box, usually filled with Cabinet Ministers, assistant secretaries, and diplomats, was empty now. Waiters idled about it; unopened bottles of champagne poked from ice buckets.

At some point during the night word flashed around that Hitler had been appointed Chancellor. Some greeted this news with forced jokes, some with optimistic constructions ('A clever chess move by Papen to checkmate him,' 'He will be the prisoner of his Cabinet,' and so on). Most made no comment at all, but drank and danced all the harder.

We left the ball with Udet, who had the knack of suddenly sobering up. He played cavalier to my mother most charmingly. 'Not another word about Hitler,' he whispered to me. 'Don't let's spoil your mother's enjoyment.'

It was, in fact, a gala night for her. We went on to Udet's house. My wife and I took a cab, declining to ride in his racing car, but my mother saw nothing against it. He had charmed her so completely that she felt no fear and later told us rapturously that he had not driven, but 'flown.'

We sat in his little 'propeller bar' until dawn. He regaled my mother with anecdotes of his adventurous life—and I really think she did not give Hitler another thought that night. I took his old guitar from the wall and sang my Brandy Songs, as I had often done before.

On the following evening the endless torchlight parade of SA and SS formations marched slowly to the Chancellery, where the new Führer of the German people stood on the balcony saluting his men.

During those two months of January and February 1933 three of my plays were running simultaneously in the theaters of Berlin: *Schinderhannes*, *The Captain of Köpenick*, and *Katharina Knie*. I was also planning a fairy-tale movie with Ludwig Berger. *A Love Story*, which I finished writing shortly before Christmas, was being serialized in the *Berliner Illustrierte*. I was also working on a new play, and the best actors in Germany were waiting eagerly for parts in it. Berlin could not offer a writer more. And more could not be taken from a man in the best working period of his life.

During the first few weeks of the Hitler regime all that continued mechanically. The tyranny needed time to organize, to close its ranks, to fix on its strategy. At the Deutsches Theater Max Reinhardt went on staging Hofmannsthal's *Great World Theater* as if nothing had happened. On February 27th, when my wife went to the dress rehearsal with Hanna Solf, her car was trapped in a crowd. The sky glowed red. 'The Reichstag is burning!'

The Reichstag building near the Brandenburg Gate had gone up in flames. Who were the arsonists?

'The Communists,' it was said.

That was the needed signal.

Next day the rabid persecutions began: the banning of the entire leftist press, the first great wave of arrests and deportations.

At Ullstein Verlag I furiously insisted that the further chapters of *A Love Story* be published—the serial had been stopped out of sheer funk, for the official interdiction of my works did not come until later. But the signs that I was in direct personal danger were multiplying. Goebbels was appointed Propaganda Minister. Many of my acquaintances had already vanished. My wife could no longer sleep at night—she expected the harsh pounding on our door every time she heard the elevator. Warnings came from all sides, even from those of my former friends who had adapted to the new regime, but still preserved a kind of loyalty toward us. Most of the people I respected had already left Germany. Reinhardt and Jessner were forced to resign. Heinrich and Thomas Mann, Bruno and Leonhard Frank, Arnold Zweig, Alfred Döblin, and many others were scattering in all directions. Prominent Jewish actors like Fritz Kortner and Ernst Deutsch had to pack up and depart overnight, after several of their colleagues had been arrested right in the green rooms of the theaters. Brecht, who had remarried at about the same time as myself, fled to Denmark with his wife and children. His wife, the brilliant actress Helene Weigel, had been a childhood friend of my wife.

Hanns Johst, who like myself had started with Pfemfert's radical leftist *Aktion*, had long since become a Nazi—out of sheer lack of talent. Now his wretched play *Schlageter* was being performed by the National Theater. It is remembered only for the one sentence he left to the world—and that sentence is often attributed to Goebbels: 'When I hear the word culture, I cock my revolver.'

That was no disappointment. Mediocrity cannot disappoint. Of those who had more than average talent and character, each had to make his own, wholly personal decision. Very few were unequal to the challenge— and nobody can know precisely how he would have acted in the place of anyone else.

When I myself left for Henndorf, as I did every spring, with my pet bullfinch in his traveling cage, my manuscripts, and my guitar,

I still refused to realize that it was forever. We kept our Berlin apartment. I gave the key to Haubach, so that it could be used as a hiding place if necessary.

At this time three of my socialist friends, Haubach, Mierendorff, and Wilhelm Leuschner, the trade-union leader and Hessian Minister of the Interior, returned to Germany from Switzerland, where they had been attending a meeting of the International Labor Office in Geneva. They came back in spite of all warnings; at this juncture they did not want to forsake the German workers, although they could no longer be of help to them. Within a short time the three disappeared behind barbed wire.

I too had it in mind to return as soon as the situation changed. In those days the members of our circle still thought a reversal was possible. We imagined that the Nazis would rapidly ruin themselves. And I did not want to be an exile. I became one because I had no choice.

During those early years Berlin and the Berliners held aloof from the Hitler regime. They adopted a wait-and-see attitude, while some fearlessly opposed the Nazis. I found it hard to part from Berlin, very hard. Half of our life remained behind there.

1939-1954
DEPARTURE AND RETURN

GOING INTO EXILE is 'the journey of no return.' Anyone who sets out on it dreaming of coming home is lost. He may return—but the place he will find is no longer the one he left, and he himself is no longer the one who left. He may return to people he missed, to places he loved and did not forget, to the region where his own language is spoken. But he never returns home. *You can't go home again* is the title of a book by the self-exiled American writer Thomas Wolfe. You cannot go back to the land of your childhood, where you were wholly at home; neither can you go back to a country you were forced to leave. For you want to find its former image, and that is gone forever.

There was only one class on the Dutch steamer *Zaandam*, on which we crossed the ocean. There were four of us in the cabin: my wife and I, our daughter Winnetou, who was then eleven (Michaela was at a girls' school in England; she still had another year there), and a small sixteen-year-old dog named Mucki, toothless and blind, whom my wife had inherited from an eccentric aunt who died in Vienna. The dog, already of an advanced age, was one of the conditions of the legacy, which consisted of silverware, jewelry, and furs. My wife had to pledge to give him a good home until his death; otherwise valuables and dog would have gone to a society for the protection of animals. When we had to flee to Austria, the silver was left behind in the sideboard, the furs in a closet, and the jewelry in a safe, for we no longer dared go to the bank for fear of arrest, and could take only a minimum of baggage. Thus the whole legacy was confiscated by the Gestapo and lost for good—but the dog went with us. My wife had become deeply attached to him in the meantime, and he to her. He looked like a cross between a bat, a jackal, and a groundhog; he growled and barked especially at customs and railway officials; he was a nuisance crossing streets, because he always tugged in the wrong direction—but he survived all our journeys and died peacefully in Vermont at the age of eighteen.

Aside from the dog, we possessed no more than the small sum in dollars which had to be shown the immigration officials in order to be admitted to the United States. It had been lent to us by friends.

329

On the ship's passenger list were many names betokening a fate similar to ours: refugee families from Vienna, from Prague, from Germany. We made no new acquaintances. We wanted to avoid the inevitable conversations about the past, about all we had lost. We wanted to shake the dust of the old continent from the soles of our shoes and begin anew. For we felt that you can make a new life only if you do not cling to memories.

We had one friend aboard ship: the American actress Peggy Wood, a clever, auburn-haired woman with a passion for extravagant hats— one of them deployed no less than six fanciful blue birds. With that hat she had created a stir even in Paris and London. We had met the year before in London, where I was doing a film script for Korda, and she was singing the lead role in an operetta by Noel Coward.

Peggy Wood knew some German, and we had worked together on a translation of my play *Bellman*, for she was eager to play the leading female role in it on Broadway. Nothing ever came of that. On the voyage she taught me 'American'—a language of which I understood scarcely a word, for the only English I had heard so far was British. She had traveled before on the *Zaandam*, and introduced us to the captain, at whose table we ate.

Captain Stamperius was a likable Dutchman with a round, smooth face and reflective, often somewhat melancholy eyes. We shared a common interest: he was an amateur ornithologist, had a sizable collection of books on birds in his cabin, and knew a great deal about the mysterious paths of migratory birds. Once he excitedly called me up to the bridge because he had sighted flocks of the golden plover, which travel from the Arctic to Mexico, Hawaii, and Argentina. 'Halfway around the world,' Stamperius said. We watched them through binoculars until they were lost from sight. The captain was in raptures.

Then we went to his cabin, where he made careful entries: Golden Plover, order *Limicolae* (shore birds), family *Charadriidae*, date, time of day, longitude and latitude, weather, direction, height and speed of flight as far as these could be estimated. . . .

'When I retire,' the captain said dreamily, 'I'll try writing a book about bird migrations.'

He was not so fortunate. During the war the *Zaandam*, which joined American convoys, was torpedoed by a submarine. Captain Stamperius died a seaman's death and his ornithological library and log lie somewhere on the bottom of the ocean.

330

On the high seas we received a cable from our New York friend Dorothy Thompson, who had provided one of our two affidavits and obtained our entry visas to the United States. Dorothy, then still married to Sinclair Lewis, was one of the most influential political journalists in America. Her name was known everywhere.

'Expecting you as guests in my apartment 88 Central Park West,' the cable read. 'Have all baggage rerouted to my address.'

We did not yet grasp the significance of this news. We were only glad to be able to stay with her during our first days in New York, instead of in the small West Side hotel in which a friend who had preceded us into exile had already reserved a room. (Had we had any inkling of the dreariness and shabbiness of that hotel, we would have been even more delighted.) The importance that cable was to have in smoothing our entry into the New World revealed itself only when we arrived.

To be precise, we were traveling with invalid passports and papers, although our visitors' visas for the United States, along with all the necessary stamps and confirmations, had already been issued. Shortly before our departure from Europe the Official Gazette of the Reich government in Berlin had published a notice of our expatriation; this meant that not only my wife and I, but my eleven-year-old daughter as well, no longer possessed German citizenship. This notice was connected with the expropriation law, under which all the property of expatriated persons became the property of the state. Our house in Henndorf had long since been confiscated. It meant further that our heirs, children who had certainly not yet committed any crimes against the National Socialist state or ideology, were stripped of any property claims.

Our German passports had not yet expired, and even though they no longer possessed legal validity we had to use them as travel documents willy-nilly. We had no others. Theoretically, the Nansen passport existed for refugees, but it would have taken many months to obtain one, and we would have lost our chance to cross on the *Zaandam,* after having so laboriously prepared everything down to the smallest detail, including the financial end.

I knew quite well that this was a precarious situation, but I had no idea of just how dangerous it was. I did not imagine that the American authorities would already have taken cognizance of a German Official Gazette only six weeks old, and none of us could imagine the thoroughness with which these authorities went through the personal papers of every single new arrival, even though he was coming only as a visitor and not an immigrant. We had had no experience with American bureaucracy. We knew nothing of the strict legalism of American officials, who recognized nothing but the letter of the law and insisted on every jot and tittle of that letter. We had not yet fully realized that it was only such legalism that had succeeded in domesticating and building into a nation a half-savage society of Western pioneers, settlers, soldiers of fortune, and adventurers of all countries and races; that what was involved was a tradition of legality which cannot tolerate the slightest impropriety or evasion without being shaken to its foundations.

We thought it amusing that we had to declare on oath on the official questionnaires that we were neither insane, leprous, nor syphilitic, that we did not live by prostitution, and that we had no intention of assassinating the President of the United States. That was an outmoded form. But the matter of exact legality cannot become outmoded. It must only be revitalized by an understanding of special situations. We had no reason to expect any special understanding on the part of the immigration officers, those hard-boiled administrators of passport control, and our friend Peggy Wood was distinctly anxious about how we would be treated on our arrival in the land of liberty.

We knew, of course, that the Ellis Island barracks were not a concentration camp; but we quite rightly did not think of a stay in such mass quarters, under lock and key, as an invigorating experience. And apart from all such awkwardnesses, a close examination of our papers and persons (not to speak of the dog) would have produced a rather hopeless situation and presented us with some ghastly dilemmas.

At four o' clock in the morning—it was the sixth of June 1939, my mother's birthday—the *Zaandam* entered Upper New York Bay. We stood shivering on the deck looking at the Statue of Liberty, which reminded us so much of the statue of Bavaria in the Munich Fairground. We saw the famous skyline, the outlines of New York's fantastic buildings, in the sallow light before dawn. Behind us, the glowing red orb of the sun arose. The ship's siren screeched three times; the reply echoed from the still distant quay. The Holland-America Line ships did not dock on the New York side of the Hudson, but across the river in Hoboken, and the vessel glided slowly, with throttled engines, along the entire city. As the daylight grew stronger we could see the towering structures of the financial district. The dark canyons among them, which the sun had not yet reached, made an uncanny and deeply moving impression on me. I realized that I was afraid of this city, afraid of the strange land, of all that was to come. Gradually it grew hot. We sweated as we stood in line outside the ship's lounge, where the immigration officials, who had already boarded the boat, had taken seats at various tables.

We had handed in our passports beforehand, along with completed customs declarations and questionnaires. Each of us had received a number and was called up by number. While we waited to be called, I tried to put myself into a confident mood, or at least to look confident, and succeeded to some extent. I thought of my flight from Austria, of that night among the brownshirts on the border, which lay only fifteen months behind me, and I grew calmer. Compared to that, whatever might threaten us now was minor.

Suddenly, from one of the the tables where a heap of passports and papers lay, I heard my number called, along with a completely incomprehensible word: that was my name.

Behind the desk sat a squarish man with a squarish face. He held our passports in his hand and another piece of paper which I did not recognize. I went up to the table and showed my number, expecting questions, cross-examination, and repeating in my mind the answers I had prepared.

But the man held out a huge paw. His broad policeman's face beamed in a friendly grin.

'How d'you do, Sir,' he said, shaking hands with me. 'You are Miss Dorothy Thompson's guest?'

'Yes, Sir,' I said as Peggy Wood had taught me (*always* say 'Yes, Sir,' to policemen in America).

Without any further questions he gave me the stamped passports and papers. 'Okay,' he said, 'everything's all right.' He picked up the other paper as if in corroboration. 'You have a special recommendation from President Roosevelt. You can debark at once.'

He beckoned to an assistant; people made room for us and we walked to the gangway. It was like 'Open Sesame' in the fairy tale.

Dorothy had uttered the magic spell. A friend had passed on the news of our expatriation. She knew, too, that the ominous Official Gazette was already in circulation. Since she herself had had to fly to Hollywood for negotiations over a film, and could not meet us personally, she had taken double precautions: provided us with the

333

protection of her own address, which might well have sufficed, and secondly, had stopped in Washington on her trip to the West Coast and called at the White House. She had only an hour's time between two planes, as she later told us, and had walked right into the President's office without an appointment—a lack of ceremony which in Europe would have been unthinkable with the president of an airline! In five minutes she had obtained from Roosevelt a signed letter to the immigration authorities stating that we were 'welcome guests' in the United States and requesting that we be spared all formalities.

On the pier a second surprise awaited us. Beside our wildly waving friend Franz Horch, who had lived through the last days in Vienna with me and was now running a literary agency in New York, stood a colossus of a man whom I did not know. He too was waving. Two Janningses and all four of the Knie brothers would have fitted easily inside his suit. The panama hat he had on must have taken a bale of straw to manufacture.

This was Hendrik Willem van Loon. His name, well known in Europe at the time, was famous in America. Of Dutch birth, he had come to America in his early youth and had done all his writing in English. He illustrated all his books himself with pen and wash-drawings or water-color sketches of a most deft and original sort. Many of his works had been published in Germany and in large editions until his forthright anti-Hitler position had brought him onto the Nazi index. These books were largely in the popular-scientific vein; they embraced world history and geography, dealt with unusual subjects and personalities in art and culture, and were so written that any intelligent high-school boy could understand and learn from them and every intelligent human being could be inspired and enriched. He had also published an uncommonly lively book on Rembrandt, the first book of his that I read. He was supremely versatile, learned in all fields, and a remarkable personality. Just as his huge proportions and enormous hands contrasted with the delicate subtle line of his drawings, so did his inner aristocracy, his human warmth, with the often ruffian style of his language and his manners. He was a hypersensitive, introverted artist, and at the same time a brilliant 'salesman' of his productions. If you were visiting him, he would be continually grumbling at the bother of having guests and the burdens which the exiles imposed upon him, to the point that you almost got up and left; but he was forever exerting himself to the utmost to rescue these exiles and to launch them on their new lives. He could be the most charming company but also the grumpiest of companions at table, especially when he had pressingly invited you. At heart he was a *grand seigneur* with an affectionate nature which he was embarrassed to show.

In 1938 he had been in Stockholm to do research for a book on the writer Carl Michael Bellman; later he published a book of translations of his songs with delightful drawings. In Stockholm he met my publisher, Bermann Fischer, and learned that I had just written a play about Bellman. He read it, obtained other plays of mine, and one day, while I was still in Switzerland, sent me a wonderfully personal and comradely letter urging me to come to America as soon as possible, and offering to serve as 'affidavit giver' for me. Since he enjoyed great prestige in the United States, including its government circles, this was of course a most welcome offer. To give such an affidavit is not only to guarantee one's protégé's moral conduct and character, but to pledge oneself to support him materially and provide his return fare if need be—that is, if the protégé should not succeed in establishing himself. That clause was viewed as a mere formality which was almost never implemented, but still there is a rather special generosity involved in making oneself financially responsible for a total stranger.

In the meantime Hendrik Willem had heard about the latest blow, our expatriation, from our friend Franz Horch, and so he was standing on the Hoboken pier at dawn to welcome us, and, if necessary, help us out of a jam. Since he lived in Connecticut, this meant he had to set out at three in the morning—and his health was distinctly delicate. Most people would make such an effort only for their next of kin. But that is the remarkable thing about arriving in America, in contrast to all other countries; you quickly find that you are among next of kin. These are people who have themselves arrived as immigrants, or whose forefathers have, and therefore they form one large family. This does not involve an exaggerated appreciation of others. Relatives are not always pleasant to have; sometimes they are a nuisance; and it is one thing to be greeted by them, another to live with them. But the first thing the new arrival feels is contact, relationship, an unforced sense of belonging.

Van Loon fell in love at first sight with our wretched mongrel Mucki. Rather like our dead friend Egon Friedell, with whom in other respects he had something in common, he had a preference for

335

mongrels, especially when they were small and ugly. The dog sensed this at once; she neither snarled at him nor tried to bite his patting hand. And all through the laborious customs procedure, huge Henrik Willem carried the little monster around in his arms and murmured comforting words to her. Finally, after all our possessions including my guitar had been acknowledged as private property, not for resale, the customs man turned to the dog. There is no health quarantine in the United States as there is in England. But since a dog is potentially salable, its import value must be estimated —or so it was in those days. However, after giving the dog a careful going over, the customs man appended to our declaration: '1 dog, object of no value.' Van Loon felt otherwise. The first time he invited us to Connecticut, he sent a telegram reading: 'Mucki invited for weekend Saturday to Monday. You may accompany her.'

Our first period in New York passed in a kind of trance. During those two or three weeks we scarcely had time to reflect, so overwhelmed were we by the plethora of impressions which this city provides, as well as by the hospitality heaped on us from all sides. Even the heat wave in which Manhattan was sweltering at the time heightened the mood because of its exotic, unfamiliar character. This was heat such as we had never known, an oven temperature that persisted day and night, softening the hard asphalt into something resembling the mud of unpaved roads. Air conditioners were not yet customary in private apartments in those days, so people left all the windows open for cross-ventilation, in spite of those fire escapes which ran from yard to roof on the backs of all the houses to simplify things for the less athletic burglar! At night we found ourselves looking with astonishment through the open windows of many rear apartments at totally unclad people slumped in rocking chairs, sitting at desks, or bustling about the kitchen, as if New York were one gigantic nudist colony. But we were soon observing the universal convention—as well as sparing our aesthetic feelings—by no longer looking. And when we occasionally groaned at the unmitigated hothouse atmosphere, Dorothy's housekeeper, a dear old sybilline Scotswoman, said: 'You only feel it at first. Once you've been in America for a while, your blood thins out and you stop noticing it. All of us from Europe,' she explained, 'have blood that's much too thick.'

We had princely quarters in Dorothy's large apartment. She herself was still in the West; Sinclair Lewis was already living apart from her, with only occasional reunions at their house in the country. She had three secretaries who, whenever they were not busy handling the mail or the telephone calls, went to a great deal of trouble, in the kindest way, to help us acclimatize ourselves. There was also an unusually large domestic staff, by American standards. Dorothy's and Sinclair Lewis's ten-year-old son Michael was already at their Vermont country house. We had the apartment to ourselves.

As new arrivals, we were constantly being invited out and shown through the most interesting parts of the city, Harlem, Chinatown, the Spanish and Italian districts, and the bars of Greenwich Village. The violent contrasts between fine avenues like Fifth and Park, with their opulent millionaires' mansions, which in those days had not yet been replaced by office buildings, and dreary, filthy Third, where the noisy elevated railway still thundered overhead; the sight of towering skyscrapers, some of them of monumental beauty, cheek by jowl with old-fashioned brownstones and the swarming districts of what we Europeans called 'the little people'—all that exerted a constant fascination for us. At first the heat went to my head like a euphoric fever; ten times a day I took cold showers in Dorothy's luxurious bathroom, and at night, since I could not sleep anyhow, I drifted tirelessly about the city, absorbing the vulgar noises and the popcorn smell of Times Square, the sudden hollow silences in side streets, the torrents of lights, the screeching of brakes, and the distant howling of ship's sirens. Here, I felt, no one dared grow tired or old or sick. Therefore you had to keep yourself young, fresh, and healthy—as long as you could.

Everything, including the dangers of the city, gave us the feeling of having landed on a wild continent where you had to be unremittingly prepared for adventures and surprises. To us the frontier still seemed to exist—and basically that was true. We also discovered the truth of the adage that the first thousand dollars is very easy to earn, the next hundred very hard. My first thousand came from the highly intelligent and genial head of Viking Press, Ben Huebsch, as an advance on a book that was never written. I was soon to find out how hard the next hundred or fifty or even ten were to come by. For what succeeded the great cordiality of arrival was the still greater coolness and matter-of-factness of daily life: Well now, you're here, we've welcomed you, patted you on the back—now fend for yourself.

The summery days of our arrival lasted for a while. It was a time

337

of astonishment, of friendships, of trustfulness, and the happiness of reunions—with so many friends whom I had missed during recent years. My greatest pleasure was seeing my friend Hans Schiebelhuth, although that was somewhat saddened by the state of his health, for he was suffering from a cardiac ailment. But at the time I did not suspect, nor did he, that death was already close to him. Both of us firmly believed he would recover, and from year to year we planned a hiking trip to Canada together. Every year he said: Next year I'll be up to it—until there was no next year.

He had come to America several years before, not with the intention of definitely emigrating but because his wife was an American and had financial affairs to settle. She had formerly been very well-to-do, had lost the greater part of her fortune during the Depression, and was now handling her remaining securities so skilfully that there was a decent livelihood for both of them. Hans Schiebelhuth could no more live by his poetry than Gottfried Benn, who had once remarked that in ten years he had earned all of 925 marks from his volumes of poetry. Schiebelhuth's masterly translations of Thomas Wolfe's novels, which Rowohlt published, provided him with years of exhausting labor, for he toiled over every word, but not with an adequate income.

Schiebelhuth had come to love America, but he kept hoping that he would be able to return, at least for a visit, to see his mother and sister, his friends and his native region. First his illness prevented him, then the war. His heart ailment dated from the First World War, the result of overstrain during mountain fighting in the Dolomites, and of severe wounds. But in the past it had manifested itself only in occasional light attacks. It had become really serious only in America; the doctors believed that the deterioration of his condition had begun after he had eaten unpeeled fruit sprayed heavily with insecticide. The poison had affected the part of his body that had the least resistance, the heart muscle. (Since then I have always peeled any fruit I eat, in spite of my conviction that the heart stops when it wants to and ought to.) His wife eventually bought a small house with a large garden in the country near East Hampton, Long Island, where the climate, tempered by the ocean and the Gulf Stream, was particularly good for him. There he spent his last years, setting poetry to music when he was not writing it, creating even when he merely breathed or did garden chores. For him—I could say this of no one else I knew—poetry was part of his nervous

338

system, creativity the essence of his being, of his body as well as his mind. Not only his wisdom, but also his concrete knowledge of the origins of language, its processes, its laws, and the methods of shaping it, which he took with him to his grave, have scarcely ever been attained by any other scholar or writer.

We reveled in the happiness of being together again. In the period of eclipse that followed, nothing so strengthened and encouraged me as his existence, nothing so depressed me and so nearly undermined what self-command I had as the loss of him at the beginning of that somber year, 1944.

On the day of our arrival he came to New York, though he had to get away quickly from the city's sultry, suffocating atmosphere. Then we visited him in his house cooled by the sea breezes. His wife Alice possessed an unlimited capacity for warmth and affection and even a talent for foreign languages. She was his companion in the arts as well as in life; and since they had no children he was her child, her husband, and her father. She did not distress him with her anxiety over his health; she simply helped him. In all practical matters she was superior to European women, for without any fuss, she took care of everything calmly, thoughtfully, intelligently. It was a technique which Europeans of both sexes had to learn in America. He lived with her in the happiness of security, she with him in the happiness of respectful adoration. In the course of our visit I once happened to wake at dawn. From the window of our guest room I saw the two of them step outside the door in the gleam of the first light rising in the east and silently wait for the sunrise. That was his sort of religious rite. Then he went tranquilly back to sleep again. Driving us all back to New York, Alice made a stop at the simple frame house where Walt Whitman had been born. To either side of the house stood a pine and a large maple.

'He saw that maple as a child,' Schiebelhuth said. 'It's older than he is. Pines grow faster; it may not have been there then, or else it was very small.' We waved our hats in tribute to the great 'camarado.'

Soon afterwards Dorothy Thompson came back from Hollywood and we followed her to the small town of Barnard on Silver Lake in the forested state of Vermont, where we were later to make our American home.

From the first day that we saw Vermont, we were struck by

339

something familiar there. It is notorious that many of the new settlers in America sought, or like us found by chance, the kind of landscape that had a familiar look to them. This continent contains all the varieties of landscapes on earth. The shore of Long Island Sound near Stamford, Connecticut, where van Loon lived, looked like the banks of the Zuider Zee. A windmill on the horizon would have been enough to transport one to Holland.

Where Swedes and Finns have settled, there is usually some resemblance to Sweden and Finland. The Amish, those Germans who settled in Pennsylvania in the eighteenth century and still speak a language of their own based on the Hessian dialect, built their farms—often half-timbered houses—in their native style, in a region that greatly resembles the countryside north of the Main River. In Vermont my wife saw the Vienna Woods and I saw the Taunus Mountains; both of us were reminded of the Salzburg area, which lies in the foothills of the Alps. Only everything was enlarged to super-dimensions—hills ten times the extent of the Taunus, fifty times as large as the Vienna Woods, stretching on, wave after wave, under a great vault of sky. Our friendly relations with Dorothy gave us a sense of neighborliness and of midsummer rest before the restless to and fro movements began: almost two years of learning how to walk in America and struggling to find a basis for a livelihood.

We had met Dorothy in 1925, before the success of my *Merry Vineyard*. At that time she was accompanied by her first husband, a Hungarian journalist from whom she soon separated. I think that must have been a very difficult period for her. Although she was married three times, she was not one of those women who divorce and remarry easily or lightheartedly. She took marriage seriously; it was due to a succession of unfortunate circumstances that she did not find the man who was truly the right one for her until years later.

At the time I met her she was living in Germany as correspondent for several lesser American newspapers. After the first night of *The Merry Vineyard* she interviewed me for her papers, and afterwards I visited her frequently at her apartment in the attic of a handsome house in Berlin's 'old West End.' Her fluent German punctuated with errors was enormously funny, and her way of speaking remained amusing even later on, when she had become proficient in both reading and writing German. The easy charm of her personality was irresistible and she was capable of addressing a Chancellor as

Du and his dog as *Sie*. In her late twenties she seemed nineteen. She was marvelously healthy; her face always looked as if she had just been running in a stiff sea breeze; and her bright, clear eyes flashed and glowed with eagerness and enthusiasm, whether she was arguing or agreeing with you. Even when her fine, well-proportioned figure was becoming a little plump, she loved to wear very light, rather girlish dresses which were wonderfully becoming on her. There was nothing about Dorothy that reminded you of the typical career woman who is intellectually overstrained or riddled by the craving for success, who never has time for herself and therefore becomes an irritant to everyone. Dorothy had time; despite all her professional work she took time to live, to be a woman and a human being. She could laugh, she loved gaiety and enjoyed simple pleasures. She cooked well; she could hold most drinks and in any quantity. The one thing that betrayed her hidden nervousness and did her no good was her incessant, hasty, uncontrollable cigarette smoking. In her greedy inhaling, her careless crushing out of a half-smoked cigarette and immediately lighting another, I saw a sign of inner restlessness which she otherwise locked within herself, as she did all the difficulties, the complications, and the tragic aspects of her life.

Without money of her own, on nothing but a small, ill-paid newspaper job, she had gone to Europe directly from college at the beginning of the twenties. She went not only out of adventurousness and a desire to see the world, but also because she sensed that in Europe, and especially in Germany, there were crises brewing which would shake the foundations of the world. Her ability to scent the atmosphere of crisis, her incorruptible eye for facts, and the boldness of her passionate—nowadays we would say: passionately engaged—opinions, added a force and interest to her reports and soon won her an international reputation. The rapid upward curve of her career coincided with the rise of Hitler, for from the start she recognized Nazism as a peril to the whole world, and she denounced and fought it when the world was still shrugging its shoulders indifferently.

One evening early in 1926 Dorothy invited me to her Berlin apartment. There I met a long-legged man with a rangy, lean, slouching frame. His face, with its elongated brow and chin, was the most interesting of all the ugly faces I have ever seen. He took his hand out of his pocket and by way of greeting shot at me a two-foot long artificial finger, the kind with the built-in springs that could be bought in joke shops. This was Sinclair Lewis, whom his friends called Red, and whose novels ushered in a new era in American literature. He knew no German and I hardly any English at the time, but we understood one another very well. At first Dorothy acted as interpreter; then the wine facilitated communication, and on his later visits to Berlin we always spent long evenings together. The first time he saw Dorothy he wanted to marry her at once, and probably she reciprocated the feeling, but some feminine instinct prompted her to flee. She escaped to Moscow; he followed, and after they had continued this game of flight and pursuit for a while they married.

Sinclair Lewis was as fascinating as he was hard to deal with and difficult to understand. He was quick-tempered and a hypochondriac. Later on those traits were aggravated to the point of being unbearable; at the time they were still leavened by a crazy humor and periods of abrupt, unexpected cordiality. For a time the two seemed to be an ideal couple—two somewhat self-centered bachelors who supported each other in their eccentricities or provided each other with mutual relaxation. But by the time we came to America their marriage had already foundered, partly because of their antithetical dispositions, partly because they were too much alike in many ways.

Dorothy had visited us in our Henndorf house and now described it in an article which, she hoped, would give me that never accomplished 'start' in America:

'The house had the bewitching smell that all really good houses have, of old wood and log fires and leather shoes with fresh snow melting from them, and of apples and warm bread.'

Later, when she visited us in our Vermont farmhouse during the war years, she would always say: 'It smells like Henndorf.' I think it did, and the same smells are here in Saas-Fee.

When the war broke out in Europe on September 1, 1939, we were still with Dorothy in Vermont, living in a small cottage she had rented for us for our summer stay. We sat by the radio, distraught and depressed as we had been ever since the news of that sinister Pact between Hitler and Stalin. We were able to hear German short-wave broadcasts: Goebbels was aiming his propaganda at America in an attempt to sway American opinion and incite German-Americans to oppose their government. Dorothy Thompson was attacked with special virulence in these broadcasts. She was denounced as 'an enemy of Germany.' That hurt. Almost weeping, she came to me, whom she regarded even in exile as unswervingly (my wife said: incorrigibly) German. '*You* know I love Germany! That I've never been against the Germans, only against the Nazis.' I knew that, and throughout the whole period of the war she was united with me in understanding of the other Germany and its desperate predicament.

At this time two friends, Lady Yvonne Rodd-Marling, the beautiful, gifted, witty daughter of an English diplomat, and Ingrid Warburg, of the well-known Hamburg family, relieved us of our great anxiety over Michaela, who had been left behind in England. Had they not acted so promptly we would not have seen our daughter for the entire war and would have had to consign her to the uncertainties of war-time England. Perhaps only women can summon up the energy and ingenuity that Yvonne displayed in obtaining an immediate American visa for Michaela, in the face of all rules. The Warburgs then managed to find the last empty berth for her on a Swedish liner. She reached America in safety before the North Sea was blocked by mines and the Atlantic became a hunting-ground for destroyers and submarines.

There came a time that I remember only as a wild, confused dream. I went to Hollywood, alone at first. An agent had summoned me with the assurance that there was a job for me there. The plane in which I left New York ran into a thunderstorm; it danced and leaped above the clouds like a bucking bronco. A child began screaming with fear and earache. In Utah the flight was interrupted because of tornado warnings. I thus saw something of the Mormon city. A film-star friend came to fetch me in his car and drove me through the salt desert and the plains of Nevada. Because of the distance we had to spend the night in a motel on the Nevada border. After dark I heard a shrill, wailing howl that sounded alternately close and far away. A taciturn fellow who was tending the fireplace said: 'Coyotes.' So these were the prairie wolves of the Wild West novels. I awoke next morning with a lingering dream of my school days. I heard a comic screech such as we boys would make when we were playing Indians. When I looked out, I saw Indians. There was a reservation of the once proud Shoshones in the vicinity, and three times a day, to earn a few coins, the redskins performed a 'war dance' for the motel tourists. They danced in a

343

circle, hopping from one foot to the other, just as we had done in the Mainz schoolyard—as if they had learned it from us.

I saw Reno and thought a movie was being shot there because suddenly a troop of cowboys in Wild West outfits, with huge hats, came galloping up the street of luxury hotels between the Chryslers and Oldsmobiles. But they were real cowboys who wanted to place a few silver dollars on the roulette wheel between roundups.

I saw glorious Lake Tahoe on the border of Nevada and California. Its color and its wooded shores reminded me of the lake of Sils-Maria in Switzerland. I crossed the Sierra Nevadas—later I would come to know that wild country in the course of a long horseback ride—and passed through the valley of the Sacramento, where a few wooden crosses still recalled the avid gold seekers who in 1849 overran and devastated the fields of General Sutter, the Swiss pioneer. I crossed the Golden Gate Bridge at twilight, swam in the Pacific near the old missionary settlements of Carmel and Monterey. The sensational landscape intoxicated me; every look and every pause was a discovery. I felt the headiness at seeing these vast expanses as it must have been felt, little more than a hundred years earlier, by those who were seeing this land for the first time. But I also felt panic, a sense of being lost in this tremendous, merciless vastness. In the West I did not feel at home as I did in the forests of Vermont, which remained friendly to me even when I lost my way in their pathless thickets. Here, I knew, I would not build a house; I would not remain.

Friends awaited and embraced me in Hollywood. There were endless reunions. Albrecht Joseph, the companion of my years in Kiel, Berlin, and Henndorf, was here; so were Bruno Frank and his wife Liesel, and Marlene Dietrich with her warmhearted camaraderie. Remarque had rented a handsome bungalow in the park of the Beverly Hills Hotel, where I took a room. He and I sat up long nights, drinking rum or vodka, just as if we were still in one of our Berlin night clubs. The German movie directors Ernst Lubitsch, William Dieterle, and Fritz Lang invited me to their houses and their parties, where I met more friends from Germany, Austria, Hungary, France, and England. These directors knew my plays and other writings, but they could not use them for the American 'market.' They needed, they indicated, seasoned Hollywood writers for their scripts.

I also met some Americans—powerful, omnipotent rulers of an

empire with feet of clay. My agent and my friends introduced me to them. At first they were very obliging, for I was a new arrival wearing the label of a 'successful writer.' They counted on my adjusting, shifting gears, fitting into their production process and their style of work. I therefore received that well-known 'seven-year contract,' which in my case began with the sizable initial salary of seven hundred and fifty dollars a week, but put the signatory totally at the mercy of the company, which for its part was entitled to dismiss him on a week's notice. One of the clauses in this contract stated: 'I hereby declare and affirm that for the purpose of this contract the concept of so-called intellectual property does not exist.' Which meant that whatever you wrote on assignment from the studio belonged to the producer like delivered goods; he could do whatever he pleased with it, use it, throw it away, have it rewritten or completely altered, without the author's having any say in it. I was shown the 'Writers' Building,' a spacious structure in which there were many large, well-furnished offices for the script writers. Such an office was assigned to me too, with a surplus of all kinds of writing materials and a secretary in the reception room. There was nothing I could do with her except give her a friendly greeting and leave her bottles of Coca-Cola, since I was not yet capable of dictating so much as a letter in English. I was also not geared to working in an office, and stayed there solely to take care of my personal mail. As for the script that had been assigned to me, I toiled at it by night in my hotel room. From time to time the telephone in my office rang, and the voice of the studio boss's head secretary asked: 'How is your work going?' 'Very well,' I said. 'Thank you,' she said. Otherwise, no one paid much attention to me, and experienced fellow exiles told me that the main thing was to be seen there—lunching, for example, in the restaurant where the celebrities ate. For the rest, there was no point in overexerting myself, they said.

In Hollywood, too, there were many invitations at the beginning, but in contrast to New York, life was very expensive. In order to count for anything you had to live in a top-class hotel or have your own showy home. To prove yourself, you had to frequent the expensive restaurants of the movie industry's upper crust. Moreover, if you wanted to 'belong' permanently, you had to begin issuing invitations yourself. You had to act as if you were rich and happy— nowhere have I ever heard the word 'happy' so often as in that anteroom to hell called Hollywood. And since nobody was, everyone drifted into drinking even when he was in no mood for it, and ended up in a morass of joyless, humorless, and dreary night life.

Some weeks after 'happiness' had come to me in the form of a contract and a weekly paycheck, I happened to be attending a Sunday afternoon party at Max Reinhardt's house. Almost the entire German colony was present. 'I'm not staying here long,' I remarked. 'This is no life for me.' Those words provoked roars of laughter. Everybody, I was told, had said the same thing after three weeks, everybody in this room, but they were all still here—some of them had been for many years. The check . . . Where else in America could you drift through life so comfortably?

There was some truth to that, but it did not console me, for I had seen that what was being drifted through could not be called life. Word spread like wildfire through the 'colony' when one of these studio serfs had his check increased or reduced. You were ranked by the size of this check. I didn't think that funny. Max Reinhardt, too, did not join in the laughter. He had become acquainted with Hollywood's tough side, just as the first wave of refugees had early encountered the tough side of Switzerland. Something had happened to him that must not be allowed to happen in Hollywood: his movie *A Midsummer Night's Dream*, done in the lavish style of Reinhardt's baroque period, had netted less money than the studio had expected. The industry had dropped him, for if a man's work does not bring in a profit, he himself is regarded as worthless, however great an artist he may be in his field. On Broadway, too, Reinhardt's rigorous directing, with its concern solely for quality, had not accorded with the laws of the box office. Now he was running a drama school in Hollywood and occasionally giving performances with the more talented of his students. But these performances were attended only by connoisseurs, professionals and Europeans. He himself did not know, and probably never learned, that his school and its performances were being secretly financed, in a most discreet and tactful way, by Gert von Gontard, a highly intelligent, cultivated, and sensitive lover of the arts and humanity, whom I later was to count among my best friends. But Reinhardt knew that Hollywood was no Garden of Allah. A few years earlier he had been the idol of international society and the theater world. Now, in his late sixties, he was once more embroiled in the struggle for status and livelihood.

In spite of the check, in spite of the presence of so many friends, Hollywood did not make me 'happy.' Never have I been so wrapped in the mists of depression as in this land of eternal spring, in whose irrigated gardens, with their chlorinated swimming pools and dream castles perched on the slopes of canyons, short-lived pleasure is at home, while in the depths sprawls a dreary, murderous wasteland: the city of Los Angeles, one of the ugliest and most brutal metropolises in the world.

All was quiet on the Western Front—for months. Not even a gesture had been made in the defense of invaded Poland. In America people talked about the 'phony war,' in France they called it '*drôle de guerre*.' Cocktail-party strategists maintained that there would not be any war at all, that secret arrangements and assignments of spheres of influence were already being negotiated between Hitler and England. At the time the ordinary American did not particularly care, so long as America itself was not drawn in. Dorothy Thompson had made a lightning trip to France. With a group of journalists she had visited the Maginot Line, was carried in an elevator like that of a grand hotel many stories below ground and there, in a spanking officers' mess safe from bombs and shells, served a six-course dinner with all the approved beverages. Over coffee and liqueurs most of her colleagues agreed that the Maginot Line was invulnerable and France the safest country in the world. She was not so sure. In reality no one knew anything. People only sensed—or at least so it was with me—the inescapable threat like a vibration of the ground underfoot before an earthquake.

At this time I received a letter from Peter Suhrkamp, who had been one of my friends since his spell as play-reader in Darmstadt in 1919. In the mid-thirties he had married Annemarie Seidel, my Mirl, and that fact had brought us even closer together. Moreover, when the heirs of Samuel Fischer were no longer allowed to run their publishing house in Germany because they were 'non-Aryans,' Suhrkamp had at their request taken over what remained of S. Fischer Verlag, whose author I had been before my books were banned. (He administered it in trust throughout the war.) The letter came from the Hotel Schiller in Amsterdam; it was dated October 12, 1939. Peter wrote:

Dear Carl, I am here for three days and taking the opportunity

347

to write to you. In Mirl's behalf, too, of course. We are very glad that you are where you are. I hope you are not having any sieges of temptation and imagining you ought to be with us now. [I was having them.] This war is in no way to be compared with 1914. Everyone lives in darkness, not only at night. We barely know what is going on in our immediate neighborhood. We wait and wait for some event whose nature we don't know and cannot imagine. We think about things, only to find that all our thoughts are mistaken. People are pale and self-absorbed. Then again they sit around trading the latest propaganda phrases with each other. Daily cares multiply like ants. The restrictions magnify needs. The day before yesterday at eleven o'clock the word spread that the British government had resigned and a ten-day armistice had been concluded. During the hour the rumor lasted people in shops and markets embraced each other, weeping and laughing.

Please do not be misled by the newspapers. The foreign press is every bit as fraudulent as ours. There's no truth in any reports. Which means that outside, too—except for ourselves, ourselves and you and yours—there is no longer anything to believe in, to cling to. . . .

I myself am naturally absorbed by the problems of the publishing house, which under present circumstances become more difficult than ever. In addition I can count on being drafted. Personally, I would not mind that. I have been prepared for death for several years. And in the end I'd rather be in the army—you will understand why. That would be a way of ending with one's hands clean. For living under communism wouldn't suit me, and this, I think, would be the other alternative; the Russians' gift to us. But then I must think of Mirl and refrain from doing anything which would mean leaving her behind. She is keeping up her courage magnificently; but she really isn't able to cope with times like these. I am terribly worried about her. About the way she is burning herself up inwardly. . . .

Carl, my dear friend, I feel more and more that I really cannot tell all of you anything. But I did want to send you a word. And Mirl's greetings too. Fondest greetings.

Think of us occasionally, but live as fully as you can. We greet you and embrace you. Don't worry. It isn't worth it.

Yours,
Peter

Along with the letter was a note explaining how things stood with my parents, who up to this point had been living in Mainz, still untouched by the war. He assured me that he would help them in any peril.

We ourselves were able to hear from our parents very rarely, by way of a friend in Switzerland. Such letters from Germany wrenched our hearts, glad though we were of any sign of life from back home. For I would rather have been there, sharing the fate of my friends.

Instead, in the midst of my serfdom to the Hollywood check and still under contract, I had to go to New York to straighten out our legal status with the immigration authorities. We would have to leave the United States once more in order to re-enter on a legal visa. In our haste we had come on visitors' visas, and I had no right to accept paid work in America. In Hollywood exceptions were made, but with limits. Now for the first time we became acquainted with the tough side of New York. We went from office to office and stood in line at consulates. We encountered nasty police officials who treated us like criminals as they took our fingerprints, who shouted at us, cursed the 'goddamn foreigners,' did not attempt to conceal their admiration for the 'strong man' Hitler and their contempt for the people he had exiled. That sort of thing existed in America, too. The recommendations I had from people such as Thomas Mann and Hemingway, Dorothy Thompson and Marlene Dietrich, Thornton Wilder and Albert Einstein, made no impression on such officials. They did not even know most of these names, except for Marlene Dietrich. Here I was a smudge in an opaque mass, already halfway a 'nothing.' This was a period of rushing around and agonizing uncertainty. At last we were able to arrange to immigrate via Cuba. That, too, was a gamble; up to the last moment we did not know whether we would make it or be stranded penniless in Havana, at that time a favorite resort for rich American tourists and a city of refugees.

This time my wife went with me to the West. It was a four-day journey by rail, first through all of Florida, with a pause in New Orleans. We saw the old French quarter, stood at the mouth of the Mississippi, wide as a lake, where the sluggish yellow river rolls into the sea. We saw giant cypresses standing deep in swamp water, wreathed with gray-green Spanish moss. Through Texas, New Mexico, and Arizona we looked out of the train window upon a landscape of endless plain, grotesque pyramids of rock, tree-high cacti. We crossed great gorges. Mountain ranges loomed in the distance. In Yuma on the muddy Colorado, where the train stopped for a while, massive Indian women were stationed along the tracks selling souvenirs, mostly amulets shaped like rabbits' feet, studded with small turquoise beads. They did not cry their wares, scarcely raised their hands to receive the money, but sat unsmiling without looking up. They gave me the impression of boundless sadness.

My wife went on to San Francisco, where we had friends and life would be more economical than if she were with me in Hollywood. I moved back into my hotel room and chrome-plated desk in the Writers' Building. I wanted to finish the work I had taken on, cash a few more checks, and then—where to? Everything was uncertain. The one thing I knew for certain was that I did not want to stay there. Desperately I searched for a gap between the bars, like a newly captive bird. Then the supreme power, in other words the studio itself, came to my aid.

I was working on material that seriously interested me: a filming of Arnold Zweig's novel *The Case of Sergeant Grischa*. It was the story of a Russian peasant soldier in the First World War who is falsely accused of espionage or sabotage, and although no one believes he is guilty and he wins the hearts of those who guard him, he is torn between the millstones of a divided bureaucracy.

In the midst of this work I was called to a projection room and without explanation shown a thoroughly ludicrous old Don Juan movie-strip from the days of the silents. Then the mighty Hal Wallis invited me into his office. Offering me a cigar and a glass of whisky, he told me to forget about Grischa. The studio had decided to drop the subject for political reasons. The Russians were currently engaged in their war against Finland, and this little country stood very high in American eyes because she punctually paid her war debts; the music of Sibelius monopolized the air-waves. At such a time it did not seem wise to bring out a movie whose hero was a likable Russian.

Instead, I was to write a Don Juan script for Errol Flynn, romantic, melodramatic, with plenty of duels and love scenes, in a Renaissance setting: Medicean Florence. . . . I objected that the Don Juan legend applied to Spain and not to Florence. That didn't matter at all, Wallis assured me. The Medici (he meant the Borgias) were a fascinating bunch. The climax would be an affair between Don

Juan and the famous lovely poisoner. This was a prime subject for a European writer, wasn't it? Yes or no? Would I let him know my decision in the morning. With a second cigar and a second glass of whisky, I was dismissed.

That evening I met the director Fritz Lang and told him what had happened. I said I had decided to turn down the project. I had been going along beautifully on *Sergeant Grischa* and could not abruptly switch to such trivial childishness. After all, I said, it was perfectly clear that they did not want a kind of poetic Don Juan done in ballad style, or a Mozartean Don Juan, or a fable, but some typical movie nonsense, and I had neither the talent nor the urge for that sort of thing. Fritz Lang, who wished me well, was horrified. In Hollywood you never said 'no' to anything, no matter what was asked of you, he advised me. To refuse an assignment was to be fired. And how could I ask for anything better than this offer? It would keep me occupied for years; that kind of expensive costume spectacular went slowly, so that I could count on staying on for the length of my contract, which provided for an increase in the weekly check from year to year. I ought to rent a nice house and hire a Filipino couple as domestics, buy a car on installments, bring my family here, and be 'happy.' Besides, I would have a three-month holiday every year during which I could do my own writing. For God's sake be reasonable and say yes, Lang urged me; otherwise I was finished in Hollywood.

But I wanted to be finished. I knew that I could live comfortably here, but at the expense of my inner independence and my productivity. All around me I saw examples to prove that three months of holiday after nine months of apathy could never lead to any true and untrammeled work, to the completion of anything of substance. I felt I would perish in this golden cage, and now at last I had a glimpse of a gap between the bars. Next morning I refused the Don Juan assignment. On Monday I found the famous dismissal slip on my resplendent desk, the specter that haunted all the serfs in Hollywood. It contained a curt notice that my services were terminated as of the end of the current week. For me it was a release. I cashed my last check and went on a spree.

My wife, too, was glad that I had cut loose from Hollywood before it had swallowed me up or sapped my vitality. We had crossed the ocean to be free. We had no idea how we would win our freedom. But anything was better than submitting voluntarily to

351

a sated, living death. Not for that had we escaped the Nazis' death camps.

It was Christmas week. I saw Hollywood one more time in all its horror. Artificial Christmas trees with electric candles in all imaginable colors, chiefly pink, orange, and silvery blue, stood in front of the houses. I had been invited to a party given in the Beverly Hills Hotel. A slide had been covered with artificial snow and men in bathing trunks, women in silk jerseys, skied down it directly into the cocktail tent. Huge crimson poinsettias bloomed in all the gardens. The sight of all this nauseated me. I said goodbye to my friends and went to San Francisco to join my wife.

Anyone acquainted with Hollywood knows (and it should be apparent to all) that this is an entirely subjective account, the personal experience, impressions, and decisions of an individual with whom the climate there did not agree. Let no generalization, no verdict, be drawn from my remarks. That would be unfair. This weird combination of artificial and artistic fragments, of business and imagination, of pointless motion, real activity, and high ambition, saw many others through the hardest years of their lives. Many magnificent productions—some that can safely be called works of art—were and are being created there. At this period I am discussing anything decent had to emerge from an obstinate battle with the monstrous industry; today the good things stem from the daring independent producers. But to achieve this takes conviction, takes total devotion to the medium, to the good and the bad sides of the production system. You have to be obsessed by the craft, or else, if you want to live a peaceful and relatively human life there, you have to practise resignation and be content with subsidiary technical contributions. Neither of these attitudes was possible for me.

We spent Christmas in San Francisco. That was the saddest, most forlorn Christmas of our lives. My wife had rented cheap quarters, set up a crèche, decorated a few pine branches with candles. On Christmas Eve we sat in an Italian basement restaurant and tried not to talk about home. Then we returned to New York.

There I obtained a job through the kind offices of Erwin Piscator, who was head of the drama school at the New School for Social Research. Piscator's school was called the Dramatic Workshop. It took in all phases of theatrical training from instruction in acting to stage designing, costuming, and even drama criticism. I was to conduct a course of lectures, discussions, and seminars for which I had selected the theme 'Humor in the Drama.' I thought that was something I knew about, but I soon made the discovery that it would have been easier for me to write half a dozen comedies—in German, to be sure—than to produce a single sentence on the theory of the subject. To this day I fall into a cold sweat whenever I think of my initial lecture. Laboriously, I wrote out the manuscript, and my translator, Elizabeth Norman-Hapgood, who was as fluent in German and Russian as she was in her native language and who had translated all the writings of Stanislavski into English, devoted no less labor to remodeling my involutions into a halfway speakable American. Then she coached me in the pronunciation of the same and tricked out my manuscript with all sorts of accents and curlicues to help me read it properly. It looked like a complicated text in ancient Greek in which someone had marked out the meter. I rejected the notion of learning it by heart because then I would have felt like a parrot. But when I appeared for this first one-and-a-half-hour lecture, the American heads of the school, who wanted to attend my debut, indicated that I must not use a manuscript at all. It was customary here, they said—and the students expected it— for the lecturer to talk to them in a free and easy manner. Ever since then the words 'free and easy' have had a highly dubious significance for me.

But the students were kind and friendly. They pretended not to notice my mispronunciations, or else when I made some particularly funny howlers they laughed in such a way that I myself was able to laugh with them. Nevertheless, this work was an agony. Once a week I had to give a lecture. Afterwards, the students openly and naïvely asked me the most ridiculous questions. Twice a week I had to conduct a so-called 'playwright' class, chiefly for ambitious ladies. Here, too, ghastly simplistic questions were asked—questions that left me helpless—for example: A good curtain line should consist of how many words? Or: After how many minutes of playing time should the sex or love interest begin? I had only two students whom I could talk to at all. One of them was a Negro who later in fact became a successful playwright, the other a fanatical Communist girl who wanted to write a Marxist drama about St Paul and early Christianity. A man came up to me who emitted a piercing smell of chemicals and wanted me to give him private lessons in humor. He was a pharmacist and explained that he had marvelous ideas for comedies that would bring in millions, but absolutely no sense of humor. He said that when he told his wife his funniest ideas at breakfast, she never gave a smile. He had heard that my successes in Europe were due chiefly to the humor in my plays. Would I impart my secrets to him at five dollars an hour? Although the five dollars was a temptation, I refused—it was too little for enduring that pharmaceutical smell.

In any case, my own sense of humor had largely drained away. By the tenth of every month I had very little left; by the end of the month, when the rent was due, none at all. The New School could pay only the most modest salaries. Although I was forever trying to find additional sources of income by writing articles for magazines and so on—articles that cost me torture to produce—we never had enough money. My wife had found a pretty little apartment. Our friends Eleonora and Francesco von Mendelssohn, who at that time still owned a house on a side street off upper Fifth Avenue, had lent us some furniture. Our windows looked out on the Hudson, the imposing arch of the George Washington Bridge, and the steep cliffs of the Palisades. I enjoyed taking long walks across the bridge, along the Palisades, then crossing the river again by ferry and tramping through the magnificent Fort Tyron Park. The Hudson became my Rhine; it soothed my heart when the sharp smell of the water entered the open windows of my bedroom at night.

But our financial situation was disastrous. We did not have to starve; there were shops in the neighborhood which let one charge things by the month, and we always regaled our friends so well it did not occur to them how poor we were. My wife, who during our good times in Europe had never touched a kitchen spoon simply because the cook could handle everything so much better, developed into an artiste of European cuisine. That had something to do with homesickness. Good food was a means of overcoming it. When we ate as we had been accustomed to do at home, we did not feel so utterly annihilated by this strange land.

But the monthly bills had to be paid: each time they descended banefully upon us. For a while Professor Max Ascoli, an exile from Italy who later became dean of the New School of Social Research, helped us out, but even so we could barely manage. We could no longer go to the movies or the theater. For years my wife depended on Dorothy Thompson's cast-off clothing, which she would alter to fit her. A man feels debased and ashamed when he can no longer buy his wife a dress or shoes.

Others were even worse off. We saw the refugees who trotted up and down stairs with suitcases full of samples, only to be insulted in a foreign language. At home these people had been prosperous businessmen. We saw wives who had to hire themselves out as domestics so that their husbands, who had been well-known doctors in Europe, could repeat their studies and take the examinations that were demanded in America. We knew old gentlemen who earned a shabby living as night watchmen in department stores. We ourselves were just barely one stage above destitution.

Fritz Kortner persuaded me to try writing a play with him. It seemed a life preserver but proved to be an absolute mistake. I could no more adapt to writing for Broadway than for the movie industry in Hollywood. That attempt made me realize fully and finally that synthetic literary products and artistic abortions would bring me neither inner satisfaction nor outward success. There was no hope of my learning to compromise, which meant there was no hope at all.

In addition to all that, the war in Europe became more and more depressing. The deceptive quiet of the phony war had ended in blitz. Norway and Denmark, Holland and Belgium, had fallen to Hitler. His armies were advancing in France; what was left of the British army had to escape as best it could across the waters. German bombers smashed the city of Coventry; that seemed like a prelude to the destruction of London. Yet we still believed the French army would manage a counterstroke, would establish a firm line of defense, as in the First World War. Every morning we turned on the radio to hear the latest news. It was preceded by a commercial which always began with the impassioned slogan: 'Better to have it and not to need it than to need it and not to have it.' There followed an invitation to purchase an idyllic cemetery plot with a pleasant view of the Hudson Valley; possession of such a plot would be a reassurance to one's near and dear. Then we heard that Paris had fallen.

All prospect of returning to Europe seemed gone forever, and the prospects we had in New York, aside from that lovely cemetery plot, were black indeed. Here, surrounded by a foreign language and an unfamiliar mentality, there were not the same chances for a breakthrough, for a sharp reversal, such as I had counted on in my early days in Berlin. Things could not get better; they could only get worse. I no longer had illusions. I would have to let go in order not to go under. I would have to retreat and start over again from the beginning.

In the spring of 1941 we finally decided to give up our New York apartment and try our luck at farming. We had no illusion about this being any way to prosperity, but it seemed to us our last and only chance to forge a life for ourselves by free, self-chosen work. For my own part, I regarded it as salvation from a demeaning and hopeless existence, and I can almost say that it saved my life. We had no inkling of the hardships that awaited us; but we knew that we would find something we could have nowhere else: a home.

We had twice been visitors and summer guests in Vermont. Moreover, we felt more drawn to the few 'natives' we had met there than to the city people, the writers, journalists, political people, and artists, who swarmed around Dorothy Thompson's house during the holiday season.

In days of tramping, always alone except for Dorothy's big shaggy farm dog, Bongo, I had roamed through the woods and become acquainted with the animals, plants, and streams of Vermont. I knew where the old and then barely discernible Appalachian Trail ran between moss-covered rocks, thickets, and gorges, the trail the Indians' had used from southwest Georgia to northeastern Maine. I had found the still unfelled 'scout trees,' huge evergreens on isolated peaks, from the tops of which they had surveyed the land. I had watched beavers laboring on their dams in hidden ponds, had encountered a large she-bear with two cubs in a dense, high stand of raspberry canes—a meeting hardly to be recommended, since the ordinarily shy and peaceable bears are often dangerous if someone approaches their young too closely. The pathless woods lured me; their solitude promised me protection, asylum, consolation.

I knew nothing about farming but was convinced that I could learn it more easily than some technical job in the city. Farming was the only practical work for which I felt that I had a certain talent and, above all, liking. I was healthy and strong, and it is not unusual in America for a man to start all over in an occupation he has never practised before, even in his riper years. Why should we not succeed in the kind of work that had provided a livelihood for many people who had lost their jobs and their savings during the Depression?

Our European friends shook their heads, but Americans gave us encouragement. There is still something of the spirit of the old pioneers in them, and they found our solution good, brave, and reasonable. Of course we would need some capital for the beginning, but not much. An American friend, intrigued by our project, offered us a loan without our asking. Alfred Harcourt, the publisher, a man of originality and simple humanity who in many respects reminded me of old Samuel Fischer, took over my still unfulfilled contract with Viking Press and in addition paid me a substantial advance. It was not that he thought I was going to develop into a best-selling American author; rather, he too was acting so generously because our project pleased him. Here was one refugee balked in his profession who was going to try to make his way in another fashion: in the authentic American fashion, by working with his hands and relying entirely on himself.

Thus we had enough, or at least the minimum, to make a start, to look for a suitable place, to come through the first winter in which there would be no income from the farm, and to obtain a basic stock of farm animals and the most essential items of equipment— the latter on installments from a mail-order company. We also bought on installments, payable over a two-year period, winter clothes: heavy shoes, woolens, snowshoes and skis, without which it was often impossible to reach the nearest crossroad. In a rickety old car bought for an amazingly low price my wife drove around the countryside to look at the farms advertised for rent or sale in the local newspaper, the *Vermont Standard*. She always returned with bad news: most of the farms were too dear, or would have demanded too much initial investment, or were unfavorably situated.

One summer day I was tramping along a grassy wood road, about three miles from the small town of Barnard, merely to see where it would lead me. Suddenly the woods opened out; I saw a big pond fed by a brook that descended the forested slope, and a bit beyond the pond, standing on a cleared hill, a solitary farmhouse with a shingled wooden roof gray with age and shingled exterior walls. The shape and proportions of the house appealed to me, with its large attached shed, a somewhat dilapidated barn, and a corn crib on stone pillars that reminded me of the barns or *mazots* of the Valais. Everything was totally utilitarian and for that reason uniquely and unintentionally beautiful. I could see at once that the house was uninhabited; most of the windows were shuttered, the

357

stone threshold was overgrown with moss, there were no signs of a tilled field or of cattle in the vicinity.

But on the open lawn between a few elms and ash trees in front of the house, where the narrow road leveled off before it continued on downhill through the woods, an old man was busy mowing the tall grass with a scythe. He was, as I later discovered, only sixty, but he looked much older: of medium height, lean, smooth-shaven, largely bald with sparse gray hair at the back of his head. He had thin lips and wire-rimmed glasses over clear, piercing eyes. Many Vermont backwoods farmers have such faces, faces that to strangers seem rather those of railroad men or postmasters. By their look they could also be engineers or bookkeepers or glaziers—perhaps a bit on the odd side, but in no way as they might be represented in the movies. There is not a touch of romanticism and adventure about them. Instead, they call to mind the fieldstones of Vermont soil, the plain wooden façades of their puritanical churches. Such faces often have an ascetic cast; they are stamped by a simple, frugal kind of life that also confers on them an expression of tranquil self-assurance, of cheerful serenity salted with a dash of hidden irony.

The man was wearing faded overalls that showed traces of many kinds of work: grass and soil stains, a few smears of paint and tree resin. Under his suspenders he had a striped shirt with rolled-up sleeves. The whetstone for the scythe protruded from an outside pocket, from another a small hammer for pounding out nicks. Lying on an old sawhorse beside the shed door I saw trousers, jacket, and white shirt; probably he had come here in street clothes. He looked at me, I looked at him. Then we both said, 'How d'you do?' For this was New England, where strangers do not greet each other with 'Hello' or 'Howdy.'

'Are you thirsty?' the man asked; he probably noticed the beads of sweat on my forehead.

'Yes,' I said.

'Come on in and have a drink,' he said. 'This is the best spring water around here.'

He opened a door alongside the shed which led directly into the kitchen. It was a huge, oblong room. The beams of the ceiling were at least twenty feet in span, I estimated, and I saw at once that they must be very old, for they were hand hewn. The kitchen was completely empty except for a chair and a black Glenwood stove. In the corner near the rear window a bent lead pipe emerged from the wall. A strong, clear stream of water flowed from it into a barrel on the wide board floor; presumably it flowed out through another pipe under the floor. This was, I was informed, the only source of water in the house.

He took a large china cup that hung on a hook beside the water pipe, rinsed it out, filled it, and handed it to me. On his face was an expression of pride rather like that of an *encaveur*, a vintner in the Rhone Valley, when he lets a visitor taste his best vintage.

I drank—and I seriously believed, and believe to this day, that never in my life have I tasted such good, pure, refreshing water, with all the coldness of the soil and the freshness of the woods in it.

'A good spring,' the man said. 'My grandfather found and stoned it. It's three hundred feet up the hill, in the woods over there. Plenty of pressure and runs just as full summer and winter.'

'Wouldn't the barrel overflow and flood the kitchen if the drain should ever get plugged up?' I asked.

He laughed.

'That drain won't plug,' he said. 'It's big enough and has plenty of pitch, the way they used to do it in the old days. Runs into a dry well ten feet deep. It can't freeze up as long as it keeps running.'

'The way they used to do it in the old days'—how often I heard him say that later on!

'You don't live here?' I asked him.

'No,' he said, 'but I was born here.'

Again there was a kind of modest pride in his voice, as when a man speaks of his ancestral castle. But also possibly a repressed sadness. 'Care to see a real old farmhouse?' he asked. 'It's been standing there since 1783. Hasn't changed much.'

Like most of the colonial houses, it was built around an enormous central chimney that served three fireplaces in the other three rooms, which, in addition to the kitchen, made up the ground floor of the house.

The largest of the fireplaces, in the room adjacent to the kitchen, seemed to me altogether unusual. I have never seen the like, not even in English or Scottish country houses. It was very high and the lintel was made of a single colossal slab of dressed granite—it was impossible to imagine how men without machinery could ever have raised it even to knee height. The interior of the fireplace was so shallow that you could not place two logs side by side in it. I asked whether it would draw properly. Given the width of the chimney above, wouldn't the smoke from the fireplace blow back into the room?

Once again the response was that good-natured, slightly mocking smile. 'In the old days,' the man said, 'they knew how to build for a proper draft. They didn't calculate it, they just knew. If you build the fire right, you don't so much as smell smoke in the room. When I was a kid we all slept here in the winter and stayed warm even on the coldest nights. Of course one of us always had to get up to stoke the fire.'

In saying this he was forecasting, before I could possibly suspect it, my fate for many winters to come.

The room was still larger than the kitchen and had longer hand-hewn ceiling beams. There was an imposing grandeur about it, but it also had a comfortable air of pleasant homeliness, all the more so since it received light through six windows. It was completely empty except for a fragile rocking chair and a small, rickety table. In one corner I saw a box spring mattress with a blanket and a thin pillow, without pillowcase. It occurred to me that this strange man probably spent occasional nights on this spartan bed. Several large old-fashioned beds in the adjoining room were unused.

A steep staircase led to the upper story, the center of which was dominated by the huge stone pillar of the chimney. There was a great deal of empty space up there, but only one room had been partitioned off. 'Would there be room for several more rooms up here?' I asked.

'Room enough,' the man said. 'We didn't need it.'

'It's a beautiful house,' I said.

'The most beautiful one I know,' he said.

We left the house through the attached shed, which was very spacious. It could be used as a garage and toolroom, I thought, and in addition would hold a vast store of firewood. Along the wall were leaning another scythe, a spade and a hoe, an ax and a hatchet, a saw and a trout-fishing rod. A grindstone, to be turned by a crank, stood in one corner. Under the high roof was a haymow. I saw a smaller room built against the outside wall of the shed. It was a privy, a two-seater of the kind you find in many old farmhouses. In some there is a third, smaller hole on the same bench for a child. A kerosene lamp was hanging in the privy; I had seen another in the kitchen, and a few wooden candle-holders. These seemed to be the sole source of light for the house.

We went out into the sunlight and sat down on the stone steps in front of the kitchen door. I was overcome by an inexplicable sense of well-being, almost of happiness, for which there was no other cause than the view of the landscape around the old house. Towards the east the woods climbed the hill; they were so thick they seemed never to have been cleared. I could make out maples, red oaks, ash and beech, white birch and yellow birch with glistening bronzed bark, and sprinkled among this hardwood small stands of dark-green pine and hemlock. In the other directions the woods also closed in to form a great frame around the house. There were fat old tree trunks and lively saplings. The gentle noon breeze swayed the treetops. Far off to the south I could see the blue peak of Mount Ascutney. I could hear the voices of a few birds, and the murmur of the brook that followed through a deep gorge, hemmed in by bushes, on the other side of the road.

The man took a small pack of cigars from his pocket. He offered me one. We smoked.

'How much land goes with the farm?' I asked.

With one finger he traced the line of the horizon.

'Everything you can see. A hundred and eighty acres. Back there is a piece of cleared land where we used to have fields and pastures, then more woods down to Gulf Road.'

That was the unpaved road from Woodstock to Barnard which ran through a 'gulf,' a deep forest gorge.

'I'd like to walk around the land some time,' I said.

He laughed.

'It would take you more than three hours,' he said. 'If you're good at walking through woods. There's lots of sedge and underbrush.'

'And all this belongs to you?'

'Yes,' he said, 'it's all mine. I have an older brother, but I bought him out. I wanted to keep the old place for myself.'

'And why aren't you running the farm any more?'

He muttered something under his breath, and his lips compressed.

'Business in Woodstock,' he said finally. 'Wife and family. I barely have time to come up here now and then, clear the grass from the door, and see that nothing is falling down.'

'What about that pond over there?' I asked. 'It's almost the size of a small lake. Is that part of the farm too?'

'We made that pond fifty years ago,' he said, his mood brightening. 'We built a stone dam across the brook. Looks just about the way it did then, except the banks have grown up some with willow.'

'It looks like a natural pond,' I said.

'Full of trout,' he said. 'But I don't use flies. I prefer grasshoppers. They kick on the water and the fish bite better.'

'Have you ever thought of renting this place?' I asked after a while.

He gave me a searching look, in which there was also a measure of astonishment. 'I haven't yet,' he said slowly. 'But I might consider it.'

We fell silent again. I began reflecting.

'I'm looking for a farm,' I said. 'But I don't think this one would do.'

'Why not?' he asked.

'Well—I'd need two or three rooms upstairs. And electric light. And a bathroom, plumbing in the house, a hot-water heater. I have a wife and two daughters who'll be spending their holidays here with us. I've been thinking of farming. The barn back there would have to be fixed up too. It would all cost a lot of money, and I don't have that much.'

He stared into space with a curiously dreamy look.

'Are you from Europe?' he asked.

'Yes, I was born in Germany and have been living in Austria.'

'Were you farming over there?'

'No. But I think I could learn.'

He chewed away at his cigar.

'I'd assume the costs of fixing the place up,' he said abruptly, 'if you want to sign a lease—let's say, for two years to begin with. I'd put in a couple of stoves, and repair the barn. We'd have to have a septic tank for the bathroom. When would you like to move in?' He had suddenly become extremely animated.

'Today if I could,' I said. 'How much rent would you ask?'

'Fifty dollars a month,' he said without reflection. 'For that you can have the house and the use of the land, and you can also cut firewood—there's plenty of it.'

For a moment he took my breath away. Fifty dollars a month for this house and these vast lands was almost a gift. And in addition the owner was going to pay for repairs and plumbing.

'It would be real nice to have the old place lived in and farmed

362

again,' he said hopefully. 'It never occurred to me. It would be nice. If you're serious.'

'Yes,' I said. 'I am serious. But you don't even know me. . . .'

'Sure I do,' he said. 'I've known you for ten minutes and you know me exactly as long. Agreed?'

He held out his hand; I took it, and with his left hand he struck both our hands.

'Agreed.'

'When do you want to draw up the contract?' I asked. 'Shall I look up a lawyer?'

'What for?' he said. 'You write me a letter—two years, fifty dollars a month. That'll take care of it. We can discuss all the rest about fixing the place. Drop by at the shop in Woodstock sometime in the next few days. I'm Joseph Ward, hardware and agricultural machinery—in the Maynes & Ward Building on Main Street. I'm always there from eight to twelve and two to six. You can come any time.'

'Fine, Mr. Ward,' I said, and gave him my name.

'Funny name,' he said good-naturedly.

'Should I write it down for you, and my address in Barnard?'

'No need. I'll learn it after a while. I'll see you in Woodstock then.'

We shook hands once more and I left.

Two days later I showed the farm to my wife. When we arrived, two deer were drinking from the pond. Shortly afterwards we sat in Mr Ward's hardware store, which was stuffed with all kinds of implements, tools, farm goods, and whatnot.

When we left, we were tenants of Backwoods Farm.

Backwoods Farm. It seems to me that I have spent half my life there. Many places had become deeply familiar to me; I had grown to love many: the old city of Mainz, the hills of Rhenish Hesse, Wiesmühl in Henndorf, the rustic hotel in Chardonne. This one had fallen into our laps like a gift—from Mr Ward, from Heaven, from all the good spirits of this earth. But we had to labor to make it our own as we did no other place before or after.

But Mr Ward came, and in this period of our lives he played th part of God, by helping as God does when He is so disposed—ł vanishing and becoming invisible like God when it seems well Him to leave His children to fend for themselves.

At first he came every day and created for us the home we had
dreamed of—not by magic or a miracle, but by performing an
almost inconceivable amount of work. But for him it was recreation,
part of his summer holiday. (It has been our experience that for
most Americans recreation does not consist in living contemplatively
lying in the sun, dreaming, walking aimlessly, as it does for us
Europeans, but in doing something, taking on some practical work
or craft, even if they have no need to do so. They like to relive the
hard work of their forefathers for a few weeks. It is a totally different
concept of a holiday from ours.)

Mr Ward had arranged to take off the entire month of August
and a week in September—he had a partner and an unmarried sister
who helped out in the store. And he spent this entire time, his only
time off for the year, making the farm habitable for us. We ourselves were still living in the small furnished cottage in Barnard
that Dorothy Thompson had earlier rented for us. Every day I
tramped the long distance to Backwoods Farm to lend a hand with
the work wherever I could. But no matter how early in the morning I arrived, Mr Ward was already there. He had a man with him
who drove an old, battered Ford and had a cleft palate; his muttering and babbling were barely intelligible, but he was a skilled
plumber and a schoolfriend or boyhood friend of Mr Ward, who was
always hiring such old acquaintances, even if they were drinkers.
He himself was a hundred per cent teetotaler. Naturally, such old
friends would work for half the wages of the standard craftsman.

In spite of all his generosity toward us, Mr Ward was anything
but a spendthrift. Rather, he was exceedingly thrifty about everything, including his personal habits. His lunch consisted of a peanut-
butter sandwich made of ordinary pre-sliced white bread. It would
have seemed to him too expensive a luxury to buy better bread
from one of the specialty bakeries in the vicinity, run by Italians,
Germans, and Russians. At most he might also have an apple in the
fall, and then a cheap cigar. For beverage he had his good spring
water, and only occasionally would he let my wife tempt him into
drinking a cup of coffee. Otherwise, he never wanted to share our
meals, even later when smells of chicken paprika and roast pork
(from our own pigs) began to waft from our kitchen. Yet he was by
no means a vegetarian; he simply loved being abstemious and
felt the better for it.

Even the low rent he had asked of us was so fixed that though

he made no money on it, he also lost none. In the two years for which I had agreed to lease the place—the two ultimately became six—the rent amounted to twelve hundred dollars, and given the price of materials in those days, he did not have to put much more into the place. But with regard to repairs he certainly did not skimp. The fact that people were once more living in his birthplace, people who thought it beautiful and loved it as he did, that animals were going to be in the barn again and the fields would be tilled and firewood cut—all that gave him a sense of profound satisfaction. Perhaps it was the greatest pleasure of his later years—all the more so since it gave him a good reason to busy himself around the old home place whenever he liked.

The pipes for the plumbing came from his own store. They were a quarter of an inch too narrow, and during the winter I had a good deal of trouble to keep them from freezing—especially in the northwest corner of the house. The two big iron stoves were also merchandise in which he dealt, as were the septic tank and the drainpipe. The latter was too wide; a shapeless, tarred colossus of a pipe which he ran from the top story down along the inside wall of the beautiful big living room, directly across from the old stone fireplace. We were horrified when we saw it, for it spoiled the room; but my wife promptly had the idea of camouflaging it by building shelves around it. We stained these dark and filled them with whatever books we owned or could lay hold of, and the appearance of the room was saved.

Apart from his friend with the cleft palate, we had no other help with all the work, including partitioning the upper floor, repairing the barn roof, and so on. We worked with picks, saws, hammers, and ax—and 'we' included me, although in the past I could not have hammered a nail in straight. Despite all the hard work, we had a lot of fun. In spite of his temperance and austerity, Mr Ward was far from a dull person. He had a sense of humor, and after work in the evenings when we sat on the doorstep he liked to tell amusing stories, and serious, even tragic ones as well—stories of the 'old days' and of present-day farm life. He knew every house and every family within a radius of fifty miles. He also knew the fates of those houses of which nothing now remained but cellar holes in the woods, overgrown with raspberry canes. He talked about families whose names could be found only on the plain gravestones of the small local cemeteries scattered about the countryside. The heavy physical work, in which he was untiring from morning to night, seemed to intensify his vitality, although he only became leaner and more gaunt in the course of it.

The stone pillar of the chimney, almost a hundred and sixty years old, was built so massively that on the upper floor we were able to hack away more than a yard of tough masonry without damaging the draft, in order to make a place for the big iron stove which would have to supply the bathroom and four small bedrooms with heat. It was beastly work up there, and I could not imagine that it would ever be finished. We nailed up new walls, created doorways, installed hinges, framed windows; and every day some other problem came to the fore which we had not considered. This 'do-it-yourself' business has become a kind of sport nowadays, and department stores furnish prefabricated materials for it. But for the backcountry farmer it was sheer necessity—and not only in the 'old days.' If you were to wait until a workman came up to repair a barn door ripped off by a storm, or a broken window, or a damaged stovepipe, or the plumbing, the animals in the barn and you yourself would have frozen to death in the meanwhile. My wife became a specialist in plumbing repairs, and even later on, especially during the early postwar years in Germany, she always carried a small box of tools in her baggage. She used them one Easter Sunday in Hamburg's best hotel, to the horror of the chambermaid. Standing on the toilet seat, she repaired the incessantly gurgling tank. Not just at the beginning but during all the years we spent on the farm, I always had cut fingers, aching muscles, one small injury or another, and every day I fell into bed dead-tired, only to get up again in the middle of the night in winter to add fuel to the stove—not so much to keep us warm as to protect the water pipes from freezing. Even so, in the autumn we had to wrap them in insulation and woolen strips so that they looked like the bandaged limbs of a wounded person.

Going to bed exhausted at night—back to work first thing in the morning. And you had to focus your full concentration on the work to master it, to get through, to survive. But it was the best thing I could possibly wish for during this period. For it was wartime, and I did not know how it would end. I knew nothing about my parents and friends back home. All we knew was that people were being killed daily, were being subjected to unspeakable horrors, and that the world was sinking deeper and deeper into a total eclipse. Although my back ached from chopping wood and my hands from milking, I was doing all this as a free man, for the sake of life—a life that accorded me an undreamed-of richness of experience and contemplation.

During the first week in September of the year 1941 we moved up to the farm. In New York we had bought a few magnificent pieces of old furniture from a German exile who had been able to emigrate in more lordly fashion than we ourselves—bought them cheaply, since he had no use for them. Among the pieces was the refectory table from an Alsatian monastery, which fitted perfectly into one of the lower rooms of the farmhouse. There was also a large, dark Renaissance cupboard which had room for all our household linens, and a Bavarian peasant table. With its long top, it made a marvelous desk and I could have worked wonderfully at it if I had ever got around to writing. Mr Ward, of Irish descent and superintendent of the Catholic parish in Woodstock, which was the central purchasing agency for all the surrounding small parishes, lent us the old wooden benches with hand-turned legs that had been removed from the parish church, St Mary of the Snows—they had been replaced by ugly factory-made equivalents. I slept on a narrow bedstead under so many woolen blankets that I could scarcely turn around, but I slept deeply and well, almost without dreaming. My wife slept in one of those enormous wooden beds in which earlier farmers' wives had slept, given birth, and died.

One September evening, after one of those crystal-clear, sparkling days with a hint of fall in the air, such as are common in Vermont, Mr Ward stood with me on the top of the hill alongside the house. As the darkness deepened, we watched a flickering greenish semi-circle in the sky give birth to a tremendous display of northern lights which are not uncommon in this region. At certain seasons they occur almost every evening. But this particular display, which was seen throughout the Northeast—my friend Schiebelhuth observed it at the same hour on Long Island—had something unusual and almost supernatural about it.

'I've never seen northern lights like that in my whole life,' Mr Ward said. And he, who was ordinarily averse to all superstitions, added thoughtfully: 'Maybe it means something. It could be an omen.'

I could not help thinking of the northern lights that had appeared

before the downfall of Austria in February 1938. What sort of end—
or what sort of new beginning—was impending now?

Early that summer, on June 22, Hitler's troops had invaded
Russia. Almost all of our acquaintances, Dorothy Thompson and
her circle, and my wife also, believed that this meant the beginning
of the end for Hitler, that he would meet destruction by penetrating
the expanses of Russia. I doubted that. I had all too strong faith in
the competence of the German General Staff. I simply could not
conceive that military minds of this caliber, so versed in strategy
and tactics, would let themselves in for a war on two fronts—not
after the experience of 1914–18—unless they were certain that
they could carry it to a victorious conclusion by a display of their
own superiority. I could not imagine that these men had become
slavishly obedient to a demented adventurer and his 'intuition.'
The fate of Napoleon, so it seemed to me, proved nothing about the
outcome of a modern military campaign. I saw the impotence of
England. It could not possibly think of reconquering the European
continent by itself and therefore would not be a serious danger in
Hitler's rear when he advanced against Moscow. We were all aware
of America's state of unpreparedness and her desire to keep out of
the war. To me it seemed likely that Russia would be finished off
as France had been; that no power would be left to put a stop to
Hitler's victories. I was wrong. But these thoughts, which I dared
scarcely express among my intimates, weighed heavily on me. And
the necessity of having to wish for the defeat of my own nation filled
me with despair. I wanted Hitler overthrown and his reign of terror
ended, but I did not want a ruined and subjugated Germany. Yet it
was becoming increasingly clear that the one was scarcely conceivable without the other. I felt caught in a conflict from which
there was no escape. And so far any chance to try to free myself
through creative work, by the catharsis of tragedy, had not appeared.
I had ceased to think about writing, and whenever my mind re-
verted to it, it was with repugnance. Therefore I plunged all the
more passionately into the multitude of tasks and adventures that
life at Backwoods Farm involved. Such work did not make me
forget, but the active life, vital contact with nature, could temporarily disperse the clouds of despair. That had been impossible in
the city. Throughout those years two sayings, one harsh, one heartening, were constantly in my mind—the words of Ecclesiastes: 'All is

vanity and a striving after wind,' and 'Where there is life, there is hope.'

During the first two years after we moved there I did not leave the farm for a single day—at most for a few hours to shop in one of the nearby towns. During these years I learned every imaginable farm, woods, and household task. My only help was a fourteen-year-old boy who came over on foot through the woods in the mornings, then had to leave to attend school, and did not come back until mid-afternoon. My wife took care of the house and kitchen, and later of the poultry. In the spring, with the help of a neighbor, we built a second barn equipped to hold a sizable flock of chickens, ducks, and geese. We bought sex-determined chicks and raised some of them for laying, some as broilers. The ducks, geese, and some of the chickens increased by brooding their own eggs.

By chance I had met a doctor who ran a small hospital about an hour's drive from the farm. He lamented that there was no goat farm in the vicinity, for he was convinced that goat milk was the best as well as the most nourishing diet for people suffering from gastric disorders. For goat milk he promised me five times the price per quart currently paid for cow miilk, and said he had private patients who would pay even more. I considered his proposal; it seemed promising to me. Cows are vastly more expensive to buy and keep than goats; a single cow provides too much milk for a single household and too little for selling. For a dairy farm to pay off at that time you had to start with a herd of at least twelve head (it is far more today). In addition, milking machines are needed, a cement-floored barn, individual drinking places for winter, and hired men—all of which were beyond my means. But goats can be kept on an old plank floor strewn with litter, watered from a bucket or a pail, and need only a fifth of the feed required by a cow, especially in summer when there was so much open pasture that I often said to the goats: 'You have all America at your disposal; kindly keep out of my vegetable garden.'

And so I decided to have a goat farm. We bought the animals from a breeder who lived several hours' drive away, and had to transport our does back there in our ancient Oldsmobile when we wanted to breed them—we would empty out the car completely and spread newspaper over everything. We had decided against keeping a buck because his smell would spoil the clean taste of the milk. My goat milk was as pure as Mr Ward's spring water. But that required an enormous amount of work in addition to the morning and evening milkings, for all implements had to be kept completely clean and free of smell. I had never milked but learned the technique in a single day, curiously enough. After two or three vain attempts I suddenly acquired the feeling in my fingers of how to make the heavy udders flow. Thereafter I only had to touch them and the milk shot out of the teats. Soon I was so familiar with the goats that they jumped onto the milking stand of their own accord as soon as I called their names. For our visitors during the summer holidays it was a special delight to go to the barn with me for the evening's milking and attend my goat circus, admission free.

I learned how to treat the goats when they came down with bloat from eating too much wet grass, for the nearest veterinarian was hard to reach and overworked. Once, in the depths of winter, I had to clean out a goat that was carrying two dead kids and was on the point of dying. She survived. When the veterinarian came two days later, he could hardly believe I had done it myself and had not been assisted by another vet. I began to realize that my childhood dream of being the director of a zoo had not been so utterly unreasonable. From the first day I began farming I knew how to handle animals as if I had done nothing else all my life.

What I did not like was slaughtering the poultry, but that was one of my inescapable duties—sometimes I even had to butcher in large numbers, for sale. I gave our broilers ugly names to make the matter psychologically easier; we thus had Ribbentrops, several Himmlers, even two Goebbels brothers (Paul and Joseph); but slaughtering even these came hard. When our pigs were taken away by a professional butcher—one job at least that I was spared—I was close to tears every time, although I had often cursed the beasts when they lunged between my legs while I was cleaning their pen.

During our first year a lady in Woodstock gave me two German shepherd pups. They grew very large and really looked like wild grayish wolves—for me the friendliest and most loyal companions, for unbidden callers a powerful deterrent, for my wife and daughter sure protection.

On the edge of the woods I found a full-grown doe who had been caught in the overgrown cattle fence and had broken her left hind leg below the knee. I carried her home on my back and managed to amputate the already gangrenous portions of leg and tend the wound until it healed. For years she lived on the farm with three and a half legs, completely tame. The dogs played with her.

I held newly hatched yellow ducklings in my hand like beating hearts. I learned to identify animal tracks—the ghostly, fingerlike pawprints of the raccoons that caught bullfrogs by the pond at night, the big, clawed track of wildcats, the larger track of the Canadian lynx, which could be recognized by the marks of clumps of hair between the claws. Once a lynx howled and hissed frighteningly at me from a granite cliff as tall as a house by the side of the forest road as I was tramping up it in the dusk of an early-winter evening, laden with mail and packages. When I turned my flashlight on the cliff, I saw two glowing eyes. Then a shadow scurried away. Next day, with a neighbor who was a dealer in timber, woodchopper, and trapper on the side, I followed the tracks in the light new snow until they were lost in the woods.

We experienced our first autumn in Vermont. It turned the Green Mountains into a sea of flame. In none of the deciduous forests of Europe had I ever seen such autumnal colors. The climax came in the first week of October, when there were already frosts at night and the sun broke through the morning mists. Then sugar maple and red oak put on mad, ecstatically loud colors. Indian summer followed; in mild, springlike weather the leaves kept falling and the woods revealed a new aspect. One morning, stepping out of the door, I saw a man standing by the brook on the steep hillside of second-growth wood. He stood absolutely motionless, staring down at the farm. It was a long time before I realized that it was a tree, a lean young pine that had hitherto been hidden by the leafage of the maples. Now a tremendous stillness and solitude spread around our house. The woods were beginning to die. We tramped often through knee-high layers of fallen leaves, the top layers covered with hoarfrost in the mornings while the lower layers were already beginning to rot. When you thrust your hand in, you felt the warmth of the ground like the heat of fading embers.

'The slow smokeless burning of decay,' Robert Frost has written in a poem about autumn.

The nights turned cold. I had to keep the stoves going briskly, and I became absurdly fond of this job. I loved the feeling of the heavy, thick bark chunks in my hand before I thrust them into the stove and helped them into the right position with the poker. I loved the motion of the fire flaring up under the sudden influx of air, before I closed the drafts to keep it down. I loved the crackling of the coal in the stove when I had cleaned out the ashes and poured in fresh coal until the small blue flames darted out of the glistening black and slowly brought the anthracite to red heat. Most of all, I loved building fires in the fireplace. There was a certain architectural pleasure in piling the three-foot split birch logs, whose bark flared brightly before the flames from the kindling beneath gradually ate into the heaped-up wood. It became my ambition not only to keep the house warm, but to be a heating artist and pile the kindling and logs in the fireplace so skillfully that a single match would suffice to light a fire that would last for hours. My wife invented a word to describe me: 'Pyromantic.'

The steep, narrow road through the woods from the highway up to the farm was passable by car only in summer, and then it required a speedy takeoff and much precision, for it had deep, wet ruts and even deeper ditches on the sides. Now it began to ice over. We had to park the car in Barnard, three miles away, and tramp down there for it if we wanted to go anywhere. I brought up food and other supplies on foot, later on skis or snowshoes, using a basket that often held forty or fifty pounds.

In November the man from the electric company, who came every month to read the meter, turned up pale and trembling. He too had now to walk up and had met a bear that growled at him. From now on, he said, would we kindly read the meter ourselves and report our consumption of electricity on a postcard. It was too wild for him up here. The bear subsequently dug himself a den for hibernating under a ruined shed by the road and did not bother us, nor we him. We never caught sight of him, but in the early spring we smelled him when the wind blew from the southwest, and then one of us would say: It's going to rain. Our bear stinks.

On the night of December 6, 1941, the big snow came.

It had begun snowing in the afternoon. All night long we heard the low moan of the storm. Yet the woods, when we listened at the door, seemed filled with a profound silence. The soft snow rose higher and higher around the house. Already it had reached to our window sill. It was as though we were going to be buried like the tree stumps and the rocks in the woods. Now and then strange sounds awakened us from sleep. The beams seemed to be groaning, and from time to time there was a loud report, like a pistol shot, from the small space under the ridge of the roof. I clambered up to investigate, but could find no cause. My wife said: 'The only rational explanation is poltergeists.'

But Mr Ward later told us it was the long wooden pegs that held the rafters. At the beginning of winter, when the heat rises from the inside and the cold snow penetrates the rafters from outside, the pegs always move a little. They could go on creaking that way for another century, he said, without affecting the soundness of the structure.

Next morning the electricity and telephone were out of action; the wires must have fallen under the weight of the snow. It was still snowing. I had to climb out through a window to shovel the door clear before I could open it. I could reach the shed, where the fire-wood was piled to the roof (we used fifteen to twenty cords in a winter), directly through the kitchen. I stoked the stoves; we had provisions in the house, and we accepted being cut off from the world until the town snowplow could break through and clear our road. We still did not know that this would always take two days, for there was only one old-fashioned plow to be used by the whole town. We also did not know that it would invariably appear in the middle of the night, making an infernal rattle and hissing. The storm passed, the pegs stopped their noise, the fires crackled in stoves and fireplaces. Otherwise everything was still as death. It was Sunday, December 7th.

Towards evening the telephone suddenly began working again. We heard our ring on the party line. Our friend Gottfried Bermann Fischer, my former and present German publisher, was calling from New York.

'Well, what do you say about it?'

'About what?'

'Pearl Harbor ... !'

That Sunday morning, when we were concerned with nothing but the snow, had brought destruction to the American fleet in Hawaii. Next day we heard the broadcast of President Roosevelt's declaration of war on Japan. There was no doubt that America would soon be participating in the war against Germany. Mournful days followed. We were alone; apart from Mr Ward and a few neighboring farmers whom at this time we barely knew, we had no acquaintances for miles around us. Our own fate was uncertain. We were the only Germans in this vicinity and in spite of having been expatriated, with the new turn of events we were legally 'enemy aliens.' We had no idea how we would be treated. The British had taken all Germans, including refugees, into custody, and had moved the majority of them into camps in Canada where they were locked up together with fanatical Nazis who abused them and made life miserable for them. What would America do? Would we be allowed to stay on the farm where we had just begun to feel at home? Would we be allowed to live as free people in this country? And how would we be regarded by the inhabitants whose sons would be going off to war against the country of our birth?

I struggled through to Barnard on snowshoes to do some shopping at the general store. I was known there. I discerned no change in the attitude of the people. They looked at me as they always had, talked about the weather, the snow, the cold—not a word about the war. Everyone was calm and friendly. Nevertheless it all seemed eerie. Could it be that they did not want to talk about the events before me, already regarded me secretly as an enemy? But we soon found out that it was good manners in Vermont not to talk about the war. It was on now, it had to be endured; people had to do their duty and made less fuss about it than if there had been a fire on a neighboring farm. There was little ardor for this war and little hate— or at most against the Japanese for their act of aggression. But there was no talk about that either.

It had been announced on the radio and in the newspapers that enemy aliens must report in writing to the nearest police station. We did so, to the station in Woodstock.

A few days later the Woodstock sheriff and a policeman came tramping up through the snow to our farm. His name was Mr Shonfield, and, unlike Mr Ward and other natives of his stripe, he looked exactly like the sheriff in a Western: a big strong man with a revolver in his belt and the familiar star on the lapel of his coat. He was reputed to be the terror of lawbreakers. When there were brawls or shooting frays among drunken woodchoppers he would simply walk right between them, so it was said, knock the weapons out of their hands, grip them by the scruff of their necks, and knock their heads together, then calmly take them off to jail. When you saw his massive arms and bull neck, you could not doubt these stories.

The two men extended their legs in their high boots towards my fire and were not the least bit coy when I offered them a drink. I showed the sheriff our immigration papers and explained that I had been expatriated from Hitler's Germany. He listened in silence, nodding from time to time. Then he looked around at our arrangements with interest, and asked in detail about our plans for the farm. Nothing more. He laughed when I told him I wanted to raise goats. 'Not a bad idea,' he said. 'But you have plenty of work cut out for you on this old place. Think you can manage it?'

I told him I was determined to—if I were allowed to stay here in spite of being an enemy alien. 'Why not?' he said. 'If you obey the law of the land, you're in as good standing as the next man.' He slapped me on the back. 'My grandparents came from Germany too, and so far as I know they never bit anybody. Oh sure, there are lots of warnings about spies posing as refugees. But what the devil could you spy on around here? How low the mercury drops and how many skunks are creeping around—I reckon such stuff wouldn't interest that skunk.' He meant Hitler.

We'd have to take our radio set to Woodstock, he said, so that the short-wave receiver could be removed; then we could have it again. Enemy aliens weren't supposed to keep short-wave receivers, cameras, and firearms. We'd also have to ask special permission for any trip of more than twenty miles from our home. (There was never any difficulty about obtaining that permission.) I didn't have a camera anyhow, and Mr Ward's double-barreled shotgun and some ammunition remained in a corner of the kitchen throughout the whole war.

'Lots of luck with the farming,' the sheriff said as he put on his fur jacket. 'And if you freeze or starve to death up here, or are murdered by a tramp, give me a ring so I can come and identify the corpse.'

That was his kind of humor.

The years rolled by.

After the snow melted that first spring, I began planting the fields: corn, potatoes, and soya beans for supplementary feed, many vegetables and herbs for our household use. But how could I have plowed those fields without my neighbor Williamson, who brought his horses and equipment over for very little money! And when I was about to begin sowing at four o'clock next morning, he came trotting through the woods on one of his big farmhorses—although he had his own sowing to begin—to tell me something he had

375

forgotten the day before: that I must treat the seed corn with a tar solution which would not interfere with its growth but would make it sticky, for otherwise all the birds in the woods would pick it out of the ground. He'd brought a pail of the stuff with him while he was about it. And he also mentioned that the seed potatoes should be treated to protect them from rust and blight. Then he trotted off without even staying for a cup of coffee. I wonder whether a European farmer would have done that—solely to be helpful to an unknown newcomer? More likely he would have stood rubbing his hands and grinned while the innocent novice looked aghast at his barren fields.

Old Mr Morgan, another neighbor, rode over on his hay wagon, which was drawn by two gigantic oxen. They looked like primeval creatures and could be guided in the ancient 'ox language' of the backwoods farmer, *Hoooo* and *Cheee* for right and left, almost without the use of rope and reins. He helped me with the building of the barn, with transporting materials, with drawing wood, and in March and April he taught me the art of sugaring. I loved going into the snowy woods to tap the maple trees and hang the big buckets on the spout. When the noon sun made the sap rise, it would drip into the buckets until evening, sounding like tiny, brittle bells. It seemed to ring far and wide over the whole forest.

The farm was now in running order. We sold goat milk, several dozen eggs a week, from time to time a sizable number of broilers. Our geese went chiefly to the more prosperous exiles in New York, who around Christmas preferred them to the customary American turkey. Ours was not an 'efficiency' farm; it was no egg factory with hens shut into mass prisons. That would not have been our style. It was, rather, an old-fashioned farm in the style of the early settlers. Our animals had the free run of natural pasture, which we improved by sowing alfalfa and ladino clover. Thanks to the dogs, our birds were not molested by foxes or other predators. The work was hard, the yield small, but we could live and survive the winter months. If my wife and daughters could have dressed in chicken feathers and goatskins, we would have been autarchic, virtually independent of civilization. But we could not quite manage to supply all our needs, and certain bills became thorny problems. It is still a mystery to me how we solved them. Sometimes we had a sudden descent of guests, especially in summer when eminent visitors turned up at Dorothy Thompson's—her country house was a few miles away, on the other side of the mountain. For these visitors an outing to Backwoods Farm was a kind of 'back-to-nature' experience. I would then fish trout out of the pond, or if we happened to have a bottle of white wine we would make Swiss fondue out of Vermont cheese. If we had recently slaughtered a pig, there would be sausage patties. We had also rented a deep-freeze locker at the freezer plant in Woodstock. Here we always had a small supply of meat, including venison and pheasants that we shot in August. We served whatever the farm produced, and the guests brought their own liquor, usually more than was drunk, which meant a few more jolly evenings for us afterwards. Then, as the summer ended, our place became quiet and lonely again—for weeks and months at a time we scarcely saw a soul.

The years rolled on, the succession of the seasons. Those who may live in the country but not on the country do not know the full meaning of these natural cycles. Woodcutting in spring, so that the wood might cure over the summer. Sowing time, haying time. Mr Ward taught me how to wield the scythe so that it cuts the grass close to the ground without the point digging into the soil. Uphill and downhill with the scythe on hot days, when flies and gnats buzz around. The scythe hisses through the grass, swing after swing; the grass falls with a faint sigh to the ground. Autumn work, corn harvest and potato digging. The big pumpkins are boiled up for pig feed, the better ones are saved for the table. Apples are gathered, and in a neighbor's press the brown, tartly fragrant cider is extracted. Mr Ward had showed me how to graft the twigs of superior varieties on wild-apple trees. We let the cider ferment and turn 'hard' in small wooden barrels. Some Vermont farmers distill the hard cider into the raw liquor called applejack which will eventually turn into a kind of calvados if it is allowed to mature in oak barrels. But most people drink it new and raw the first winter, as a medicine against the intense cold. It bites in the throat as the cold does in the face, but it warms the bones.

Winter preparations, splitting wood, sawing and piling it, banking the house with pine branches and dry leaves after protecting the lower clapboards up to the window frames with building paper. I acquired muscles like a boxer; my hands were permanently callused. I could carry bags of cement on my·shoulder up the ladder to the attic. And during all this time, except for a rib I broke at work and a bout of pneumonia from a visit to the city I was never sick. In the summer before milking, I would go through the dewy grass to the pond for a swim in the cold water, in which I could see the speckled trout swimming. On winter mornings I jumped naked into the deep snow, rolled in it, then dried myself in front of the glowing coal stove—a kind of simplified sauna. Then the first rays of the sun rose above the margin of the woods, the trees cast pink and delicately blue shadows on the snow. If I had a free hour around noon, I skied over the hills. There would be nothing but my own track in the snow, at most the pawprints of an animal.

Except for a very few friends, I had little contact with other political and literary refugees. Many of them looked askance at me because of my obstinate faith in a different Germany, in a true German spirit which, I insisted, must not be equated with the Nazi filth. Americans had an understanding and respect for an exile who nevertheless believed in the forces for good in his own nation. But as is almost inevitable in the course of a long war, a prejudice against Germans in general gradually developed; it is an old prejudice which to some extent still exists and in certain aspects resembles anti-Semitism. Many people now felt that way, but they did not make me aware of it. Aside from farmers, woodcutters, and workmen we had contact with a few persons of culture and education and some of these acquaintances ripened into lasting friendships. There were Sven and Harriet Gundersen. He was of Norwegian descent, chief resident in internal medicine at the hospital in Hanover; she was a woman of great charm and intelligence. In her house and in her company we felt almost as if we were in Europe. There was Bill Storey, who looked like Paul Bunyan; he was a scion of Boston society and had studied law. But now, during the war, he was running a herb farm near us, and when we called on him for the first time to buy seeds of certain herbs, expecting to meet an ordinary farmer, we found a man with a library encompassing the whole of what was then modern literature, including virtually all of German writing that had been translated and published in America. We went on skiing tours together over trackless mountain ridges where a man alone could very easily be lost or in case of a minor accident lie helpless and freeze to death. On such adventures, when one man must rely on the other, intimacy grows without many words. Later I was godfather to his first son, Charley.

Julia and John McDill were a kind of Vermont aristocracy. With her tall slenderness she looked like an English duchess, and at first glance she seemed to have a noble calm and reserve. After one knew her better she radiated the kind of warmth and cordiality found only in a few unusually vital, spirited, and intelligent persons. John, forever diverted from his proper literary work by the responsibility for his family and a large going farm, met us, the foreigners, with a spontaneous friendliness and understanding that broke through all conventions. Now and then the McDills invited us to their Thanksgiving dinner, and we admired the simplicity and generosity of their traditional way of life.

The neighbors came to regard us more and more as one of them. We became members of the Grange, attended its meetings and familiarized ourselves with the simple, cheerful, rather childlike social life—including the custom of the men's sneaking out to their parked cars (since the old rule was that nothing alcoholic might be drunk at such meetings) to empty a bottle of whisky or applejack and hastily tell a few dirty jokes. The majority were friendly, naïve people of great integrity. We attended their barn dances, learned the many steps and turns of square dancing.

One gay festival during these dismal times was Dorothy Thompson's marriage to Maxim Kopf, the Prague painter whom we had already met when he was staying with Dorothy as a summer guest. Of all the visitors to the farm, he was one of our favorites, a person of strong, manly nature and original sense of humor. I shall never forget how Dorothy, already a mature woman at that time, stood in the plain church of Barnard and in a clear, girlish voice spoke the words: 'Till death do us part.' They remained together until death parted them after happy years, and she soon followed him.

My wife regularly visited the Dartmouth College library in Hanover, New Hampshire, and there I made a new friend whose personality, knowledge, and wisdom meant a great deal to me: Professor Eugen Rosenstock-Huessy. With the coming of Hitler he had emigrated from Germany, where, before the end of the Weimar Republic, he had been among those searching for new forms of community life, for an organic union of the creative intelligentsia and the working people. Every encounter with this courageous, bold, independent thinker—it would take a separate book to write about his lifework—gave me more in the way of intellectual intensity than the reading of many books would have done. In any case I had little time for reading, almost none for writing.

At the beginning of September 1943 I left the farm to go to New

379

York, in order to celebrate Max Reinhardt's seventieth birthday among a group of his closest friends. It was my first trip to the city in two years, and I had to go without my wife—we were never able to leave the farm both at the same time. That evening Reinhardt seemed healthy and vital; he was just back from a seaside vacation and his face was taut and bronzed, his hair like a cap of silver. A few weeks later I had to go to New York again for his funeral. Death had struck suddenly, wholly unexpectedly, after two strokes and a brief period of cruel suffering.

Whenever I went to New York for a few days then and during the later years of the war, my visits were made brighter by my friend Gert von Gontard, who has since won high regard in both nations by organizing guest performances of German theater troupes in America. Knowing how starved I was for any social life, he arranged small parties for me during these visits, and invited old friends from Berlin: Karl Vollmöller, who after being mistakenly taken for a Nazi and being clapped under dreadful conditions into Californian prisons, was leading a retired life in New York, broken in health and spirit; Remarque; and above all George Grosz, who had adopted the pose of talking and acting like a thoroughgoing American, though he suffered more than most others from his alienation from Germany. Out of repressed homesickness as well as an apocalyptic horror at the way things were going in the world, he was becoming more and more of an alcoholic, the kind that drinks not for pleasure but out of inner turmoil and desperation. His health could no longer stand it; sometimes after a 'sazerac,' a mixture of absinthe and bourbon, he almost lost consciousness. When once more back in Germany, he died a few days later, tragically, in Berlin.

The years rolled by, for us resembling the waves of Vermont's Green Mountains in their evenness, their endlessness. We did not think about returning. One night the news came over the radio that the city of Mainz had been bombed. The report was brief, laconic, like the accounts of the bombings of so many other cities. But our hearts felt briefly numbed. Then there was an aerial photograph in the *New York Times* showing the bombed city. The area around the railroad station looked erased. There, five minutes' walk from the station, stood my parents' house. That was the first bombing of Mainz, and it had been directed chiefly against the station and the bridges. The second, in 1945, almost completely destroyed the city. Many months passed before we learned through the Red Cross that my parents had survived the bombing and burning of their house and had been taken by friends to Oberstdorf in the Allgäu. My father was at that time almost eighty, my mother five years younger. Such messages delivered through the Red Cross, comprising only a few words, took six months before reaching us; the answers took even longer. We hoped we might see my parents again, though I no longer dared to believe in a reunion. We tried to imagine life in that distant, vanished realm of our native land, the life of relatives, friends, resistance fighters, soldiers in the army; but we had not the slightest thing to go by.

During this period, the more the harsh realities of our own existence involved me in a multitude of problems, the more the life itself seemed unreal, strange, spellbound. I did not know what had died within me, what was asleep, what was still awake. I saw omens in the snow, in the clouds, in the night sky. Sometimes, before daybreak, my eyes still heavy with sleep, I saw a star I thought I had never seen before: big as a fist, it sparkled threateningly or promisingly in the sky. Once, alone in a solitary patch of woods where I was marking trees for cutting, I experienced a miracle. I had kicked aside a loose stone, and from under the stone, with a gurgling sound that resembled a cry, a summons, a spring bubbled up. It was clear and pure; I dipped my hands into it and cooled my face. At that moment I knew that some tight knot within me had been released. Soon afterwards I began writing again.

In December 1941, shortly after the United States entered the war, the American newspapers had carried a brief item: Ernst Udet, Chief of the Air Force Supply Service of the German Army, had suffered a fatal accident in trying out a new weapon and had been honored with a state funeral. That was all. There were no commentaries, no surmises about his death. Fatal accident; state funeral.

I kept thinking about it all the time. Again and again I saw him as I had seen him in 1936, during my last reckless visit to Berlin. We had met to dine in a small, not particularly popular restaurant. 'Not at Horcher's,' he had said—that had formerly been our regular meeting place. 'It's full of the top brass now.'

He was in civilian dress, but he was already a high-ranking officer in the Luftwaffe. 'Shake the dust of this country from your shoes,' he said to me. 'Clear out of here and don't come back. There is no more decency here.'

'And what about you?' I asked.

'I'm completely sold on flying,' he said lightly, almost casually.
'I can't disentangle any more. But one of these days the devil will
fetch us all.'

We talked no more about the matter. We drank, and when we
bade each other goodbye we embraced.

Now, on that late fall evening in 1942, a year after Udet's death,
I was trudging back to the farm with my carrying basket. The two
dogs sometimes leaped up at the basket, which contained several
pounds of meat.

Suddenly I paused. 'State funeral,' I said aloud.

The last word of the tragedy.

I did not know what had happened in reality, and did not care.

The whole story was there in my mind—without a gap.

If my daughter Winnetou had not come home for the Christmas
holidays in 1942 and brought a school friend with her, if these two
young people had not taken over my work in the barns, and had not
carried the wood and fed the stoves for three weeks, until the middle
of January 1943, my play *The Devil's General* would never have
been started.

As it was, during the hours between six and nine in the evening
I wrote the first act in a kind of trance (I never changed a word
afterwards) and the outline of the last act.

My wife did not know what was occupying me, like one possessed
up there in my small bedroom. In the mornings, when I milked the
goats, I myself did not know what would be set down that evening.
I had to write. That was like a grace restored to me. One freezing
night at the end of January 1943 I read my wife the first act and the
outline of the entire play. She sat wrapped up to her nose in blankets, for the northwest wind was howling. We drank all the beer
and what whisky remained in the house. 'This is the first play I
have written for the bureau drawer,' I said. 'It will never be performed, but I had to do it.'

The Stalingrad disaster was then building to a climax, but this
was not known as yet; the great counteroffensive came at the beginning of February. It seemed unlikely that such a play could ever
have an audience in Germany. And as far as other countries were
concerned, it was peopled by too many likable Germans, especially
army officers. It was a task without prospects, but it filled us both
with a kind of ecstatic enthusiasm.

'Yes,' my wife said, 'that is what it's like. It must be like that.'

That night I fell into bed half dead, delirious, happy, despairing, and I forgot—the only time in all those winters—to refill the stoves.

Next day the water line was frozen. I worked for thirty-six hours, along with the farm chores, to start it running again. My wife, who had come down with a severe bout of sciatica from the cold in the house, was ensconced in a chair wrapped in blankets, as close as possible to the fireplace, where she sat as if on a throne, flanked by two days' worth of unwashed dishes and a cauldron of snow that we melted for water.

The first act and the outline of the last were done in barely three weeks. It took more than two years for me to complete the whole play. For weeks the daily chores kept me from writing. But I was living with the play, was living with Germany. And when the war was over, the play was completed. A year after the end of the war, when the manuscript of the play was already circulating in Europe, one of the first letters about it to come in was from Alexander Lernet-Holenia. He wrote: 'You have never been away.'

The darkest year was 1944. Towards the end of January my friend Schiebelhuth died in East Hampton. Two days later I received the news that Carlo Mierendorff had been killed by a bomb in Leipzig. Stefan Zweig had taken his life in Brazil in 1942. Max Reinhardt was dead. A year later Franz Werfel and Bruno Frank died in Hollywood. And the war was taking untold lives; it was a time, it seemed, for universal dying.

On March 10th I spoke at a memorial service for Carlo Mierendorff in New York. Among other things, I said:

> When a Carlo Mierendorff has lived in Germany, has worked all his life for the German people and remained faithful to it in time of crisis and suffering—then that people is not lost, then it deserves to live and will live. And as I write and say this word—*live*—the full force of the fact strikes me: that Carlo is really dead, that along with him a part of our life is gone, that in our hearts we have participated in his senseless death. . . .
>
> Germany, Carlo's fatherland and ours, has passed through a tragedy that in fearfulness equals death. Germany's fate reminds us of that mysterious saying of Christ's: that offense must come into the world—but woe to him from whom it cometh. Germany is

guilty before all the world. But in this universal trial, we who could not avert her guilt do not belong among her judges, nor will we be accepted as her advocates. Therefore our place is on the witness bench, where we sit side by side with our dead. And although we can never be reconciled to her torturers and hangmen, we will always raise our voices for the German people.

On July 20, 1944, the radio announced the desperate, death-defying, hopeless uprising of the German army officers and resistance. Thereafter began the merciless slaughter which carried off so many of my friends, among them Haubach, Leuschner, and Count Moltke. We learned of this only after the war. But even at the time we were aware of the terrible implications and lived in fear and sorrow.

There were brighter hours. One summer afternoon my daughter Winnetou came back from the barn where she had been tending a pair of cows we had temporarily taken over, and reported: 'There's an odd-looking man hanging around the house. A seedy fellow, maybe one of the Canadian woodcutters.'

I went out and saw a man with a leather cap, ill-shaven, wearing a loose-fitting leather jacket. It was Brecht.

At the time we had found a summer place in the vicinity of Woodstock for Elisabeth Bergner and her husband, Paul Czinner. She had invited Brecht up to work with her on the adaptation of an Elizabethan play, John Webster's *The Duchess of Malfi*, which was to be put on in New York. He had found his way from there to our farm.

'Bert!' I shouted. We looked at each other, and burst into helpless laughter. We were still laughing when we went inside and sat down.

'You're someone I can laugh with when there's nothing to laugh about,' Brecht said.

Then we sat together for a few hours and talked gaily and seriously as if it were only yesterday that we had been walking along the banks of the Isar in Munich. He looked carefully at all our domestic arrangements.

'It has the note of home,' he said several times. 'Yes, it has the note of home.'

The spring of 1945 came, a harsh spring with late snowstorms. Morning and night we sat anxiously at the radio. The communiqués were a welter of contradictions. Some announced the imminent capitulation of Germany, others that Hitler would be withdrawing with part of his forces that were still intact to the alpine redoubt in southern Bavaria and western Austria, where the last decisive battle would be fought. We had only the faintest notion of the destruction and misery inside Germany. But my parents were in Oberstdorf; we had had no word of them for months and did not know whether they were still alive. And the thought that death and destruction would come to that vicinity, that our beloved Salzburg countryside would at the very end be a theater of war, was like a nightmare.

Early in May we learned of the suicide of Adolf Hitler. On May 5, 1945, the radio reported the capitulation of Germany. The war in Europe was over.

All that we had lived through crashed down on us once more. Now it seemed more than we could bear.

On May 6th I received a cable from my friend Henry Goverts, who had managed to escape to Switzerland at the last moment, just as he was about to be arrested by the Gestapo. It read: 'Parents living.'

Now the hour of return was approaching, but it came falteringly, after a long waiting period. And now, in fear and hope, nostalgia revived. During the early postwar years it was almost impossible to enter Germany unless one was with the troops of the Occupation Powers or was admitted by them on some special assignment. Germany and Austria were cut off from the world by our Occupation Statutes. Only in the rarest cases could someone from outside travel to these countries. At first there was still no normal civilian travel from America to Europe. Letters and packages to Germany were banned. It was some time before such helpful organizations as CARE were set up; through them it at least became possible to send a minimum of essential provisions to one's family. But at first the only way to do it was to evade the official restrictions by sending letters and packages to personal acquaintances in the Army of Occupation, with the request that they be transmitted to the German addresses. Many things were lost in this process because between the time of sending and the time of arrival the station and address of the go-between had changed. For us the problem was further complicated by lack of money. During the first postwar year, until

the late summer of 1946, I had no choice but to continue running
the farm, which barely yielded the minimum for our own livelihood.
During this period I gave up smoking and drinking. With great
labor I wrote short stories and essays in English, and sometimes
placed them in magazines, earmarking the small proceeds for food
packages to my parents. My wife put the packages together with
loving solicitude, and it was a matter for despair when they did not
arrive.

In the summer of 1946 we learned that my father, then eighty-
two, was dangerously ill. We knew an American officer stationed
near Oberstdorf and sent him some penicillin, which was simply
not available in Germany yet—or could be had only for American
military personnel. The shipment saved my father's life, but the
helpful officer and my parents barely escaped arrest by the American military police. There had been a postal check, and they were
charged with 'smuggling medicines.'

As long as the war had lasted there was nothing to do but accept
the inevitable, and we had tried to keep our composure even in the
face of the most terrible events. But now we were consumed by
impatience, and by the fear that my parents might die of hunger and
inadequate care before we could be with them and take responsibility for them. My brother, too, who was then still in Turkey, had
no way of traveling to Germany—the less so since he was still a
German citizen. My wife and I had by this time acquired American
citizenship—not for practical reasons, but because we felt gratitude
towards the country which had sheltered us for so long and had become our second homeland. Now I applied for a civilian post with
the American government, hoping that I could be sent to Germany
on some cultural mission, for there lay my only hope of returning
to the country of my birth within the foreseeable future. For those
American citizens who had been born in Germany were subject to
a particularly strict ban on private travel; this ban was relaxed only
gradually in the course of the years of Occupation. And I also
thought that through such a mission I might help to bring about
a reconciliation of the two nations to which I felt I belonged.

My application led at first to a protracted and wearing struggle
with red tape. I think that in six months I filled out more questionnaires than any Hitler Youth leader during the first four years of
the Occupation. In the end it was Pare Lorentz who smoothed the
way for me. Before he entered the army he had distinguished him-

self by producing documentary films of unusual artistry. Now, after an equally remarkable career as a pilot and wing commander in the Far East, he had become chief of a foreign Section in the War Department. I was entrusted with the Section for Germany.

I had come to know Pare Lorentz through his wife Elizabeth, whom I had met in London long before her marriage. She subsequently visited us in our Henndorf home; we became friends and remained close in America. She also introduced us to her parents: Eugene and Agnes Meyer, people of an altogether extraordinary character and conduct, such as is rarely found in Europe. Eugene Meyer, scholar, writer, and diplomat, as well as owner and editor of the *Washington Post*—which under his guidance became one of the principal liberal newspapers in the country—held the post of President of the World Bank for a time after the war. Agnes Meyer, a woman of singular vitality and intellectual alertness, befriended Thomas Mann during his by no means easy or comfortable years in exile. German by descent, she was familiar with the German language and literature from childhood, and in the broadest sense with European cultural life. The French poet Paul Claudel was also one of her closest friends. We admired and revered both Eugene and Agnes. The two had a deep social and philanthropic bent. Without ever falling into the pose of humanitarian 'charity,' they were forever concerned for the welfare of their fellow men and their nation.

Had it not been for the help and intercession of these friends, I would scarcely have obtained such a post, which was generally reserved for people from the military.

At the beginning of July 1945 I started work in a skyscraper office on Madison Avenue. My job was to study the reports of the various bureaus for cultural and artistic affairs set up by the Army of Occupation in Germany. On the whole I found this work virtually useless; it was impossible to judge the effectiveness of a program or make improvements from a distance. What I did learn there was the life of a New York office building, peopled by innumerable employees, managers, and secretaries who at six in the evening rushed like a flock of poultry half dead of thirst—and with the same sort of cackling—into the bars of the neighborhood to fortify themselves with a drink before riding home in jammed subway cars and buses. I too had a few drinks, and I blessed every day of the past years that I had spent among genuine poultry, far from the big city.

Before going off to this job, for which I had signed a year's contract, I had reduced that genuine flock of poultry to the minimum needed for the household, but I continued to lease the farm. For economic reasons my wife had remained there for the time being, together with our daughter Winnetou, who was already going to college in California but had long summer vacations. The animals we were attached to were later boarded with a farm where we knew they would be well treated. At the time I still thought that if I were sent to Germany my wife would be coming along. In fact, that was against the regulations: only a member of the army with a long-term post in the Army of Occupation was allowed to take his wife overseas. Only gradually did we become familiar with these complications and difficulties built into the bureaucratic procedures. Now I had to apply my energies to getting to Europe myself and not remaining stuck in the New York government office. The prospect of a limited orientation trip to Germany had been dangled before me for September, but week after week passed and still approval of it did not arrive. I myself had to go to Washington to try to get things moving.

That was my first visit to the Pentagon, that legendary five-cornered building where the destinies of much of the world are decided. The structure was new at that time, and to me it seemed the misbegotten product of an abstruse fantasy. It was the sort of place a director like Fritz Lang might have conceived to symbolize the horror of a depersonalized world in a surrealist science-fiction movie. I repeatedly lost my way in the endless, uniform corridors and uniform floors, whose walls were marked with varicolored lines, letters, and numbers for purposes of orientation. Again and again I wandered into a wrong elevator and a wrong office. In the halls I met rapidly striding men in uniform who had neither the time nor the desire to give information to a bewildered civilian—or else female officers in close-cut uniforms, tight around their backsides and bosoms, who walked at the same hasty pace, always in pairs and always giggling over something. These would pause when addressed, and give information amiably enough, but it was almost always wrong, so that I went on wandering around the labyrinth without an Ariadne's thread. I had to go from colonel to general, from male sergeant to female sergeant, to a variety of indoctrination centers, political personnel checkups, physical examinations—after three days of this I was finally told that my official travel order would come through by the end of October. My assignment read: To visit the larger cities in the American Occupation Zone of Germany and Austria—and in the other zones as well—and draw up a detailed report on the status of all cultural institutions, together with proposals for their improvement and for activating the cultural life in the occupied countries. It was a good assignment; it did not put upon me the burden of discriminating or prohibiting, had nothing to do with political interrogation or indoctrination, but represented simply an effort to build new bridges between Germany and the world. Moreover, it enabled me to intercede in cases where injustices had been done. A period of five or six months was allotted for my journey. For transportation, food, and shelter, I would be dependent on the American army, but I would not be a member of any army formation. I remained a civilian, was not required to assume any military rank or wear a uniform, but my salary was set at the level of an American colonel, which I thought would permit me to offer material help to people. Not until I reached Europe did I learn that money was not very important. Only cigarettes counted; they were the only secure medium of exchange during the years of hunger.

Before my flight across the ocean there came another leave-taking, and I had not realized how hard and painful it would be. On my last weekend in America I had a chance to go home once more. Home— that meant the farm. It was October. The woods were aflame with their full autumnal color. I walked around alone, around the house, around the barns, down to the pond, the stillness humming in my ears. There was a fence of unpeeled birch saplings, there another of crudely sawn wooden posts and wire. I remembered every hammer- blow, every thrust of the spade, that I had put into building this fence. Over there was the small wood path I had cleared myself, up to the slope where I had cut firewood. I closed my eyes, inhaled the spicy evening odor of the woods. The evening turned cold; I stoked my stove and fireplaces once more. Tears came to my eyes—I could pretend it was from the smoke.

The destination written in my travel order was Berlin. When I read the word, I felt hot and cold shivers, similar to the feeling with which we had listened to the radio accounts of night air raids and the destruction of German cities.

Three days later I took the plane from Paris to the Tempelhof air- field in Berlin. It was an overcast afternoon; soon we were enveloped in fog and rain. Further flying was impossible and we landed at the Rhine-Main airport.

That same evening I walked through the city of Frankfurt—the first large city I had seen as a child. I heard passers-by speaking German, in their local dialect, and each time I gave a start. I walked through the shattered Old Town, stood on the ruins of the Römerberg, and felt as if I were in a nightmare from which I could not awaken. I no longer knew a soul in this city where many of my friends had lived; I had not a single address and had no idea whether most of the people I knew were still alive. The theaters were destroyed; I did not know whether any performances were still being given, or where, nor whether there might be any actors and directors of my acquaintance here. The rubble crunched underfoot and I was alone.

But then, in the small hotel requisitioned by the American army, where I had been assigned a room for the night, something altogether unexpected happened. When I showed my billet with my name on it, the old, starved-looking desk clerk stared at my face. Then he said in thick dialect: 'Are you by any chance the *Merry Vineyard* Zuckmayer?'

When I nodded, he gripped my hands.

'Oh, what a pleasure,' he said again and again, 'what a pleasure you've come home. You know what? You'll get a white towel in your room. We never give them out nowadays, see, because the soldiers take them. But you'll get a towel and two pillows.'

That was my welcome home.

The following night I rode to Berlin in a military train, because all airports were fogged in. It stopped at a small suburban station; the main stations of the city had been destroyed. From there a bus took me to the headquarters of the military government in Dahlem.

That arrival: the ride through the ruins, past the bare Tiergarten—all the trees had long since been cut down for firewood and even the stumps rooted out; all that was left was a huge potato field across which you looked from one belt of rubble to another; the first days in the freezing, starving city—when I write all this down, I no longer know whether I really experienced it. It all lies behind a gray, misty veil. I can tear it away, blow it away like smoke, but even then something vague and clouded remains, a dimness before my eyes. There are flickerings of light: the reunions with friends. But even so, it is as if I had been in Hades and dare not look back after emerging. Probably this is the origin of that curious amnesia that repeatedly surprises me in so many persons in Germany. It is as if they had not really lived during those times of distress, as though they passed through those miserable years like sleepwalkers.

That was the coldest autumn and winter of the postwar era. Scarcity had reached its peak, had become a permanent condition. And its impact was felt the more now that the direct cruelties of the war had passed. Only a few suburbs had been spared the bombs, such as Dahlem, part of Grunewald, and Litchterfelde. The Allies had requisitioned these intact areas—in fact, it was whispered that they had deliberately spared them with a view to using them as headquarters for the Occupation. Aside from these places, there was hardly an unblasted street or row of houses in the whole city. Wherever houses were wholly or partially habitable, you saw things that looked like black snail's horns protruding from every window. These were the pipes of drum stoves that had been set up in the rooms. Except for the intolerably overheated quarters of the Occupation forces, there was no longer any central heating in the city, and in any case there was so little fuel that the emergency stoves could be used for a few hours a day at most. Even then they warmed only a bit of the room, where inhabitants and visitors crowded together, while in the farther corner, where the windows were, crystals of ice glittered on the walls.

I spent many evenings with many friends in many cities gathered around the slowly dying stoves, all of us in overcoats with collars turned up. In Berlin that winter you saw long lines of women standing every morning in front of the emergency hydrant set up by the American armed forces. They carried pails for water—the water lines were frozen almost everywhere. The women wore heavy woolen men's trousers, often tightened around the ankles with wrappings of rags, and a variety of shoes ranging from the ski boots of long-ago winter vacations to fur slippers and wooden clogs. Almost every night the electricity was cut off and we sat around a smoking tallow candle. If old people and children fell ill, there was no hope for them. Whatever hospitals were available were overcrowded and lacked medicines or staff. Berlin, that liveliest of cities, had become a kind of necropolis. The blatant noisiness of the new places of entertainment set up for the Occupation forces did not change that atmosphere. One evening I stood alone near the Kaiser Wilhelm

Memorial Church—the Gedächtniskirche. A jagged shattered tower rose from the ruins. This had been the intersection of Tauentzien-strasse and Kurfürstendamm, the main artery of the city between the Zoo Station and the entire West Side. Here the big movie palaces had stood. Here, in the past, everything would have been bathed in glaring light at night, and filled with the hubbub of an incessant stream of automobiles and pedestrians. Now everything was pitch-dark, except for dim emergency lights on the street corners, and quiet as a grave. There was not a soul in sight, not a sound to be heard. Here and there, where half a floor had remained suspended like a swallow's nest among the ruins of the buildings, candlelight flickered. Suddenly I heard a noise: a rattling and squeaking. Diagon-ally across the street, where at this hour not even a single American jeep was likely to be passing, a boy in tattered clothing was dragging a small handcart. It was loaded with firewood he had probably filched from the ruins. The boy's wooden shoes clattered loudly on the cracked pavement. I heard him for a long time while he tugged his cart in the direction of Wittenbergplatz. That was in November 1946—barely twenty years ago.

On my first day in Berlin, during an interval in calling at various military government offices, I had let Mirl and Peter Suhrkamp know I was there. They were currently living in a house in Zehlendorf to which they had also moved whatever they had salvaged of the former S. Fischer Verlag—Suhrkamp was already engaged in re-viving the publishing firm. Toward evening I took the subway to the station Mirl had indicated. She was standing, pale and thin, wearing a battered overcoat, at the top of the stairway. She held out her hands to me. For a long time we could not speak as we walked down the quiet side street to her apartment.

Peter Suhrkamp lay in bed, hollow-eyed, equally pale. The room was unheated. He was down with another of those bouts of pneu-monia and pleurisy he was prone to; his health was permanently broken from his long stay in one of the worst concentration camps. When I looked at him I thought I was confronting a dying man. But his blankets were heaped with manuscripts, proofs, and letters; he was holding a pencil in his tremulous hands. If ever I had seen an example of the fact that the mind can dominate the body, he was providing it. Without removing her coat, in heavy woolen stockings, Mirl fussed in the kitchen cooking on an alcohol burner. The only thing she could prepare was a thin but hot potato soup; there was not a morsel of fat in it, and it had little nutritive value. For two years longer, such soup was to be the principal food of most Germans. At best, only men engaged in hard physical labor received a scant supplementary ration. Students and intellectuals had to subsist for an entire month on a ration of calories which would scarcely do for a single day in the German Federal Republic now.

In spite of his weakened condition, Peter Suhrkamp had little desire for food. But he did crave alcohol, which warmed him and had a tonic effect on his constitution. I had not yet had the chance, on this first day, to try and find any food supplies, but I had with me a bottle of whisky and a bottle of brandy brought from America. We spent the night over these. My heated room in Harnack House, where visitors on American governmental assignments were quartered, remained empty.

The first thing Peter did—before we had exchanged more than a few words—was to place a long-distance call to my parents in Oberstdorf. I had tried to do so that morning, on my arrival at American headquarters. But I had been informed that the army lines were to be used only for official purposes.

It took hours before the call went through, and it was repeatedly interrupted. The line was noisy; it was hard to communicate. Dimly and very far away, I heard my mother's voice. She had been routed out of bed in the small boardinghouse where my parents were living. She could not understand that I was not allowed to come to them at once, that I was 'on duty' and would have to wait until my assignment took me to Munich, where permission could be secured for a weekend furlough. The long waiting period was still not over for us. But at least I was in the country and we could count the days.

That night Peter Suhrkamp told me the story of how he and Mirl had survived. His recital was often interrupted by fits of coughing. He spoke with a kind of feverish need for completeness, but nevertheless with a remarkable, aloof calm, as if he were reporting historical events. They had been bombed out four times, each time barely escaping death, and had lost all their possessions. He also spoke of his arrest, of the disgraceful denunciation that had brought it about, and of the terrible ordeals in the camp. He had to go over it all once more, he said, because he felt that he had to give an accounting to himself before a witness. But he made me pledge never to tell others about the details of his experiences, the cruelties he had had to watch in concentration camp, and the horrors he himself had experienced. Above all I must pledge never to write about these things. Description of atrocities, he contended, did not act as a check, but rather stimulated the instinct for cruelty present in man's subconscious mind. It aroused a secret pleasure in imagining, inflicting, and suffering cruelty, and therefore would evoke the evil spirit once more. The same thing applied to war books, he said, even though they were directed against the war. I have kept my promise and think that he was right. To be silent in this matter is not to veil facts, but to vanquish and go beyond them. Imagination is a deep and dire as well as a saving force. It is better not to awaken the diabolic elements slumbering in its depths. Let us rather seek its brighter regions, attune our hearing to its *vox coelestis,* its *vox humana.*

That first reunion took place in a spirit of unbroken closeness that years of separation had not changed. Innumerable other such reunions followed, as well as new encounters marked by the same sense of belonging. Every time, it was as if a spark had been struck; no cable had to be laid, no bridges of reconciliation needed to be built. There was no strangeness, no gulf. The years in which we had not heard from one another no longer counted; in our inner depths we had nevertheless known what was happening to one another. We had never lost touch.

There was scarcely anyone in Germany, least of all in Berlin, still to be found in his old haunts. Most people had lost their homes and possessions; many had been driven hither and yon. Earlier, and in a different form, the same thing had happened to us. We had undergone the same fate, and it was altogether senseless, without any human significance, to measure and weigh the tears shed on both sides, to try to decide who had suffered more, those who had remained or those who had been forced to leave. The time for a great settlement seemed to have come, for turning toward a new humane spirit born of man's horror of his own potentialities. That was how many felt at the time, especially many Germans, burdened as they were then by shame and suffering, as they would be for years afterward by the calamities and afterpains of the war.

Among the German people a kind of intellectual ravenousness accompanied physical starvation, a virtually insatiable craving for clarification and insight, a thirst for inner renewal, a chiliastic hope that went deeper and embraced far more strata of the population

than the similar phenomenon after the First World War. For all the
the wretchedness, it was also a magnificent period. Whatever cultural
nourishment came from 'outside,' plays, books, reportage, every
type of artistic and intellectual utterance, from Sartre to Eliot, as
well as everything repressed inside the country during the twelve-
year reign of terror, was absorbed with passionate eagerness.

Everywhere the unheated theaters were crammed with people
who often had to walk for hours to reach them, people in tattered
clothing, with hunger written on their faces, but whose eyes burned,
who were full of receptivity, ready for any challenge to their emotions and their minds. In Berlin, for example, I saw Thornton
Wilder's *The Skin of Our Teeth,* which I had earlier seen performed
in New York before a highly literary, aesthetically pampered
audience. Now the people in the house were the same as those on the
stage, who had only just survived the Ice Age and the Flood by the
skin of their teeth. The audiences in Berlin could still feel the shudder of menace, were still caught up in the perils of their own fate.

At that time Russians and Americans were still treating each
other as equal allies, although an undercurrent of mistrust was already palpable. But the two Powers governed the city jointly, and
people could cross from one sector into another without hindrance.
As yet civilians were well advised not to walk on the streets in the
Russian sector after dark; the women still hid when a uniformed
Russian pounded on the door. But the Russians, in their childlike
enthusiasm for *kultura,* had been the only Occupation Power to open
a club for German artists, actors, and writers. This was the Möwe
('Seagull') on Neue Wilhelmstrasse. Here club members could have
borscht and sausages, beer and vodka, at very low prices. Here the
whole art world of Berlin met; and here too the Russian cultural
officers arranged a first 'reception' for me. Representatives of the
other Allies and German theatrical people from all sectors were
invited.

Upon my arrival Herbert Ihering had spoken the first public
welcome to me on the Berlin radio. He was now working as dramaturgist in the Deutsches Theater in East Berlin. At that time a
division of the city, a partition of Germany, was inconceivable.

From Berlin my duties took me westwards again. I saw battered
Darmstadt and stood at the grave of my friend Carlo Mierendorff.
I walked, half stunned, through the ruins of my own city of Mainz,

stood before the rubble of my parents' house, and could no longer trace the streets I had walked to school. I saw the heart-rending notes posted in the railroad stations, covering the walls, one beside the other, from all the people who had lost touch with one another. I saw those ghostly railroad stations, full of waiting, hopeless, and hapless people, full of monsters and murderers, cripples and refugees, of worn and broken returning prisoners of war, black-marketeers, starvelings, of male and female prostitutes, and the Occupation soldiers who pursued such prey and were preyed on by them.

I went to Munich. In the cold November rain it was a city of dampness, shabbiness, wretchedness. Crowds of people in pitiable clothing stood at the streetcar stops. The cars came seldom and were jammed. People hung in clusters on the running boards and were swept down by the rubber truncheons of the MP's in their tight breeches and white leggings. Hordes of hungry children, some hopping about because they had lost a leg in the bombings, still hung around the hotels where American troops were quartered, hoping for a little chocolate, chewing gum, or cake that some soldier might throw them. The black rain dripped and dripped all the time I was there. I saw soldiers, most often Negro soldiers, pick up such children, and feed and kiss them. I saw others who made a game of tossing out cigarettes and watching the cripples run for them. Among these 'Amis', too, beastliness and decency dwelt side by side—as in the German people.

We knew that the murderers were still among us. For that reason friends clung all the closer together.

And at last, on the last Sunday in November, after vanquishing many difficulties, I succeeded in going to Oberstdorf, to my parents.

During this time I experienced two kinds of happiness. The one was being able to help, to alleviate suffering. The other, and perhaps it was the greatest and most blessed happiness that has ever come my way, was:

Not to have to hate.

I do not know how I would have felt if my mother had been killed, if my father—who could not have gone on living without her, nearly blind as he was, and would not have wanted to—had died in grief and misery. But they were living, both of them; I could see them again. And my mother had even received kindness from a

'Nazi'—such things happened too! When she had registered in Oberstdorf after being bombed out of her home in Mainz, the local Group Leader had glossed over the 'non-Aryan' descent recorded in her papers, in order to spare her possible persecution or humiliation. An unknown person, wearing the devil's mask, had shielded my parents. And my friends, executed by the devil's henchmen, had gone to their deaths for a good cause. There were glorious as well as bad examples.

I did not need to hate.

When we had left Europe—it seemed to me as if a century lay between that time and my present return—we had had a certain idea of what it would be like when we came back. That idea was wrong, and we knew it. Moreover, for reasons of self-preservation we did not cling to such thoughts. We banished them from our minds, from our conversations, even from our dreams, so that we would be able to live where we were. Nevertheless, all of us had that secret, unspoken conception of what it would mean: to come back. And in my own conception the city of Zurich held a special place.

For in Zurich there was the theater. At the time of our departure it was the only free theater of any stature in German-speaking countries. There, in 1938, I had attended my last opening night in Europe. There, something was to happen which I no longer imagined possible.

Before too long my wife crossed to Europe on a Dutch liner, a sister ship of the boat on which we departed. Since Germany was closed to her, she went to Switzerland. There friends gave her a glorious welcome. Immediately after the end of the war we had received a cable from Pierre and Françoise Pelot, in whose Hotel Bell-Vue in Chardonne we had spent our last year in Europe:

'*Toujours invités venez vite!*'—'Always welcome here—come quickly!'

Heinz Hilpert was living in Zurich with his Nuschka, whom he could not marry, according to the Nuremberg Laws, since she was Jewish. But he had managed to get her to Switzerland before the worst could befall her. There, after many years, they were reunited and married. He himself had suffered acutely from the war; his only son by his first marriage, a gifted young cellist to whom he was deeply attached, had been killed shortly before the surrender.

But Hilpert still had his old vitality where work was concerned, and now at the Zurich Schauspielhaus he was rehearsing my play, *The Devil's General.*

The first night was set for the second half of December. I had never heard the name of Gustav Knuth, the actor who was taking the lead, his rise having occurred during our absence. But people in Germany who knew something about the theater always exclaimed: Knuth—marvelous! And Hilpert, my friend, who had put on the best performances of my plays, was the director. I simply had to go!

But a wall of obstacles lay between me and Zurich.

My employment contract did provide for a Christmas vacation, but not for leaving occupied Germany. I had never imagined special permission would be needed for that, and that I would have to apply to Washington. What that meant was clear: the application would be approved, the approval arriving in three months at the earliest, by which time I would probably be on my return flight to America. The frontiers of Germany were still closed, and even within Germany special permission and formalities were required every time anyone wanted to cross the boundaries between the different zones of occupation.

There I was in Munich and on the verge of despair. It was three days before opening night. Then chance brought my way my old friend Günther Stapenhorst, a former German naval officer, later production head of UFA, who had voluntarily gone into exile at the beginning of the Nazi rule, out of disgust and horror. Now he was in Munich for a day in connection with movie business. That same evening I was on my way to Zurich with him, in his Swiss car.

It was an obstacle race, for I was traveling 'illegally,' like a refugee during the war. I had obained a visa from the Swiss consulate, but had not considered that at Bregenz we would have to drive for a few miles through the French Occupation Zone of Austria. There the French authorities made difficulties about letting me through. Only the fact that I was able to curse in French finally moved the heart of a young officer of the border guard.

Suddenly, in the darkness, I sensed that we were in the land of peace. I felt it physically; the country smelled different. That was the first thing I noticed—before I became aware of the paved roads, the comforting orderliness of brightly lit villages with their small, neat inns.

An hour before midnight we saw the lights of Zurich. It was a dream of a city—an unchanged European city—for although I had passed through Paris on my way to Germany, it had still looked depressed, unkempt, and gloomy, not yet recovered from the war. I was too excited to go right away to the small hotel where my wife was waiting, without knowing whether and when I would arrive. I felt I first had to grasp where I was. . . .

I asked my friend to stop at the Kronenhalle restaurant. It was about to close, but there was time enough for me to be served a glass of Pilsen and a triple 'Chrüter.' The waitresses seemed like friendly nurses. I felt secure and well cared for. There was something of comforting normality even about the way the chairs were stacked on the tables and the closing hour strictly observed.

Next morning I went to the rehearsal with my wife. No one knew that I would be coming. I walked slowly through the sunlit, wintry city, stopping frequently—to watch the swans by the lakeside, where you can see the snow-covered mountains in the distance and the twin peaks called the Mythen; to look into the window of Oprecht's bookshop on Rämistrasse; and finally at the Pfauen corner, where hotel, restaurant, and playhouse are lodged in one building. I still needed time for reflection—it was like passing through the stages of gestation, and I should have taken nine months to do it. . . . For here, right now, I was to be reborn. I felt as if I ought to utter a prayer as I walked from Zeltweg across the courtyard to the stage entrance. Softly, I opened the familiar door and tiptoed in. At that moment I heard my friend Hilpert's voice saying: 'Yes, yes, Gustav, I know, the part's longer than Lear, but it's time you had it down cold.'

I was home.

Hilpert had been standing up front near the footlights. As if he sensed something behind him, he turned around. 'One moment,' he said to the actors. And then we were embracing each other.

Those days in Zurich were one single bacchanal, a prolonged festival of friendship. All the friends whom I could possibly have expected were there, and many whom I had not hoped to see—even Franz Czokor, still wearing American uniform, after an incredible Odyssey through Poland, Hungary, Rumania, Yugoslavia, and Italy, always just ahead of the German tanks, and Henry Goverts. It was all unreal and it was all sharply actual. A hundred threads were knotted into a fabric that was timeless. I had a long telephone conversation with Countess Freya von Moltke, the widow of my friend Helmuth, who had founded the Kreisauer Kreis, the most important civilian group in the German Resistance, and who had been executed by the Nazis. She was on her way to Geneva and could not come to Zurich, but she told me about his last days, his defense in the 'People's Court,' and his brave death. I had never met her, but I saw her through her voice.

All our friends were with us, the living and the dead.

I cannot talk about the first night. I watched it with a special kind of intentness, following every smallest aspect of the splendid performance. But there are feelings and experiences that resist description. If a man has been buried alive in a coma, then disinterred and resuscitated, presumably he could not talk much about it either.

On the day after the opening, while we were still dazed by the success of the play and the strong reactions to it, I heard from my friend Goverts that a man who had seen the play, and wanted to say a few words about it, would like to meet me. He was Carl Jacob Burckhardt. I had not yet read anything of his—his correspondence with Hugo von Hofmannsthal had not yet been published, and I read his *Richelieu* and short stories later. I only knew who he was: great-nephew of Jacob Burckhardt, the Basel historian, High Commissioner in Danzig before the war, President of the International Red Cross after the war. We met in the apartment of friends. This man's approval of the play meant more to me than the approval of the literary critics, for he had experienced and understood as had few others the complexity of what the Germans had been through and had done in the years of Nazi rule. He was the first to tell me what I afterwards heard from countless Germans: that was what it was like—the way I had presented it in this play; that I had captured the truth which cannot be found in documents, only in literature, and which cannot be delineated with hatred, but only with love. This first meeting laid the foundation for a later friendship, one of the richest and most rewarding in my life.

On New Year's Eve—laden with smuggled Swiss rarities: chocolate, canned milk, and cigarettes for the inescapable clandestine barter—I was back with my parents in Oberstdorf. I stayed a few days; then I had once more to be on my official rounds. In spite of many reunions these became more and more difficult for me—and not only because I scarcely slept, for I was working with American officialdom by day, attending the theater in the evenings, and spending the nights with my friends in Germany and Austria. The main trouble was that my position entangled me in almost insoluble conflict.

From the first moment I set foot on German soil, from my first meeting with people who spoke German, from my first walk through a bombed German city, I knew that I was not an American, although I had a home in America and in Vermont had achieved a real sense of belonging. I felt more and more strongly that my identity was not with those who had sent me here and who regarded me as theirs. Rather, I belonged to the nation whose language and ways were mine, in which I had been born and grown up. But in Germany, too, we were no longer really at home. There was a shadow that could not be ignored, even though I rejected all the terrible simplifications, all the charges of collective guilt: the shadow of a frightful crime. To be sure, other nations could conceivably have committed it, but ours *had* committed it, and that should have been out of the question for this nation as we knew it and had loved it and continued to love it. I did not belong to one of the victor nations, but neither did I belong to the defeated. Now, after returning home, I had really become homeless, and I did not know how I would ever find a homeland again.

The Devil's General was not performed in Germany until a year after the first Zurich performance. Until then it was banned by the American authorities (despite the fact that its author was for a time assigned to these authorities) for reasons that remain unclear. Partly there was fear of the play's having a 'reactionary' political effect, fostering a legend about the German officer class; partly it was thought that there might be riots, brawls, public disturbances. The play did not fit into the so-called re-education program, which in any case proved vain, for no nation can educate another, least of all with an army as teacher.

The first night took place in Frankfurt at the end of November 1947. I had meanwhile returned once more to America to deliver my report, had resigned my job, and returned on my own—this time accompanied by my wife. Obtaining permission to re-enter Germany had been difficult even then, but I had managed to overcome the bureaucratic obstacles.

Hilpert staged the play as magnificently as he had done in Zurich. The performance was given in the former Frankfurt Stock Exchange, which had been refurbished to make a temporary theater.

401

The actors were a fiercely dedicated group, although some were on the verge of physical collapse from sheer hunger. During the last rehearsals we had to keep up their strength with Swiss canned food, Nescafé and sandwiches we smuggled in from American PX's. Opening night was marked by an uncanny tension. People everywhere had been talking about the play ever since the Swiss performances. How would the German public take it? Many officers of the Occupation forces sat in the audience that evening, mistrustful and skeptical. But they witnessed, as we did, a surge of universal emotion such as a play can rarely evoke. The Germans saw themselves in the mirror of their own times. Many of those present had been in concentration camps, in penal battalions, in the Resistance, or simply in the army. They could not understand how this play could have been written by a man who had been living abroad, who had not been on the scene during those years, who had not personally shared their experiences. The play corresponded to the reality as they had known it, down to the smallest detail. Nevertheless it probably could not have been written without the perspective of time and place; it would scarcely have been possible under the incessant assault of new events. And if you had once been a German soldier, though in the First World War, you knew how a German soldier speaks and feels. If you had once known the Nazis, though before they came to the full flush of power, you knew what they were like.

Two days later, after another performance at the Stock Exchange, I held a first discussion of the play with young Germans. It was arranged by Peter Suhrkamp. Questions were asked, confessions made, with a spontaneous candor that overwhelmed all of us. The hearts of these young people seemed to be wide open.

From then on I knew what I had to do.

I devoted two years thereafter to a long dialogue with the young, at student meetings, youth group sessions, in discussion clubs and union halls—wherever they wanted me. I even talked to young people who had belonged to the Waffen-SS and were now being held in the camp at Dachau. I addressed myself to German youth, who had emerged from the collapse in a state of deep moral confusion.

I received several hundred letters that began: 'I am your Lieutenant Hartmann . . .' That was the young officer in my play who enters the war an enthusiastic adherent of the Hitler Youth, believing in its ideals, and who is converted to the opposition by his encounters with terror and baseness. Surely the same conversion had not taken place in every single one of these young people, but I felt it as the sign of a great awakening, of a transformation, that they wished to interpret their experience in such a light.

I myself felt an enormous responsibility, from which I neither could escape nor wished to withdraw. And in meeting that responsibility I belonged to my nation, though I could no longer feel Germany to be my home. Month after month I traveled around the country, going from one meeting or discussion group to the next. It was more than my strength could stand. At the end of January 1948, after a lecture and discussion tour through the Rhineland and the Ruhr, in the course of which I had kept myself going on liquor, I collapsed with a heart attack.

I was in my early fifties; I came through. I recuperated in the Stillachhaus Sanatorium near Oberstdorf. There I was close to my mother. There, a year earlier, my father had died. On the eve of his death my wife and I had been with my parents in Oberstdorf for a brief visit, for our visa for occupied Germany had expired and we had to return to Switzerland the next morning. That night I had two odd experiences. One of them seemed really to be an encounter with death.

My parents were still living in the small boardinghouse where they had been quartered during the war, for no other housing could be found. Just after darkness fell I stepped out of their living room into the hall. The hall was unlighted, for electric power had to be husbanded. There I suddenly confronted the figure of death as it appears in old engravings of the Dance of Death: a tall white figure and naked skull with large, dark eye sockets. When I switched on my flashlight I saw it was a Catholic priest in a long white surplice whose handsome gray pate had gleamed skull-like in the darkness. It was the venerable Pastor Rupp, who a few days later would conduct the funeral service for my father. He was here to give the last Sacraments to a sick old woman and was looking for the right door in the dark hallway. Later I met him frequently and spent many an hour in his parish house. But at that time he seemed to me the embodiment of death, whose presence I physically sensed at this moment. I thought, however, it was old Frau Schmidt's death that it was his office to see to.

We spent this last evening with my father in a gay mood; he himself was the gayest of us. My mother was concerned, for he showed signs of an incipient bronchial catarrh, and was in fact particularly susceptible to respiratory illnesses. But he seemed unconcerned, although his voice grew more and more hoarse. When we had arrived that afternoon we had found him sitting in his armchair rather exhausted, saying very little and drumming his right hand on the table in a curious rhythm. 'Why are you drumming like that?' my mother asked. 'I hear drums,' he had said.

That evening we had prepared a meal that was wildly extravagant for current conditions. My wife had brought all sorts of eatables from Switzerland—delicacies that had become mythical in Germany during the war, and more so thereafter. There was even a can of lobster. She cooked on an alcohol stove. I think there was turtle soup and veal ragout—a feast for people who had been wretchedly nourished for years. It was intended as a celebration of our reunion, for we could still see each other only at intervals. My parents loved my wife as if she were their daughter—and she, who had grown up without a father and whose own mother had been long dead, found in them the parents she missed.

Ever since my first return to Germany I had managed to supply my parents now and then with wine, which was still being produced in occupied Germany, but was either 'confiscated' or disappeared into the black market. Now I had brought two bottles of champagne from Frankfurt, in response to my father's particular request. He had drunk regularly, though never immoderately, all his life; and as a Rhinelander the absence of wine had been harder on him and done more to weaken him physically than the shortages of food. We drank to our next reunion, we drank to the happiness of being together again, we drank to the welfare of my brother, who had not yet been able to come, we drank to a new and redeemed Germany. I had also brought my father a good cigar—my mother was inclined to forbid it, because of the accumulating mucus in his throat, but he insisted on smoking it. 'I still enjoy it,' he said. 'Who knows how much longer I will?' He was eighty-three years old.

Late that night he held out his glass to my wife and asked: 'Is there any left?' She poured out the remainder of the bottle for him and said, touching his glass and alluding to the bottle: 'The last drop.'

As she spoke those words I knew that I would not see my father again.

We had to leave early in the morning while my parents were still sleeping. My father died the next day. I received the news by telegram, while we were at the Zurich Schauspielhaus. Brecht and his wife were in the box with us. I have never seen him so kind and affectionate. He knew what my father had meant to me. 'Go ahead and cry,' he said. But I did not cry. My mind was occupied with thoughts of how to return to my mother's side at once.

I managed it by one of those fantastic, no longer altogether believable shifts that frequently came to our rescue in those days. I had to go alone; my wife could not obtain a permit. Later, at Christmas, she was able to be with my mother when I could not get permission.

I had feared that I would find my mother completely broken and helpless. She was not. Now the strength of a true marriage, a lifelong partnership, was revealed. There is no strength like it. Her composure banished all sentimentality. For many years she had cared for her nearly blind husband. Now she would not let anyone take from her the last care she could give him. She laid him out, dressed him, as if she were tending a child—without tears. There was a problem of obtaining a cross for the grave—everything was a problem then. We solved it with American cigarettes. We buried him in a corner of Oberstdorf's wooded cemetery, under the dark pines he had loved.

I had also feared that my mother, after nearly sixty years of marriage, would not be able to bear the loneliness of widowhood. I need not have worried, she was never alone. To her, her husband had not died; he had only changed. Into what? Where had he gone? That did not trouble her. For her he was always there, as present in death as he had been in life. In her last years she was perfectly able to be gay with us, and we sensed that he was always there for her.

I was able to arrange for her to live permanently at Stillachhaus, the sanatorium to which I owed my own recovery. There I knew she was well looked after, especially when we had to leave for protracted periods to return to our second home in Vermont.

Death was as kind to her as life had been. One night in August 1954 she fell asleep and did not wake.

1966
THE HIGH STAIRWAY

W HEN MY WIFE and I with knapsacks on our backs tramped up Kapellenweg from Saas-Grund to Saas-Fee one July evening in 1938, we did not know that we were going home. We walked along that path for the first time with growing inexplicable emotion, such as one rarely feels on outings, even outings in a new, exciting landscape. It was as if we had some premonitory sense that up there something unexpected and wonderful was awaiting us.

That was four months after our expulsion from Austria, ten months before our departure for America.

It had become very hot among the vineyards of Chardonne on Lake Geneva, where we had found refuge at the time. Since I had a difficult writing job ahead of me, we decided to look about in the mountains of the Valais, where the summer climate was good, for lodgings we could afford. We were certainly not thinking of seeking a permanent place in which to live.

There was no road then from Saas-Grund, which lies on the valley floor at an altitude of somewhat more than five thousand feet, up to the resort of Saas-Fee. There was only a path on which mail, baggage, materials, supplies for the hotel, and visitors disinclined to walk could be brought up on mules. The mule-path led into Kapellenweg, 'Chapel Path,' which ran in steep serpentines along a deep gorge through which Fee Brook, fed by glacial waters, roared down to the valley.

This was an old pilgrims' path, lined by fourteen small stone chapels, each representing a Station of the Cross and containing seventeenth-century carvings. They were done with a harsh, primitive realism—especially the torturers, the scourgers, the soldiers, and the mocking onlookers of the Passion. In many of these groups Jesus is shown small as a child, while figures of the powerful men to whom He must submit appear almost more than life-sized. The Holy Mother is always portrayed as a gentle peasant beauty.

We did not meet a soul on this path—it was already dinnertime. It kept leading us along the margin of the gorge whose precipitous granite walls barred our view of the higher mountains. We passed rocks worn to a high polish by the passage of the glacier, light-dappled young woods, and tiny fields planted with potatoes and barley—fields that seemed glued to the slope just above the plunging chasms.

The rocks and fragments of cliffs strewn about everywhere delighted me: blue basalt and green-striped serpentine, pale gray gneiss, dark-red porphyry, shimmering quartz, which suggested the possible presence of crystals, and broadly stratified layers of mica-schist.

As yet we could not see the high mountains. Only now and then did we catch a glimpse of shimmering blue ice, the sudden gleam of a snowy peak that vanished again around the next serpentine. The woods closed in more densely, then suddenly opened out to a bright, grassy slope with scattered larch trees, ancient and massive, with furrowed reddish bark. A fieldstone bench had been built around one of them. And nestled against the crags, almost built into it, was the pilgrimage church called Maria zur Hohen Stiege, 'Mary of the High Stairway.' Over the arched doorway the date 1661 was carved. The church was crowned by a delicate bell tower of ocher-colored tufa. Above the roof and through the lightly swaying crowns of the larches we looked into a tremendous brilliance, a supernatural radiance, so bright as almost to force us to close our eyes. It was the sunset glow from the thirteen-thousand-foot peaks.

We stood still, dazzled and deeply stirred by the stillness, the enclosedness, the humble dignity of this last station before the last climb to Saas-Fee.

That climb, called the Hohe Stiege after the church, consists of a steep path made of ninety stone steps hewn into the wall of rock beyond the church. Once again you see nothing but the walls of the gorge. Then, already at the level of the village, you turn a corner of rock and suddenly meet with a sight such as I have never seen anywhere else. You are standing at the end of the world, and simultaneously at its origin, its very beginning, and in the middle of it. An arc of snowy peaks arranged in inexpressible harmony frame the horizon toward the south, while on the west loom a chain of Gothic spires. At first you can do nothing but look up; it takes your breath away. Then you see Saas-Fee lying before you—at that time still a village of mountain farmers counting 466 souls, its coherence scarcely affected by the few hotels built for English tourists in the first decade of the century. Encircling it are broadly curving meadows, then forests of larch and stone pines rising up the mountains, and the vault of sky above is so vast that you feel freedom and openness to all sides, as if you were on the high seas. That sky was blossoming now, at evening, with a deep dark-blue tinted almost violet, while the eternal snows still flashed and glittered with the reflections of a sun that had already sunk below the horizon.

All around the foaming white ribbons of streams descended from the bastions of the glaciers, their rushing and ringing filling the air and only deepening the stillness. And everywhere, almost up to the tongues of the glaciers and the walls of the cliffs, incised into the edges of the woods and the open pastureland, were the squares and oblongs of those tiny fields, brown with grain and green with herbage, looking at us like the faces of old people who quietly lift their heads from their work.

We could not speak for a long time. We could only breathe deeply. The air was sweetened with the smell of hay and a pungent, ice-born purity. 'Here,' one of us said then, 'if only we could stay here!'

Twenty years later, in July 1958, we moved into our house here, the most beautiful and—God grant—the last house of our lives.

I did not seek this one either. Rather, it came to me, like our house in Vermont. I had often passed by it and admired its magnificent structure, true to the original form and proportions of the old Saas farmhouses, and the surrounding land, ringed by stone pines, firs, and spruces. But we did not know that the builders had died, that there were no heirs who wanted to keep it, and that the present owner was on the point of offering it for sale. A chance meeting acquainted us with all these facts.

In the meantime, since the end of the Second World War, we had come to Saas-Fee fourteen times; something drew us here again and again. I had done some rope climbing in the mountains in the good, taciturn company of one of the older guides, who also gave us lodging. I had come to know the old goat paths and the sheep pastures of the vicinity as well as I had the wood roads and the game trails in Vermont or the paths and mountain forests near Henndorf.

I had imagined I knew a few things about wood, hardwood and softwood—certainly I'd had enough splinters of both in my fingers during my time in Vermont. But I first learned what proper lumber is like when I saw the mighty old beams of larch of which this house was built. On the outside they have weathered almost black; inside, where they show through the plastered walls, they have retained their warm reddish hue.

All the beams of this house, whose foundation is built of blocks of gray gneiss and whose roof is sheathed with slabs of the native mica-schist—all these beams are sawed out of the heartwood of the larch. And I learned that the heartwood does not die for many years after the tree is felled. It goes on living and imperceptibly working. It groans and creaks, girding itself for the load it must bear; it snaps the rings of its youth with the bony force of an old man's fist; it tears long wounds around its pith, jagged cracks that never heal. But the core endures and the strength of the structure is only increased by the calculated 'working' of the wood. These cracks permit the invisible to enter, the health-giving air. Sills, trusses, purlins, the 'dead space' between rafters and roof, the area between overhang and support, the right angle formed by corner post and plate—all these constantly admit air to empty spaces. And I learned that it is not the stone and the timbers, but the air in the empty spaces, the relationship of the empty spaces to one another, that sustains a house.

It is the same, I think, with all lasting works.

Living in Saas-Fee is not 'escape.' Nowhere else do I feel so much in the midst of the vital world.

There are a few solitary larch trees above the tree line which are a good six hundred or a thousand years old, some gnarled by storms and bent by the weight of winter snows, one split by lightning yet towering upright. In autumn their colors change to Van-Goghesque ochers and oranges; then the needles yellow and fall, but every spring the branches of these methuselahs are covered again in the tenderest, palest youthful green. Every time I pass one of these giants I doff my hat. Who could possibly deserve more respect?

I look out the window of my study, under the gable; I look into the moonlit night and know that as long as I stand here drawing breath, as long as the afflictions neither of old age nor of the age expel me from here, I am a powerful man. More powerful than the rich or the wielders of power. I cast my shadow, a moon shadow, over the slope; it covers it wholly, and what my shadow covers is mine.

This house is not so old as Wiesmühl in Henndorf, which stood there three hundred years before we moved in; not so old as the farm in Vermont, which was built by the first settlers. This house was the work of this century, but it is old enough to have its voices. I hear them talking on winter nights when the wood cracks and sighs, calls and whispers. They are the voices that go on talking when ours have fallen silent. They soothe my dreams; they fill me with peace and confidence.

I have neighbors; I have made friends in this place; and over the whole world I know where my friends are, or their graves. Where they are, I am at home. Here and everywhere.

I shall close this book with a sentence not of my writing. It heads a document drawn up by my fellow citizens of the commune of Saas-Fee when they took me into their midst. The document is called CERTIFICATE OF CITIZENSHIP.

'Eternal rights and eternal friendship should be confirmed and fixed in writing, since in the course of time past things are soon forgotten.'

The meaning of my story is to be found in that sentence.

INDEX

Index

Index

417

Index

Index

Index

Index

Index